THE RETURN OF
CULTURAL TREASURES

THE RETURN OF
CULTURAL TREASURES

Jeanette Greenfield

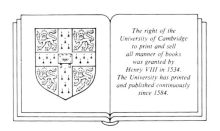

The right of the
University of Cambridge
to print and sell
all manner of books
was granted by
Henry VIII in 1534.
The University has printed
and published continuously
since 1584.

CAMBRIDGE UNIVERSITY PRESS

CAMBRIDGE

NEW YORK   PORT CHESTER

MELBOURNE   SYDNEY

Published by the Press Syndicate of the University of Cambridge
The Pitt Building, Trumpington Street, Cambridge CB2 1RP
40 West 20th Street, New York, NY 10011, USA
10 Stamford Road, Oakleigh, Melbourne 3166, Australia

First published 1989

Printed in Great Britain at the Bath Press, Avon

British Library cataloguing in publication data
Greenfield, Jeanette
The return of cultural treasures.
1. Art objects. Restitution
I. Title
707.5

Library of Congress cataloguing in publication data
Greenfield, Jeanette.
The return of cultural treasures.
Bibliography.
Includes index.
1. Cultural property, protection of.
2. Cultural property, protection of (international law)
3. Restitution.   I. Title.
CC135.G74   1988   363.6'9   88-2878

ISBN 0 521 33319 9

AN

Contents

Illustrations

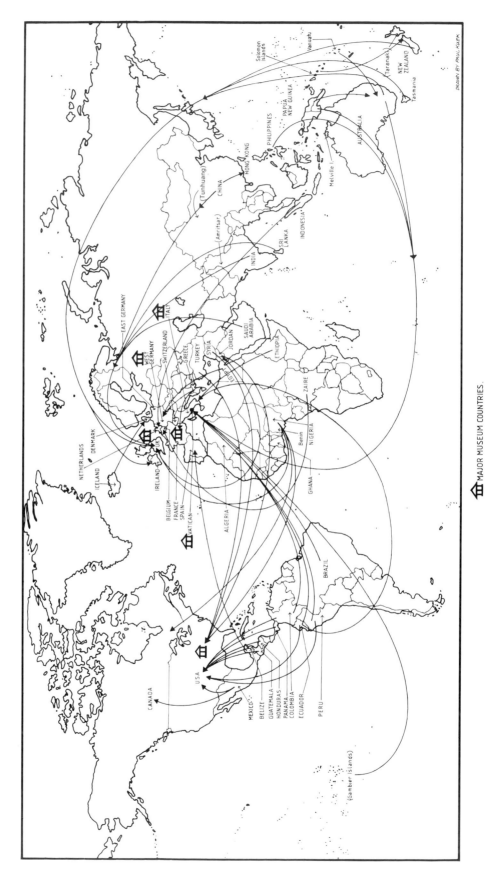

MAJOR MUSEUM COUNTRIES.

Map 1. General removal trends, indicating some relevant major museum countries

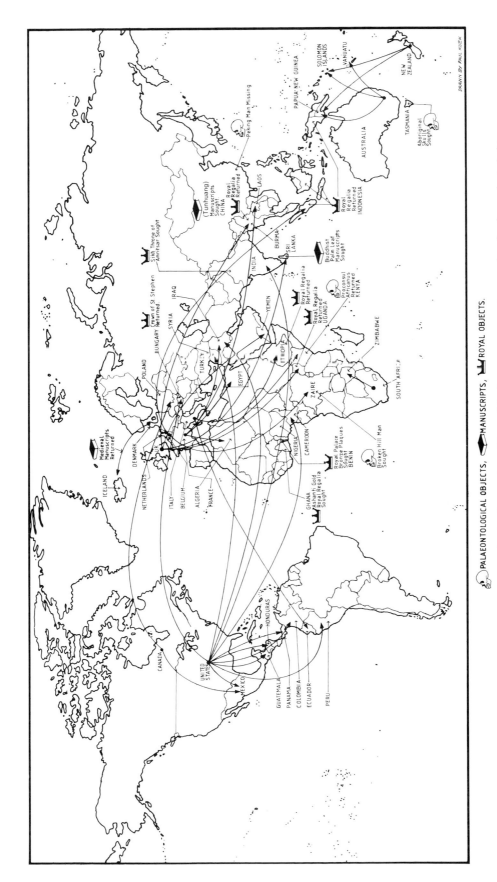

PALAEONTOLOGICAL OBJECTS, 𐃘 MANUSCRIPTS, ♛ ROYAL OBJECTS.

Map 2. Returns, indicating general trends and isolated examples, with special reference to manuscripts, royal and palaeontological objects

DRAWN BY PAUL KUEK

CHINA
(Tunhuang)
Manuscripts
Sought

Royal Regalia
Returned
LAOS

Sikh Throne of
Amritsar Sought

BURMA

SRI
LANKA
Buddhist
Palm Leaf
Manuscripts
Sought

Peking Man Missing

PAPUA NEW GUINEA
SOLOMON
ISLANDS
VANUATU

NEW
ZEALAND

AUSTRALIA

TASMANIA
Aboriginal
Skulls
Sought

Royal Regalia
Returned
INDONESIA

INDIA

Crown of St Stephen
Returned
HUNGARY

POLAND

IRAQ
SYRIA

TURKEY

YEMEN

EGYPT

ETHIOPIA

Royal Regalia
Returned

Royal Regalia
Returned
UGANDA

Proconsul
Africanus
Returned
KENYA

ZIMBABWE

ZAIRE

SOUTH AFRICA

Medieval
Manuscripts
Returned

ICELAND

DENMARK

NETHERLANDS

ITALY
BELGIUM
ALGERIA
FRANCE

NIGERIA
CAMEROON

Royal Palace
Bronze Plaques
Sought
BENIN

Broken Hill Man
Sought

GHANA
Ashanti Gold
Royal Regalia
Sought

CANADA

UNITED
STATES

MEXICO

GUATEMALA
PANAMA
COLOMBIA
ECUADOR

HONDURAS

PERU

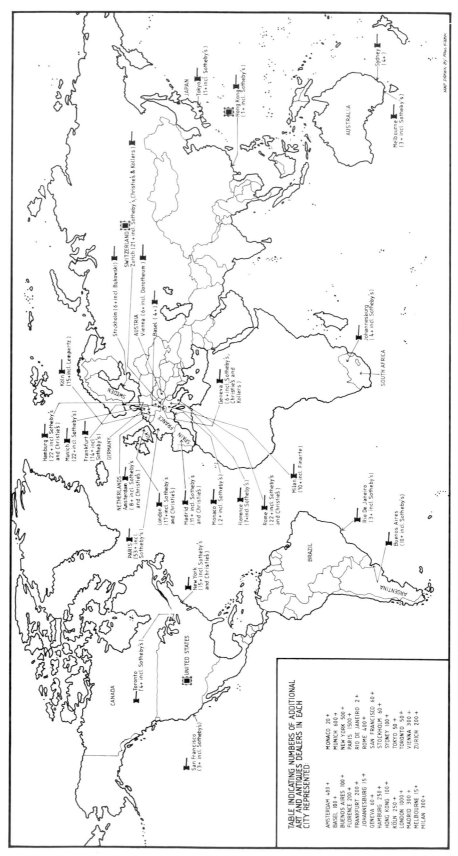

Map 3. The contemporary art market (data from *International Directory of Arts*, vol. 2, Frankfurt: Müller, 1988)

◄ SOME CITIES WITH PRINCIPAL AUCTION HOUSES (AND ESTIMATED NUMBERS OF AUCTION ROOMS).   ▣ REPUTED BUYERS MARKETS FOR STOLEN ART.

TABLE INDICATING NUMBERS OF ADDITIONAL
ART AND ANTIQUES DEALERS IN EACH
CITY REPRESENTED

AMSTERDAM 400+	MONACO 20+
BASEL 100+	MUNICH 600+
BUENOS AIRES 100+	NEW YORK 500+
FLORENCE 200+	PARIS 1500+
FRANKFURT 200+	RIO DE JANEIRO 2+
JOHANNESBURG 15+	ROME 400+
GENEVA 60+	SAN FRANCISCO 60+
HAMBURG 250+	STOCKHOLM 60+
HONG KONG 100+	SYDNEY 100+
KÖLN 250+	TOKYO 50+
LONDON 1000+	TORONTO 50+
MADRID 300+	VIENNA 300+
MELBOURNE 15+	ZURICH 200+
MILAN 300+	

Tokyo (1+ incl. Sotheby's)
Hong Kong (1+ incl. Sotheby's)
Sydney (4+)
Melbourne (3+ incl. Sotheby's)
Stockholm (6+ incl. Bukowski)
SWITZERLAND Zurich (21+ incl. Sotheby's, Christie's & Kollers)
AUSTRIA Vienna (6+ incl. Dorotheum)
Basel (4+)
Köln (15+ incl. Lempertz)
Geneva (6+ incl. Sotheby's, Christie's and Kollers)
Johannesburg (4+ incl. Sotheby's)
Hamburg (22+ incl. Sotheby's and Christie's)
Munich (22+ incl. Sotheby's)
Frankfurt (14+ incl. Sotheby's)
NETHERLANDS Amsterdam (8+ incl. Sotheby's and Christie's)
London (17+ incl. Sotheby's and Christie's)
Madrid (11+ incl. Sotheby's)
Monaco (2+ incl. Sotheby's)
Florence (7+incl Sotheby's)
Rome (22+ incl. Sotheby's and Christie's)
Milan (10+ incl. Finarte)
PARIS (53+ incl. Sotheby's)
New York (15+ incl. Sotheby's and Christie's)
Toronto (4+ incl. Sotheby's)
San Francisco (3+ incl. Sotheby's)
Rio De Janeiro (3+ incl. Sotheby's)
Buenos Aires (10+ incl. Sotheby's)

MAP DRAWN BY PAUL KLEEK.

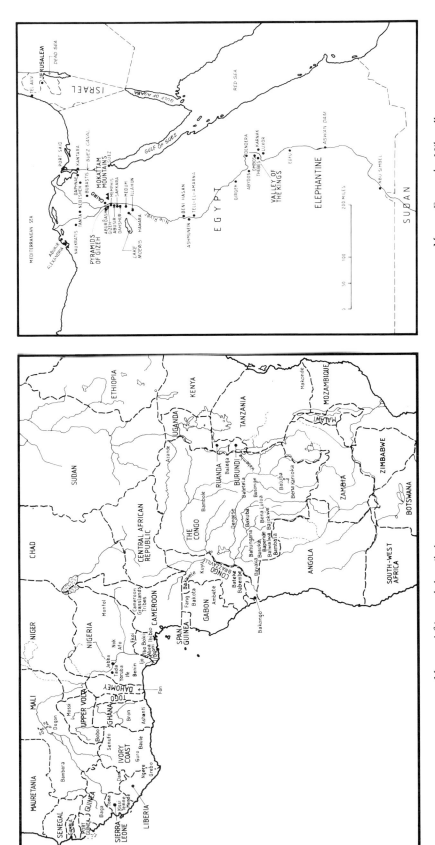

Map 5. Egypt: the Nile valley

Map 4. Africa and the tribal areas

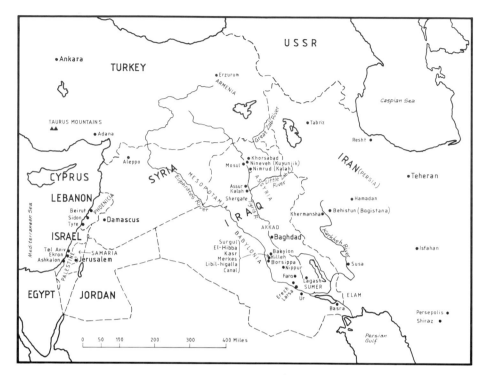

Map 6. Mesopotamia

Map 7. The eastern Mediterranean

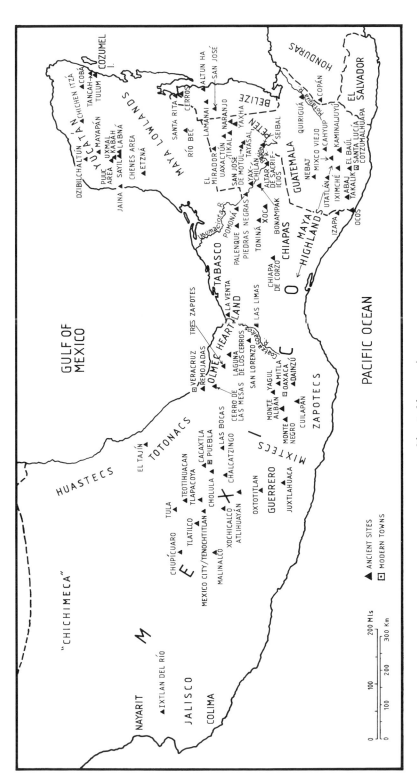

Map 8. Mesoamerica

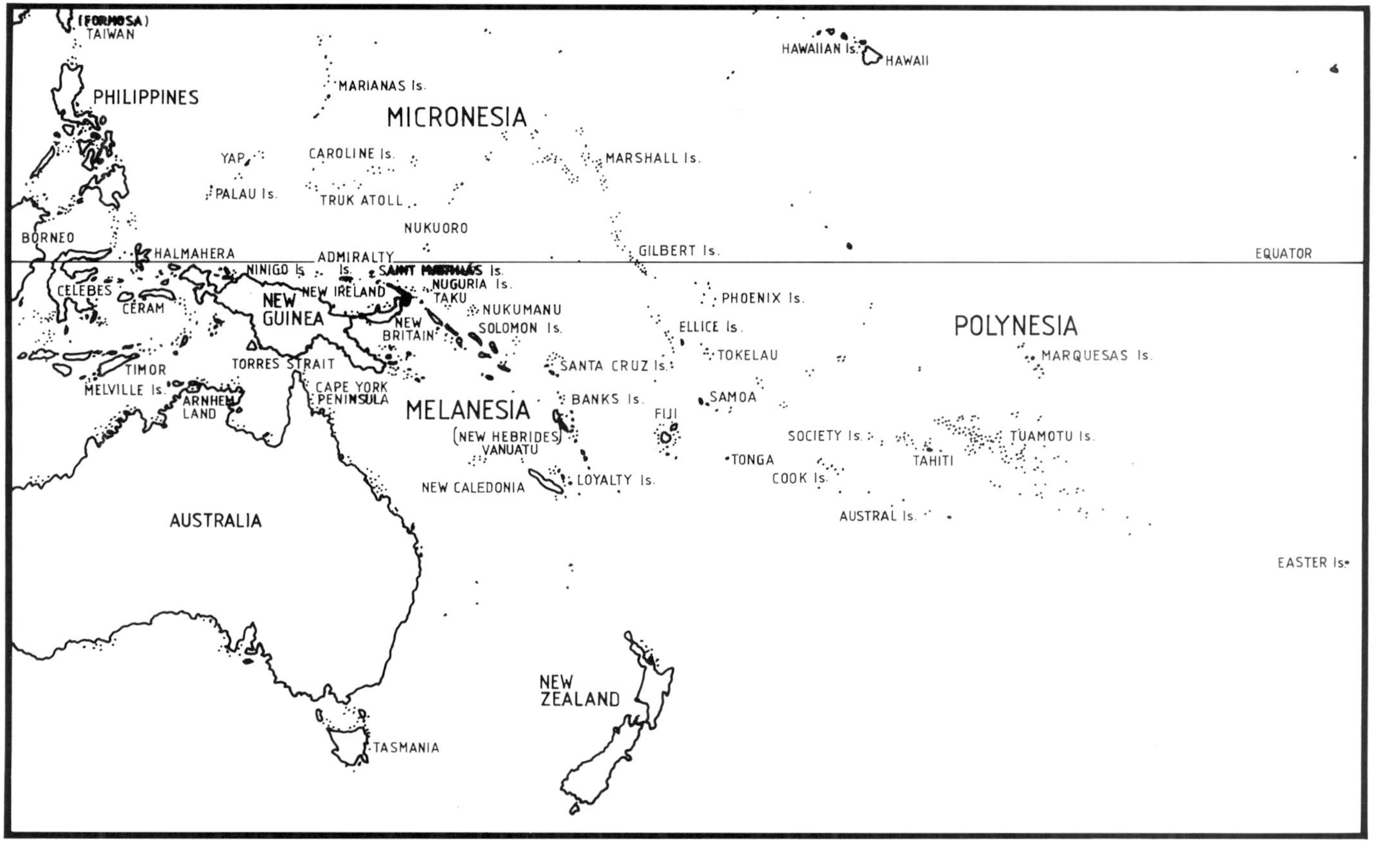

Map 9. Oceania

Preface

A visit in 1980 to the caves of Tunhuang, China, denuded of their scrolls and Buddhist manuscripts by Aurel Stein over seventy years earlier; a book of essays by Magnus Magnusson, one of which described the elation in the 1970s at the return of Iceland's greatest national treasures, the medieval saga manuscripts; the unending debate over the *cause célèbre* of cultural return cases, the Elgin Marbles; fascination with the magic of archaeology; curiosity about ethnology and the museum and art collecting phenomenon; international chagrin over the un-resolved claims and contentions of cultural return; historic and contemporary resolutions to this dilemma; and the perspectives of international law. These are the main threads woven into the fabric of this book.

But despite its title this is not a book about emptying the great museums of the world of their many treasures. 'Return' is part of a wider movement of cultural treasures and need not only mean restitution in the sense of reparation for wrongful taking. It may also refer to other kinds of restoration, reinstatement, and even rejuvenation and reunification. Inevitably museums are often central to this issue. What emerges is that objects 'migrate' sometimes legitimately and sometimes not. There are historical, political, legal, material and aesthetic con-siderations which govern this. A congruent feature of war, colonialism, mis-sionary and archaeological expeditions and other cataclysmic events has been the transportation of art treasures on a global scale. Sometimes objects have also been peacefully and uncontroversially collected and bought. Such movements are a fascinating reflector of human history. Hardly a nation or tribe has remained untouched by this experience. All manner of individuals have participated, from common looters to men who attained high rank and office. The route of objects has sometimes been no less colourful and dramatic than that of the persons who initiated their journey.

There is a distinction to be made between historically removed treasures and the contemporary illicit traffic in art objects. The issue of return should be determined on the criteria of the means of acquisition and the nature of the object. This book makes out a case primarily on historic and aesthetic grounds, but within a legal framework, for the return of certain kinds of objects. It points out that such 'returns' have taken place under different guises in the past and that it is by no means a novel occurrence setting into motion unacceptable precedents. The role to be played by the scholars and conservators in the great institutions in this course of action is not to be underestimated. A purely politicized view of the locations of cultural treasures can be shown to be quite futile, as evidenced by the many instances of wasteful returns resulting only in the reappearance of the same treasures on the international art market. A legalistic approach can be applied as leverage in obtaining returns or stemming the illicit flow of art treasures. The United States especially has followed that course of action, whereas the United Kingdom has no such approach. European institutions remain conservative while the Oceanic countries, such as Australia and New Zealand, take a more liberal view.

The issue of cultural return remains a perennial one which arouses passions and emotive argument, often because it is connected more with a restitution aspect than any other, and connected too with the existential dilemma of identity. There are cynical and material aspects, but the issue also has something to do with the charisma of objects and their language, or semiology. They represent creativity, continuity, and concreteness in the face of what is evanescent.

On the whole it has to be said that there is in this matter no magnanimity without duress, no voluntary codes applied voluntarily, no easy restoration of loaned materials recalled, no internationally accepted code of practice, no simple formulas to resolve cultural return.

There is a romantic, educative, inspirational aspect to museums. But there is another. It serves us well to remember that the Prague Museum of Judaica, which contains an unparalleled collection, was established by the Nazis and called the 'museum of an extinct race'. The Tasmanian Aboriginal Centre in 1985, seeking the return of the human remains of their people, were informed by the Natural History Museum of Vienna that the Tasmanian aborigines are 'extinct'.

This book deliberately crosses 'territories' in more than one sense in order to understand a phenomenon which has been debated for hundreds of years and to appreciate the real worth of the objects fought over. Sometimes enlightened co-operation emerges and the result can be a noble one, as in the case of the Icelandic manuscripts returned from Denmark. In the words of Iceland's Literary Nobel Laureate, Halldór Laxness, without the sagas Iceland would have remained 'as just another Danish island'.

JEANETTE GREENFIELD

Introduction

On 21 April 1971, a Danish frigate called *Vædderen* ('The Ram') came steaming into the harbour bay of Reykjavík, the capital of Iceland, bearing priceless gifts. There were 15,000 Icelanders cramming the quayside; but throughout the rest of Iceland, it was as if a plague had struck. No one moved in the streets. Shops and schools were closed. The whole nation, just over 200,000 souls in those days, was listening to the radio or watching television for a live account of the historic event that was taking place at Reykjavík harbour.

Just after the *Vædderen* tied up, off came three members of the crew. Each of them was carrying a carefully wrapped package. These three packages had been locked in a cabin all the way across from Denmark to Iceland. Only the captain had had a key to that room; and twice a day he and an Icelandic representative had solemnly unlocked the door of the cabin to see if the three inmates were all right and the temperature and humidity at optimum level.

They contained, these packages, two books which are by any standard priceless. On the quayside they were snugly installed on the back seat of a black police car. Various dignitaries such as the Prime Minister made speeches of welcome. Then the car was driven slowly through the streets of Reykjavík, past thousands of cheering people, to the university. It was like a royal wedding. And that afternoon Mr Helge Larsen, the Danish Minister of Education, got up behind a battery of microphones, picked up the old leather-bound volumes, handed them to his Icelandic counterpart, and uttered the immortal words: 'Værsgo! Flatøbogen og Kongebogen.' ('There you are! *Flateyjarbók* and *Codex Regius*.')

To any Icelander (and here I must declare a passionate interest, for I am an Icelander myself) it was a magic moment, and these were magic words. For *Flateyjarbók* (the Book of Flat-Island) and *Codex Regius* (the King's Volume) were, and are, two of the most valuable manuscript treasures of Iceland's medieval literature; and they were being returned by one country, Denmark, to a former colony, Iceland, from which they had been removed 250 years earlier.

The long story behind this historic event is carefully documented in the first chapter of this important book by Dr Jeanette Greenfield. It has not, to my knowledge, been told so fully or so well in any English-language source. But it is well worth the telling, because it is of paramount significance to the issues involved in *The Return of Cultural Treasures*.

Flateyjarbók is a magnificent manuscript codex, containing a great collection of Icelandic sagas and royal histories of Norwegian kings. It was made for a wealthy farmer in the north of Iceland in the 1390s, who employed two priests as scribes for two years to copy and illuminate the material. They wrote on vellum, calfskin; and it took the lives of 113 calves to make the 225 leaves of the codex. Later, this book passed into the possession of a farmer on the little island of Flatey in Breidafjördur on the west coast of Iceland, and became known as *Flateyjarbók* as a result. In the seventeenth century it came into the possession of Bishop Brynjólfur Sveinsson of Skálholt, a distinguished scholar and collector of manuscripts, and he sent it as a gift to the king of Denmark in the hope that it would be printed and published there.

The other manuscript, *Codex Regius*, which was also presented to the king of Denmark by Bishop Brynjólfur, is tiny by comparison but incomparable in stature. It was written around 1270, and its significance lies in the fact that it is the only surviving vellum copy of the *Edda*, the major repository of the mytholo gical and heroic lays of Germanic literature, composed in Icelandic (Old Norse) and preserved only in Iceland. Without it, our knowledge of Norse mythology and heroic legend would be vastly the poorer.

Their value to world scholarship is inestimable. But their value to Iceland was, and is, if anything greater, for between them they symbolized Iceland's great heritage of medieval prose and poetry. Denmark could not have chosen two more suitable gifts to hand over to her former colony.

But these two books were only a forerunner, an earnest of the future. They were simply the first instalment of nearly 3,000 manuscripts and other docu ments that Denmark promised to return to Iceland – a process which is now almost complete.

These manuscripts had all been removed from Iceland in a hectic period of manuscript collecting that covered barely more than fifty years, from around 1650 onwards. Iceland by then had been a colony, first of Norway and then of Denmark, for some four centuries. Danish imperial policy, coupled with severe climatic conditions, had reduced the people of Iceland to unbelievable penury and misery. Yet the seventeenth century had seen a flowering of Renaissance learning amongst Icelandic scholars, whose Latin treatises about the geography and culture of Iceland had kindled a revival of antiquarianism among scholars in the rest of Scandinavia. Fired by a desire to learn more about their past, these scholars began to realize that the main sources were to be found in the ancient writings of the Icelanders in their vellum books. Expeditions were sent out from Denmark and Sweden to find and fetch them as if they were rare botanical specimens. Indeed one Royal Antiquary, despatched by the king of Denmark,

was drowned in 1684 when his ship, laden with a cargo of uncatalogued manuscript books, was lost with all hands on the voyage back to Denmark.

Much the most significant manuscript collector, however, was a brilliant
young Icelandic scholar called Árni Magnússon (1663–1730). He was brought
up at the farm of Hvammur, on the west coast of Iceland, celebrated as the home
of a prominent settler and matriarch of the Dales district in *Laxdæla Saga*. He
grew up in an environment where, despite the endemic poverty, learning and
culture were revered. His grandfather was a clergyman and also the local teacher,
who taught him Latin from the age of six; his uncle, another clergyman, started
him on Greek and algebra from the age of twelve. A precocious scholar, the boy
was sent to the university of Copenhagen, which was then the only seat of higher
learning open to young Icelanders. He quickly graduated in theology, but his
burning interest was in the literary antiquities of his homeland. He became a
secretary in the Royal Archives, and in 1701 he was appointed to a new chair at
the university of Copenhagen as Professor of Danish Antiquities – the first
Icelander ever to hold a university chair.

In 1702, Árni Magnússon was sent to Iceland by the king as one of two
royal commissioners to carry out a land census of property throughout the country, and to carry out a general investigation of conditions in the country and the
conduct of Danish officials and merchants. It gave Árni a unique opportunity
of seeking out antiquities on his own account at the same time. For ten years,
from 1702 to 1712, he travelled the length and breadth of the land, looking for
manuscripts wherever he went, cajoling, wheedling, haggling, begging, borrowing and buying up every single scrap of vellum he could find, whatever the
price, and paying for them out of his own pocket. People said of him that he
could sniff out old manuscripts like a bloodhound. He found one piece of
vellum that had been cut to make an insole for a shoe; another had been trimmed
by a tailor to make a pattern for the back of a waistcoat. Eventually he had
amassed fifty-five cases of vellum manuscripts and paper copies and medieval
documents. There were long delays before they could be shipped to him in
Copenhagen, where they arrived in 1720. Árni installed them in his professorial
residence in Kannikestræde, in the University Quarter, and set scribes to work
to make copies of every item.

But then disaster struck. On 20 October 1728, the Great Fire of Copenhagen began. For several hours, Árni Magnússon thought himself safe; but on
the second day the flames reached the University Quarter. Only then did Árni
start to take precautions. All day long, until five o'clock in the evening, he and
two helpers tried to empty the library as fast as they could. But by then it was too
late to save all but the best books. The oldest and most valuable manuscripts

were rescued, but the bulk of the library, including all the printed books and paper copies and other documents, perished in the flames. Árni Magnússon never really recovered from the tragedy, and within fifteen months he was dead. On his death-bed he bequeathed the remnants of his great collection to the university of Copenhagen, to create an institute for their study.

The significance of these saga manuscripts to the people of Iceland would be impossible to exaggerate. They have been the root and stock of Icelandic culture, the life-blood of the nation, the oldest living literature in Europe, enshrining the origins of Icelandic society. The sagas not only preserved the old language as a living tongue and a written language that is closer to modern Icelandic than Shakespeare is to modern English; they also helped to keep alive the Icelanders through the worst centuries of natural disasters and colonial oppression. Indeed, when the Icelanders took up the struggle for freedom and independence from Denmark in the nineteenth century, the saga literature was both their inspiration and their justification. In the long independence campaign, the demand for the return of the manuscripts was a constant theme. And when Iceland eventually achieved full independence in 1944, the first claim that the Icelanders made on their former colonial masters was for the restitution of the saga manuscripts to their homeland.

The wrangle that ensued lasted for more than twenty-five years, and absorbed public opinion in both Iceland and Denmark. Iceland never brought a legal action against Denmark, either nationally or internationally. Instead, it was left to the political will of the Danish parliament, which reflected the response of Danish public opinion to the appeal of 'natural justice'; and in the end, the Danish judiciary rejected a massive claim for compensation from the Danish institutions involved, thus clearing the way for the start of the hand-over on that memorable day in Reykjavík in 1971.

This striking example of magnanimity and goodwill stands out in my mind like a beacon in the rather murky conditions that befog the whole issue of the restitution of cultural objects. The Icelandic experience, I confess without shame, has put me firmly on the side of those who sympathize with others who would like to have their national cultural treasures returned – like the Greeks and their Parthenon Marbles (the so-called Elgin Marbles in the British Museum). For me it is not a matter of morality or even legality, but of decency and civilized behaviour.

Happily, there are signs that people's consciences are being stirred, all over the world. The matter of the Icelandic manuscripts is not so exceptional now as those who base their arguments for stubborn retention on the grounds of the danger of setting a precedent seem to realize. Dr Greenfield listed a remarkable number of cases of restitution in an article in *Antiquity* ('The Return of Cultural Property', March 1986): let me cite some of them here.

In 1950 there was an agreement between France and Laos about the restitution of Laotian objects of art.

In 1962, when Uganda became independent, special objects relating to the Kabaka of Uganda were returned by the Cambridge University Museum of Archaeology and Anthropology.

In 1964, the Mandalay regalia were returned to Burma by the Victoria and Albert Museum.

In 1968, there was an agreement between France and Algeria returning some three hundred paintings which had been exhibited in the Museum of Algeria.

In 1970, Belgium returned at least forty objects to Zaire.

In 1973, the fragment of a stela stolen from the Piedras Negras was returned by the Brooklyn Museum to Guatemala.

In 1974, a fifth-century mosaic from the ancient city of Apamea was returned by the Newark Museum in New Jersey to Syria.

In 1974, a mask was returned to Papua New Guinea by the National Museum of New Zealand.

In 1977, Belgium returned several thousand cultural objects to Zaire, on top of the 1970 consignment.

In 1977, the Netherlands concluded an agreement to return a number of important historical and cultural objects to Indonesia.

In 1977, two major American institutions returned a number of cultural items to Panama.

In 1977, too, Australia (which now has a good track record in these matters) started returning artifacts to Papua New Guinea, perhaps inspired by a growing awareness of its own aboriginal cultural heritage.

In 1980, France and Iraq came to an arrangement about the return of fragments of Babylonian law codes to Iraq.

In 1981, a French court ordered the restitution to Egypt of a stolen Amon Min statue which had been illicitly traded.

In 1981, South Africa returned some carved birds to Zimbabwe.

In 1981, New Zealand returned more than a thousand cultural objects to the Solomon Islands.

In 1981, the Wellcome Institute in London returned a collection of Himyarite items to the Yemen.

Throughout the 1980s, indeed, restitution has continued unabated, to the gratification of countries like Vanuatu (New Hebrides), Honduras, Kenya, Iraq, Ethiopia, Ecuador, and Peru.

Some of these returns have been the outcome of protracted and often bitter wrangling. Some have been the outcome of patient and sympathetic negotiation between governments. Some have been the outcome of spontaneous gestures by the museums and institutions involved. Some restitutions have been enforced when the objects were shown to have been illicitly imported or illegally acquired.

Some museums are more obstinate than others, even about returning items that originally came to them on loan. It took many years for Kenya to prise back from the British Museum of Natural History the seventeen-million-year-old skull of *Proconsul africanus*, which Mary Leakey had brought back to London on loan for display. It was not until 1982 that the Trustees reluctantly agreed that it should be 'de-accessioned'.

The main impetus for return is coming from those countries which feel that they were in no position to resist the original removal of the antiquities, for colonial or other reasons – naturally enough. The wholesale looting and plundering and (sometimes fraudulent) 'purchasing' of objects by dominant countries is a continuing blot on the saga of the growth of archaeological learning. Nor is Lord Elgin with his notorious acquisition of the Parthenon Marbles alone in the hall of dubious fame. What about André Malraux?

For those who think of André Malraux only as a distinguished writer (the author of *La Condition humaine* about the Kuomintang Revolution of 1927, and *L'Espoir* about the Spanish Civil War, in both of which he took part) and in his latter years as a statesman (Minister of Cultural Affairs in the 1960s), it may come as a surprise to learn that in his younger days he was charged and sentenced to three years' imprisonment (reduced on appeal in Saigon to a suspended sentence of one year) for using his official position on a study expedition to dislodge and steal a cargo of massive stones and bas-reliefs from a protected temple in Cambodia. No doubt his rationale had been impeccable; he claimed that the temple of Bantea-Srei had been abandoned, and that he was indulging in 'rescue archaeology' to put into circulation treasures that had been 'lost'. No doubt his youthful experiences in Cambodia helped to inform his views on art in such classic books as *Les Voix du silence* and *La Psychologie de l'art*.

Taking the law into one's own hands can work both ways, however. When the so-called Stone of Destiny was stolen by young Scottish Nationalists from Westminster Abbey on Christmas Day in 1950, there can have been few Scots who did not feel a guilty tinge of secret pleasure that a historic piece of Scottish nationhood had been spirited back to its homeland: deplorable, of course, but, well...

Something very similar happened in June 1982, when a Mexican journalist called José Luis Castaneda de Valle stole an ancient eighteen-page Aztec codex known as the Tonalamatl Aubin from the French National Library in Paris and spirited it back to Mexico. By the time the loss was discovered and Interpol had been alerted, the codex had been given to the Mexican Institute of Anth- ropology and History. The French were naturally indignant and demanded it back, but the buccaneering aspect of the whole business inspired a wave of nationalism: this was part of Mexico's cultural heritage that had been plundered, like so much else, in the past. It had come into the possession of the Spanish viceroy as early as 1740, and later was acquired by a Spaniard called Antonio de Leon y Gama. On his death it was sold to a German traveller called Max Waldeck, who sold it in Paris to a French scientist called Joseph Aubin (hence its name). It was bequeathed to the National Library in 1848 by its last private owner, a Frenchman called Eugène Goupil. The French government can argue that it has proper legal title to the codex — twenty sheets of tree bark, folded like a concertina; but the people of Mexico claim that it *ought* to be in Mexico, its original home, and the Mexican authorities are not being exactly helpful about its return to France.

Some might think that there is a kind of poetic justice about this bizarre situation, and might even relish it; but it does the cause of orderly return little good. How much better it is to be able to point to dignified agreements such as the one in 1978 when the US government returned to the Hungarian people the crown, orb and sceptre of St Stephen, the first Hungarian king, who had re- ceived them from Pope Sylvester II in 1001. The regalia had been lost and stolen, lost and stolen again several times over before finding asylum in Fort Knox after the Second World War.

The United States of America, indeed, has a notable record of restitutions. The Maya Room of Mexico's National Museum of Anthropology now boasts a magnificent temple facade which had been shipped to New York in 1968 and offered for sale to the Metropolitan Museum there for some $400,000. The Mu- seum refused the purchase, however, and the dealer who had organized its illicit removal from a remote site in Campeche was 'persuaded' to donate it to the Mexican Museum.

The current international market in illicitly acquired art and archaeological treasures is a huge business now, by all accounts, and all too many auction houses and institutions are prepared to turn a blind eye to the dubious provenance of some of the illegally excavated items put up for sale. But the Americans are setting the rest of the world a fine example with their strenuous efforts to return treasures, particularly pre-Columbian artifacts, when they can be proved to have been illegally removed.

In Europe, many major national institutions, especially the Louvre and the British Museum, are against the return of anything if it can possibly be avoided.

The *cause célèbre* at the British Museum is the Elgin Marbles, whose return to Greece is so passionately advocated by Melina Mercouri, the celebrated actress, in her ministerial role with the Greek government. Many of the greatest treasures in the British Museum were acquired in circumstances that reflect little credit on the ethics or honesty of the 'finders'; today's 'keepers' therefore find themselves occasionally having to bat on an extremely sticky wicket and rely on stonewalling techniques. The wholesale plunder of antiquities in Egypt and Mesopotamia by the giant Italian, Giovanni Battista Belzoni, in the first decades of the nineteenth century was as unscrupulous then as it is indefensible today. Sir Aurel Stein's removal of a whole library of ancient Chinese documents from a sealed room in one of the Tunhuang Caves in China in 1907 was devious, to say the least, and has aroused considerable bitterness amongst the Chinese.

It is my belief, however, that the climate of opinion is now changing to one of greater willingness to consider, at least, the possibility of return of certain objects. Men of great distinction and renown in the world of scholarship, like the late lamented Professor Glyn Daniel, for many years editor of *Antiquity*, have expressed themselves as being firmly on the side of restitution of *some* of the objects in Western museums to their place of origin, such as the Benin bronzes to Africa, or the Rosetta Stone to Egypt.

Obviously, this is not something that could, or should, be done overnight. Every single object has its own particular history, its own peculiar circumstances of acquisition, and the merits of each case must be weighed. These merits should obviously include such factors as the capacity of the home country to house, protect, study and display any material that is returned, just as much as the gratification of national pride or the soothing of national injury for political or sentimental reasons.

In this book, Dr Jeanette Greenfield has documented a great number of these cases, and takes the reader through the tangled legal undergrowth that surrounds them. She chronicles and analyses the work of international agencies like UNESCO and the various international conventions and resolutions that have been drawn up in an attempt to establish workable principles that all can follow. In her final chapter she offers her own working formula for the assessment and resolution of national claims for the recovery of historic treasures that might be considered to be 'cultural property'.

On the whole issue of cultural return there is often a confusion between historically removed objects, and those objects which have been removed illicitly in more recent times. The latter category is, on the whole, the easier to deal with through existing legal machinery. Historically removed objects, however, are harder to assess. It should be possible to claim legally all materials that have been taken by force, by unequal treaty, by theft or by deception; such material is more often than not held in state institutions. Dr Greenfield argues that the class of object in which title should not be deemed to have passed would be: (a) the historic records or manuscripts of a nation, including the narrative representation of its history in an art form which has been dismembered; (b) objects torn from immovable property forming part of the sovereign territory of the state whence they were taken; and (c) palaeontological materials.

It can be argued that many of the objects that were moved in the past were so removed for safe keeping, and that without that removal they would not now exist. That may well have been true then, but it does not necessarily pertain today. Can anyone argue that the Elgin Marbles are still so important to scholars of the history of Western art that it would be unsafe to return them? And now that the Rosetta Stone has been deciphered, is it anything more than a trophy of war?

One sometimes wonders whether the attitude of the British establishment to the return of cultural property would be different if Stonehenge had been sold abroad? The possibility actually arose in 1898 when Sir Edmund Antrobus offered to sell it to the British nation for £125,000. The offer was refused, and it was not until 1915 that it was bought by Cecil Chubb for £6,600; but it must be considered providential that there were no American millionaires around at the time who wanted to buy it at all costs, like London Bridge in 1968.

Dr Greenfield concludes her original and penetrating study with these words:

> The case of the Icelandic manuscripts is the outstanding example of a major state-to-state return of cultural property. It was an unusually civilized and rational act in the face of all the common legal, political and historic arguments against return. With time, the view that certain major treasures selected under certain fixed criteria ought to be returned may not be regarded as the pipedream of misguided liberals and scholars . . . nor as a precipitate action which will cause the ultimate absurdity – the return of everything.

It is a view with which I find myself in total sympathy.

MAGNUS MAGNUSSON

CHAPTER ONE

THE ICELANDIC MANUSCRIPTS[1]

The Icelandic manuscripts case is of particular interest and relevance because it involved the successful restitution of cultural treasures from one country to another. One country (Iceland) petitioned for the return of treasures which had been removed into the care of another country (Denmark) during a period of colonial status. These treasures – vellum and later paper manuscripts of the medieval saga literature of Iceland – were perceived to be symbols of Iceland's nationhood and cultural identity, and the question of their return to Iceland aroused powerful passions and prejudices in both countries.

The story goes back to the seventeenth century, when Renaissance scholars in Iceland and elsewhere began to take a growing interest in Icelandic studies based on the medieval manuscripts written in Iceland from the twelfth century onwards, particularly the Icelandic sagas. To facilitate the publication of these works at a time when Iceland was a Danish colony, the Icelandic bishops sent some of the most treasured manuscripts from their bishoprics to the king of Denmark. Among these were two priceless books, *Flateyjarbók* (Figs. 1 and 2) and *Codex Regius* (Fig. 3), which were deposited in the newly founded Royal Library in Copenhagen.

Later in the century two rival emissaries, one from Denmark and one from Sweden, were sent to Iceland to collect as many manuscripts as possible. Yet the greatest manuscript collector of all was a brilliant Icelandic scholar and antiquarian, Árni Magnússon (1663–1730). Born in Iceland, he studied at Copenhagen University (where his name was Danicized to Arne Magnussen), and became a Secretary in the Royal Archives. In 1701 he was appointed to the new chair of Danish Antiquities at Copenhagen University and in the following year he was sent to Iceland with the lawyer Páll Vídalín to compile a National Register of all the farms and estates of Iceland. This took them ten years, a period during which Árni scoured the country in search of manuscripts for his own private collection, begging, borrowing or buying wherever he went, at almost any price. At the same time, he employed scribes to take copies of some 6,000 medieval documents and letters.

This great collection of manuscripts – fifty-five crates in all – eventually reached Copenhagen in 1720. Arne Magnussen continued to collect from every available source, and made many further notable acquisitions. But in the Great Fire of Copenhagen in October 1728, Arne's home was destroyed, and only

Fig. 1. A page from the magnificent *Flateyjarbók* codex, one of the manuscript treasures in the Royal Library, Copenhagen, that was returned by Denmark to Iceland in 1971. It is a compilation of sagas, made in the north of Iceland in the 1390s. This page contains the start of the Saga of St Olaf, king and patron saint of Norway; the illustration in the illuminated capital depicts the king's death at the Battle of Stiklestad in 1030.

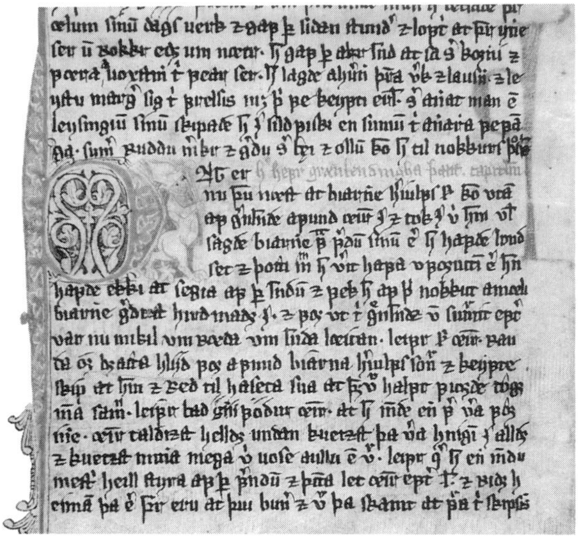

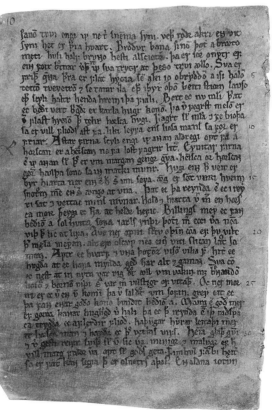

Fig. 2. A page from *Flateyjarbók*, showing the start of *Grænlendinga Saga*. This tells the story of the expedition of Leif the Lucky to Vínland (North America), and the Norse discovery of the New World five hundred years before Columbus. In the 1890s the Americans wanted to put *Flateyjarbók* on display at the Chicago World Fair because it contained this particular saga. They offered to send a battleship to fetch it, and to insure it for one million dollars, but the offer was refused after an outcry in Iceland: *Flateyjarbók* was priceless and irreplaceable, and even battleships had been known to sink.

Fig. 3. A page from *Codex Regius*, the precious vellum manuscript copy of the *Edda* that was one of the first books handed over by Denmark to Iceland. It was written in the second half of the thirteenth century. It is 90 pages long, measuring a mere 20 cm by 12 cm. The *Edda* is a collection of thirty-five mythological lays and heroic poems that date back in their inspiration to the very roots of Germanic mythology and legend. This page shows a section of *Hávamál* (Words of the High One).

about a third of his library was saved. Mercifully this included most of the oldest manuscripts.

When Arne Magnussen died in 1730, he bequeathed his collection to the university of Copenhagen, along with a handsome endowment to look after it and encourage publication of documents. For the first few years after his death the collection was neglected and little used, and it was not until 1760 that Arne's will was at last translated into actuality with the foundation of an institute, the Arnamagnaeanske Stiftelse, in Copenhagen. In that year a royal charter based on the will set up a Fundation for det Arnamagnaeanske Legat to manage the capital. Later, by an ordinance of 1772, a permanent Kommission for den Arnamagnaeanske Stiftelse was established as the governing body of the institute. This commission subsequently published many fine editions of Icelandic manuscripts.

The story of Iceland's efforts to have the manuscripts returned goes back as far as the 1830s, but the issue did not come to a head until 1945, when Iceland, following her final constitutional separation from Denmark, celebrated her independence by embarking on what turned out to be a long, and sometimes acrimonious, campaign for their return. The wrangle was to last for nearly thirty years, eventually involving litigation within Denmark and between Danish institutions and finally reaching the Danish Supreme Court. Though the Danish parliament passed a bill concerning restitution as early as 1961 (ratified in 1965), the constitutional validity of the Act was challenged in the courts and the decision in the case in favour of return was not finally made until 1971.

To understand the great importance of the manuscripts to Iceland one must appreciate the history of enormous literary activity of that comparatively small country and the ultimate rarity of its medieval works.

The great Danish historian, Saxo Grammaticus, writing about 1200, made a famous and profound remark about the Icelanders, who supplied him with most of his material for the older history of Denmark: *Inopiam ingenio pensant*, 'They make up for their poverty by their wits'. He had gathered from his acquaintance with Icelandic court poets and other visitors from Iceland that historical knowledge and literary activity were forms of compensation for the drab life of farming and fishing. Later scholars and historians elaborated this observation, taking the view that traditional Viking vigour and aspirations, pent up in the isolated island, found an outlet in memories, imagination, and story-telling. Indeed the 'bookishness' of the Icelanders, both in earlier and later centuries, came to be regarded as a national characteristic.

Besides a considerable volume of national literature, in the form of sagas, the period 1100–1400 saw the production of adaptations of foreign books of a religious or historical nature. Many of these are preserved today only as fragments. In addition there was a great deal of transcribing and copying-out of books, much of it now also lost.

According to an estimate made in 1929 by Professor Halldór Hermann-sson,[2] there are now extant some seven hundred vellum manuscripts, including fragments, that were produced in Iceland, or written by Icelanders, earlier than the middle of the sixteenth century. Yet it is incredibly rare to find among these a complete volume. Many of the fragments consist of a few leaves or even a single leaf, and one can only guess at the numbers of manuscripts that have been entirely lost.

Of all the works composed and translated in Iceland before 1400, only one, a book of annals written in the fourteenth century, appears to have been pre-served in its original manuscript. Twelfth-century fragments are very few, and of saga manuscripts older than about 1250 scarcely anything is left. Besides the books which have been entirely lost, several old and important works – among them the *Íslendingabók* by Ari Thorgilsson, written about 1125 – are preserved only in copies on paper dating from the seventeenth century.

When several vellums of a book are available, comparison generally reveals not only that the original has been lost, but also some links between the original and the surviving manuscripts. The extent of literary interest in the Icelandic manuscripts can be measured not only by the number of copies which must have existed of the most popular books still surviving – there are, for instance, twenty-one vellums left of *Njáls Saga* and thirteen of *Egils Saga* – but also by the curious fact that many, or even most, of the books which were translated into Norwegian are preserved only in Icelandic transcriptions. Even of the chief work of Old Norwegian literature, the *Speculum Regale*, which dates from the middle of the thirteenth century, there seem to have been more copies in Iceland than in Norway itself. Of the numerous books in Latin which are known to have been in Iceland, scarcely any survived the Reformation.

Of the *Jónsbók*, the Icelandic code of laws lasting from 1281 down into the nineteenth century, about eighty manuscripts from the period 1300–1550 re-main. No other book was of such a practical value to so many people, which explains both the great number of copies made and the number that were excep-tionally well preserved through the following centuries. Even so, it is estimated that at least ninety per cent have been lost.

It was in April 1971 that the first two manuscripts were formally handed back to Iceland, the remainder in Denmark to be returned over a period of twenty-five years. These two were of particular significance because they were the two books that had been sent to the King of Denmark in the middle of the seventeenth century, *Flateyjarbók* and *Codex Regius*. *Flateyjarbók* (Flat-Island Book) is a magnificent two-volume collection of Icelandic sagas and other historical material, written for an Icelandic chieftain, Jón Hákonarson of Víðidalstunga, at the end of the fourteenth century. 450 pages long, it had been copied onto vellum cut from over one hundred calfskins using the quills of ravens or swans, and black glossy ink made by boiling bear-berry plants. The margins were filled with 'illuminations', used principally to decorate the initial letter of each chapter. By comparison, *Codex Regius* (the King's Book) is a tiny book, ninety pages long and measuring only twenty centimetres by thirteen. Written around the year 1270, it is Scandinavia's most valuable literary treasure for it contains the *Elder Edda*, the major existing source of Norse mythological and heroic poetry.

The strength of feeling that the manuscripts issue generated is vividly reflec-ted in the fact that on the day these two manuscripts left Denmark the National Librarian at the Copenhagen Royal Library ordered the flag to be flown at half-mast and that on the day they arrived in Iceland on board the Danish frigate *Vædderen* (Fig. 4), the ceremonial hand-over (Fig. 5) was broadcast live on Icelandic television and hardly a soul was to be seen out of doors anywhere in the country.

Before considering the sequence of events that led up to this memorable climax it is as well to bear in mind the fact that the manuscripts involved were, and are, by no means the only Icelandic manuscripts in foreign libraries. Apart from those in the Royal Library and the Arnamagnaean Institute in Copen-hagen, and some 14,000 (mainly paper) documents in the National Library in Reykjavík, there are some three hundred Icelandic manuscripts in the Royal Library in Stockholm, 250 in the British Museum in London, 150 in the Bodleian Library in Oxford, 100 in the National Library of Scotland in Edin-burgh, 50 in Uppsala University Library in Sweden, and 45 in Harvard Uni-versity Library in the United States. No attempt has been made to have these manuscripts returned. The Icelandic case has always rested on the fact that the university in Copenhagen was also Iceland's university at the time of Arne Magnussen's will, its own university in Reykjavík not having been founded until 1911.

In the nineteenth century, a strong independence movement inspired by revolutionary and nationalistic movements elsewhere in Europe began to flower in Iceland, and the Icelandic manuscripts came to symbolize its national heritage. In the 1830s the bishop of Iceland made a formal request for the return of all documents relating to the former bishoprics of Skálholt and Hólar, but this was refused.

Political pressure for Home Rule was partially satisfied with a revised Icelandic Constitution in 1904. Three years later, in 1907, the Althing, the Icelandic parliament, made its first call for the return of 'all those documents and

Fig. 4. Reykjavík harbour on the morning of Wednesday, 21 April 1971. Three sailors carry the first manuscript gifts from Denmark to Iceland. The two larger packages contain the two volumes of *Flateyjarbók*; the smaller package contains *Codex Regius*. Stepping off the gangway is the Danish Minister of Education, Helge Larsen.

Fig. 5. The moment of the handing-over of the first two manuscript treasures from Denmark to Iceland. On the right, Helge Larsen, the Danish Minister of Education; on the left, accepting custody of *Codex Regius*, Dr Gylfi Gíslason, the Icelandic Minister of Education and Culture, who had campaigned tirelessly for the return of the manuscripts. On the table, the two volumes of *Flateyjarbók*.

manuscripts formerly granted to Árni Magnússon which had originated from the archives of bishoprics, churches, monasteries and other offices and in-stitutions', a request which included also the documents and manuscripts in the Royal Library. Again the Danish government refused the request.

Between 1924 and 1927 the request was renewed. This time it resulted in an exchange of documents bearing upon the governance of the two countries, whereby Iceland received from the Royal Library and the Arnamagnaean In-stitute some seven hundred documents and four manuscripts which concerned Iceland exclusively. For its part, Iceland handed over various papers from the archive of the Iceland Office in Copenhagen. The National Librarian in Copenhagen wanted an assurance from Iceland that no further demands would be made, but this the Icelanders refused to give as long as treasures such as *Flateyjarbók* and *Codex Regius* were still at issue.

The Althing repeated its demand for the return of all Icelandic manuscripts in Denmark in 1930 – the millennial anniversary of Iceland's parliament – and again in 1938. But all discussions were brought to an end by the outbreak of war in 1939 and the German occupation of Denmark.

When, in 1944, Iceland became a fully independent republic, all remaining political and monarchical ties with Denmark were severed. When the war ended in 1945 and discussions took place between the two countries to clear up any outstanding problems caused by Iceland's declaration of independence, it was made clear to the Danes that the manuscript issue had been one of the factors leading to the break, and that it should be resolved forthwith before fully normal relations between the two countries could be expected.

In response, the Danish government set up in 1947 a Commission of politi-cians and scholars to consider the whole matter, a burning issue now in Den-mark as well as in Iceland. In that year, for instance, a group of forty-nine headmasters of Folk High Schools in Denmark published a petition supporting return on historical and moral grounds, under the heading 'Give Iceland her treasures back'.

Though the Commission published its report in 1951, it came to no con-sensus. Some members wanted to return a few manuscripts, others wanted to return rather more, and only one member supported the Icelandic demand in all its particulars. In the aftermath of the report, moreover, a group of Danish university lecturers published an open letter arguing strongly against restitution on the grounds that the Icelandic manuscripts were not specifically Icelandic but 'Old Nordic' (*oldnordisk*), and therefore a pan-Scandinavian treasure. They argued that it was only by accident that the manuscripts were written in the Icelandic language.

In the spring of 1954 the Danish government prepared its own proposals to resolve the dispute. The nub of these proposals was that the manuscripts should be considered a joint Danish–Icelandic possession to be shared between two national institutions: one in Iceland to deal with specifically Icelandic materials, the other in Denmark for more generally 'Scandinavian' documents. As it happened, these proposals were 'leaked' and published by the Danish newspaper *Politiken* on 5 March 1954, before they had been formally presented to the Icelandic government. This caused a great outcry in Iceland and, in the ensuing debate in the Althing, the proposals were emphatically rebuffed on the grounds that they were wholly out of accord with Icelandic national feeling. As a consequence the Danish proposals were never formally presented to the government in Reykjavík, and all formal discussions between the two countries lapsed for the time being.

Diplomatic activity continued behind the scenes, for in 1951 Iceland had appointed as her ambassador to Copenhagen the distinguished scholar Sigurður Nordal, the leading authority on Icelandic saga literature. But it was not until 1957 that the Althing proposed a resumption of formal discussions through a joint Icelandic–Danish commission. Danish government ministers declared themselves in favour of this proposal, but the opposition in parliament refused to co-operate and the matter was once again shelved.

In 1959, the Althing decided that a five-man committee under the chairmanship of professor Einar Ólafur Sveinsson should be appointed to work with the government to help the progress of the manuscript negotiations. Its remit was to study the earlier Danish proposals and assess whether they might form the basis for discussion. At the same time, the committee was to try to formulate the foundation on which Iceland would base its case: which manuscripts could be called 'Icelandic', and which could most readily be claimed from Denmark?

The committee was of the unanimous opinion that the natural criterion to use was the *nationality of the scribe*: an Icelandic manuscript was one that had been written by an Icelander. The main burden of their report was that, with few exceptions, Iceland should get back all the manuscripts in Denmark that had been written by Icelanders. The Danes should retain sagas specifically relating to Danish kings, along with any Icelandic manuscripts which had come to Denmark from Norway, and any from Danish private collections which had been deposited in the Arnamagnaean Institute or the Royal Library.

In the autumn of 1959 there was a general election in Denmark which resulted in a Social-Democratic and Radical victory over the Conservatives, the party which had most consistently opposed the return of the manuscripts. This brought a possible resolution of the matter much closer and in February 1961 the new Danish government asked for a full statement of Iceland's position and requests. This was presented in the following month, along with a long list of both the categories of manuscripts, and the individual manuscripts that Iceland was claiming. There was some hard horse-trading behind the scenes, but an agreed list was reached by April 1961.

In general, it is fair to say that the Icelandic politicians acknowledged that their country had no absolute judicial right to the manuscripts in Danish possession, but argued that there was a moral obligation to return them, particularly in the light of the ending of the monarchical union with Denmark in 1944. On the other hand the opponents of restitution argued that the manuscripts constituted a pan-Scandinavian heritage which ought to remain in Copenhagen. In their view Iceland lacked both the technical resources to conserve the manuscripts properly and the scholarly resources to study and publish them. Copenhagen, in contrast, was a recognized centre for Old Norse studies and already possessed all the technical and institutional resources necessary to house them and make them available for study.[3]

It was also argued that the will of Arne Magnussen was inalienable, and that any removal of manuscripts from the Arnamagnaean Institute in Copenhagen would be tantamount to an illegal expropriation of private property. Nonetheless, in April 1961 the Danish government laid before parliament a bill changing the provisions of Arne Magnussen's will and a draft agreement between the two countries concerning the restitution of the manuscripts. In June 1961 this bill was passed by a large majority of 110 to 39. However, parliamentary opponents of the bill argued that the new Manuscript Act amounted to an expropriation law, which, under Article 73 of the Danish Constitution, had to be held in abeyance until such time as a new parliament could confirm it, unchanged, following a general election. In the event, when it came to the vote, a sufficient number of MPs – sixty-one in all – was mustered to enforce this requirement.

Although the campaign within the Danish parliament to secure the return of the manuscripts was for the moment checked, the fierce debate in the Scandinavian world continued unabated for years. Intense lobbying took place and a pamphlet war ensued.

Professor Poul Andersen,[4] writing in 1961, developed the case against return. The basis for his argument was that Article 25[5] of the Danish Constitution did not allow the necessary authority for giving away the manuscripts, which was a far greater measure of intervention into the integrity of the Foundation than those changes in Foundations which had been practised hitherto. The handing-over would deprive the Arnamagnaean Foundation of the right of ownership of the manuscripts and would serve an irrelevant purpose in relation to the Foundation: namely, the improvement of relations between Iceland and Denmark. The property of a private citizen was to be used for a purely political purpose, and the Icelandic desire to move the manuscripts sprang purely out of nationalistic feeling. Generally, he said there are distinctions between Foundations under private and public management. The Commission had a right to bring a case in this instance because it was not so subordinate to the Minister of Education or the Senate of the University that it could be obliged to give away manuscripts (even by a decree). Nobody in the normal sense is the owner of the property of a Foundation because of the limited right of disposal by the Deed of Foundation. Generally in a Foundation the right of disposal rests with the Board limited by the purpose of the Foundation. It is protected. When the Foundation is regarded as an owner, it must be regarded as an owner with respect also to the expropriation law. In practice the question had never given rise to any doubt. He asserted that Article 73(2) of the Danish Constitution operated where the law, as here, was an expropriation law.

Dr Gylfi Gíslason, who was the Icelandic Minister of Culture from 1956 to 1971, stressed the literary merit of the manuscripts.[6] This literature was one of the most important contributions of Northern man to world culture. Because of the Icelanders, the *Edda* poems had been preserved. Much of the historic worth of the sagas lay in the fact that they were written in Icelandic, and not in Latin, which was then the world language; in Iceland alone among the Scandinavian countries was the vernacular being used as a written language. It was at the end of the sixteenth century that the outside world began to discover this literature as the result of copies made on paper, in which the many abbreviations found in the vellum manuscripts were written out in full.

In connection with an exhibition in 1963, the Arnamagnaean Institute, the university of Copenhagen and the Danish Royal Library published a pamphlet about Arne Magnussen. One contributor to the pamphlet was Professor Christian Westergård-Nielsen, the Chairman of the Arnamagnaean Commission. He claimed that much of the collection comprised seventeenth-century copies of earlier manuscripts, some of which were Arne Magnussen's own copies. There was a tradition in Iceland for doing this – twenty-six manuscripts were written or owned by his maternal grandmother. In 1688 Arne Magnussen had met Thormod Torfeus, the Royal Antiquary, who had in 1662 acted as intermediary between the bishop of Skálholt and the Danish king (who received *Codex Regius* and *Flateyjarbók*). Other contributors to the pamphlet explaining the background of the Arne Magnussen Foundation were Kåre Olsen, the Head Librarian of the Royal Library, and the Icelandic scholar Jón Helgason, then director of the Arnamagnaean Institute. They pointed out, among other things, that the original will of Arne Magnussen, drawn up in 1730, was no longer extant.

In 1964 the Danish Manuscripts Committee, which was a private committee under Professor Brøndum-Nielsen, published *Facts on the Manuscripts* (*Fakta om Håndskrifterne*), a booklet in which they put the case against return in question-and-answer form. This publication caused enormous offence in Iceland. Thus they asked:

Q: What are the Icelandic manuscripts?
A: These manuscripts are spread all over the world.
Q: How did they come into being?
A: Copying was used to transmit literature on vellum and parchment. After the year 1600, paper was used.
Q: What do they look like?
A: They are stained by the soot and smoke from Icelandic farms; they use a special language. Not everyone who reads Icelandic can read the Icelandic manuscripts.
Q: Why did interest decrease in them?
A: Once transferred onto paper, these older manuscripts were not so useful.
Q: What do the old manuscripts contain?
A: They are a monument to Nordic peoples and life in antiquity. They contain not only Icelandic material, but communal Germanic and Nordic material – sagas about Nordic kings and Vikings. The Norwegian material includes *Flateyjarbók*; the Faroese material tells about the discovery and colonization of the Faroes; the Greenland material is about the discovery of Greenland and America. Some of the manuscripts are single sagas; others hold collections; sometimes very different contents are bound together.
Q: What do the more recent Icelandic manuscripts contain?
A: They contain the earlier sagas and literature dating from 1500 to 1850.
Q: Where are the Icelandic manuscripts today?
A: Most are still in Icelandic ownership.
Q: How are the 12,000 manuscripts in Reykjavík treated?
A: They have been neglected; only recently have they been preserved.
Q: Has Iceland the scholarly prerequisites for studying the manuscripts? And what else has been taken back?
A: In 1927 manuscripts and letters were handed back. There has been no scholarly research done on them.

The booklet explained that *Codex Regius* consisted of thirty poems and fragments of mythological poems, including *Völuspá* ('Sybil's Prophecy') and *Thrymskviða* ('The Lay of Thor'). The text also included heroic poems with subject matter drawn from Germanic legend, on, for example, Wayland the Smith and Attila the Hun, which is the foundation of our modern knowledge of old Germanic and Nordic mythology and history. Though it was the greatest of all the manuscript treasures in Denmark the Icelanders had refused to nego-tiate without it.

According to the booklet, *Flateyjarbók* was a large collection of legends about the Norwegian kings, beginning with sagas about King Olaf Trygg-vason, the international fame of which was due to its unique account of Norse voyages to Greenland and Vínland (America).

Furthermore, the booklet continued, Iceland did not meet scholarly pre-requisites. Academic teaching in philology at Reykjavík was confined to Icelan-dic language and history, and there was no access to a sufficiently comprehensive scholarly library. Copenhagen, on the other hand, had a fully established uni-versity with scholars in all the subjects necessary for studying the manuscripts, and had for centuries been a centre for research into Nordic antiquities. All the necessary ancillary books, both old and new, together with sophisticated modern technical aids, could also be found there.

In conclusion the Danish Manuscripts Committee was united in regarding the decision to hand over the manuscripts as a catastrophe, and was concerned that it had been reached hastily and without co-operation and trust between government and the academic and legal experts.

In Iceland, a rebuttal of this pamphlet was published by Professor Einar Ólafur Sveinsson, of the university of Iceland, in which he refuted a number of points made by the Danish Committee. On the condition of the manuscripts and whether interest in them had waned, he commented: 'The Danes have suggested that the Icelanders did not value the manuscripts. However, they can normally be read without aids, and the vellum books have been taken care of.' On the manuscripts' contents he said that what Shakespeare is to English, the manuscripts are to Icelandic. As to the suggestion that most of the manuscripts were already in Iceland, he said this was unfair, since no distinction had been drawn between paper and vellum. There were only a few such vellum books, of little value, in Reykjavík, and as to the 13,000 manuscripts in Iceland, it was also unfair to allege that no research had been done into them. They consisted of copies of known older manuscripts, and were of no value for publishing. *Codex Regius*, he said, was written by Icelanders, and was not the original copy of the poems. It represented a stage in the development of Icelandic literature in the thirteenth century. *Flateyjarbók* was an Icelandic book which had been copied by named scribes for a named Icelandic chieftain, and contained sagas written by Icelandic authors. Most of it was about Norwegian kings, but also much of it, sometimes complete sagas, was about Icelanders, including the section about the discovery of America. It bore witness, he said, to the art of Icelandic book-making and of historical writing for Icelandic chieftains at the end of the four-teenth century. It was, in short, a unique monument to the history of Icelandic books, not only because of its size and condition, but also because it declared when it was written, by whom it was written and for whom it was written.

Poul Møller, the Conservative Danish MP, in his book *De Islandske Hånd-skrifter i dokumentarisk belysning* (*The Icelandic Manuscripts seen from a Documentary Point of View*), suggested a Nordic solution whereby the manuscripts should not leave Denmark but remain in a combined Nordic Research Institute. He em-phasized that, in the last few hundred years, the Nordic countries had freed themselves from each other without severing their ties, and that the basis for close co-operation has been established. However, some of his arguments against any return of the manuscripts to Iceland were based on his disapproval of the separa-tion of Iceland from the monarchical union in 1944. These arguments were to be countered by another Dane, the Conservative politician Christmas Møller, who pointed out that the Icelandic people had every right to their freedom, that in the years 1928 to 1937 the Icelandic parliament had previously given notice of its intention to take advantage of the anticipated dissolution of the union in 1943,[7] and that it was impossible to prolong the union in any event, especially in the light of the war situation.

In the course of the dispute, other Nordic countries issued statements to the effect that the matter was exclusively between Danes and Icelanders. However, this did not prevent Nordic writers from expressing their views. In an Icelandic newspaper article, entitled 'Do the manuscripts have to stay in Copenhagen?',[8] a Swedish writer, Peter Halberg, entered the fray in favour of Iceland. He said the Danes had been taken by surprise because in fact no one had ever taken the slightest notice of the manuscripts before. He referred to the manuscripts as Iceland's *only* treasures. Ninety-nine out of a hundred people in Denmark did not understand the language of the manuscripts, whereas in Iceland nine out of ten had read the sagas. As for the precedent of a hand-over, this was, he said, a typical scare to frighten other libraries and museum authorities: legal precedent was a legalistic term. The question here was the matter of a gift from one nation to another, unique in its nature, and having a special background.

In the event, the Manuscript Act had to be held in abeyance until the next general election in Denmark, which took place in September 1964, and resul-ted in a minority Social-Democratic government. In October of that year the new government laid before parliament the 1961 Act, unchanged, and it was eventually passed, by 104 votes to 58 with three abstentions, and thus became law in May 1965.

At long last, it seemed, this thorny issue had been settled. But it was not to be. In June 1965 the Arnamagnaean Institute brought an action against the Danish Ministry of Education to oppose the restitution of the manuscripts, initiating an internal Danish legal dispute to which Iceland was not itself a party at any time – although it was of course to be the beneficiary of its ultimate outcome.

In order to understand this last phase of the dispute, it is necessary to look back at the 1961 Proposal for the Law of Change to the Arnamagnaean Foundation which was finally passed in the Danish parliament on 19 May 1965, and ratified on 26 May.

The proposed law contained the following provisions:

CLAUSE 1: Regardless of the rules in the Deeds ratified by King Frederick V on 18 January 1760 for the Arne Magnussen Legacy, the Foundation is to be divided into two departments in such a way that the manuscripts and archive documents from the bequest that must be re-garded as Icelandic cultural property are to be transferred to Iceland's university, to be kept and managed there in accordance with the Rules and Title Deeds of the Foundation.

CLAUSE 1(2): All documents extant in the original or copies concern-ing Iceland and such other archive documents which can be presumed to have pertained to Icelandic local and private archives are regarded as Icelandic cultural property.

CLAUSE 1(3): Manuscripts are regarded as Icelandic cultural property if the work in question is known to be, or with considerable certainty must be regarded as being, composed by or translated by an Icelander and moreover if [this work] in terms of contents solely or to a consider-able degree concerns Iceland and Icelandic affairs or [if it] belongs to the Icelandic fictional literature of the late middle ages. These criteria are brought to bear whether the manuscript is the original formulation or a copy. Mixed manuscripts are regarded on an equal footing with a manuscript composed or translated by an Icelander if they come under the above criteria to a considerable degree ...

CLAUSE 2: Simultaneously with the division of the Arne Magnussen Foundation, such manuscripts can [also] be given from the Royal Li-brary to the Icelandic Institute as can essentially be put on an equal foot-ing with those [manuscripts] which fall to Iceland as a result of the divi-sion. Moreover, *Flateyjarbók* and *Codex Regius* are given from the Royal Library to the Icelandic Institute.

CLAUSE 3(1): A committee consisting of two representatives of Copen-hagen University and two appointed by Iceland's university are given the authority of examining the manuscripts and archive documents in the Foundation's possession, and [also the task of] making a recommendation concerning which of these [manuscripts] are to be given to Iceland's university according to the regulation in Clause 1.

CLAUSE 3(2): The same committee has the responsibility of going through the manuscripts in the possession of the Royal Library [and making a recommendation] concerning which of these should be given to the Icelandic Arnamagnaean Institute by virtue of the regulation of Clause 2.

CLAUSE 3(3): The recommendation is to be put before the Prime Minister [who] after consultation with the Danish and Icelandic Ministers of Education shall make the final decision on both questions.

CLAUSE 3(4): Similarly the Prime Minister shall make the decision that a suitable part of the capital of the legacy is transferred to Iceland's university simultaneously with the carrying out of the division.

CLAUSE 4: The Danish government is given the authority to complete an agreement with Iceland about the transfer of the manuscripts in question.

Dr Jónas Kristjánsson, the Director of the Manuscripts Institute in Reykjavík, subsequently wrote a critique of this Danish law.[9] He pointed out that according to Danish law, it was not actually clear who owns the manuscripts; it only said that they were to be kept by the university of Iceland. When the matter was completely concluded and the manuscripts had come home, he suggested, the matter of who definitely owned them should be looked into.

For the meeting in April 1961, the Icelanders had produced a 'Wish List' of manuscripts which they would like to have returned. At the meeting, the Danes produced another list which was referred to in the Danish press as the 'Secret List' ('den hemmelige liste'). This list was designed simply to give the Icelanders a general indication of what the Icelanders might expect to receive, within the terms of the proposed law.

The 1959 Icelandic Manuscripts Committee had based their 'Wish List' on the nationality of the scribes. But other considerations came to the fore later: who had commissioned the making of a manuscript, who the owners had been in the past, how it had reached Denmark – or whether it had perhaps actually been written in Denmark, and for a Danish owner. Thereby several factors were introduced to induce the Icelanders to drop their claims to certain manuscripts even though they had been the work of Icelanders.

The basis of the Danish law, however, was somewhat different. It stipulated that Iceland should receive those manuscripts which would be categorized as Icelandic 'cultural property' – *islandsk kultureje*. This was defined as follows: a work composed or translated by an Icelander, and in addition whose content was wholly or chiefly concerned with Iceland or Icelandic conditions. An exception was made for Icelandic works from the late medieval period, all of which were to be returned unconditionally.

This definition was formulated exclusively by the Danes. It seems that they wished to resolve the matter as far as possible without Icelandic interference, and in Dr Jónas Kristjánsson's view they had their own reasons for this. However, in terms of practicality and clarity, the definition contained in the law was open to criticism, particularly from the Icelandic point of view.

In the first place, it rejected the view of the 1959 Icelandic Manuscripts Committee that it should be the nationality of the *scribe* that counted; instead, it proposed to apply the nationality of the *author* or the *translator* of the work and its contents. Usually, it is easy enough to decide whether a particular manuscript is *written* by an Icelander or not; but it can be extremely difficult to determine the nationality of the original *author* of the work. A large part of Icelandic works from the medieval period is preserved without the name of the author, and in trying to follow the Danish manuscript law, it has been difficult to decide whether a work is Icelandic or Norwegian, since during the main period of Old Icelandic literature, Iceland and Norway were one cultural area. It is exceptional for an Icelandic or 'Norwegian' saga to be preserved in the handwriting of the original author; for the most part, the manuscripts have descended from the original through many lost links – sometimes much changed in language or style. Therefore there is uncertainty about the author or nationality of the *preserved* work even though the nationality of the original author or translator is thought to be known. Secondly, from the Icelandic standpoint, it is ridiculous that 'Icelandic cultural ownership' has such a narrow meaning as the law indicates. For example, the *Heimskringla* by Snorri Sturluson is not Icelandic under the Danish definition, even though it is written by an Icelander, because it deals mainly with the history of Norway.

Thirdly, the definition is unclear. What do the words 'concerning Iceland' or 'Icelandic conditions' mean? With regards to the later Middle Ages, what is 'fiction literature'? Which Icelandic works from this period should be included under this heading? Fourthly, according to the findings of the Manuscripts Commission in 1951, it was apparent that most members wished to hand over works from the post-medieval period, and it was obvious those works appealed less to other nations than the medieval works. Therefore it is strange that in the law reference is made only to *later* medieval fiction literature, as if post-medieval literature is not to return to Iceland. This is an omission. Fifthly, there is no clause concerning the archive documents in the Royal Library. This is not an understandable omission, because it is hardly believable that the law intended to leave these in Denmark. In the Commission's conclusions in 1951 there is unanimous agreement on the handing over of Icelandic documents. In the law on the return of the manuscripts there are special clauses on the return of documents concerning Iceland from the Arnamagnaean Institute, and it is not understandable why this should not also refer to documents in the Royal Library. Among the lists from the Copenhagen meeting of 1961 there is one in particular which included some Icelandic documents in the Royal Library which are to be returned to Iceland; this is also not included in the Danish law. This omission has tied the hands of the committee working on the return.

Icelanders had agreed to forgo their claims to certain other manuscripts to get *Codex Regius* and *Flateyjarbók* back. For example they gave up the *Ormsbók* version of *Snorra Edda*, now in the Arnamagnaean Institute, and two manuscripts of *Njáls Saga* kept in the Royal Library (and preserved in many old manuscripts).

This much-criticized law had nevertheless been passed in 1965, but not without considerable debate in the Danish parliament. The political divide was generally between Social Democrats, who favoured return, and Conservatives, who were against it.

At the first reading in October 1964 before the re-elected Danish parliament, the debate over the proposed amendment to the Arne Magnussen Foundation document of 1760 was a lively one. In part it went as follows: Dupont, a Social Democrat, spoke on behalf of the government for the return of the manuscripts. He considered it a very touchy subject, but to the Social Democrats it was clear that they had to carry out the return. He said that the gesture was built on the pre-requisite that it was a gift that was being referred to, and by dividing the Foundation's holdings they were doing something historic, and ensuring the return to Iceland of a heritage which was placed in Denmark in 1760 when there was no university in Iceland. The Social Democrats, he said, clearly had to re-propose the Act as a matter of principle and for historical reasons. From the government's point of view this had to happen with the same wording as before, as it had no wish for any further postponement with reference to article 73(2) of the Constitution.

He went on to say that the background of this Act dated to the beginning of the twelfth century. From a decision in 1117 of the Icelandic parliament, the Althing, the Icelandic laws began to be put in writing and this meant the beginning of a comprehensive activity of copying and writing.

Descriptions of the history of Iceland and Norway such as the family sagas, the *Edda* and Nordic mythology, were written down in manuscripts which consisted of parchment and hide bindings (vellum). Not until the sixteenth century did Denmark become interested in this Nordic literature. While it was Icelanders who wrote the books, through the patronage of rich chieftains and church schools and monasteries, it was King Frederick III and a few Danish men of means who during the period of absolute monarchy acquired the manuscripts. Nor should it be forgotten that the interest in the Icelandic manuscripts also coincided with the knowledge that there were rival Swedish buyers in the market. Arne Magnussen was instrumental in acquiring the manuscripts for the Danish Royal Library, but it seems most unlikely that the manuscripts would have come to Copenhagen at all had there been an Icelandic university at the time or if Arne Magnussen could have envisaged the developments which had taken place since then.

Dupont said that no one doubted the scholarship and publishing activity which the Danes had achieved through the Arnamagnaean Institute and Danish scholarship. But the fact was being ignored that a large number of scholars who had been engaged in this work had been Icelanders.

True, Iceland had no legal right to the manuscripts, but the consideration of reasonableness played a part. The greater part of the manuscripts concerned Icelandic matters, and they were written by and for Icelandic people. Those manuscripts which concerned Norwegian matters were likewise written by Icelandic people, for it was the Icelandic people who for the greatest length of time concerned themselves with the copying and reproduction of these prehistoric things.

Dupont disagreed with the Manuscripts Committee in their opposition to the return and over their publication *Facts on the Manuscripts* (*Fakta om Håndskrifterne*, 1964). In it Professor Brøndum-Nielsen had opposed the return on the grounds that it represented an encroachment on the university's access to free research, and had even compared the conduct of the Danish government with that of the Nazi government against German universities. Dupont supported the return of a cultural heritage to Iceland, which for more than five hundred years in one way or another was under Danish rule. He asserted that the government and the majority of the general public believed that there was a duty to carry out this action. It behoved the professors and teachers and students at the university and all concerned not to promote national egoism over the matter of free research but to promote instead understanding for Nordic community.

Dupont acknowledged the argument that when Iceland was under Danish rule the manuscripts were not properly taken care of by the Icelanders. However, he said that such maltreatment of historic heirlooms had also occurred in the past in Denmark. Although the Icelanders were without legal rights, he urged consideration of their wishes from the point of view of morality and reasonableness.

On the question of expropriation, he said, learned people disagree violently; but at least two professors agreed that the collections could be removed from the Foundation by law, while the university itself in a declaration to the previous parliamentary committee had established that it is within the powers of parliament to make changes in the Foundation. Dupont ended by recommending that the present proposals for the Act should receive very favourable treatment.

Ib Thyregod, a Liberal, also favoured return. He adopted an historical perspective, stating that the debate for the manuscripts' return began in 1961 and was revived by the present claim. The background for this situation had been dealt with in a report on Icelandic manuscripts by a commission of experts and political representatives which was set up in 1947: this had been published in 1951. In 1772 the Arne Magnussen Foundation had been set up, which ever since had been the administering board. The manuscripts had been housed in various places.

Historically, he said, one should look at the demands that had been made to the government to date. In 1817 the so-called Schwerin Letters had been handed over from the collection after negotiations previously carried out with the Arnamagnaean Commission who had accepted this. In 1851 there were negotiations with Norway for an exchange of papers which did not succeed. The Commission agreed to a proposal but on the Norwegian side obstacles prevented the exchange. In 1891 the Danish State Archives put forward a demand for documents. Negotiations were entered into but opposed by the Commission. In 1907 various demands were put forward by Iceland. The Commission did not agree to these demands, after which the question was shelved. In 1922 a new demand from the State Archives was put forward about the letters; once again negotiations were carried out with the Commission, which split into a majority and minority, and handing over of the letters took place. Finally, in 1927 about seven hundred documents and four manuscripts were handed over to Iceland. Once again negotiations were carried out with the Commission, which accepted the proposal on condition that thereafter there would not be any further demands from the Icelandic side.

Thyregod continued by reporting that before the war there were various further demands from the Icelandic side. These demands were dealt with by an Icelandic–Danish Board. In 1939 this question was passed on to the Arnamagnaean Commission. Finally in 1939 there was a handing over to Norway of a number of documents – also after negotiations with the Commission, which agreed to the transfer.

He argued that there was one clear line running through all these cases – namely that from the point of view of different governments it was a duty that they should negotiate with the Commission, and also that the Commission in all these cases bar one (through disagreement in the Commission) had agreed to these transfers. He also pointed out that there was no legal demand from the Icelandic side. The question of referring the case to the International Court of Justice would not arise.

Thyregod continued in an historical vein. In 1947 the question was raised again and a parliamentary commission set up. At that time Professor Brøndum-Nielsen and Professor Carsten Høeg (and the Commission) stressed that all the members of the Commission agreed that from the Icelandic side no watertight legal case had been or could be put forward for any part of the Icelandic manu-scripts which are in Danish possession. They insisted that it was a self-evident rule that to give away irreplaceable cultural heirlooms in the state's legally unas-sailable possession must always be seen as an exception, when arguments of a very special nature are put forward.

In the present case they were of the opinion that such arguments could be put forward. The reason why so many Icelandic manuscripts were to be found in Denmark was essentially due to the former but now dissolved union of states. Iceland, whose greatest cultural contribution lay in medieval literature and where book culture both in the Middle Ages and in the present day had been unusually rich and deep, was almost entirely without those heirlooms through which this medieval book culture had been transmitted to the present day. There was widespread feeling amongst the Icelandic people concerning the manu-scripts, and it would show a lack of Nordic community spirit to disregard their wishes. Therefore they favoured a considerable gift of manuscripts to Iceland. A proposal was drawn up to make such a gift but there was not the time to accomplish it. This was seen as a matter of negotiation with the university and the Arnamagnaean Commission.

In 1961 the then Minister of Education put forward a suggestion for a splitting of the Arnamagnaean Foundation and a transfer of manuscripts partly from the Foundation and partly from the Royal Library. An Act was proposed in April 1961. He maintained that there were no proper negotiations with the University and no negotiations with the Foundation. Instead, there were secret negotiations with Iceland.

If there were to be a gift, preferably it should be voluntary and without a court case to determine the constitutional validity of the parliamentary Act. This gift should be donated with the concurrence of as many members of parliament as possible. There should be negotiations with the Foundation.

Thyregod concluded that his party was divided: some thought the legal and scholarly research arguments went against return, others from a Nordic point of view and in line with the view put forward by the principals of the Folk High

Schools favoured return. From the point of view of the populace they agreed that a gift should be made to Iceland.

Poul Møller, a Conservative, argued against return:

> Clearly Iceland has no legal right to the manuscripts. It is exclusively a question of a Danish gift.
>
> Arne Magnussen's gift to the Foundation was a purely private one, received privately by an Institution not on behalf of the state, and which had its own legal personality. This is not something amounting to spoils of war or something acquired on the strength of the union of these two states. These are things legally bought in Iceland in the sixteenth and seventeenth centuries. This is not state property and never has been.

Møller was opposed to interfering with private ownership. He continued by asserting that the price for good relationships with the Icelandic people should not be the break-up of the Foundation. This was a matter for all Nordic people and not just Icelandic people. He said 'cultural ownership' was not defined. He stressed that the determining factor should be that the handing over should be accepted by Danish scholars who best knew the facts of the case. There should have been free negotiation of this matter in parliament, so that the donors of the gift and the judiciary would determine the extent of the gift, and these two bodies should not be dictated to by the terms of the 1961 agreement reached by the government.

Helveg Petersen, a Radical Liberal, maintained that there had been parliamentary negotiations. Denmark had no other relationship with another country like that with Iceland. Such a gift to Iceland would not be a commitment to other countries to make similar gifts. This was a special case.

Aksel Larsen, a member of the Socialist People's Party, favoured return. He said that it was the Icelandic people who had preserved and handed on the contents of the manuscripts orally for centuries until Icelanders wrote the contents on vellum (parchment) and then paper.

The whole population of Iceland knew the contents of these manuscripts and lived with them to a greater degree than those who had never been to Iceland could ever conceive. Therefore they had a special right to physical ownership of the manuscripts, now that external circumstances permitted this. Larsen believed it was a question of moral right and a question of whether one people would make a gift to another people. In principle Iceland should have everything that was written by Icelanders in Iceland regardless of the contents. This case was a special one and not a precedent for cultural property elsewhere.

The Icelandic people who live in Iceland are the same people who lived in Iceland a thousand years ago. That made it more reasonable to present the manuscripts to this people as a gift. The decision to do so could only rest with parliament.

Rimstad, an Ultra Conservative, said that the manuscripts were a Danish cultural heritage which it had a duty to preserve.

Rosing, of Greenland, said that in 1961 he favoured (among sixty-one signatories) the postponement of the passing of the law on the basis of Section 73 of the Constitution. He said he personally sympathized with returning Iceland's cultural heritage. But if it was regarded as natural that the Danish National Museum should hold a collection of Greenland Eskimo items open to scholarly research, then this was analogous to the Icelandic manuscripts. An undivided collection best served the purposes of good research, and so the manuscripts should not be handed over.

Diderichsen, a Liberal, was against return. He said that popular cultural heritage and hereditary possession of manuscripts are two totally different things which we have no right to confuse. Iceland's popular cultural heritage would be as much alive whether the manuscripts were in Copenhagen or Reykjavík.

Thestrup, a Conservative, said that Iceland had no legal right to the manu- scripts. In Iceland there had been a great literary achievement, to which was owed knowledge of the culture and life of the Nordic countries before the in- troduction of Christianity, carried out by a people closely related to the Danes and to the peoples of Norway, Sweden and Finland. These old books were for the Icelandic people a national shrine; for the other Nordic people it was not the books themselves but their contents which had this importance. He would have liked to see the case decided through a referendum.

K. B. Andersen, the Minister for Education and a Social Democrat, said that this was an exceptional case, since Iceland had so few heirlooms left. But there was a limit to any compromise because there was already a treaty as well as the 1961 law.

At the second reading of the 1964 bill (in May 1965) Poul Møller said that 1,178 people had signed a protest petition after the publication of the Interim Committee Report, including art historians and scholars. He criticized the Icelanders and the Icelandic Minister of Education for refusing to negotiate the matter with the Danish parliament. It had been said that nothing could be changed in the 1961 law. Møller said it was not known if the majority in parliament was in tune with the majority of the people. 'Kultureje' – 'cultural ownership' – was a word which previously did not exist in the Danish lan- guage, but was a term that emerged in Section 1 of the proposed (1961) law. It was a word that had been constructed ad hoc. Cultural heritage – 'kulturarv' –

may have been an accepted term, but cultural ownership – 'kultureje' – was unknown.

He said of clause 1(3) of the law, which attempted to define Icelandic cultural property, that it was extremely difficult to interpret a stipulation with expressions such as 'composed by Icelanders to a considerable degree' or 'with considerable certainty', in relation to something which had occurred three hundred to six hundred years ago. He went on to quote seven professors of law to the effect that the law was a question of a compulsory renunciation of property.

Rimstad, an Ultra Conservative, questioned the idea of a 'people's gift', the so-called 'folkgave'.

Diderichsen, a Liberal, said that *Codex Regius* and *Flateyjarbók* had been in Copenhagen for three hundred years, and had been given as a present to King Frederick III. He referred to 'a UNESCO principle that cultural and historic items in archives should stay where they are now'.

Per Møller, a Liberal, said that this matter was concerned with historical justice.

Hanne Budtz, a Conservative, favoured the return of the manuscripts to Iceland.

Poul Andreasen, Faroes, favoured the return of the manuscripts to Iceland.

K. Axel Nielsen, a Social Democrat and Minister for Justice, speaking for the government, said that this intervention meant that all that was happening was a change in the Deed of the Foundation.

Opinion remained divided but throughout these debates the hope was that the issue would not result in any form of legal action, and the point was often made that it was not a legal issue.

However, in the course of the third (and final) reading of the bill in May 1965, it emerged that if the law was passed the Arnamagnaean Commission had unanimously decided that the matter would go to the courts.

Poul Møller claimed that about 20,000 people had protested to him. He said that according to Section 42 of the Constitution, a minority consisting of a minimum of sixty members had the right to demand that a law be put to referendum when it had been passed by a majority in the House. The two main books were state property. Therefore the people should have a say: this was a mixing of private and state property.

Thyregod said that according to Section 42(2) of the Constitution there could be no question of a referendum.

Helveg Petersen, a Radical Liberal, said that less than 1 per cent of the people amongst voters had actively protested against the return of the manuscripts.

Per Hækkerup, a Social Democrat, speaking for the Foreign Ministry, said:

> There is to be no ratification of the law until there has been a judicial
> determination on the matter [whether there was to be a court case]. If we
> ratified the treaty before such a determination and if the court went
> against the majority of parliament – there would be a conflict between
> state law and international law, because then the government would
> have no power to fulfil the treaty in practical terms, while as seen from
> the point of view of international law we would be forced to fulfil the
> treaty.

Therefore the treaty should be signed first and ratified when the practical possibilities for its fulfilment finally and clearly and unambiguously had been determined, either by there not being any legal case put forward or by the fact of no
referendum being carried out.

The law was passed by 104 to 58, with 3 abstentions. Therefore on 22 May
1965, it was determined that the law (effectively transferring the manuscripts to
Iceland) would then be sent to the Prime Minister. Despite the politicians'
persistently expressed dread of any form of legal proceedings, that is precisely
what ensued.

Professor Christian Westergård-Nielsen, of Århus University, who was
chairman of the governing body of the Arnamagnaean Institute, was the
moving force behind the action taken against the Ministry of Education. The
plaintiffs demanded that the Ministry of Education should acknowledge that the
new law was invalid, because it involved the compulsory surrender of property,
in violation of Article 73 of the 1953 Danish Constitution.

This stated

> Private property: freedom of business
> 73. (1) The right of property shall be inviolable. No person shall be
> ordered to surrender his property except where required in the public
> interest. It shall be done only as provided by statute and against full
> compensation.
> (2) Where a bill has been passed relating to the expropriation of
> property, one-third of the members of parliament may, within three
> weekdays from the final passing of such bill, demand that it shall not be
> presented for the Royal Assent until new elections to the parliament
> have been held and the bill has again been passed by the parliament
> assembling thereafter.
> (3) Any question of the legality of an act of expropriation, and the
> amount of compensation, may be brought before the courts of justice.

The hearing of issues relating to the amount of the compensation may
by statute be referred to courts of justice established for such purpose.

A High Court judgement was given on 5 May 1966 to the effect that the law
did not violate the Constitution, and cleared the Ministry of Education.

The Arnamagnaean Institute appealed to the Danish Supreme Court but
the decision of the lower court was upheld, on 17 November 1966 (see Appendix 1, in translation from the Danish). The provisions in the Constitution as to
the second reading of such a bill had been met. There was no basis for assuming
that the carrying-into-effect of the Act was not justified by consideration of the
common good and the fact that no provision was incorporated into the law for
compensation did not render it invalid.

On 23 November 1966, Westergård-Nielsen informed the Ministry of
Education that the governing body of the Institute would demand compensation for the loss of the manuscripts from the Danish government. The Ministry
replied (19 December 1966) that the government did not think it was liable for
the payment of any compensation, but wished the matter to be legally settled in
court at the earliest opportunity. To that end, the Ministry of Education brought
an action against the Arnamagnaean Institute on 17 February 1967.

The plaintiff (Ministry of Education) claimed that, in connection with
enforced renunciation, compensation should be given only for proven financial
loss. It was irrelevant that the body to whom the property went might be enriched by it. The loss for which compensation should be given was to be evaluated at the time of expropriation, and any possible expectation on the part of the
Institution concerning future profit on its capital should be left out of consideration. In the present case the Institution suffered no financial loss, as no encroachment would take place into the property value of the Institution. The manuscripts could not be sold or otherwise made the subject of transactions, and they
were exempt from creditor proceedings; of the usual rights of ownership remaining to the Institution, the sole question at issue was the opportunity to have the
manuscripts at its disposal.

The defendant (Arnamagnaean Institute) contended that this was a case of
compulsory surrender of rights protected under Section 73 of the Danish Constitution, and that such a surrender could only take place on receipt of full
compensation. The function of Section 73 was founded on the same considerations as other compensation regulations. Its function was preventative and re-
storative. Here the financial loss could be objectively established by expert evalu-
ations at an international level. The limitations on the Institute's right of disposal
did not mean that the benefits of the institution were without financial value.

The Eastern High Court made its judgement on 13 March 1970 (see Ap-

35

pendix 1), to the effect that the Manuscript Institute was obliged to return, *without compensation*, such manuscripts as the law required. In addition, the Arnamag-naean should hand over, also without compensation, a suitable portion of Arne Magnussen's endowment.

In particular the court determined that the defendant's interest in the collec-tion was not of a financial nature. Therefore there was no basis for determining that the defendant had sustained a loss for which the plaintiff, as the body carrying out the expropriation, was liable to give compensation.

Danish editorial opinion, following this High Court judgement in which the Ministry of Education won the case, suggested that a new precedent was being established in Danish law; in particular, that institutions which became closely involved with the state would in reality lose the legal protection of the Constitution that any other institution would enjoy. It was said that it was probably an innovation in Danish legal history in that a measure which clearly amounted to compulsory surrender could not fall under the Constitution's expropriation provision.

Two Ministers for Justice had testified in front of two parliaments that the law for handing over the manuscripts was not tantamount to a compulsory surrender. So far they had been contradicted by the High Court. It was left to the Supreme Court to pronounce final judgement in the 'Manuscripts Case'. The surprising submissions in the High Court case had made the decision in the highest court of the land even more necessary and more exciting than before.

An appeal against the High Court judgement thus went to the Supreme Court, which pronounced its judgement on 18 March 1971. The details were as follows:

The appellant (Arnamagnaean Institute) argued that this was a case of enforced renunciation. In reality there was to be a handing over of property to a foreign state. This was indicated by the use of such words as 'renunciation', 'gift', 'giving over', etc. There had been no judicial demand for the manuscripts, and there was legal opinion to the effect that this was a state intrusion into the affairs of a private foundation, for which there were neither grounds nor precedent.

It was also alleged that parliament had not had the opportunity to consider whether the renunciation had been justified by 'the common good', and had had no chance to decide on compensation.

Regarding the concept of 'the common good': the plaintiff had argued that in Article 73 of the Constitution, the reference was only to the *Danish* common good. Consideration of this could have made renunciation not only desirable, but necessary; in this case, however, handing over the documents favoured *Iceland's* interests. Whether or not it was seen as desirable and reasonable to fulfil the Icelanders' wishes, no necessity for handing over the manuscripts had been established.

Reference was made to protests by scholars, from Norway and Sweden as well as Denmark, against handing back the manuscripts. And it was argued that legal theory as well as judicial practice recognized that the question as to whether an expropriation was required by the general good could be determined judicially by the court.

Furthermore, the absence of any provision for compensation in such a law also invalidated it, so it was argued, whether or not there was any question of giving compensation.

The respondent (Ministry of Education) argued that according to their origin and character, the manuscripts were a national treasure for the Icelandic people and were their only historical records. Iceland was practically denuded of manuscripts. Although Arne Magnussen was a private citizen, the nature of his public office made him particularly successful in collecting the manuscripts. It was because people saw the cause as important for the relationship between the two countries that this law had been carried by a large majority which had crossed party lines.

The Foundation, it was argued, was set apart from ordinary Foundations, and must really be regarded as a state institution. For example, since the setting up of a permanent Commission in 1772, its management has been appointed by the state authorities. An 1850 Royal Resolution (Section 5) shows clearly that the ultimate authority rests with the Ministry of Education, while the Senate of the university has the right to express itself and have general supervision of the Foundation. This situation is upheld in Article 6 of the Royal Decree of 25 May 1936. The Foundation is clearly set apart from ordinary grant-giving bodies in that it is not to serve individual interests, but to act through scholarly research and publication of the manuscripts. This is purely a state purpose and the expense of the Foundation is covered by the state. Furthermore, as a result of the circumstances of the setting up of the Foundation, it does not enjoy the same protection against change as it would have if set up by the testator himself. In the past a number of changes in administration and even in the wording of the Deed of Covenant have been made without establishing an absolute necessity for them. And in 1817 the Commission agreed to hand back some letters.

The Ministry also put forward the case that whilst it is true that under Danish jurisprudence protection under Section 73 of the Constitution also includes foundations and legacies, such foundations vary greatly, ranging from purely private family funds to purely state institutions. The determinant factor in deciding whether a foundation was an independently protected legal subject had to be the identity of the owner of its capital funds. As far as the Arnamagnaean

Foundation was concerned it had to be assumed that the funds belonged to Copenhagen University. According to Arne Magnussen's and his wife's will, the manuscripts had been added to the university; the fact that according to the Deed the manuscripts had been put under the Foundation's protection made no difference to the issue of possession. The Deed had only set up an administrative body to manage the capital. As the university was purely a state institution, the capital of the Foundation was also state property. Even if the university rather than the Commission were to be regarded as the owner of the capital, then it would (bearing in mind the character of the Foundation) still be state property. Therefore the Foundation could not be regarded as being protected under Section 73.

The Ministry also argued that under Section 73 there is no expropriation in this case. According to this law, which is imprecisely formulated, it must be assumed that it is only the right to realizable property which enjoyed such protection. It is clear that the right of the Foundation to the capital is not a right to realizable property, but only a right to administer the capital. The capital cannot change hands nor be made the object of distraint or of further inheritance. Even the Foundation's actual access to the capital was subject to very considerable limitations, because it was the Foundation's duty to use the capital in accordance with the purpose of the Foundation. It was required to preserve the capital and give others access to it. Moreover, even in the event of the Foundation not being considered a state institution as such, then it was still of such a special character that it differed decisively from private Foundations.

The Ministry also argued that the division of the manuscripts was not a surrender in the sense covered by Section 73. The concept of 'surrender' was, in Section 73, of undetermined content and had to be interpreted with regard to individual circumstances. Emphasis could not be placed on expressions used during debates in parliament; 'splitting up', 'conserving', and the expression 'gift' did not necessarily mean a transference of property right. What was involved was a sharing-out or splitting-up of the capital of the Foundation – in such a way that the part handed over to Iceland must be preserved and administered at the university of that country, in accordance with the rules of the Foundation. There was therefore no breach of the aims of the Institute.

Even if the court found an expropriation, the Ministry further argued, the constitutional conditions had been met. As to whether the division was required by the 'common good', the final decision rested with the judicial powers' *general* estimation of this principle as the determinant factor. In the present case it must be clear that there was no basis for disregarding this general notion which had been reached from certain *factual and societal* considerations. By meeting the strong and rightful wishes of a state close to the heart of Denmark, the Danish general good was obviously also being acknowledged; and the law had been passed twice with a large majority.

Regarding compensation, it was argued that Section 73 was of no importance in this case. Only financial loss had to be compensated, and such loss was not suffered by the Foundation, which could not *absolutely* dispose of the capital. The Foundation's right of use over this capital had no financial value either. The law making the division had no compensation clause, but this could not render it invalid.

Concerning the claim of the appellant that the law was invalid, since it was not clear to parliament that it was dealing with an expropriation law, the Ministry argued that the question of expropriation had been raised several times during the debate in parliament. In any event, unawareness of expropriation would not result in the invalidity of the law, if expropriation was required out of consideration for the common good.

The Ministry finally argued that the measures set out in the law would presumably have simply been carried out in an administrative fashion since the purpose of the Foundation was not adversely affected; and the defendant also put forward the view that the measures taken into consideration in the setting up of the Foundation – especially the founding of the university of Iceland – must be taken to fit into the intention of the founders.

The court took the view that the manuscripts and archive documents, and the capital from the Foundation, *belonged to* the Foundation; and that the Foundation, regardless of the close connection with the Copenhagen University, was an autonomous institution set up according to a private legal will.

In judging the case, however, the following factors had to be taken into consideration:

All of the members of the Board of the Foundation are appointed by the state authorities. Of these, five are chosen by the Ministry, which also chooses the chairman of the Board, and the expenses of the Foundation are by and large covered by the Ministry. These circumstances give the Foundation a special character. As a result the Ministry has considerable influence over the Foundation. Against this background the Ministry also had reasonable occasion to participate in the creation of the law of 26 May 1965, which, by meeting the Icelandic people's wish to possess part of the manuscripts, solved an important problem in the relationship between Denmark and Iceland.

Regardless of the fact that the settlement as set out in the law, Art. 1(1), divided the Foundation into two departments which are both to be preserved and administered in accordance with the rules of the Foundation, the court found that the handing over to the university of Iceland, against the will of the Foundation, of some of the manuscripts and part of its capital must in itself be described as compulsory surrender.

The rights of the Foundation over the objects were, however, found to deviate to a great degree from those rights of property which are clearly protected against expropriation according to Section 73. The setting-up of the Foundation was not to serve individuals, but exclusively to preserve the manuscripts with a view to researching them and publishing them, which could still be achieved regardless of the decision that had been made.

In deciding whether the Foundation should accept the renunciation of some of the manuscripts, the court also found that it should attach importance to the fact that Arne Magnussen, as Archive Cabinet Secretary and Professor at Copenhagen University, and in his capacity of Land Registry Commissioner to Iceland, had a position which had given him a great opportunity for contacting people who were willing to give him their manuscripts. Moreover, a consideration of the Ordinances of the Foundation amongst others revealed that Icelandic grantholders and scribes were to research and copy the manuscripts, and indicated that the founders, in so far as was possible, wished to further Icelandic interests. Thus it was found that the 'interference' caused by the law to the Foundation was not covered by Section 73(1) of the Constitution and the Ministry was to be absolved.

There was some difference of opinion about various aspects of the case; ten of the judges sought largely to absolve the Ministry of the compensation claim whereas two of the judges supported the claim of the Institute. By a majority decision, the judgement of the lower court was upheld, but it was decided that the Institute should be allowed compensation for that portion of the *endowment* alone which should go to Iceland. The sum was not significant. If the Danish state had been obliged to pay the Institute the full market value of the *manuscripts* that were being returned to Iceland, the amount would have been prodigious and their return would have been impossible. It has been suggested the figure could have been as much as £50 million.

When the manuscript law had first been passed in 1961, an agreement was made between Denmark and Iceland about the transfer of some of the manuscripts from the Arnamagnaean Institute to the university of Iceland. It was agreed then between the Danes and Icelanders to delay its full ratification until all the court cases were over. After this last Supreme Court judgement on 18 March 1971, the final agreement was ratified on 1 April 1971.

According to the terms of the agreement there was an obligation to establish an Árni Magnússon Institute in Iceland. A special Manuscript Institute had already been set up in 1962, and it was thought proper to change the name, in accordance with the agreement, to 'Stofnun Árna Magnússonar á Íslandi'. This change was ratified by the Icelandic parliament in the spring of 1972, and came into force on 28 May.

The treaty between Denmark and Iceland about the transfer of parts of the Arnamagnaean Foundation's manuscripts to be kept and managed by Iceland's university (1965, ratified in 1971), took the following form:

Transfer to Iceland of manuscripts regarded as Icelandic cultural property

ARTICLE 1. As soon as the division of the Foundation into two sections has been carried out according to Danish Law 26 May 1965 concerning the change of the Deed of 18 January 1760 for Arne Magnussen's legacy (the Arnamagnaean Institute), those manuscripts and archive documents that are to be kept and managed by Iceland's university are to be transferred to Iceland.

ARTICLE 2. The Icelandic government undertakes the responsibility through Iceland's university of keeping and managing the manuscripts and archive documents transferred to Iceland in accordance with the rules in the Deed in the Arnamagnaean bequest.

ARTICLE 3. At the same time as the transfer of the manuscripts, a division is to be carried out of the capital of the Arnamagnaean Foundation which at present constitutes 100,000 Kroner, and a sum to be established in Article 3(4) of the law is given to Iceland's university with the duty for the same to manage and use the financial resources in accordance with the title deeds of the Foundation.

ARTICLE 4. The manuscripts and archive documents covered by this treaty, along with the capital, are to constitute the Arnamagnaean Foundation in Iceland, which designation is to be ratified by Iceland's government.

ARTICLE 5. To the Arnamagnaean Foundation in Iceland are given from the Royal Library in Copenhagen those manuscripts which are covered by the decisions reached according to Article 3(3) of the above-mentioned law.

ARTICLE 6. The contracting parties are agreed that the arrangement that has been reached is to be recognized as a complete and final resolution of all Icelandic wishes concerning the transfer of national Icelandic heritage items, of any kind, residing in Denmark. In accordance with this it will not be possible in future for Iceland to raise or support demands or wishes for the handing over of any further such heritage items from Danish archives or collections, either public or private.

ARTICLE 7. The transfer to Iceland of such manuscripts which, according to the Board of the Danish Foundation, are vital to the compilation of a new Icelandic dictionary which is presently in progress in Denmark, will not be started until this work has been completed. However, [this will be] no later than twenty-five years after the taking effect of this Treaty.

ARTICLE 8. By agreement between the two Ministers of Education of the two countries, rules will be established concerning mutual access for the two divisions of the Foundation, for documents and manuscripts for use in scholarly research.

ARTICLE 9. [Any] possible dispute concerning the understanding of the present treaty is to be the subject of discussion via diplomatic channels. If a satisfactory solution is not reached in this way then the question is to be passed for final decision to a committee consisting of two members appointed by the Danish government, two members appointed by the Icelandic government, and an arbitrator appointed by the four members of the Committee. If no agreement regarding the choice of an arbitrator can be reached, then the parties will ask the President of the International Court of Justice in the Hague to make the choice.

ARTICLE 10(1). This treaty, which has been written in Danish and Icelandic so that both texts shall have the same validity, must be ratified, and the instruments of ratification are to be exchanged in Copenhagen as soon as possible.

ARTICLE 10(2). This treaty takes effect from the date of exchange of instruments of ratification.

1 July 1965. Sealed. Copenhagen.

In the Danish manuscripts law, it had been indicated that a joint committee of four was to decide which manuscripts should be returned to Iceland in the light of the new law; two of them were to be nominated by the university of Copenhagen, and two by the university of Iceland. The bill allowed for the return of 1,700 manuscripts and documents from the Arnamagnaean Institute, and 106 manuscripts and thirty documents from the Royal Library. It also provided for the return of some 1,350 original documents and some 6,000 copies of documents from the Arnamagnaean. The law referred particularly to the two immensely important manuscripts to be returned from the Royal Library of

Copenhagen upon the confirmation of the new law, *Flateyjarbók* and *Codex Regius*.

On 21 April 1971 when these two manuscripts were returned, by Danish frigate, to Icelandic soil and ceremoniously handed over in Reykjavík, the day was a momentous one for Icelanders. All activities were suspended as the whole nation watched on television one of the most extraordinary episodes of cultural restoration.

The Manuscript Committee was appointed on 13 September 1971, and held its first meeting in July 1972, meeting thereafter four times annually, alter-nating in Iceland and Denmark.

The first of the other manuscripts, after *Flateyjarbók* and *Codex Regius*, reach-ed Iceland on 27 June 1973. When the Icelanders held a ceremonial celebration of the tenth anniversary of the manuscripts law, on 21 April 1981, 835 manu-scripts and 2,855 copies of old documents had been returned from the Arna-magnaean Institute, as well as thirty-eight manuscripts from the Royal Library in Copenhagen (Fig. 6).

When the forty-first meeting of the Committee took place in May 1983, it had nearly finished its work. Manuscripts had been sent back continuously since 1971, and it had only to agree on a few cases that were disputed. More than 1,000 manuscripts had been sent from the Arnamagnaean Institute, along with sixty files of copies of manuscripts, and a total of forty-six manuscripts from the Royal Library. The Commission had come to a decision on 1,539 manuscripts and other documents from the Arnamagnaean, and 144 manuscripts from the Royal Library. The final consignment was expected before 1996.

In Jón Samsonarson's[10] view, the manuscripts war between Denmark and Iceland had died down. Seen politically, patience and co-operation on both sides had helped to settle the matter. He expressed the hope that bigger nations could take this as an example. For the cause of research the dispute had ended well. All the publications which needed to be done from the manuscripts could be done through the co-operation of the two institutions. For the Icelanders the tangible outcome of the dispute was the establishment of the Manuscript In-stitute in 1962, which has become the cornerstone of Icelandic philological scholarship. In the view of Dr Jónas Kristjánsson, director of Iceland's Manu-script Institute, the direct influence of the homecoming of the manuscripts has not been easy to estimate, but there has been an increased interest in the language and literature of Iceland, and an increased attendance in Icelandic studies at the university of Reykjavík. Undoubtedly the homecoming of the manuscripts has strengthened Icelandic national feeling and cultural consciousness. Historically, the appeal of these literary masterpieces and lesser works amongst a largely literate

Fig. 6. A page from the Icelandic manuscript known as *Gráskinna* (Greyskin). It is one of the oldest of the manuscripts of *Njáls Saga*, mightiest of all the Icelandic sagas, which was written around 1280. The manuscript dates from the early fourteenth century, and is one of the cultural treasures returned by Denmark to Iceland.

44

population played an important part in preserving the Icelandic language as it is spoken today.

In reality the arguments over the return of the manuscripts had gone through many phases between 1907 and 1971. Icelandic experts such as Einar Ólafur Sveinsson had argued that as cultural treasures – 'menningarfjársjóður' – these works had kept the nation alive for centuries, and were still an anchor of Iceland's culture today. They were and are today the cornerstone of Icelandic nationality and language, and it had been a matter of regret that, after independence, the key to their cultural identity remained so far away from Iceland. It had been predicted that the restoration of the manuscripts would become one of the most important events in its cultural history, and this prediction proved to be true.

What was so exceptional about this case? The materials in question had been removed from Iceland while there had been a colonial but none the less legitimate political union between Iceland and Denmark. They were removed by an Icelander in the course of his official duties for his own private collection, and then deposited in Copenhagen. Sometimes the ensuing debate over the manuscripts sank to invective when aspersions were cast on the scholarship of Icelanders or their political integrity. Sometimes the arguments for return were sublime. In the end Danish public opinion, which responded to the appeal of natural justice, the political will of the Danish parliament, and the authority of the Danish judiciary, combined to produce a result of astonishing goodwill. Iceland never brought a legal action against Denmark either nationally or internationally. Yet, as the result of the legal action to which Iceland herself was never a party, substantial numbers of Icelandic manuscripts were returned. Although there had been a compulsory surrender of property, there had not been such an expropriation of property as would under the Danish Constitution have justified compensation. Moreover, included amongst the returned cultural property were the two most historically valuable manuscripts, *Codex Regius* and *Flateyjarbók*, which were after all never part of Árni Magnússon's own collection and were kept at the Royal Library.

The question of a national referendum had been mooted. In 1961, when the Danish Manuscript Law had been passed by 110 votes to 39, the bill had been postponed because of the issue over Section 73 of the Danish Constitution regarding expropriation. When the vote was taken again in 1965 the bill was passed by 104 votes to 58. The opposition fell two short of the minimum of sixty votes which would have been required to bring about a referendum. Therefore the arguments in parliament about the validity or appropriateness of a referendum under the Constitution proved to be academic. There never was a referendum, and to that extent Danish public opinion was not gauged.

Nevertheless the extraordinary feat of return was accomplished. Danish regret for its sometimes harsh colonial rule spanning five hundred years must have played its part. But in 1965 Icelandic editorial opinion had already hailed the handing-over of the manuscripts as a unique step in Nordic and world history – an example and incentive for the rest of the world on how to resolve sensitive disputes. Given the many different twists and turns to this particular case its outcome was an extraordinary one by any standards, and its implications far-reaching. The extent to which this case serves as an international model for other cultural restitution cases is discussed in the following chapter, and in the conclusion to this book.

CHAPTER TWO

THE ELGIN MARBLES DEBATE

One of the most controversial items sought for return from Britain has been the Elgin Marbles, or Parthenon Marbles, as they are referred to by Greeks, in particular by the Greek Minister of Culture, Melina Mercouri. The marbles, kept in the British Museum, comprise a 247-foot length of fifth-century frieze that adorned the Parthenon, the Temple of Athena on the Athenian Acropolis, and a collection of larger than life-size figures. It is almost half of the original frieze, which was 524 feet long. It has been stressed by the Greek Minister for Culture that the marbles, removed by Lord Elgin one hundred and eighty years ago, are an integral part of the Acropolis, which symbolizes Greece itself, and are part of its psychological landscape. They have been argued about ever since their transportation to England and have become the *cause célèbre* amongst the cultural return cases.

The Parthenon stands on the highest point of the Acropolis, or citadel, of Athens (Fig. 7). From the earliest times the Acropolis served both as citadel and religious centre, the principal cult being that of the goddess Athena. The temple was conceived by the Athenian statesman Pericles and was designed by the architects Ictinus and Callicrates to house a statue of the goddess Athena, patron and protector of the city, and the Athenian treasury. Pheidias, the famous sculptor, was commissioned to create a colossal statue in gold and ivory. The Parthenon was erected in the fifth century BC (Fig. 8) and took about sixteen years to complete. It was to remain in use as a temple for nine hundred years. It is considered to be unusual in its almost total concentration on the goddess Athena, to whom it was devoted and who gave it its name, which means 'the shrine of the Virgin'. It has been assumed that Pheidias supervised all the sculptures and that their themes were arrived at through discussions with Pericles. There has been some speculation about the authorship of the marbles but the long-established opinion which credits Pheidias primarily with the sculpture of the Parthenon is generally considered the most plausible view. The other principal building on the Acropolis was the Erechtheion (Fig. 9), a complex group of sanctuaries incorporated into a single building around 400 BC and considered to be of great refinement and beauty.

It is believed that at least four temples were erected successively on the Parthenon site. A new temple was under construction when the Persians invaded Greece for the second time (480 BC) and destroyed it. In 450 BC, a decree

Fig. 7. The Parthenon. Photograph by Alfred Eisenstadt.

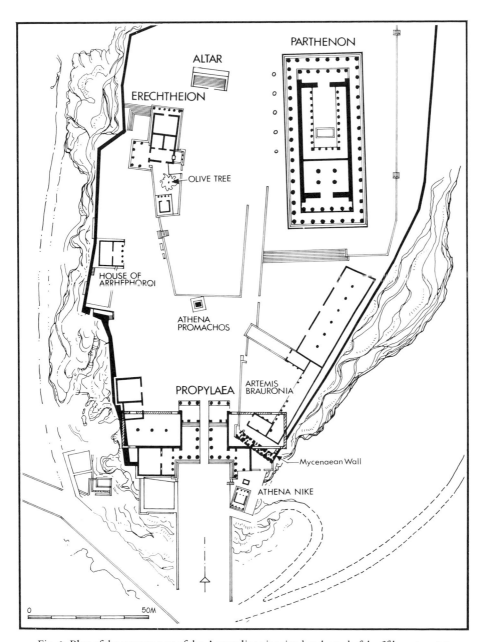

Fig. 8. Plan of the western part of the Acropolis as it existed at the end of the fifth century BC.

49

Fig. 9. 'Pillars of the Parthenon'. With a view of the Caryatid porch on the Erechteum.
Photograph by Edward Steichen, 1921.

was put through the Athenian Assembly by Pericles which made it possible for the city of Athens to draw from the funds contributed by her allies for defence against the Persians (the alliance known as the Delian League, with the Athenians acting as leaders) in order to rebuild the temples destroyed during the Second Persian war. Work on the Parthenon started in 447 BC, and in 438 BC the temple was ready to receive the 40-foot high statue of Athena made of ivory and gold on a wooden core. The sculptures of the Parthenon were completed by 432 BC. After the Roman conquest of Greece (87–86 BC) the Parthenon remained a place of worship. In the third and fourth centuries Athens was attacked by the Vandals and then the Goths but it is believed that the cult statue of Athena was still in place in the fifth century AD, and the Panathenaic Festival was still celebrated. However, around that time the gold and ivory Athena Parthenos was taken to Constantinople and disappeared. A bronze statue of Athena Promachos which was also taken away was destroyed by the Crusaders in the sack of Constantinople in 1204. The first major change to the building itself came in the sixth century when the Parthenon was converted to a Christian church under the Byzantine Emperor Justinian (AD 527–65), and was dedicated to Saint Sophia (Holy Wisdom). The north-west and east metopes were defaced because of their pagan images. The Crusaders later dedicated it to the Virgin Mary and it became the Metropolitan Church of Athens. In 1458, shortly after the fall of Constantinople, when Athens was taken by the Turks, the Parthenon was turned into a mosque and the Christian bell tower, erected in Byzantine times, became a minaret. These were almost the only changes in two thousand years. Structurally the Parthenon remained unaltered, as the 400 drawings made by the French artist Jacques Carrey in 1676 show (Figs. 10–13).[1] In 1678 the Venetians under their general Francesco Morosini besieged the Acropolis, where the Turks kept their gunpowder in the Parthenon. The Venetian bombardment ignited the powder, which exploded, blowing up the centre of the Parthenon; eight columns fell on the north side and six on the south, together with their entablature. Morosini added to the damage by attempting to remove from the west pediment the horses and chariot of Athena; their weight was misjudged and the tackle broke during the removal, shattering the statues. By 1766 a small mosque was built within the ruins. Following this, the building succumbed to the passion of collectors. In 1787 the Comte de Choiseul-Gouffier removed to France one detached piece of the frieze. In 1801 Lord Elgin obtained the 'firman' (written authority) from the Porte 'to remove some stones with inscriptions and figures'. The Italian artist Lusieri supervised the removal of the greater part of the frieze and the metopes from the structure of the Parthenon. To achieve this he purportedly had to remove the superstructure and thus destroy the architecture. Part of the Erechtheion was also removed. Over the

Fig. 10. The French artist Jacques Carrey in 1676 made four hundred drawings of the Parthenon. These are now preserved in the Bibliothèque Nationale, Paris. They indicate the state of preservation of the buildings up to the date of the drawings. Details of west pediment (left side).

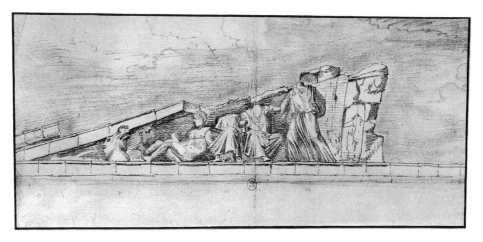

Fig. 12. Drawing by Jacques Carrey in 1676. Details of east pediment (left side).

Fig. 11. Drawing by Jacques Carrey in 1676. Details of west pediment (right side).

centuries the main building suffered a number of privations which only cul⁄
minated in Elgin's action and in the contentious collection now housed in the
Duveen Gallery in the British Museum.

The Parthenon lay east to west, and its interior was divided by a blank wall
into two chambers of unequal size. The principal compartment, whose door
was to the east, held the gold and ivory statue of Athena Parthenos; the lesser
chamber, opening to the west, was intended as a strong room to house the

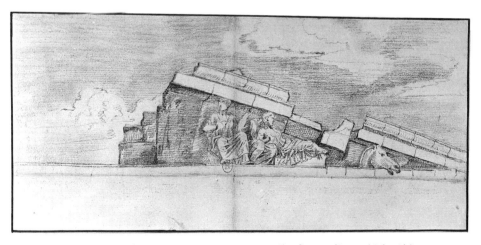

Fig. 13. Drawing by Jacques Carrey in 1676. Details of east pediment (right side).

53

treasures belonging to Athena and the accumulated revenue from the empire. In front of each doorway was a porch supported by six columns, and round the whole structure ran a continuous colonnade, with eight columns at front and back and seventeen on the long sides. The building, with its facade of eight columns instead of the more usual six, was exceptionally wide in proportion to its length. It is built throughout of fine-grained local marble, and is of the Doric order, with fluted columns which taper upward; each one supports a spreading capital and square abacus, upon which rest the horizontal beams or architraves running from column to column. The architraves in their turn carry the metopes, panels of marble approximately four feet square; each is separated from the other by a narrow grooved block or triglyph, and two metopes with their intervening triglyph fill the space between two adjacent columns, so that in all there were ninety-two carved metopes, thirty-two on a long side and fourteen on a short one. Above them runs a horizontal cornice; on the short side a second cornice rises with the gable end of the roof, framing a triangular space known as the pediment.

The sculpture of the Parthenon (Fig. 14) consisted firstly of groups in the round in the gables or pediments and contained about fifty figures. Secondly there were square panels sculptured in high relief, the metopes on the external order. Finally there was the frieze, with the scene of the Panathenaic procession, which surrounded the central chamber.

The metopes, carved in high relief, mainly portrayed mythical battles between humans and superhuman creatures. The east end is devoted to the single story of the war between the gods and giants who tried to storm Mount Olympus. On the west end, the theme is the battle between Greeks and Amazons. On the north side the main theme was the sack of Troy and on the south side the struggle between the Lapiths (a people living in northern Greece) and the Centaurs (half horse, half man). The frieze, carved in shallow relief, was about thirty-nine feet above floor level, and, until one came close to the building, was masked by the architraves of the outer colonnade, so that the angle of view was extremely steep; the upper parts of the figures on the frieze are carved in higher relief to compensate for this. The blocks which form the frieze are about three feet three inches in height; out of an original total length of about 524 feet, over 420 have survived, a further 56 feet are known from the drawings made by early travellers, and 45 feet are lost.

The whole frieze is devoted to a single subject, the Panathenaic procession (Figs. 15 and 16). The Panathenaea, as its name suggests, was a festival in honour of Athena. The event which in particular gave meaning to the occasion was the solemn procession, formed from representatives of all classes of the community, which ascended the Acropolis to offer sacrifice to the goddess

Fig. 14. A view of the east end of the Parthenon showing the position of pediments, metopes and frieze.

whose name the city bore. It was the main religious event of the year in Athens and took place annually in early August on the day traditionally regarded as the birthday of the goddess. Every fourth year was marked by an important addition to the ceremonies: the wooden statue of Athena which stood in another temple on the Acropolis was draped with a new robe, woven to a traditional pattern. It has also been suggested that the procession depicted on the frieze was not an

55

ordinary one, but is an assembly of the gods to receive the 192 Athenian heroes who died at the battle on the Plain of Marathon (which was fought to rout the Persian army). This was the number of men or youths who appeared on the frieze, and there is also a proximity in date between the Great Panathenaic Festival of 490 BC and the battle of Marathon.

The frieze begins on the west side of the temple, with cavalrymen preparing for the parade. The action unfolds from right to left, and around the corner of the building, at the start of the north side, there is a last glimpse of the preparations. In front of the cavalry come the chariots, each one drawn by four horses. There follows a group of elders and musicians and young men carrying offerings. On the south side the procession again moves from east to west, repeating the same theme, but not identically. On the east side the two streams of the procession converge. Two groups of seated figures, larger in scale than the rest, look out-ward at the two divisions of the procession. They are the twelve major gods of Olympus, with two younger divinities standing beside them. On the left, in the place of honour nearest the centre, is Zeus, ruler of the gods and father of gods and men; he alone has a throne. Beside him sits his consort Hera, holding her veil in the traditional attitude of a bride; in the background is a winged girl who may be Victory or Iris. Next is Ares, the god of war, his unquiet temper expressed by the restlessness of his pose; then the corn goddess Demeter, holding the long torch which was her attribute. Her right hand touches her chin; the gesture, in anti-

Fig. 15. Frieze of horsemen from the Parthenon Marbles. North frieze, Slabs xxxv–xxxviii, figures 109–18. Photograph by David Finn.

Fig. 16. Frieze of horsemen and a boy from the Parthenon Marbles. North frieze, Slab xlii, figures 130–4. Photograph by David Finn.

quity an expression of sorrow, alludes to her mournful quest for her daughter Persephone, who was carried off by Hades to the kingdom of the Dead. In front of her sits Dionysus, leaning carelessly on the shoulder of Hermes, the messenger of the gods, who is dressed ready for the road with boots, cloak and broad, brimmed hat. On the right, in a position of importance comparable to that of Zeus, is Athena, watching the ceremonies performed in her honour; she has a bronze spear, attached by rivets, but as it is a festal day she has laid aside her helmet and her aegis lies in her lap. Beside her and turning to speak to her sits Hephaestus; his body and shoulders are powerful but a slight distortion of his ankles and the stick beneath his arm hint at the tradition that he was a cripple. The bearded figure next to them is probably Poseidon, with a youthful pair who are surely Apollo and his twin sister Artemis; the goddess at the extreme right is Aphrodite, and against her knee leans her son Eros, who shades her with a parasol.

In the centre, framed by the two groups of divinities, are five figures, a man and a boy folding up a large rectangle of heavy cloth, a woman taking a stool from a girl who carries it on her head, and a second girl with another stool moving up behind. For the key position of the whole frieze the artist has selected

Fig. 17. The Chariot of Helios, Dionysus, and three goddesses from

the climax of the ritual; the peplos, the new robe for the statue of Athena, has reached its destination and has passed into the care of a magistrate and his acolyte. The rest of the scene is obscure. The frieze thus was exceptionally long, unmatched in any other Doric temple.

The pediments (Figs. 17, 18) are over ninety feet long and about three feet deep, measured from the back wall; their height rises to over eleven feet in the centre. The space was originally filled with figures carved completely in the round, the largest of them being nearly twice life size. Pausanias, who wrote a *Description of Greece* in the second century AD, states explicitly that the pediment above the entrance – that is, at the east – represented the birth of Athena, while at the other end was the contest between Athena and Poseidon for the land of Attica.

The frieze consisted of 111 panels, of which about ninety-seven survive, intact or broken. Of the surviving panels, fifty-six are in the British Museum, forty *in situ* or in the Acropolis Museum, and one in the Louvre, collected by the French consul in Athens, Fauvel. Broken fragments exist in the Copenhagen, Vienna, Heidelberg, Palermo and Vatican museums. Of the original ninety-two metopes, thirty-nine are either *in situ* or in the Acropolis Museum and fifteen

:henon Marbles. East pediment, figures B–G. Photograph by David Finn.

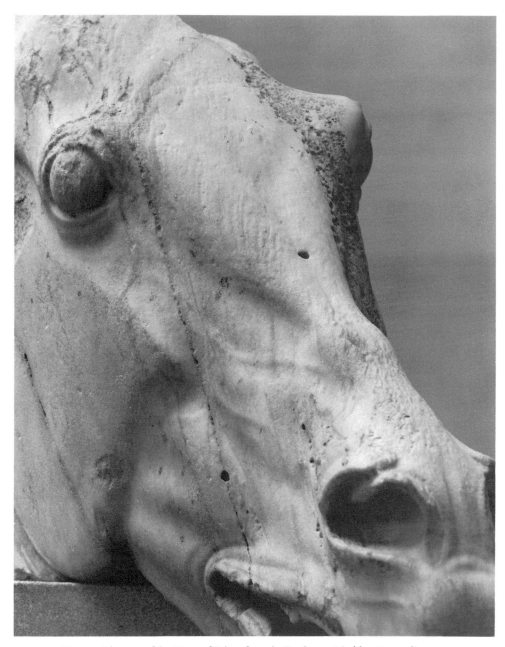

Fig. 18. Close-up of the Horse of Selene from the Parthenon Marbles. East pediment.
Photograph by David Finn.

are in the British Museum.² The British Museum also has seventeen pedimental figures, as well as sculptures taken from other buildings, notably a caryatid and column from the Erechtheion.

From the time of their removal up to the present day, the action of removing the marbles from the Parthenon has caused debate, and Elgin himself has been both praised and vilified. Four factors contributed to the removal of the Parthenon Marbles by Lord Elgin at the beginning of the nineteenth century: the conquest of the Greek people by the Ottoman Turkish empire in 1453, which lasted about four hundred years; the British victory against Napoleon, which altered the balance of power in the Mediterranean and won them favour with the Turks; the practice of acquiring antiquities to embellish grand country houses, which Elgin at least originally sought to copy; and the special nature of Elgin's office.

Lord Elgin was made ambassador to the court of the Sublime Porte in 1799. He had earlier engaged a young architect, Thomas Harrison, to build a new mansion, Broom Hall, in Scotland, on the occasion of his marriage. With Elgin's new appointment, Harrison would have the opportunity of making detailed drawings and copies of Greek architecture and sculpture. Elgin also employed a personal secretary, William Richard Hamilton, and a Neapolitan topographical draughtsman, Giovanni Lusieri. Hamilton, Lusieri and a team of craftsmen including several Italian architects, Vincenzo Balistra, and Sebastian Ottar, were to go to Athens to measure and make casts of the ancient monuments whilst Elgin himself and his wife went to Constantinople.

When Elgin's team arrived in Athens the Parthenon was reportedly being used as an ammunition storehouse, and much of the building had been destroyed earlier, in 1678 by the Venetians. The local governor of the fortress imposed restrictions on Elgin's men, and they could only make limited copies. However, Elgin was encouraged in 1801 by Dr Philip Hunt, chaplain to the British embassy in Constantinople, to apply for a firman to permit him to take away sculptures which did not interfere with the works or walls of the citadel. A copy, in Italian, of the firman is now said to exist to show that Lord Elgin had permission to take the marbles in 1801. It is from the Turkish government in Constantinople to the governor of Athens, giving Lord Elgin permission to dig at the Acropolis and take things away. It is the only known document supporting Lord Elgin's claim that he was entitled to bring the sculptures back to Britain. It is said to be in the possession of Mr William St Clair, joint chairman of the Byron Society in London. It belonged, with many other papers, to Philip Hunt.

The existing copy of the firman in Italian contains the clause giving Elgin permission to take 'qualche pezzi di pietra con iscrizione e figure'; 'some [or 'any' – 'qualche' can mean either] pieces of stone with inscriptions and figures'. It concludes that no one should meddle with the work of Lord Elgin and his team 'nor hinder them from taking away pieces of stone with inscriptions or figures'. Dr Hunt, it has been said, had insisted on the translation into Italian, the *lingua franca* of the time, when the firman was issued.

It has been suggested that the document was ambiguous because it was probably a misinterpretation of the meaning of the words to say that permission to dig and take away meant that Lord Elgin could take sculptures from the building. It has also been said,[3] and generally assumed, that the document was subsequently shown to a British Parliamentary Select Committee before it was persuaded in 1816 to approve the acquisition of the marbles and their ultimate purchase by the British government for £35,000.

Ostensibly on the basis of the firman, three hundred of Elgin's workmen took one year to dismantle the frieze. Most of this was done in his absence. By 1803 hundreds of pieces of sculptured marble, including a column from the Erechtheion, seventeen figures from the Parthenon pediments and fifteen metopes, were boxed for shipping to Scotland. Elgin was captured in the resumption of hostilities between Napoleon's France and England and was a prisoner of the French between 1803 and 1806. He was on parole until 1814. It was not until 1812 that all the marbles were consigned in about eighty cases of sculptures, vases and medals to England. All in all Elgin took almost all the substantial pedimental figures that survived, most of the remaining north, south and east frieze (leaving the west) and the best metopes from the south side.

When he finally returned to England he found his marriage was over, his diplomatic career ended; he lost his seat in the House of Lords and the marbles were the subject of controversy. He was attacked by an archaeologist, Richard Payne Knight, and the poet, Lord Byron, but praised by the artists Canova and Benjamin Robert Haydon. 'What the Goths spared, the Scots destroyed', said Byron, and through such poems as 'Childe Harold's Pilgrimage' he helped to establish Greek nationalism as a cause and the Parthenon as a national monument, a view which others have alleged was not justified. The term 'Elginism', which is attributed to the French, came to describe the plunder of cultural treasures in general.

At first Elgin's collection was exhibited in his London home at Piccadilly and at Burlington House. In February 1816 he presented a petition to the House of Commons requesting an enquiry into the value of his collection, which he desired to sell to the government for the use of the public.

In June 1816, a Parliamentary Committee was convened to consider 'Whether it be expedient that the collection mentioned in Earl of Elgin's petition should be purchased on behalf of the public and if so what price it may be reasonable to allow for same'. The Committee heard from leading artists that the marbles were in the very first class of ancient art, and also heard from others including Elgin's secretary, Hamilton, and from Dr Hunt that the Acropolis was in a bad condition, and that it was desirable to preserve such treasures of the past.

The Report on the Elgin Marbles of 1816 (see Appendix 11) shows precisely what the Committee considered in making its decision:

> When the Earl of Elgin quitted England upon his mission to the Otto-man Porte, it was his original intention to make that appointment bene-ficial to the progress of the Fine Arts in Great Britain, by procuring ac-curate drawings and casts of the valuable remains of Sculpture and Architecture scattered throughout Greece, and particularly concentrated at Athens.

> With this view he engaged Signor Lusieri, a painter of reputation, who was then in the service of the King of the Two Sicilies, together with two architects, two modellers, and a figure painter, whom Mr Hamilton (now Under-Secretary of State) engaged at Rome and des-patched with Lusieri, in the summer of 1800, from Constantinople to Athens.

> They were employed there about nine months, from August 1800 to May 1801, without having any sort of facility or accommodation af-forded to them; nor was the Acropolis accessible to them, even for the purpose of taking drawings, except by the payment of a large fee, which was exacted daily.

> The other five artists were withdrawn from Athens in January 1803, but Lusieri has continued there ever since, excepting during the short period of our hostilities with the Ottoman Porte.

> During the year 1800, Egypt was in the power of the French: and that sort of contempt and dislike which has always characterized the Turkish government and people in their behaviour towards every de-nomination of Christians, prevailed in full force.

> The success of the British arms in Egypt, and the expected restitution of that province to the Porte, wrought a wonderful and instantaneous change in the disposition of all ranks and descriptions of people towards our Nation. Universal benevolence and good-will appeared to take the place of suspicion and aversion. Nothing was refused which was asked; and Lord Elgin, availing himself of this favourable and unexpected al-teration, obtained, in the summer of 1801, access to the Acropolis for general purposes, with permission to draw, model, and remove; to which was added, a special licence to excavate in a particular place.

Lord Elgin mentions in his evidence, that he was obliged to send from Athens to Constantinople for leave to remove a house; at the same time remarking that, in point of fact, all permissions issuing from the Porte to any distant provinces, are little better than authorities to make the best bargain that can be made with the local magistracies. The applications upon this subject, passed in verbal conversations; but the warrants or fermauns were granted in writing, addressed to the chief authorities resi-dent at Athens, to whom they were delivered, and in whose hands they remained: so that your Committee had no opportunity of learning from Lord Elgin himself their exact tenor, or of ascertaining in what terms they noticed, or allowed the displacing, or carrying away of these Marb-les. But Dr Hunt, who accompanied Lord Elgin as chaplain to the em-bassy, has preserved, and has now in his possession, a translation of the second fermaun, which extended the powers of the first; but as he had it not with him in London, to produce before your Committee, he stated the substance, according to his recollection, which was, 'That, in order to show their particular respect to the Ambassador of Great Britain, the august ally of the Porte, with whom they were now and had long been in the strictest alliance, they gave to his Excellency and to his Secretary, and the Artists employed by him, the most extensive permission to view, draw and model the ancient Temples of the Idols, and the Sculp-tures upon them, and to make excavations and to take away any stones that might appear interesting to them'. He stated further, that no remon-strance was at any time made, nor any displeasure shown by the Turk-ish government, either at Constantinople or at Athens, against the ex-tensive interpretation which was put upon this fermaun; and although the work of taking down, and removing was going on for months, and even years, and was conducted in the most public manner, numbers of native labourers, to the amount of some hundreds being frequently em-ployed, not the least obstruction was ever interposed, nor the smallest uneasiness shown after the granting of this second fermaun. Among the Greek population and inhabitants of Athens it occasioned no sort of dissatisfaction; but, as Mr Hamilton, an eye witness, expresses it, so far from exciting any unpleasant sensation, the people seemed to feel it as the means of bringing foreigners into their country, and of having money spent among them. The Turks showed a total indifference and apathy as to the preservation of these remains, except when in a fit of wanton destruction they sometimes carried their disregard so far as to do mischief by firing at them. The numerous travellers and admirers of the Arts committed greater waste, from a very different motive, for many of those who visited the Acropolis tempted the soldiers and other people about the fortress to bring them down heads, legs, or arms or whatever other pieces they could carry off.

The report then clearly sets out the circumstances and local atmosphere prevailing at the time the marbles were taken.

The second part of the report continues:

Upon the Second Division, it must be premised that antecedently to Lord Elgin's departure for Constantinople, he communicated his intentions of bringing home casts and drawings from Athens, for the benefit and advancement of the Fine Arts in this country, to Mr Pitt, Lord Grenville, and Mr Dundas, suggesting to them the propriety of considering it as a national object, fit to be undertaken, and carried into effect at the public expense; but that this recommendation was in no degree encouraged, either at that time or afterwards.

It is evident from a letter of Lord Elgin, to the Secretary of State, 13 January 1803, that he considered himself as having no sort of claim for his disbursements in the prosecution of these pursuits, though he stated, in the same despatch, the heavy expenses in which they had involved him, so as to make it extremely inconvenient for him to forgo any of the usual allowances to which Ambassadors at other courts are entitled. It cannot, therefore, be doubted, that he looked upon himself in this respect as acting in a character entirely distinct from his official situation. But whether the Government from whom he obtained permission did, or could so consider him, is a question which can be solved only by conjecture and reasoning, in the absence and deficiency of all positive testimony. The Turkish ministers of that day are, in fact, the only persons in the world capable (if they are still alive) of deciding the doubt; and it is probable that even they, if it were possible to consult them, might be unable to form any very distinct discrimination as to the character in consideration of which they acceded to Lord Elgin's request. The occasion made them, beyond all precedent, propitious to whatever was desired on behalf of the English nation; they readily, therefore, complied with all that was asked by Lord Elgin. He was an Englishman of high rank; he was also Ambassador from our Court: they granted the same permission to no other individual: but then, as Lord Elgin observes, no other individual applied for it to the same extent, nor had indeed the same unlimited means for carrying such an undertaking into execution. The expression of one of the most intelligent and distinguished of the British travellers, who visited Athens about the same period, appears to your Committee to convey as correct a judgment as can be formed upon this question, which is incapable of being satisfactorily separated, and must be taken in the aggregate.

The Earl of Aberdeen, in answer to an inquiry, whether the authority and influence of a public situation was in his opinion necessary for accomplishing the removal of these Marbles, answered, that he did not think a private individual could have accomplished the removal of the remains which Lord Elgin obtained: and Dr Hunt who had better opportunities of information upon this point than any other person who has been examined, gave it as his decided opinion, that 'a British subject not in the situation of Ambassador, could not have been able to obtain from the Turkish Government a fermaun of such extensive powers'.

It may not be unworthy of remark, that the only other piece of Sculpture which was ever removed from its place for the purpose of export was taken by Mr Choiseul Gouffier, when he was Ambassador from France to the Porte; but whether he did it by express permission, or in some less ostensible way, no means of ascertaining are within the reach of your Committee.

It was undoubtedly at various times an object with the French Government to obtain possession of some of these valuable remains, and it is probable, according to the testimony of Lord Aberdeen and others, that at no great distance of time they might have been removed by that government from their original site, if they had not been taken away, and secured for this country by Lord Elgin.

This part of the report makes clear that Elgin was not encouraged to remove the marbles as a state enterprise. It clearly recognizes that he nevertheless used his special office to accomplish something which would otherwise have been impossible. It also significantly casts doubt on the full extent and interpretation of the Turkish authorization to him. It is quite clear therefore that the Select Committee did not overlook such considerations in making the decision, as is sometimes alleged.

The third part of the report concerned itself with the artistic worth of the marbles:

The testimony of several of the most eminent Artists in this kingdom, who have been examined, rates these Marbles in the very first class of ancient art, some placing them a little above, and others very little below the Apollo Belvidere, the Laocoon, and the Torso of the Belvidere. They speak of them with admiration and enthusiasm; and notwithstanding the manifold injuries of time and weather, and those mutilations which they have sustained from the fortuitous, or designed injuries

66

of neglect, or mischief, they consider them as among the finest models, and the most exquisite monuments of antiquity.

With this estimation of the excellence of these works it is natural to conclude that they are recommended by the same authorities as highly fit, and admirably adapted to form a school for study, to improve our national taste for the Fine Arts, and to diffuse a more perfect knowledge of them throughout this kingdom.

The fourth part of the report then proceeded to deal with the valuation of the marbles, and provided a detailed account of their condition, merit and classical context. Lord Elgin's total outlay was around £74,270, although none of this was attributable to the actual purchase of the marbles. The marbles were acquired by Lord Elgin without any significant recorded payment. On the strength of this report, the British government finally purchased them for less than half that sum, at £35,000. The report emphasized the importance of maintaining the collection as a whole.

The directions of the House in the order of reference imposes upon your committee the task of forming and submitting an opinion upon the fourth head, which otherwise the scantiness of materials for fixing a pecuniary value, and the unwillingness, or inability in those who are practically most conversant in statuary to afford any lights upon this part of the subject, would have rather induced them to decline.

The produce of this collection, if it should be brought to sale in separate lots, in the present depreciated state of almost every article, and more particularly of such as are of precarious and fanciful value, would probably be much inferior to what may be denominated its intrinsic value.

The mutilated state of all the larger figures, the want either of heads or features, of limbs or surface, in most of the Metopes, and in a great proportion of the compartments even of the larger Frieze, render this collection, if divided, but little adapted to serve for the decoration of private houses. It should therefore be considered as forming a whole, and should unquestionably be kept entire as a school of art, and a study for the formation of artists.

. . . Your committee refer to Lord Elgin's evidence for the large and heavy charges which have attended the formation of this collection, and the placing of it in its present situation; which amount, from 1799 to January 1803, to 62,440 *l.* including 23,240 *l.* for the interest of money; and according to a supplemental account, continued from 1803, to 1816, to no less a sum than 74,000 *l.*, including the same sum for interest.

All the papers which are in his possession upon this subject, including a journal of about 90 pages, of the daily expenses of his principal artist Lusieri (from 1803 to the close of 1814) who still remains in his employment at Athens together with the account current of Messrs Hayes, of Malta, (from April 1807, to May 1811) have been freely submitted, of your committee; and there can be no doubt, from the inspection of those accounts, confirmed also by other testimony, that the disbursements were very considerable; but supposing them to reach the full sum at which they are calculated, your committee do not hesitate to express their opinion, that they afford no just criterion of the value of the collection, and therefore must not be taken as a just basis for estimating it.

...Your Committee cannot dismiss this interesting subject, without submitting to the attentive reflection of the House, how highly the cultivation of the Fine Arts has contributed to the reputation, character, and dignity of every Government by which they have been encouraged, and how intimately they are connected with the advancement of every thing valuable in science, literature and philosophy. In contemplating the importance and splendour to which so small a republic as Athens rose, by the genius and energy of her citizens, exerted in the path of such studies, it is impossible to overlook how transient the memory and fame of extended empires, and of mighty conquerors are, in comparison of those who have rendered inconsiderable states eminent, and immortalized their own names by these pursuits. But if it be true, as we learn from history and experience, that free governments afford a soil most suitable to the production of native talent, to the maturing of the powers of the human mind, and to the growth of every species of excellence, by opening to merit the prospect of reward and distinction, no country can be better adapted than our own to afford an honourable asylum to these monuments of the school of Phidias, and of the administration of Pericles; where, secure from further injury and degradation, they may receive that admiration and homage to which they are entitled, and serve, in return, as models and examples to those, who by knowing how to revere and appreciate them, may learn first to imitate, and ultimately to rival them.

March 25, 1816.

It is said that the Committee thus did its best to evaluate the matter of purchase, accepting the view that the collection was of extraordinary interest and setting new standards of merit.

Although the Parliamentary Committee's recommendations were followed by the House of Commons in June 1816, it cannot be said that no voice was strongly raised against the purchase of the Elgin Marbles for the nation. At the February debate on the petition to investigate their value, Mr Thomas Babington said that the mode in which the collection had been acquired 'partook of the nature of spoliation'. It was of the greatest importance, he said, to ascertain whether this collection had been procured by such means as were honourable to this country, and he hoped the Committee would be careful in seeing that the whole transaction was consonant with national honour. Otherwise, the government should have nothing to do with it (Hansard, *Parliamentary Reports*, 1816, vol. XXXII, 828).

In the June debate on the actual purchase Mr Hugh Hammersley said he would oppose the resolution because of the dishonesty of the transaction by which the collection was obtained. As to the value of the statues, he agreed with the bill's sponsor, but he was not so enamoured of those headless ladies as to forget another lady, namely Justice. He should propose as an amendment a resolution, which stated:

> That this Committee having taken into consideration the manner in which the Earl of Elgin became possessed of certain ancient sculptured marbles from Athens, laments that this Ambassador did not keep in remembrance that the high and dignified station of representing his sovereign should have made him forbear from availing himself of that character in order to obtain valuable possessions belonging to the government to which he was accredited; and that such forbearance was peculiarly necessary at a moment when that government was expressing high obligations to Great Britain. This Committee, however, imputes to the noble Earl no venal motive whatever of pecuniary advantage to himself, but on the contrary, believes that he was actuated by a desire to benefit his country, by acquiring for it, at great risk and labour to himself, some of the most valuable specimens in existence of ancient sculpture. This Committee, therefore, feels justified, under the particular circumstances of the case, in recommending that £25,000 be offered to the Earl of Elgin for the collection in order to recover and keep it together for that government from which it has been improperly taken, and that to which this Committee is of opinion that a communication should immediately be made, stating that Great Britain holds these marbles only in trust till they are demanded by the present, or any future, possessors of the city of Athens; and upon such demand, engages, without question or negotiation, to restore them, as far as can be effected, to the places

from whence they were taken, and that they shall be in the mean time carefully preserved in the British Museum.

(Hansard, 1816, vol. XXXIV, 1031–3)

To his voice was added that of Mr Serjeant Best who thought that Lord Elgin had not acted as he ought to have done, whatever the opinion about the works of art which he had imported into this country. He regarded greatly the improvement of national taste, but he valued the preservation of national honour still more. He could not approve of a representative of His Majesty laying himself under obligations to a foreign court, to which he was sent to watch the interests of and maintain the honour of his country. Such an officer should be independent, as by his independence alone could he perform his duty. He had obtained the firman out of favour, and had used it contrary to the intention with which it was granted. What, he said, would be thought of an ambassador at an European court, who should lay himself under obligations by receiving a sum of £35,000? But even the firman Lord Elgin had obtained did not warrant him to do as he had done. It could have achieved nothing without bribery, nor could the words in which it was written admit the construction that was put upon them. It merely gave the right to view, contemplate and sketch them. Did this mean, he asked, that these works were to be viewed and contemplated with the design of being pulled down and removed? Lord Elgin himself did not say that he had authority to carry off anything by means of the firman and he was surely the best interpreter of the instrument by which he had acted. If he erred, Mr Best continued, he erred knowingly, though his design might have been excusable or praiseworthy. Dr Hunt's evidence, he said, had been quoted to show that his lordship had authority from the governor of Athens for what he had done, but his words would not bear such an interpretation. Dr Hunt had said only that the voivode (governor) was induced to allow the construction put upon the firman by Lord Elgin. The powerful argument by which the voivode was induced to allow this had been a present of a brilliant lustre, fire-arms, and other articles of English manufacture. But were these, he asked, arguments that ought to have been used by a British ambassador? Was he to be permitted to corrupt the fidelity of a subject of another state, and a servant of a government in alliance with and under obligations to the British government? It had been said that if the works of art had not been brought here, they would have been destroyed by the Turks. This, he said, would not have been the alternative. The Turks would have been taught to value these monuments, had they seen travellers coming from distant countries to do them homage. They could not help but learn their value now, after they had been deprived of them, by hearing that £35,000 had been paid for them to the person who imported them to England. It had been said that Lord Elgin would advance the arts by lodging these remains of antiquity in a country where eminence in arts was studiously attempted. Mr Best thought this doubtful. Such works always appeared best in the places to which they were originally fitted. Besides, with this example of plunder before their eyes, the Turks would be a little more cautious in future whom they admitted to see their ornaments. The marbles had been brought to the country, he said, in breach of good faith and therefore he could not consent to their purchase, lest he render himself party to the guilt of spoliation. He said he did not object to the bargain on the ground of economy, but of justice (Hansard, 1816, vol. XXXIV, 1037–8).

Arguments were also raised against the purchase by other members of the House on the basis of economy, but when the House divided the vote was eighty-two in favour and thirty against (Hansard, 1816, vol. XXXIV, 1040). Apparently Mr Hammersley's amendment was not put to the House.

An Act of Parliament was passed on 11 July 1816 'To Vest the Elgin Collection of Ancient Marbles and Sculptures in the Trustees of the British Museum for the Use of the Public'.

It was enacted that:

> (I) the Lord High Treasury of Great Britain was authorized and em-powered . . . immediately after the passing of the Act . . . to issue and advance the sum of 35,000 pounds to the Trustees of the British Mu-seum or any person appointed by the said Trustees to receive the same . . . and shall be applied in the purchase of the said collection, and that the Trustees shall on or before the first day of September 1816 require the delivery of the Collection . . . and on delivery of the same shall pay the said sum of 35,000 pounds to the said Thomas Earl of Elgin, his Executors, Administrators and Assigns.

[And] (II) On payment of the said sum the said Collection shall be vested in the Trustees for the time being of the said British Museum and their Successors in Perpetuity . . .

[And] (III) The said Collection shall be preserved and kept together in the British Museum whole and entire and distinguished by the name or appellation of 'The Elgin Collection'.

It is amusing to recall that in fact the Trustees of the British Museum en-countered some initial difficulty in obtaining actual delivery of the marbles despite this enactment. Elgin was already indebted to the Treasury and to a number of other creditors to an amount in excess of £35,000. In keeping with the somewhat bizarre passage of the Elgin Marbles, two of these creditors (a Mr Booths and a Mr Leggatt) had, under an Extent from the Crown and an assignment, secured actual possession. They were said to be stored under a shed within the walls of the courtyard at Burlington House. Elgin eventually assigned the moneys due to him on 31 July 1816. Thus he never directly received any money for the marbles at all and once the purchase was completed he considered his active part in their disposition to be concluded. They were duly delivered and first went on public display after the Christmas recess of 1816, although they were not properly displayed together in the completed Duveen Gallery until 1961 (Fig. 19).

Since the purchase of the marbles, there has never been an incentive towards relinquishing ownership. There has not been the political will to effect such a return although the question continued to be put before successive Prime Ministers in the House of Commons. Whether or not the actual *removal* of the marbles was an act of preservation, it can be fairly said that the *purchase* by the British government was an act of preservation, because it sought to hold the collection together to be housed safely in one of the finest museums in the world. Given that the House of Commons Committee was confronted with a *fait accompli* in the transportation of the marbles to Britain, it is unreasonable to attack, as many writers do, the British government's action in purchasing them for the nation.

The removal of the Elgin Marbles thus came to be seen in the light of a rescue operation, ostensibly against further loss through vandalization. In Stuart and Revett's *Antiquities of Athens*, 1816, Lord Elgin's activities were eulogized: 'The highest praise and sincerest thanks are due from an enlightened public to Lord Elgin for stepping forward at the critical moment, and rescuing these precious remains of ancient art from the destroying hand of time and from the more destroying hand of an uncivilized people.'

In 1882 a German archaeologist, Adolf Michaelis, said of the Elgin Marbles, that 'the removal of the Statue of the Erechtheum, in particular, had severely injured the surrounding architecture'. He said it was doubtful whether Lord Elgin was discreet in using his official office to further his private ambitions, or whether the firman was interpreted accurately in accordance with the Turkish government's wishes. But taking the prevailing conditions at that time into account he concluded 'Only blind passion could doubt that Lord Elgin's act was an act of preservation.'[4]

There was contradictory evidence at the time as to the actual or imminent danger to the marbles, and there is of course no way of establishing with certainty whether they would have suffered further or simply remained as they were, given that they were removed towards the end of Turkish rule. It is extremely unlikely that in their very removal they did not suffer substantial damage; and some may have been lost in transit. It was recorded at the time of Elgin's activities that the backs of the architectural sculptures were cut off if their thickness made them

Joseph Duveen in 1928 made a donation to build a new gallery for the Parthenon sculptures. Although this was completed in 1938, the war intervened. The frieze was stored in the London Underground railway and the pediments and metopes went to the museum vaults. The gallery was damaged in 1940 and not restored or completed until 1961.

inconveniently heavy for any methods of transport then available. Apart from the actual removal of the Parthenon's sculptural decorations, the cornice above the south metopes, and a part of the south angle of the east pediment were destroyed. Moreover, the second shipment of the marbles to England was ship-wrecked *en route* in September 1802 aboard the brig *Mentor*. Seventeen cases of antiquities in the passage from Athens to Malta went down on the coast of Cerigo. Salvage operations were not commenced until December and not com-pleted until two years later, in October 1804. It was recorded that the salvage operations were completely successful, and all the marbles at Cerigo were re-covered. Somewhat ironically, in 1828, Lusieri's drawings[5] were lost in the wreck of the *Cambrian* near the island of Grabousa at the extreme north-west of Crete.

Much has been made of Elgin's motives and conduct in the marbles affair. One must consider whether this is particularly relevant to the issue of return. It seems clear from the evidence that the actual removal was not initially planned, in that it was not a premeditated act. It was not even a personal act but done almost vicariously and seems to have happened more by chance and opportun-ism than design. When the opportunity arose to take away as much as was practically possible, Elgin and his men seized upon it to stretch the terms of the firman. It was of course by no means an isolated act of 'collecting' on his part. Lord Elgin was a voracious collector of antiquities whose activities were wide-spread.[6] The marbles were his greatest acquisition and attracted the widest notor-iety. On balance one should not make too much of the nobility of his intentions, as many of the politicians of the time did.

Various individuals and bodies have, since their removal, championed the return of the marbles. In 1890 Frederick Harrison, an English historian, advo-cated their return, writing, 'But for the glorious tradition of Athens, of which these pathetic ruins are the everlasting embodiment, Greece would never have attracted the sympathy of the civilized world, and would not have been assisted to assert herself as a free state . . . The existence of the Acropolis made any capital but Athens impossible . . .'[7]

In 1832 Greece achieved independence from Turkish rule, and one of its first acts of statehood was to start work on the restoration of the Acropolis. The Parthenon became a national symbol, and with it came the call for the return of the marbles. It was repeated on the centenary of Byron's death in 1924 and was mooted again during the Second World War.

In 1941 Miss Thelma Cazelet, National Conservative in the House of Commons, asked whether the government was prepared to introduce legislation allowing the return of the marbles 'as some recognition of the Greeks' magnifi-cent stand for civilisation', since Greece was then fighting alone in continental

Europe against the Nazi invaders, and in answer to her question, Anthony Eden, the Secretary of State, advised Clement Attlee, the Lord Privy Seal, that the decision to return the marbles should be taken once the war was over. Attlee informed the Commons that the moment was 'inopportune for a final decision'.

The Foreign Office prepared a memo[8] on the subject and arrived at its position largely on advice from the British Museum and the Courtauld Institute.[9] Neither of these establishments put up the anticipated absolute opposition to the restoration of Lord Elgin's collection.

However, an examination of the Foreign Office papers of the period clearly shows that the marbles were regarded as a pawn in the propaganda war with the Germans, and as a useful instrument of possible future foreign policy strategy. To this end the possibility of making a gift was strongly considered.

In his memo of 15 January 1941 Sir Alexander Cadogan, Permanent Under-Secretary of State wrote:

> I don't know where this is going to end. Where is the Bellini portrait of the Sultan which, unlike the Elgin Marbles, was obtained by direct fraud on the part of the enemy? Public attention has been focused on the Elgin Marbles, but they were actually acquired in a manner no more disreputable than many of the contents of European and American museums.

Prevailing opinion within the Courtauld Institute was that, 'provided they were not exposed to the weather, scholarship would not suffer if the Elgin marbles were returned to Greece'. However, a report[10] noted that it would be 'in Greece's best interests to leave the marbles here – though in all probability Greece would not take that view'. It was suggested that one solution would be for casts to be placed upon the Parthenon, leaving the originals in London.

A memo from the British Museum dated 31 December 1940 declared: 'The principle of tying works of art to their places of origin is not recognized by Western Nations, and the frequent claims that such as have got out shall be returned has never been admitted and seems to be preposterous.' It continued: 'The point is that the Acropolis of Athens is the greatest national monument of Greece and that the buildings to which the marbles belonged are still standing or have been rebuilt . . . Greek pride may reasonably be offended by the patronage (assumed in recent newspaper correspondence and in this Parliamentary Question) which proposes the return as a favour rather than a right.'

Mr Knight of the Foreign Office Greek Section, in his memo of 14 January 1941, came to the view that the return of the Elgin Marbles, if decided on, should be in the nature of a gesture of friendship to Greece and should not be based on the principle that antiquities should be put back where they came from, which would be a most awkward and dangerous precedent. For the gift to be complete it should include the caryatid and column of the Erechtheum. He also recommended that the British government should be assured of a share in perpetuity in the control of the arrangements to be made for the marbles' preservation. Their restoration 'would thus set the seal on Anglo-Greek friendship and collaboration . . . in the way that would most appeal – short of the cession of Cyprus – to Greek patriotic sentiment'. His superior, Sir Philip Nichols, head of the South-Eastern Europe department, added: 'Personally I am strongly in favour of returning the marbles not because I think such a gesture would be warmly welcomed by the Greeks and by public opinion throughout the world, but also I believe that it might to some extent deflect Greek eyes from Cyprus.' Mr James Bowker, deputy head of the South Eastern Europe department, wrote: 'Everything points to a decision on principle to return the Elgin marbles to Greece on certain conditions as enumerated in Knight's memorandum.' Sir Alexander Cadogan, the Permanent Secretary, endorsed the recommendation for 'careful and sympathetic consideration' by the government. Most notably, Anthony Eden told Attlee that the marbles should be returned after the war as 'a gesture of friendship to Greece but not on the principle that antiquities should be returned to their place of origin'. No further decision was taken.

The arguments against returning the marbles have also since been voiced by Sir David Wilson, Director of the British Museum. He has suggested that it would mean the end of the museum as an international cultural institution, which was doing a service for the international community. But this is to perhaps confuse the nature of an institution with the nature of its collection. The British Museum is undeniably a national museum. To counter the museum view, which the Foreign Office has shared, a group called the British Committee for the Restitution of the Parthenon Marbles, headed by Professor Robert Browning of London University, was set up. This group has supported the view that the marbles should be restored to their spiritual home. In particular the Committee was set up in response to the (UNESCO) World Conference on Cultural Policies attended by Ministers of Culture in Mexico in 1982, and at which a specific recommendation concerning the return of the Parthenon Marbles was made.

Recommendation No. 55[11] of the Final Report went as follows:

> *Recalling* resolution 4/09 adopted by the General Conference of Unesco at its twenty-first session, on the return of cultural property to its countries of origin,

Recalling the recommendations adopted by the Intergovernmental Committee for Promoting the Return of Cultural Property to its Countries of Origin or its Restitution in Case of Illicit Appropriation at its second session (Paris, 14–18 September 1981),

Considering that the removal of the so-called Elgin marbles from their place in the Parthenon has disfigured a unique monument which is a symbol of eternal significance for the Greek people and for the whole world,

Considering it right and just that those marbles should be returned to Greece, the country in which they were created, for reincorporation in the architectural structure of which they formed part,

1. *Recommends* that Member States view the return of the Parthenon marbles as an instance of the application of the principle that elements abstracted from national monuments should be returned to those monuments;

2. *Recommends* that the Director-General give his full support to this action which comes properly under the heading of the safeguarding of the cultural heritage of mankind.[12]

The wording of this recommendation actually states that the marbles should be returned to Greece *for reincorporation* into the architectural structure of which they were a part. This condition has in the past been considered to be physically impossible to fulfil, something which is overlooked by some commentaries on this recommendation.

The International Council of Museums held its thirteenth General Conference in London ending with its General Assembly sessions on 1 and 2 August 1983. This was the first occasion on which a Greek national section participated in an ICOM Conference. The Greek delegation was admitted to the Conference's Working Group on the Return of Cultural Property to its Countries of Origin for three years.

The leader of the Greek delegation, Yannis Tzedakis, Director of the Department of Antiquities at the Ministry of Culture in Athens, made a statement to the ICOM General Assembly concerning the Parthenon Marbles, whose 'regrettable, not to say notorious removal from their original position', he said, 'had destroyed the unity of a unique monument'.

He continued:

We consider it right and just that the Parthenon marbles and those taken from the Erechtheum should be returned to Greece, the country in which they were created, in application of the principle – to quote – 'that all countries have the right to recover the most significant part of their respective cultural heritage lost during periods of colonial or foreign occupation'.

The Assembly passed a resolution on the 'Return of Cultural Property to its Countries of Origin'. While not referring to any particular examples, this noted that the initial distrust shown by certain countries was disappearing and that certain returns had already been effected, 'motivated by considerations of a moral, cultural and scientific nature'.

The resolution also noted 'the moral rights of people to recover significant elements of their heritage dispersed as a consequence of colonial or foreign occupation', and went on to declare ICOM's continuing support for the UNESCO intergovernmental committee on this question. It urged ICOM members 'both at the individual and institutional levels, to initiate dialogues with an open-minded attitude, on the basis of professional and scientific principles, concerning requests for the return of cultural property to the countries of origin'.

In a short discussion that ensued the British Museum representatives took no part, but French delegate M. Victor Beyer expressed reservations over the return of the marbles because of the levels of atmospheric pollution in Athens. However, one of ICOM's three vice-presidents, Alpha Oumar Konare of Mali, pointed out that conditions in the country of origin could never be invoked as an argument against the return of cultural property, and that this was merely a way of avoiding the issue.

The leader of the Greek delegation added that this was not an issue since, until after the Second World War, London was one of the most polluted cities in Europe. Moreover, the state of the marbles in the 1930s had led the British Museum to try to clean them, which caused serious damage to the surface.

The ICOM resolution was passed with no votes against, but with ten abstentions, including those of the five-member British delegation.

After the session, the director of the British Museum, Dr (now Sir) David Wilson, also a delegate, said that he did not think the resolution would make any difference. He remained convinced that the marbles would stay in Britain.[13] However, Greece claimed that the proceedings constituted a 'moral victory', especially in so far as they contributed to an awareness of the issue among public and professional opinion. It was not believed however that this would persuade the Trustees of the British Museum or the British government to hand over the marbles.

After the Conference, the chairman of the British National Committee of the International Council of Museums, Mr Max Hebditch, was at pains to stress that no resolution had been passed supporting the return of the Elgin Marbles. The resolution, he said, was a much more general one. It committed ICOM to advising the UNESCO intergovernmental committee which was examining this issue, and to providing information about, and evaluating the needs of, countries which had lost a significant part of their cultural heritage.

While sympathetic to the needs of some countries to acquire material related to aspects of their culture which is not represented in their museum collections, ICOM has not sought to become involved in specific issues. Indeed its present advice to UNESCO is that a claim for the return of cultural property from one museum to another requires an extremely full and careful consideration of all the issues involved, including the use to which the material is being put by the holding museum. These are obviously matters primarily for trustees and curators rather than governments. Max Hebditch explained that the UK Committee had abstained from voting because the resolution could be interpreted as the moral victory which the Greek delegation had claimed.

However, in September 1983 the cause of the return of the Elgin Marbles was dealt a blow by a resolution and report on the return of works of art issued by the Parliamentary Assembly of the Council of Europe.[14] This Council was founded in 1949 and has nineteen member states including Greece and the United Kingdom, its aim (by Article 1 of its Statutes) being 'to achieve a greater unity between its members for the purpose of realizing the ideals and principles which are their common heritage and facilitating their economic and social progress'. In the opinion of some it has not become a political force, turning its attentions instead to technical matters, especially in the field of legal co-operation.

A resolution was passed regarding the return of works of art which, among other things, stressed 'the unity of the European cultural heritage' and declared its belief that 'claims for the return of cultural property within the European area must be considered differently from claims for the return of property outside this area'; it therefore called 'on governments of member states to recognize that the European cultural heritage belongs to all Europeans and to ensure that the diversity of this heritage remains easily accessible in each country'.

This resolution was adopted by fifteen votes to one with three abstentions. It was in effect another way of saying that the Elgin Marbles are 'European' and need not be transported back to their place of origin, since they belonged to and could be appreciated by 'all Europeans'. This was suggested as an exceptional approach vis-à-vis Europe; in Third World states principles of cultural restitution would apply.

From the Greek point of view this resolution must be regarded as implying that, by accepting the generic label 'European', it and other states abdicate their sovereignty and unique individual history. It appears to represent a convenient device for declaring a moratorium on the return of treasures taken by one European state from another, saying in effect that who holds such treasure shall keep it. The resolution of the Council has no binding effect, and there seems to be little foundation for the notion that a loose confederation of states into a 'European' entity could justify the abrogation of sovereignty or the creation of a special exception, applicable to the return of cultural property. This ignores the very different cultural civilizations involved within 'Europe', which defy such bureaucratic assimilation.

The accompanying report states that the return of specific objects is a matter for bilateral negotiations between the states concerned, which, it admits, is not something for which the Council of Europe is competent. It points out that it is concerned with 'return' and not 'restitution', which implies illegal possession, and it goes on to state that 'the current bona fide ownership of the objects in question is not at issue. Return is not a question of law, but of judgement on cultural, historical and social terms, if not political. Admittedly the question of compensation may arise, but it is secondary.'

This is very presumptuous since the legal validity of continued possession may well be in issue, and the legal question will inevitably arise in conjunction with the criteria of culture, history and other social considerations.

The Council explained the special problem of return within Europe. With reference to the Icelandic sagas it acknowledged the precedent of negotiated return but proceeded to distinguish that case from the claim by Greece for the Parthenon Marbles.

It stated:

> Whereas the Icelandic case was a matter of calm negotiation, the Greek claim to the Parthenon sculptures has attracted a considerable amount of press attention. It has moreover been closely linked to the policy of UNESCO regarding the return of cultural property. This is unfortunate for a number of reasons. First it turns the (reasonable) case for the return of objects for the reconstitution of representative national collections into a claim for the return of major pieces. This consideration is perhaps one of the reasons for most major holding countries not coming forward to ratify the UNESCO Convention of 1970. The recent move by Greece [of making a formal claim] has further justified this reticence.

These comments do not bear close scrutiny. An examination of the Icelandic manuscripts case indicates that 'calm negotiation' is far from the truth. The fact that the matter was fruitfully resolved after a long period is a reflection of the continuous special relations between Denmark and Iceland. It also reflected the strong political will for return in Denmark, which was backed by legal process and supported by general goodwill between the Danish and Icelandic peoples. It may also have had something to do with a more integrated notion of 'Scandinavian' culture. That these factors are lacking in the case of the marbles is hardly reprehensible.

The Icelandic manuscripts case also received great public attention in the Scandinavian press for years, was a subject of great interest for a long time, and did not reach its conclusion without great debate, and some bitterness. The English press hardly mentioned this subject at the time. The reason why the Elgin Marbles case appears to have been more publicized is because it concerns the British Museum, because the marbles have always been the subject of controversy, and because the formal claim of Greece comes at a time when the world has been made generally more conscious of such issues. That such a claim causes embarrassment or inconvenience should not detract from its merits, although it may fairly be argued that diplomatic and discreet negotiations are the best way to achieve the desired result.

The Council in its report also distinguished the reasonable 'reconstitution of representative national collections' from the return of 'major pieces'. It is difficult to see what distinction there is, and no criterion was suggested. A 'major piece' can easily be an essential part of a 'reconstituted representative national collection' and it is hard to see why this should be less rather than more important. Moreover, it seems unjust to lay the blame for the failure of the 1970 Convention to be widely ratified, as the report appears to do, at the door of Greece for claiming a major piece. Between 1970 and 1983, the date of Greece's formal claim to the marbles, only fifty-three states ratified. Major holding states like the UK had ample opportunity to ratify in the intervening years but did not do so. This cannot be attributed specifically or retrospectively to the deterrent effect of the Greek claim.

Four concepts, according to the Council of Europe, had to be 'balanced' in the European context: individual artistic creativity, national cultural identity, European cultural identity and the heritage of mankind. It sees Europe as recognizing the 'contribution [of] the smaller community to the larger'. Thus, the problem of 'return' can be seen more positively in the light of sharing and extending appreciation of the 'cultural heritage'. Such claims to universality are dangerous because they are open to any state that has the power to impose them. In the past they have been used to vindicate the requisitioning of one state's arts treasures by another, and the usurpation of unique civilizations.

Anthropological arguments about race and ancestry have also been taken to extremes. Some writers have pointed to the early lack of homogeneity of the

Greek people who, making up a quarter of the Ottoman Empire, were widely scattered all over the Mediterranean. The chief cities of the Greek world in Elgin's time were Constantinople, Smyrna and Bucharest. It has been suggested that the modern Greeks are not the pure Hellenic descendants of the ancient Greeks. One must ask whether this really matters since no culture is 'purely' inherited. No civilization exists which is not hybrid or is uninfluenced by others. This cannot detract from the nexus between the sculptured marbles, the Parthenon building, the Greek people and Greece. To be accurate, the Parthenon is essentially *Athenian* and the Athenians were Ionian by race. In the words of Plutarch, Pericles' plan for the construction of the public buildings of Athens 'was [the] one measure above all which at once gave the greatest pleasure to the Athenians, adorned their city and created amazement among the rest of mankind, and which is today the sole testimony that the tales of the ancient power and glory of Greece are no mere fables . .' Professor John Boardman of Oxford University has written:

> the story of the Parthenon begins with the arrival of the Greeks in Greece, with the Greek land itself. It embraces the beginnings of organized religious life in Greece and Greek religion; the absorption into Greek life and thought of foreign ideas and acts; the history of architecture and sculpture; the development of the narrative and symbolic functions of myth; the physical, political, economic, social and military history of Athens itself.

Yet the Council of Europe Report in 1983 said:

> It is as difficult to see any realistic connection between the people who built the Pyramids and the modern Egyptians as it is between those who built Stonehenge and the citizens of the United Kingdom. The same applies for the civilization of the Incas and Ancient Greece. These claims are all the more difficult to substantiate when one considers for example the extent of ancient Greek contact between Ionia (Asia Minor) and Magna Graecia (Sicily and Southern Italy).

This view must be startling to some archaeologists and historians, since it seems to deny the legitimacy of any cultural continuity. Such distinctions can never be clear-cut. All descendant cultures do not resemble their antecedents but that seems little ground for denying the link. This argument also ignores the additional factor of geography, since objects may sometimes belong not so much *to* a people as *within* a particular landscape.

As a matter of archaeological reassembly, arguments about the purity of the modern inheriting culture are irrelevant. For reasons of geography alone there is sufficient historic link between modern Greece and its classical antecedents. It is difficult to see how the Council of Europe could deny any 'realistic connection' between Greece and the marbles or, for instance, Stonehenge and Great Britain. Certainly Stonehenge no more belongs in Greece than the Parthenon does in Britain. Each is part of the mysterious history in stone of its original location.

It has actually been stated that the marbles never belonged to Greece but to the Athenian republic, and that when they were removed by Lord Elgin, Greece was not an independent entity. However, this overlooks that the Athenian republic was at the time occupied territory. Moreover, the marbles are part of an Athenian ancient monument, and the Greek people are the in-digenous descendants and inheritors of the Athenian republic. The link be-tween Greek civilization, Athens and the marbles appears to be inexorable, and does not even bear comparison with any possible link that Britain may have with pieces of classical Greek sculpture, transported thousands of miles from their home. Ninety-five per cent of the exiled sculptures are in the British Museum. The only other substantial items surviving outside Athens are a single slab of the frieze and one metope which are in the Louvre. Elsewhere there are two heads in Copenhagen and a handful of fragments in Heidelberg, Vienna, Palermo and the Vatican.

Despite such international setbacks as the Council of Europe Report, the decision formally to request the return of the marbles was taken unanimously by the Greek Cabinet on the recommendation of the Minister of Culture. The terms of the formal request by the Greek ambassador, Mr Kyriazides, to the Foreign Office on 12 October 1983 were based on the following:

- that the Parthenon Marbles are an integral part of a unique building symbolic of the Greek cultural heritage;
- that it is now universally accepted that a work of art belongs to the cul-tural context in which (and for which) it was created;
- that the marbles were removed during a period of foreign occupation when the Greek people had no say in the matter.

This last term, it has been said, seriously questions the legality of the acquisition.

To effect a change in the status of the marbles it would be necessary to convince a majority of the members of the incumbent British government that their return would be an act of restoration in keeping with the original intention of conservation. The political complexion in the United Kingdom has re-mained such that only a minority of Members of Parliament have openly com-mitted themselves to the return of the marbles.

The British Restitution Committee conducted a survey to which (as at the end of 1983) they had received 250 replies. This indicated that only forty MPs gave their full support – the greatest majority (twenty-eight) being Labour MPs, four Social Democratic MPs,[15] and only two Conservatives. Another eleven MPs gave support but with reservations, and of these five were Conservatives, and two Labour. Another twenty MPs were 'open to argument'. The rest, a total of 178, were 'non-committal', made an 'acknowledgement' of the survey only, were 'absent' or simply were opposed. The formal request for return, which, despite the history of debate and controversy surrounding the marbles, was not made by the Greek government until 1983, was formally rejected in 1984.

Undoubtedly the issue of return will always be the subject of political debate. Nevertheless when a subject becomes politically fashionable this is also an indication that the time is right to address some serious consideration to it. Since the act of return must inevitably be a political act apart from anything else, then political differences between the governments involved may well be a bar to return. As the government of Greece which requested the marbles was Socialist, the Labour Party of the United Kingdom indicated that it was well disposed to returning the marbles, and there was even a pledge to that effect from the Opposition Labour leader, Mr Neil Kinnock. However, it was clear that this had not been given any deep consideration, from the rather impractical suggestion that the marbles could somehow be shared on a rotation basis. This undertaking was attacked in a London *Times* editorial as submission to Greek chauvinism, the manifestation of post-imperial conscience, and as a threat to the common heritage of art. Predictably the British Museum reacted with concern at the other implications of such an undertaking.

The attitude of the British public to the return of the marbles has been hard to gauge from the informal opinion polls conducted in the press. One suspects that the average English man or woman could not care less about the marbles, and has never seen them. In Greece, on the other hand, it is said that even in the most remote village or island the average Greek is well aware of the great historical and cultural significance of the marbles and remains concerned about their ultimate fate. Fifty thousand Greek schoolchildren have been organized by the architect Yannis Nazlides to make a postcard appeal to MPs and museum directors. In the words of the Greek Minister of Culture, the marbles remain a 'part of the deepest consciousness of the Greek people'. In 1986 she participated in an Oxford Union debate which carried the motion 'that the Elgin Marbles must be returned'. In 1987 the Onassis Public Foundation declared that it would seek the return of the marbles.

Most editorial opinion in the UK, however, has opposed return, with the exception of the *Guardian* and *The Scotsman*. Sometimes the objections to return have been little more than subjective vitriol. This appears to be the peculiar aberration of an avowed love and appreciation of art coupled with a contempt for the indigenous people from whom the art in question has sprung. It is an attitude which appears to have been rife amongst many 'collectors' in the past. One contemporary instance manifested itself in a newspaper article[16] which attempted to discredit the link between the Greek people and the Parthenon by deploring the state of modern Greece.

In October 1983, a debate took place in the House of Lords over a proposed amendment to the British Museum Act.[17] This was not about a bill to return the Elgin Marbles, but about an enabling bill to give the Trustees wider powers of disposal. The debate inevitably proceeded with the possibility of having to return the Elgin Marbles firmly in mind.

It was stated that the Elgin Marbles were not plundered. Sympathy was expressed for the Greek position, and their contribution to classical Greek cul-ture acknowledged. But it was added that the Elgin Marbles had been well cared for in the British Museum and that their return would constitute a precedent. Moreover, it was said, the Trustees of the museum opposed it as detrimental to their objective in maintaining a great universal museum; the limitation on the Trustees' right to dispose of objects served as a protection in maintaining the integrity of the museum. It was precisely because there was a formal Greek request pending that Lord Nugent was able to say 'What [would] the Trustees [have to] do except take a decision in a political context? It is surely wiser – in the interests of the British Museum . . . – to defend it against [such] pressures . . .'. Thus an amendment was finally moved to defeat this bill. The only strong expression of a possible solution, particularly in respect of the marbles, came from Lord Donaldson, who advocated special national legislation for particular cases rather than a general enabling bill such as was being proposed.

In November 1983, during Question Time in the House of Commons,[18] two questions were tabled, concerning the acquisition of the marbles, and the Greek request for return.

Sir David Price [Conservative] asked the Under-Secretary of State what reasons the Greek government had given in support of their request that the Elgin Marbles should be handed over to them without payment; and what had been the government's reply. Mr Christopher Murphy [Conservative] also asked the Under-Secretary of State if he would make a statement on the request by the Greek Government for the return of the Elgin Marbles.

In reply, Mr William Waldegrave, the government spokesman on the arts in the Commons, said: 'A formal request for the return of the Elgin marbles was made by the Greek ambassador on 12 October. It will, of course, receive careful consideration. As my noble friend said in Parliament recently, the Government are aware of no general wish to change the existing powers of the British Museum's trustees, and do not propose to seek authority to do so.'

The following exchange then ensued:

Mr Michael Foot [Labour]: [Is the Minister] able to recall that the circumstances and the manner in which the so-called Elgin marbles were taken from Greece were bitterly denounced at the time by most leading English people, headed by Lord Byron? Is he further aware that Lord Byron pronounced a terrible curse on those who were engaged in the transaction? Will the Minister undertake that the Government will seriously examine the proposition that has been made by a friendly, democratic country?

Mr Waldegrave: Lord Byron may have been against it but the right honourable gentleman doubtless knows that a Select Committee which looked into the matter believed that the marbles had been acquired legally. What my honourable friends say is doubted by few — if the marbles had not been taken away they would have been more seriously damaged.

Mr Andrew Faulds [Labour]: To take this matter seriously, does the Minister not consider that it might be time to accept that there is an argument in Third World countries and others that a limited range of objects should be returned? Is it not likely that if we in the West do not draw up a limited range of objects for restitution, we shall eventually face commercial and economic pressures to do so when dealing with other matters?

Mr Waldegrave: The honourable gentleman is right. This matter raises wide and general issues. That is why we must consider carefully the implications for the British Museum and other great international collections.

Mr Denis Canavan [Labour]: Is it not a historical fact that Lord Elgin used his position as British ambassador to get his hands on the Parthenon Marbles, without the consent of the people of Greece, and that he then proceeded to sell them to the British Government for £35,000? Will the Government now, belatedly, do the decent thing and send the marbles back to Greece so that they can be exhibited in their proper homeland? Should the Government not make reparation for an act of piracy by Lord Elgin, which even Byron described as plundering the Parthenon to decorate a villa in Scotland?

Mr Waldegrave: It was not described as plunder by the Select Committee which looked into the matter, nor have I ever heard any serious criticism of the way in which the British Museum displays the marbles.

The British government delivered its formal reply to the request for return of the marbles to the Greek ambassador in London in April 1984. It declined to return them on the grounds that the marbles were 'secured' by Lord Elgin 'as the result of a transaction conducted with the recognized legitimate authority at the time'. This was stated in a written reply to the Commons by Mr Ray Whitney, Under-Secretary of State at the Foreign Office, who said that legislation would be necessary to empower the Trustees of the British Museum to part with them, and such a bill to so empower the Trustees had been rejected by the Lords in October 1983.

The Greek government responded by indicating that it would continue to pursue the matter in all appropriate forums. On 20 September 1984 Greece formally requested the return of the marbles through the newly formed UNESCO documentary procedure for seeking the return of cultural treasures. This system allowed Britain a year to respond and in 1985 the Foreign Office formally rejected this claim.

The Greek application to the UNESCO Committee, apart from recounting all the well-established arguments, also contained a number of general concepts. It was argued that any part of a cultural treasure belongs to the owner of the whole, so that the totality of the Parthenon property belongs to the Greek government. It was also argued that the marbles have been held on trust. The following Conventions were also cited: the 1954 Hague Convention on the Protection of Cultural Property in the Event of Armed Conflict, the 1969 European Convention on the Protection of Archaeological Heritage, and the 1972 Convention on the Protection of World Cultural and Natural Heritage.[19] It is difficult to see what practical effect such application could have. There was no mandatory consequence for non-compliance by the United Kingdom, who subsequently withdrew from UNESCO (for general reasons). The United Kingdom is not party to the 1972 Convention, and, interestingly, perhaps, the Parthenon Acropolis site is also not on the World Cultural Heritage list drawn up in connection with that Convention. The particular pertinence of the other Conventions was not elaborated upon in the Greek application. This approach through UNESCO did not have any constructive effect on the issue of return.

The debate naturally continued and in 1986, in a House of Commons debate on the condition of the arts, Michael Foot called for the British Government to celebrate the two hundredth anniversary of the birth of Lord Byron in 1988 by giving back the marbles to Greece. The government response was then, as always, apprehension about the precedent that would be set in relation to the other collections held by Britain. In 1986 the UK Art Historians Association also entered the debate, passing a resolution at their annual meeting to the effect that such treasures as the Elgin Marbles should be allowed home on the proviso that: (i) they were properly protected; (ii) it was mutually agreed that the objects were centrally important to a country's heritage; and (iii) that negotiations were not intergovernmental.

Arguments have also continued to be made against the practical possibility of returning the marbles. It has been said that the marbles would face destruction by the pollution of Athens. Sir Bernard Braine, at the time Tory MP and chairman of the British–Greek parliamentary group, has expressed reservations against return without a museum to receive them. But there have also been arguments over the preservation techniques employed by the British Museum on the marbles, including the use of a thin film of a ten per cent solution of polyethylene glycol, a polymer which can be washed off. Dr Theodore Skoubikidis, a member of the Acropolis Conservation Committee, has criticized the process as not only ineffectual in halting decay, but possibly also as having the reverse effect. Mr Brian Cook, keeper of Greek and Roman Antiquities, has stressed that despite competing claims over the marbles, conservation information should be shared.

Sir David Price, a Conservative, made the point in the 1983 Commons debate[20] about the dangers that would face the marbles on return to Greece:

> Would the Minister remind the Greek Government: 'No Elgin, no marbles and no British Museum, no marbles'? The present level of sulphur dioxide in the Athenian atmosphere is as destructive of what remains of the Parthenon as Turkish gunfire, Turkish gunpowder and the vandalizers and marauders of the Greek people.

This valid argument that the returned marbles would face the hazard of air pollution, which is a serious problem in Athens, was countered by the steps taken by the Greek government to acquire a special building as a museum to house the marbles. This was part of a several million dollar government plan to restore ancient monuments and build museums all over Greece. Some short-term measures were taken to prevent atmospheric pollution in Athens and yielded the following results:

> All the sculptures of the Acropolis monuments have already been moved into the Acropolis Museum where some are displayed in transparent cases with nitrogen circulation to avoid further attack from sulphur dioxide. All ornaments are covered *in situ* in such a way as to avoid contact with rain water.
>
> A 20 per cent decrease of the local concentration of sulphur dioxide was achieved by forbidding access of buses to the Acropolis area, by

reducing the sulphur content in central heating oil and by new industrial regulations.

A Committee for the Maintenance of the Monuments of the Acropolis (ESMA under its Greek acronym) was set up in 1974. Its task was to initiate and supervise studies on the complex problems of the monuments and to put into action specialized programmes for their restoration and maintenance. To begin with, this work comprised three main elements: problems of restoring architecture and statues; methods of repairing broken or degraded marble and making sure that it stays repaired; and scientific investigation of the physicochemical problems involved in the surface deterioration of marble and how to protect the marble against such deterioration. ESMA's first action was to put its experts to work on the problems of restoring the Erechtheion. In December 1977 its plans were revealed to an international symposium of experts in Athens and universally adopted. Work began early in 1979 and in the autumn the caryatids were removed to the Acropolis Museum, where the problem of protecting their surface was studied. About seven hundred stones, weighing 1,200 tons, damaged by the restoration of 1902–10, were removed from the temple; systematic repair was commenced, with titanium pins where appropriate, and the work of replacing them begun. In December 1988 the newly restored Erechtheion temple was opened by Melina Mercouri. The mode of restoration has been controversial and the original caryatids have been replaced by concrete casts.

A comprehensive fifteen-year programme has been worked out, taking in not only the principal monuments (Parthenon, Erechtheion, Propylaea, temple of Athena Nike) but all the other man-made additions to the sacred rock. It comprised the following: restoration and maintenance of the Acropolis walls; creation of paths following the roads which existed in ancient times; restoration of the Roman temple to Augustus and Rome, a circular building to the east of the Parthenon; restoration of the foundations of the pre-Parthenon temple to Athena (between the Parthenon and the Erechtheion); measures to protect the stability of the whole perimeter of the Acropolis rock. This work is expected to cost over one billion drachmas.

In addition, in September 1983, an International Meeting for the Restoration of the Acropolis Monuments was held in Athens. The proposed plan for the restoration of the Parthenon provided a twelve-point programme for the substitution of the corroded iron clamps which hold the marble members together; the strengthening and safeguarding of the temple against pollution and earthquakes; and the restoration of thousands of marble fragments, scattered around the monument, which have now been identified as part of the building.

The International Conference recognized that the restoration work will reach completion only when the sculptural parts are returned.

As part of the restoration programme the Greek government pledged to proceed with plans to build a modern museum which would house all objects from the Acropolis and provide all necessary safeguards for proper display, accessibility to the public and preservation of archaeological treasures. However, it would appear that total restoration has not been planned, nor is it regarded as feasible. That is to say, the incorporation of the marbles into the actual building was not envisaged, since it would involve considerable rebuilding, although it has been suggested that modern techniques make this possible.

In the past, the sculpture of the west pediment used to dominate the entrance to the Acropolis from the Propylaea (the famous gateways and approaches). But the original entablatures on which the marbles rested were destroyed and the Greeks now prefer to leave the question of using reproductions to the future. Total rebuilding or restoration, as has been indicated, is not going to be possible, a point which has been made much of by some British politicians in arguing against return, and it is true that the Greek plans will not actually meet the terms of recommendations made at the 1982 Mexican Cultural Conference.

It could, however, be legitimately suggested that where incorporation into the original structure is not feasible, restoration could be effected by means of archaeological reassembly which involves placing the integral pieces of an ancient monument in as close proximity to each other as to make possible the optimum appreciation of the whole – a kind of jigsaw restoration.

In 1985 an exhibition concerning the restoration programme for the Parthenon actually went on display at the British Museum. And in 1986 an operation to rebuild the Parthenon partially was reported to be in progress in Athens. Mr Manolis Korres, the architect in charge, said the plan was to dismantle the building, stone by stone, for treatment, bringing down the marble blocks at the rate of one or two a day and replacing corroded iron clamps of earlier restorations, which cause the marble to crack, with rust-proof titanium joints. At the same time hundreds of marble blocks and fragments blown to the ground by the 1678 explosion, which left the Parthenon in two ruined halves, were to be put back in place, as in a gigantic jigsaw puzzle. It was thought that it would be possible, using enough authentic material, to add another eight per cent to the monument's volume. However, any restoration can at best only slightly alter its aesthetic appeal as a ruin. Much of the building will remain a mystery: there is so much of it which is destroyed and lost. The question of missing figures and their composition will remain the subject of scholarly speculation, as reflected in the interesting work carried out in the Cast Gallery of the University of Basel under Ernst Berger's direction (Fig. 20).

WEST

A–hero 'Ilissos'. B–F–Kekrops, his daughters and son (?). G–Nike. H–Hermes. I,K–Triton (?) supporting horses. L–Athena. M–Poseidon. N–Iris. O–Amphitrite. P,Q,R–woman with two children, Oreithyia (?). S–W–other Attic royalty or heroes.

EAST

A–C–Helios (Sun) and chariot. D–Dionysos. E,F–Demeter and Kore. G–Artemis. a–c, i–k–conjectural chariot groups (Ares and Iris; Hermes and Amphitrite?). d–Hephaistos. e–Hera. f–Zeus. g–Athena. H–Poseidon. K,L,M–Hestia, Dione, Aphrodite (?). N,O–Selene (Moon) or Nyx (Night) and chariot.

Fig. 20. The pediments. The drawings are those of the reconstruction in Basel by Ernst Berger, combining extant fragments with Carrey's drawings (left plain in the west pediment).

The further argument that more people see the marbles in the British Museum than would see them in Greece is difficult to validate, although the British Museum is said to have about three million visitors a year. Moreover, it seems that this is a diversion from the real argument about the legal, historic or aesthetic merits of return. The issue is whether the marbles should be where they are at all, or should form part of an archaeological reassembly. Many of the hypothetical arguments against return are couched in terms which distract from this central issue.

It is often presupposed that the legal position regarding the marbles is beyond serious dispute. This point of view has never been closely examined, and demands serious scrutiny. The Explanatory Memorandum to the 1983 Council of Europe Resolution on return said: 'The bona fide ownership of the objects in question is not at issue. Return is not a question of law . . . Existing legal rights are not at issue . . .' The view of the British government has also always been expressed in terms of the legality of the acquisition of the marbles. The Trustees and officials of the British Museum have often gone on record as saying that the marbles were legally purchased even if Greece was under Turkish tutelage at the time. In the House of Lords debate on the proposed amendment in 1983 to the British Museum Act, Lord Nugent declared that the 'question of legal ownership is beyond all doubt . . .'. However, no legal question is ever beyond all doubt, of course, and certainly not before it has been properly considered by a properly constituted legal authority. There are a number of issues which should be more closely examined. The first is the question of the status of Greece in the Ottoman Empire, and the nature of the Turkish authority at that time.

Sometimes the legal arguments become confused, especially when they are introduced as an aside. Thus an American writer, James Wiseman, has stated:

> The support that England gave to Greece in its war of Independence
> from Turkey is some evidence that England came to the conclusion,
> even within the lifetime of Elgin, that the Ottoman Empire had no right
> to the domination of Greece. There is therefore a selfcontradiction in
> the argument that Elgin received a legal permit for activities in Greece
> from a Government that Elgin evidently concluded had no legal rule in
> Greece.

However, the legal power of a state rests on its authority over its subjects and territory. This is internally derived, and not abrogated by the disapproval or even subsequent political conduct of other states who otherwise formally recognize its *de jure* (legal) and *de facto* (effective) authority. Lord Elgin was after all ambassador to Constantinople. England had given the fullest recognition to the Ottoman Empire, and Turkish authority. Moreover the presence of Turkey was not a provisional state of affairs, without the transfer of sovereignty. It was not a case of a shortlived belligerent occupation but of total absorption into the Ottoman Empire for over three and a half centuries. It would not be feasible to challenge retrospectively the legal status of the Turkish authority throughout that period.

The second issue which should be examined is the firman upon which so much reliance has been placed over 180 years for legally validating Lord Elgin's removal of the marbles. It is necessary to reexamine carefully a particular passage of the 1816 Parliamentary Committee Report:

The success of the British arms in Egypt, and the expected restitution of that province to the Porte, wrought a wonderful and instantaneous change in the disposition of all ranks and descriptions of people towards our Nation. Universal benevolence and goodwill appeared to take place of suspicion and aversion. Nothing was refused which was asked; and Lord Elgin, availing himself of this favourable and unexpected alteration, obtained, in the summer of 1801, access to the Acropolis for general purposes, with permission to draw, model, and remove; to which was added, a special licence to excavate in a particular place. Lord Elgin mentions in his evidence, that he was obliged to send from Athens to Constantinople for leave to remove a house; at the same time remarking that, in point of fact, all permissions issuing from the Porte to any distant provinces, are little better than authorities to make the best bargain that can be made with the local magistracies. *The applications upon this subject, passed in verbal conversations; but the warrants or fermauns were granted in writing, addressed to the chief authorities resident at Athens, to whom they were delivered, and in whose hands they remained: so that your Committee had no opportunity of learning from Lord Elgin himself their exact tenor, or of ascertaining in what terms they noticed, or allowed the displacing, or carrying away of these Marbles. But Dr Hunt,* who accompanied Lord Elgin as chaplain to the embassy, has preserved, and has now in his possession, *a translation* of the *second fermaun, which extended the powers of the first: but as he had it not with him in London, to produce before your Committee, he stated the substance, according to his recollection,* which was, 'That, in order to show their particular respect to the Ambassador of Great Britain, the august ally of the Porte, with whom they were now and had long been in the strictest alliance, they gave to his Excellency and to his Secretary, and the Artists employed by him, the most extensive permission to view, draw and model the ancient Temples of the Idols, and the Sculptures upon them, and to make excavations and to take away any stones that might appear interesting to them'. He stated further, that no remonstrance was at any time made, nor any displeasure shown by the Turkish government, either at Constantinople or at Athens, against the extensive interpretation which was put upon this fermaun; and although the work of taking down, and removing was going on for months, and even years, and was conducted in the most public manner, numbers of native labourers, to the amount of some hundreds being frequently employed, not the least obstruction was ever interposed, nor the smallest uneasiness shown after the granting of this second fermaun. Among the Greek population and inhabitants of Athens it occasioned no sort of dissatisfaction.

What does this part of the report mean? It says that in 1801 Elgin had access to the Acropolis and permission to draw, model and remove, together with a special licence to excavate *in a particular place*. But the Parliamentary Committee *never saw* these permissions since they remained in Athens. Dr Hunt, whom history records as the one most responsible for encouraging Elgin in his extensive enterprise, had in his possession a translation of a *second* firman, which *extended* the powers of the first. But even this translation of a second firman was never presented to the Parliamentary Committee, 'as he had it not with him in London'. Therefore he stated the substance 'according to his recollection'. He remembered the words being to the effect that Elgin had the most extensive permission 'to view, draw and model . . . and to make excavations and to take away any stones . . .'.

Much has been made of interpreting this wording in the years since that report. But the fact is that the Committee never had sight of *any* legal document or documentary evidence of any kind authorizing the removal of the marbles. Dr Hunt's *recollections* were only hearsay. That a liberty was taken with such permission as had existed is practically admitted in the report; that, in Elgin's own evidence, 'all Permissions issuing from the Porte to any distant provinces, are little better than authorities to make the best *bargain* that can be made with the local magistracies'.

One must inevitably question whether any second firman even existed, since neither the original nor its translation have ever been produced; and one can only speculate on the contents of the first firman and licence. Indeed, the Committee itself admits it had '*no* opportunity of learning from Lord Elgin himself *their exact tenor*, or of *ascertaining in what terms, they noticed, or allowed the displacing or carrying away of these marbles*'.

The documentary authority to take the marbles does not appear to exist. In addition it should be noted that although the Parliamentary Committee was making a general report on the suitability of the marbles for purchase by the British government, it was not constituted to determine any legal issues. It was Lord Elgin's position as ambassador which lent credence to the extent of the authority which he exercised, but on no concrete evidence. Further justification was drawn from the failure of the Greek population to object to his conduct, but it is unclear whether their circumstances prevented them from doing so. Some travellers' tales of that period recount that there was Greek and Turkish displeasure over the removal of the marbles.[21] Indeed in 1985 Professor Robert Browning of London University unearthed a letter from Lord Elgin to the Prime Minister Spencer Perceval, written in 1811.[22] This casts doubt on the assistance which Elgin is always believed to have received from the Turkish government. It refers to the fact that the succeeding British ambassador, Mr Adair, understood in his dealings with the Turks that 'the Porte denied that the persons who had sold those marbles to me [Elgin] had any right to dispose of them . . .'.

Law Professor John Merryman of Stanford University[23] has relied upon the subsequent acts of ratification by the Turkish authorities to overcome any arguments about those actions taken in excess of the original terms of the firman. In particular there were said to be two such instances of acquiescence, namely the issue by the sultan of additional firmans addressed to the voivode and disdar of Athens, in which he generally sanctioned what those local officials had done for Elgin and his party, and written orders by the Ottoman government to the Athenian government releasing a shipment of marbles to England when they were held up at Piraeus, the port of Athens.[24] Again, whilst these events are referred to in correspondence, there are no authentic original documents in existence.

A British Museum publication[25] says of these matters that the Parliamentary Committee vindicated all of Elgin's claims. From an aesthetic point of view this was so. It also adds that although Elgin was acting as ambassador he had collected the marbles as a private person. Yet the Earl of Aberdeen and Dr Hunt, who both testified to the Committee, clearly stated that it was the office which Lord Elgin held which had made his actions possible, and that no private individual could have accomplished this.

A close examination of the whole matter of Elgin's collection was made in a detailed report in the 1916 *Journal of Hellenic Studies* based on correspondence which passed between Elgin and Hunt and Lusieri and Logotheti (the British Consul in Athens). This reveals that there was indeed prolonged difficulty in obtaining an appropriate firman. The documentary evidence clearly suggests that the original intention had only been to model and draw the figures on the building.

As regards the government of Athens at the time, the city had been under the patronage of the Kislar Aya, or Chief of the Sultan's black eunuchs since the middle of the seventeenth century, and its chief officer the voivode was his nominee. The chief military officer was the disdar, or commandant of the citadel, who regulated the access of strangers to the Acropolis and who lived within its walls.

It is said that no letters survive from Lusieri describing the opening of the campaign at Athens, but some details may be gleaned from the letters of Logotheti.

In September 1800 he wrote to Lord Elgin: 'With reference to the Temple of Minerva, your Excellency must be aware that, inasmuch as Turkish families live round it, when the scaffoldings are made all the Turkish houses and courts will be in view, and since they are very particular on that point we shall meet with difficulties.'[26] A letter was therefore needed, addressed to the voivode, and commending the artists and Logotheti. Accompanied by 100 piastres to the disdar, and another 100 to the neighbouring Turks, this letter would serve. In February 1801 he reported that he had arranged without the aid of the firman for the artists to get admission to the fortress. There had, however, recently been a change of voivode, and it was therefore still desirable to have the firman. In March, work was continuing, but a powerful letter of recommendation was much to be desired. By May 1801, according to Lusieri, a firman of some sort was apparently obtained and forwarded to Logotheti, but it failed to reach him for a long time, and, according to Hunt, turned out to be an illusory document.

In the same month Lusieri reported to Lord Elgin that he had found the company in good health, and was well satisfied with the quality of their work. The architects had finished measuring all that there was on the Acropolis and the best of what was in the town. He proposed to set them to measure all that remained in the town after they had finished their elevations of the most remark-able monuments. There had, however, been a change for the worse:

> The Formatori were ready to begin work on the Temple of Minerva, in the citadel, when the commandant prevented their going on. The same cause prevents Feodor from drawing the bas-reliefs of the same temple, the architects from making new observations, and myself from taking views. That is because they lack the necessary firman for that purpose, which your Excellency sent to Signor Logotheti before my departure, and which he has never received. Everything that has been done up till now in the citadel has been by means of presents to the Disdar, who is the commandant. He, however, has been threatened by the Cadi and Voivode if he should continue to admit us to the fortress, and has just told us that henceforth it was impossible for us to work there without a firman. I therefore beg your Excellency to have one sent to us as soon as possible, drawn up in such terms as to prevent us meeting with new dif-ficulties in resuming and peaceably continuing our work. I also require one of the same effect in case I shall go elsewhere.

Meanwhile it was Hunt who waxed enthusiastic about the prospects of the expedition:

> Of the Temples of Minerva, Theseus and Neptune, I can say nothing that would convey an idea of the effect they produce. They must be seen to know what the union of simplicity and beauty is capable of: and after having feasted the eyes with those exquisite specimens of Athenian arch-itecture, every deviation from them, even the edifices of Rome itself will

almost disgust . . . Luisieri is employing his pencil on two general views of Athens, one from the Pnyx, the other from Mount Anchesmus [i.e. Lycabettos] which will embrace all the monuments and classic spots of the Citadel and the Town. He has also commenced near views of the Temples of Theseus, Minerva and Pandrosos. Positive Firmans must, however, be obtained from the Porte, to enable the Architects and Modellers to proceed in their most interesting labours. Unfortunately the Temple of Minerva, called the Parthenon, and those of Neptune Erech-theus of Minerva Polias, and Pandrosos, as well as the famous Propylea, are all within the walls of the Acropolis, now a Turkish fortress, gar-risoned by mercenary and insolent Janissaries, so that every obstacle which National jealousy and Mohometan bigotry, seconded by French intrigue, could produce, have been too successfully used to interrupt their labours. Till those Firmans are obtained, the bas-reliefs on the frieze, and the Groupes on the Metopes can neither be modelled nor drawn. The architects, therefore, in the mean time, are proceeding to make the elevations and ground plans, from the measures they had taken, and the Calmuc Theodore employs his almost magic pencil in copying such remains of Sculpture as are beyond the walls of the citadel.

Also in May 1801 Logotheti was no less active than Lusieri and Hunt in urging the need for a firman. He had asked for it during the previous winter. In May, however, the difficulties he had clearly foreseen began to be a problem, and Logotheti explained in detail what Hunt had only described in general terms. Having finished their plans, the artists had erected their scaffolding for moulding and drawing, and had just begun work 'when a firman arrived here which advised the governor to keep good watch, and to guard the citadel, because a French fleet has gone out of Brest, and has reached Toulon. He has put new difficulties in the way of the progress of the work on the ruins of the citadel.' Logotheti had endeavoured to meet the difficulty by a formal call on the com-mandant in company with Mr Nisbet as the ambassador's kinsman. The com-mandant had promised that such facilities as had been previously granted would be renewed after a few days, but Logotheti still urged the advisability of the firman.

Hunt proposed to leave Athens to return to Constantinople on 23 May 1801, with a conviction, shared by Lusieri and by Logotheti, that a strong firman must be obtained.

Hunt is presumed to have reached Constantinople early in June 1801, where he would have been able to urge by word of mouth the case for an extended firman. A written memorandum exists (*JHS*, 1916, p. 190), showing the points which Hunt considered of importance:

Pera, July 1, 1801. Mr Hunt recommends that a Firman should be procured from the Porte, addressed to the Voivode and Cadi of Athens, as well as to the Disdar, or Governor of the Citadel; stating that the Artists are in the service of the British Ambassador Extraordinary, and that they are to have not only permission, but protection in the following objects:

(1) to enter freely within the walls of the Citadel, and to draw and model with plaster the Ancient Temples there.

(2) to erect scaffolding, and to dig where they may wish to discover the ancient foundations.

(3) liberty to take away any sculptures or inscriptions which do not interfere with the works or walls of the Citadel.

However, it has been reported that there were no written records of the actual negotiations with the Porte, and Lord Elgin subsequently testified that such offices were purely oral.

Because he had previously been deceived as to the pretended contents of a firman, Hunt advised Lord Elgin to apply for one which embraced the particular objects he had pointed out to him, and was accompanied by a literal translation.

A firman,[27] or official letter, from the Kaimacan Pasha (who filled the office of grand vizier at the Porte, during that minister's absence in Egypt), which was addressed to the cadi or chief judge, and to the voivode or governor of Athens, in 1801, read as follows, in its translation from the Italian:

[After the usual introductory compliments, and the salutation of Peace]
– It is hereby signified to you, that our sincere Friend his Excellency Lord Elgin, Ambassador Extraordinary from the Court of England to the Porte of Happiness, hath represented to us, that it is well known that the greater part of the Frank [i.e. Christian] Courts are anxious to read and investigate the books, pictures or figures, and other works of science of the ancient Greek philosophers: and that in particular, the ministers or officers of state, philosophers, primates and other individuals of England, have a remarkable taste for the drawings, or figures or sculptures, remaining ever since the time of the said Greeks, and which are to be seen on the shores of the Archipelago and in other parts; and have in consequence from time to time sent men to explore and examine the ancient edifices, and drawings or figures. And that some accomplished Dilettanti of the Court of England, being desirous to see the ancient buildings and the curious figures in the City of Athens, and the old walls remaining since the time of the Grecians, which now subsist in

the interior part of the said place; his Excellency the said Ambassador hath therefore engaged five English painters, now dwelling at Athens, *to examine and view, and also to copy the figures remaining there, ab antiquo:* And he hath also at this time expressly besought us that an Official Letter may be written from hence, ordering that as long as the said painters shall be employed in going in and out of the said citadel of Athens, which is the place of their occupations; and in fixing scaffolding round the ancient Temple of the Idols there; *and in moulding the ornamental sculpture and visible figures thereon, in plaster or gypsum; and in measuring the remains of other old ruined buildings there; and in excavating when they find it necessary the foundations, in order to discover inscriptions which may have been covered in the rubbish*; that no interruption may be given them, nor any obstacle thrown in their way by the Disdar (or commandant of the citadel) or any other person: that no one may meddle with the scaffolding or implements they may require in their works; and *that when they'd wish to take away any pieces of stone* ('qualche pezzi di pietra') *with old inscriptions or figures thereon, that no opposition be made thereto.*

We therefore have written this Letter to you, and expedited it by Mr Philip Hunt, an English gentleman, Secretary of the aforesaid Ambassador, in order that as soon as you shall have understood its meaning, namely, that it is the explicit desire and engagement of this Sublime Court endowed with all eminent qualities, to favour such requests as the above-mentioned, in conformity with what is due to the friendship, sincerity, alliance and good will subsisting ab antiquo between the Sublime and ever durable Ottoman Court and that of England, and which is on the side of both those Courts manifestly increasing; *particularly as there is no harm in the said figures and edifices being thus viewed, contemplated, and designed.* Therefore, after having fulfilled the duties of hospitality, and given a proper reception to the aforesaid Artists, in compliance with the urgent request of the said Ambassador to that effect, and because it is incumbent on us to provide *that they meet no opposition in walking, viewing, or contemplating the figures and edifices they may wish to design or copy*; or in any of their works of fixing scaffolding, or using their various implements; It is our desire that on the arrival of this Letter you use your diligence to act conformably to the instances of the said Ambassador, as long as the said five Artists dwelling at Athens shall be employed in going in and out of the said citadel of Athens, which is the place of their occupations; or in fixing scaffolding around the ancient Temple of the Idols, or *in modelling with chalk or gypsum the said ornaments and visible figures thereon; or in measuring the fragments and vestiges or other ruined edifices; or in excavating, when they find it necessary, the foundations, in search of inscrip-*

tions among the rubbish; that they be not molested by the said Disdar nor by any other persons, nor even by you [to whom this letter is addressed]; and that no one meddle with their scaffolding or implements, *nor hinder them from taking away any pieces of stone* ['qualche pezzi di pietra'] *with inscriptions or figures*. In the above-mentioned manner, see that ye demean and comport yourselves.

(*Signed with a signet*) SEGED ABDULLAH KAIMACAN

The tenor of this translation has been accepted ever since as the legitimate authorization for the removal of the marbles. Ordinarily some courier or sea captain would have conveyed the firman from Constantinople or Athens. But history records that it was Dr Hunt who conveyed it to Athens in July 1801. In describing the letters he had obtained, Hunt referred to the object of his mission as 'to create an impression in favour of our views and of our power . . . On such Classic ground investigations into the remains of Antiquity, and an attempt to procure such as are interesting and portable will naturally come in as a secondary object; and as I shall carry a Ferman to enable our Artists to prosecute without interruption their researches in the Acropolis of Athens, I will take care to see it put properly into execution . . .' (*JHS*, 1916, pp. 193, 199).

It is clear from records that when Hunt arrived back in Athens he proceeded to generate a favourable atmosphere for the activities of Lord Elgin's men, by impressing on the Turkish voivode the matter of disrespect to Englishmen by the Turkish authorities. It was recorded that a conference with the voivode 'ended with repeated assurances that henceforward the gates of the Citadel are open to *all* Englishmen, from Sun-rise to Sun-set, and to draw or measure any of the old buildings they please, and that your Lordship's Artists are to consider them-selves at full liberty to model, dig, or carry away whatever does not interfere with the works. Hitherto all this has been most faithfully performed. The Citadel is now as open and free to us as the streets of Athens' (p. 196). Thus followed all the activity which has so divided opinion ever since. Posterity has made Lord Elgin the villain, but it is clear that Hunt's role deserves closer scrutiny.

In its frustrated quest for the return of the marbles, there are several possible forums to which Greece might have turned for a legal judgement.

A member state of the United Nations is automatically a member of the International Court of Justice (based in The Hague and inaugurated there on 18 April 1946) and a party to its rules. The court has jurisdiction in contentious cases between states, and in such cases Article 36 (2) (referred to as the Optional Clause) of the statute of the court provides:

The States parties to the present Statute may at any time declare that they recognise as compulsory, *ipso facto* and without special agreement, in relation to any other State accepting the same obligation, the jurisdiction of the Court in all legal disputes concerning:

(a) the interpretation of a treaty;

(b) any question of international law;

(c) the existence of any fact which, if established, would constitute a breach of an international obligation;

(d) the nature or extent of the reparation to be made for the breach of an international obligation.

The United Kingdom has deposited a declaration under this Article. Greece has not. However, states which make no declaration under the Optional Clause, but which are parties to the court's statute, may make a declaration at any moment, and by drafting it so as to gain reciprocity secure the court's jurisdiction over a dispute involving another state which has made a declaration. Furthermore, it can limit the duration of its declaration so as, in effect, to invoke the jurisdiction for the instant dispute and then exclude it for future disputes. Thus the consent of the parties is necessary, and preliminary objections as to jurisdiction and as to admissibility may be raised before the merits of a case can be considered.

In the case of the court's advisory jurisdiction, Article 65 (1) of the Statute provides:

> The court may give an advisory opinion on any legal question at the request of whatever body may be authorized by or in accordance with the Charter of the United Nations to make such a request.

All states, including Greece, would have to seek this through a majority of the General Assembly, which together with the Security Council is empowered under Article 96 to request an advisory opinion. Objections to jurisdiction could also arise and this is a matter for the court's discretion. There are therefore many technical and jurisdictional constraints, and many practical difficulties. Whilst judgements of the International Court are binding, there is an absence of a mandatory power attaching to them and an opinion of the International Court commands only some moral force. There is, however, a precedent of an International Court of Justice judgement on the issue of the return of cultural property. This occurred in 1962 in the *Case Concerning the Temple of Preah Vihear*.[28] The land on which the temple was situated was the subject of a dispute between Cambodia and Thailand. The majority opinion of the court was that it was under Cambodian sovereignty. Cambodia had also claimed sculptures, stelae, fragments of monuments, sandstone models and ancient pottery which had been removed from the temple by the Thai authorities. The majority of the court found in principle in favour of the Cambodian claim for restitution.

If Greece sought to bring an action before an English court there would also be private international law questions to be dealt with, such as *locus standi* (the right to appear as a party before the court), because of the succession of the modern Greek state to the Athenian republic, from whose territory the marbles were taken. Laws vesting the archaeological relics of Greece in the state would be recognized but would be retroactive. Greece would also not be able to invoke any of its subsequent protective legislation regarding export or removal because of its retroactivity and because an English court will not enforce a foreign state's public laws outside its own territory. On the question purely of title, however, Greece would have a strong case to argue because, as this chapter has shown, although it has been endlessly reiterated by numerous parties that the marbles were acquired legally, this is an assertion open to grave doubt upon close examination.

There appears to have been no sight taken of the original document entitling Elgin to remove the marbles, and the subsequent production to the Parliamentary Committee of 1816 of a copy would arguably not be adequate to give concrete proof or valid documentary evidence of title. In retrospect it seems extraordinary that the purchase was effected on so meagre a basis. The mere accomplishment of removal from Greece without final hindrance from the Turkish authorities is not proof *ipso facto* of legal title.

The Sale of Goods Act 1893 embodied the principles of English law relating to transfer of title upon the sale of goods. This was amended in 1979 and provides in Section 23 for 'Sale under voidable title':

> When the seller of goods has a voidable title to them, but his title has
> not been avoided at the time of the sale, the buyer acquires a good title to
> the goods, provided he buys them in good faith and without notice of
> the seller's defect of title.

The operative words in the present context would be 'voidable title', 'in good faith'[29] and 'without notice of the seller's defect of title'. If it can be shown that property is stolen and there is no title in the vendor, then even a purchaser in good faith would not acquire title against a party who had superior title.

In addition the *purchase* of the marbles by the British government is arguably suspect because of a possible notice of defective title since (i) The existence of the firman original is not confirmed. It was not seen in England in 1816. It is presumed lost, and the absence of an original document means there was no proper documentary proof of title. (ii) Even if the terms of the firman as translated are accepted as accurate, it is clear that Elgin exceeded them. He acted in breach of the conditions allowing him to remove items from the Parthenon site, and what he did remove was not included within the descriptions contained in the firman. Any arguments as to estoppel because of subsequent acts of ratification by the Turkish authorities are also subject to the challenge of the absence of documentary proof. (iii) Lord Elgin did not *buy* the marbles, and there was no appropriate consideration given for them even to the Turkish authorities. (iv) The Parthenon was a public building and a religious monument. Whilst the authority of the Turks over it cannot be challenged, there is a strong *prima facie* presumption (because of the nature of the building) against any state authority divesting itself of title to its own public property. This presumption is now embodied in all the international conventions dealing with the protection of such buildings in war and peace.

Indeed it could be argued that Elgin's men did in peacetime what would no longer have been acceptable even in time of war. According to the international jurist Henry Wheaton:

> By the ancient law of nations, even what was called *res sacrae* were not exempt from capture and confiscation ... But by the modern usage of nations, which has now acquired the force of law, temples of religion, public edifices devoted to civil purposes only, monuments of art, and repositories of science, are exempted from the general operations of war.[30]

In discussing the term 'Elginisme' the jurist Professor Charles de Visscher wrote of Elgin's actions:

> Despite the reasons given by Lord Elgin to justify his action it was severely judged even in England. It is very doubtful however, whether the arguments put forth can actually justify the irreparable damage resulting from his action. The fact is that the principle of the unity and integrity of a monument of such extraordinary and historic value clearly outweighs any other consideration here.[31]

Many treaties confer 'property' or 'title' without referring this to the national law of the states or to any other local law.[32] Greece could also argue that there is a general principle of international law contained in numerous conventions, bilateral agreements and state practice, which holds it as a *prima facie* presumption of public policy that title to 'immovable property' never passes, regardless of how acquired. Clearly, since the marbles were transported, they were physically movable. However, they are in a class of object which belong to a building or monument or some other natural formation as, for example, a cave, and are part of sovereign territory. Therefore they are legally 'immovable'. In the *Temple of Preah Vihear* case the International Court held that a claim for restitution of cultural property was implicitly included in the claims for territorial sovereignty. It could be argued that the continued retention of the marbles, however they were initially acquired, is contrary to such a principle of international law, to which the United Kingdom is also subject.

At best the situation is legally doubtful. Certainly the great reliance which was placed, seemingly by all parties concerned, upon the firman for over 180 years was quite erroneous.

Professor Merryman has considered the possible loss of litigation rights in England, which may have been proscribed by the passage of time.[33] He concedes that in international law there is no such thing as a Statute of Limitations, but points out that the Greeks have had 155 years in which to pursue any possible legal remedies. Viewed as a possible action for the return of stolen property he concludes that the Greeks have lost their right to litigate in the English courts because under the 1939 Limitation Act (s. 2) the time limit for any such claim is six years. However, national legislation cannot prescribe any rights in international law and could not have any effect on any international historic delict. Greece could argue for redress on the basis that title has not passed or is defective (for the reasons previously referred to) and voidable under contemporary international law. Emphasis in the British case for retention of the marbles is placed upon the passage of time, and upon the law at the time of removal. There was no body of international law governing *removal* or protection at that time. Moreover, international law does recognize a bar of claims by lapse of time, although this argument is more likely to succeed where there is estoppel through acquiescence. However, it may be argued that the issue is the continued *retention* of certain kinds of cultural property. In recognition of superior title, or where title could be regarded as voidable, the principle of the physical return of cultural property is becoming, through increasing state and institutional practice, a custom of international law.[34] This has especially been true in the case of objects of religious, royal and palaeontological significance and in the case of historic records and 'immovable' state property. It is becoming established practice in the case of the illicit and contemporary removal of archaeological treasures. That is to say, Greece may argue that the Parthenon belongs to a class of property which was removed in such past circumstances that title never passed. Both the British Museum and the British government have stressed the legality by which the marbles were acquired. The British Museum position has also been that it would in any event be precluded by statute (the British Museum Act) from returning objects held in its trust. Additionally it should be remembered that the marbles were specifically vested in the Trustees in perpetuity by a separate Act of Parliament in 1816. The British government position has been that the Museum Trustees must be protected from political pressure, and that legislation enabling return would create the climate for such pressure and set the precedent for uncontrolled cultural returns. Indeed comparisons have been drawn between the marbles and other treasures whose return is sought. For instance, the Indian Arts Council in Britain has pointed to the Amravati marbles[35] removed to Britain in 1880. The Eleventh Earl of Elgin and descendant of Lord Elgin, who removed the marbles, has said he would not in principle oppose their return to some great museum although he linked this possibility with returns from other sources as well.[36] In 1987 the Onassis Public Foundation entered the fray by declaring its support for the making of such approaches for the return of the Elgin Marbles as would not set an unacceptable precedent. The manner by which this would be achieved was not clearly stated. The complexities of having to deal with both government and museum are dealt with in the next chapter.

CHAPTER THREE

BRITISH AND OTHER EUROPEAN APPROACHES

The seventeenth and eighteenth centuries bore witness to the zenith of the European passion for 'collecting' antiquities. The extension of colonial empires, the activities of travellers and traders, and the growth of a class of wealthy private collectors made it possible to amass an astonishing quantity of objects from all over the world. The scale, both in numbers and bulk, of the items brought back to Europe over considerable distances and with great difficulty testifies to the zeal with which this pursuit was widely undertaken.

The British Museum, in particular, was a great beneficiary of that era, and in the words of one of its own publications,[1] 'by its non-exclusive approach to collecting and by its abiding concern with scholarship and the study of cultures [it] has inherited and enlarged the tradition established by the best early private collectors'. It was the collection of one such private individual, Sir Hans Sloane, which formed the nucleus of the initial British Museum collection, especially in the area of Egyptian antiquities.

The United Kingdom stands out as a principal holder of some of the major cultural treasures of the world, primarily because of her colonial history, although not all the treasures were acquired as a direct result of this. Many were acquired simply as the result of long-distance archaeological raids and these were not always carried out by archaeologists. The United Kingdom was not alone in this; all the European countries which maintained colonial interests abroad mounted archaeological expeditions and amassed collections containing items which are of special cultural significance in their homeland. These countries included France, Belgium, Germany, Holland, Italy and Denmark. Often objects were collected in the spirit of intense competition and rivalry, and this only hastened the destruction or removal of countless treasures.

An example of this was the different expeditions sent out to Chinese Turkestan at the turn of the century. These included the French, notably Professor Paul Pelliott, the Germans, notably Albert von Le Coq, the Japanese, notably Count Kozui Otani, the Americans, notably Langdon Warner, and the Russians. The blame for starting this international race for antiquities has been attributed to the Swedish explorer and writer Sven Hedin and the British Orientalist Aurel Stein. The result has been that the treasures of Central Asia are today scattered throughout the world in over thirty museums and institutions.

In Greece, the rivalry was between the French and the British, especially over the Elgin Marbles. Many other major pieces were transported away to the museums of Bavaria and France. For instance, the frieze of the temple of Aegina, excavated by Charles Cockerell, an Englishman, went to Bavaria in 1811.

In Egypt, the rivalry of Bernardino Drouetti and Giovanni Battista Belzoni whose collections went to France and England, respectively, took on epic proportions, and the scale of their activities in bringing back major pieces was much publicized and glamorized. These two men were little more than grave robbers. Belzoni collected without regard for archaeological significance. Among other things, Belzoni found a colossal head of Ramesses II, the Younger Memnon, weighing several tons, buried in the sand in a temple complex near Thebes and brought it back to the British Museum. Near Thebes he also discovered the tomb of Sethos (Seti) I, and the empty sarcophagus was brought to the Soane Museum in London. In the Valley of the Kings he opened the second pyramid of Gizeh, tomb of Chephren, and entered the royal chamber. He was used as a collaborator by Henry Salt, British consul general in Egypt, to collect many important pieces for the British Museum.

The Germans were also active in Egypt. In the mid-1800s the German archaeologist Richard Lepsius brought together the treasures now held at the Egyptian Museum in Berlin, although his primary brief was orderly classification. In particular, he investigated the interment chambers (*mastabas*) around the pyramids. The removal from Egypt to Germany of one of the world's most famous and prized pieces of sculpture is attributed to Ludwig Borchardt. As Director of the German Institute in Cairo in 1912, he was active in digging at the 'library' of Tell el-Amarna. The beautifully coloured limestone bust of Queen Nefretiti, the wife of the pharaoh Akhenaten, appears to have been removed to Germany some years before its actual appearance in Berlin in 1923. Its removal caused a worldwide Egyptological scandal.

In contrast with the old archaeological plunderers there was Auguste Mariette, sent out to Egypt in 1850 by the Louvre, who regulated excavations in Egypt as the director of the Egyptian Service of Antiquities. He did pursue the search for precious objects and impressive monuments but his priority was excavation and discovery. The most famous excavations with which he is associated are those of the Serapeum at Memphis, the cemeteries of Sakkarah, and the temples of Osiris-Apis, the Sphinx at Gizeh and those of Abydos, Medinet et Habu, Der el-Bahri and Edfu. He devoted himself strenuously to preventing the exportation of Egyptian antiquities to Europe. In the early 1850s he created a National Museum of Egyptian Antiquities at Bulak in Cairo, the world's largest museum of such objects. He felt that with such a museum in Egypt it would no longer be possible for agents of European missions to justify removal of treasures from Egypt on the grounds that the Egyptians were not fit to look after them. He effectively stopped the plunder and irregular sale of Egyptian antiquities. The creation of the first National Museum in the Near East and the birth of conscience about the expropriation of antiquities are among Mariette's great achievements.

In Mesopotamia the first excavations were carried out in 1842 by Paul Emile Botta, who was French consul at Mosul. In particular, in 1846 he excavated Khorsabad (Dur Sharrukin, city of the Assyrian king Sargon II (721–705 BC)). The king's summer palace stood on the outskirts of Nineveh, and was the first Assyrian palace to be discovered. The site contained a huge number of sculptures and reliefs, many of which were made of alabaster and deteriorated seriously upon exposure to the sun. Botta succeeded in loading a number of sculptures onto rafts to be transported down the Tigris, but the stream proved to be too fast-flowing and these were lost. A second attempt to load sculptures onto an ocean-going vessel at the river mouth was successful and the first collection of Assyrian sculptures was sent to Europe, where they remain in the Louvre.

The Englishman Sir Austen Henry Layard excavated at Nionicede from 1845 to mid-1847, and later at Kuyunjik and at Ashur. Many of his finds reached the British Museum in 1848, but some were stolen *en route* at Bombay. Some of the treasures which the British Museum thus acquired include the huge winged bulls, the Black Obelisk of Shalmaneser III and the sculptures of Ashur-nasirpal, which are among the Museum's most valued possessions today. It is said that Layard's main criterion for the success of his excavations was the finding of portable antiquities. Layard's assistant Hormuzd Rassam, a Moslawi who was an English national, also excavated over the whole of Mesopotamia to the frontiers of Syria and the shores of Lake Van in search of as many works of art and inscriptions for the British Museum as possible. In 1878 he discovered at Tell Balawat the famous bronze gates of Shalmaneser II. In 1880, he excavated Abbu Habbah, the site of biblical Sepharvaim, and discovered a large collection of tablets and cylinders which provided a chronological record of the first known archaeological activities in history by Nabonidus, the last king of Babylon. Rassam left his excavations unsupervised, and tablets from them found their way on to the market both before and after he completed his excavations. Sir Wallis Budge, an Englishman, was able to recover hundreds of these tablets from Baghdad dealers in 1888, although he used his own unusual methods of getting the tablets out of the country which Professor Seton Lloyd described as a 'very blatant piece of sharp practice';[2] his outspoken comments on the leakages from Rassam's digs involved him in an action for slander brought by Rassam.

In Africa, South-East Asia and South Asia, the pattern of exploration, colonization, tribute, and then the punitive removal of treasures was repeated, with the result that many African and Asian nations were deprived often of the central core of their own art, as in the case of Benin, or of invaluable documentary records, as in the case of Sri Lanka.

The Christian missionaries were major suppliers of ethnological objects from the New World, the Pacific, and Australia to the museums of Europe. A notable example is the George Brown collection of Pacific tribal art which was bequeathed to Newcastle University but which was broken up by sale in 1986. About 3,000 unique masks and other items were gathered between 1860 and the turn of the century, while Brown worked as a Methodist missionary in the Western Pacific.

A vast collection of ethnological objects is held by the Vatican Ethnological Museum in Rome. There are more than 60,000 objects, with approximately 10,000 from Africa, 10,000 from the Americas, 20,000 from Asia, 6,000 from Oceania, and another 15,000 labelled 'prehistoric'.

In 1692 the missionary Fray Francisco Romero brought wooden carvings from a shrine in northern Colombia to Rome. He presented these to Pope Innocent XII, who instructed that they be housed in the Palazzo di Propaganda Fide. These objects formed the basis of the collection of non-European archaeological objects in the Ethnological Museum.

In the nineteenth century many new objects were sent to European missions by missionaries from all over the world. These were ultimately deposited in the then Museo Borgiano in the Vatican. In particular, a number of carvings were sent from the Gambier islands of Polynesia. These were sent by Father Francis Caret, the first Catholic missionary on Mangareva. A Vatican exhibition in 1887 resulted in the addition of yet further objects.

In 1925 Pope Pius XI organized a missionary exhibition extolling missionary work all over the non-Western world. About 100,000 items were sent and after the exhibition only about half were returned. The Pope proclaimed the formation of a new museum, Pontifico Museo Missionario–Etnologico, so that [the] 'dawn of faith among the infidel of today can be compared to the dawn of faith which . . . illuminated pagan Rome'.[3] The part of the museum which dealt with contemporary mission work and included ethnographic material was completed and opened to the public in 1927, and was rehoused in modern galleries in 1973. Its contemporary object is to show that man is by nature religious.

Included among the 1925 exhibits were wooden carvings and masks from Papua New Guinea collected by Father Franz Kirschbaum, who continued to send objects to the Vatican. In its collection there are also at least two hundred

aboriginal artifacts sent from Australia by unknown missionaries. These include ten sculpted, decorated funeral poles from Melville Island (Fig. 21). There
are also thirteen painted stones from the Drysdale River zone of Western Australia kept in a glass case labelled 'totemism'. These depict animals such as the
kangaroo, lizard and dingoes (Figs. 22, 23, 24). On others are apparently spirit
figures as well as colour patterns. The documentation which accompanied the
stones suggested that one dates from 1917. There are eight wooden shields from
Darwin and the Benedictine mission of New Norcia in Western Australia.
Together with two coloured vegetable fibre crowns or headbands, they are
labelled 'ceremonial objects'. They are all believed to have been used in initiation
ceremonies. Their provenance is uncertain but all the artifacts are from the
Northern Territory or from Western Australia.

The aboriginal collection was rediscovered accidentally in 1985 as a result
of the Australian National Museum seeking material for its own collection. The
director, Don McMichael, drew attention to the issue by speaking on the subject
to the Institute for Conservation of Cultural Material Conference in Perth in
1985. He sought the return of these materials for the aboriginal people on the
grounds that they were of secret or sacred importance to a particular tribal group,
or were skeletal remains. Three federal government departments became involved in negotiations with the Vatican Museum: Aboriginal Affairs, Foreign
Affairs, and Arts, Heritage and Environment. There are, however, more extensive collections of aboriginal materials in other museums, such as the Peter the
Great Museum of Anthropology and Ethnology in Leningrad.

The two great European museums of the nineteenth century, the Louvre
and the British Museum, also face a re-examination of the past in the light of the
many historic and social changes that have occurred since their establishment.
The British Museum, housed in the Duke of Montague's residence in London,
was set up under the British Museum Act in 1753, which has since been re-
pealed and amended a number of times up to the present 1963 Act. In its
235-year history it has become established as one of the finest and greatest museums of the world, attracting a very considerable number of international visitors. It is probably one of the two or three most important museums in the world,
and is described in one of the British Museum's own publications as the first
public, historical and secular museum in the world.

The museum's official position on claims for the return of cultural property
has been understandably defensive. The line taken has always been that legislation has prohibited it from permanently disposing of any object, other than
duplicates, and that its aim is to preserve exhibits 'for the benefit of international
scholarship and the enjoyment of the general public'.[4]

Fig. 21. These Australian aboriginal tomb poles from Melville Island, measuring around two metres, were used in funeral rites. Part of the Australian collection brought to the Vatican in 1925.

Figs. 22–24. Australian aboriginal totemistic emblems on stone, about eight inches in diameter, depicting dingo, emu and snake; all on display in the Vatican Ethnological Museum.

There are twenty-five Trustees of the museum responsible for its general management and control: one appointed by the Queen, fifteen by the Prime Minister, four by the Secretary of State, and five by the Trustees of the museum.[5] Their period of appointment varies but cannot generally exceed ten years, or five years if reappointed within twelve months.[6]

Under Section 3(4) of the 1963 Act, objects vested in the Trustees as part of the collections of the museum cannot be disposed of by them, other than as is permitted by Sections 5 or 9 of this same Act. Section 9 only deals with 'internal' transfers between British institutions. Therefore we must look at Section 5. This provides:

> 5. Disposal of objects
> (1) The Trustees of the British Museum may sell, exchange, give away or otherwise dispose of any object vested in them and comprised in their collections if —
>   (a) the object is a duplicate of another such object, or
>   (b) the object appears to the Trustees to have been made not earlier than the year 1850, and substantially consists of printed matter of which a copy made by photography or a process akin to photography is held by the Trustees, or
>   (c) in the opinion of the Trustees the object is unfit to be retained in the collections of the Museum and can be disposed of without detriment to the interests of students:
>   Provided that where an object has become vested in the Trustees by virtue of a gift or bequest the powers conferred by this subsection shall not be exercisable as respects that object in a manner inconsistent with any condition attached to the gift or bequest.
>
> (2) The Trustees may destroy or otherwise dispose of any object vested in them and comprised in their collections if satisfied that it has become useless for the purposes of the Museum by reason of damage, physical deterioration, or infestation by destructive organisms.
>
> (3) Money accruing to the Trustees by virtue of an exercise of the powers conferred by this section shall be laid out by them in the purchase of objects to be added to the collections of the Museum.

This appears to be a very limited right of disposal and is generally regarded as limited to duplicates of coins and such like.

Subsection (1)(c) of Section 5 is interesting, however, since it permits the Trustees to sell, exchange, give away or otherwise dispose of an object if, in their opinion, 'the object is unfit to be retained ... and can be disposed of without detriment to the interests of the students'. What does 'unfit' mean in this context? Clearly the 'opinion of the Trustees' is a most subjective judgement but it is unclear what criterion is to be applied. Would it be stretching a point to argue that this could mean no longer suitable, or appropriate, for one reason or another, to be kept by the British Museum? Clearly, even if this interpretation could be placed on this clause, it would still remain a matter for the discretion of the Trustees. It is a point which has not been tested. But certainly 'unfit to be retained' does not mean only the possibility of physical unfitness since a separate provision is made for that in Section 5(2). This interpretation appears to be borne out further by a comparison with the provision in the National Heritage Act 1983, which deals with the rights of acquisition and disposal by the Victoria and Albert Museum. That is Section 6: Acquisition and disposal of objects. In particular subsection 3 states:

> The Board may not dispose of an object the property in which is vested in them and which is comprised in their collection unless –
> (a) the disposal is by way of sale, exchange or gift of an object which is a duplicate of another object the property in which is so vested and which is so comprised, or
> (b) the disposal is by way of sale, exchange or gift of an object which in the Board's opinion is unsuitable for retention in their collections and can be disposed of without detriment to the interests of students or other members of the public, or
> (c) the disposal is by way of sale or gift made to, or exchange made with, any institution mentioned in subsection (4), or
> (d) the disposal (by whatever means, including destruction) is of an object which the Board are satisfied has become useless for the purposes of their collections by reason of damage, physical deterioration, or infestation by destructive organisms.

This more recent statute actually uses the words 'unsuitable for retention in their collections' – in subsection 3(b), and also has a separate clause like that of the British Museum Act which deals with physical unfitness. The general powers under Section 6 of the National Heritage Act allow for disposal by sale, exchange or gift. It is possible to submit that Section 5(1)(c) of the British Museum Act was meant to have a similar meaning to that of Section 6(3)(b) of the National Heritage Act – except that the wording of the latter is clearer. One may ask what difference there is between the words 'unfit to be retained' in the British Museum Act and 'unsuitable for retention' in the National Heritage Act. It appears, however, to be always presumed that the British Museum Act requires amending before Trustees can act in returning objects on the grounds that their mandate under the Act is not wide enough. There have, however, been minor acts of return, although under which Section of the Act is unsure. Certainly under Section 4 of the Act, the Trustees can *lend* any objects, whether in the UK *or* abroad. Thus Section 4 provides:

> 4. Lending of objects.
> The Trustees of the British Museum may lend for public exhibition (whether in the United Kingdom or elsewhere) any object comprised in the collections of the Museum:
>> Provided that in deciding whether or not to lend any such object, and in determining the time for which, and the conditions subject to which, any such object is to be lent, the Trustees shall have regard to the interests of students and other persons visiting the Museum, to the physi-cal condition and degree of rarity of the object in question, and to any risks to which it is likely to be exposed.

Return of original objects on the basis of 'permanent loan' with retention of replicas for scholarly purposes would therefore not be an impossibility under the existing Act, if the will of the Trustees was so disposed. The powers under Section 5 generally are to 'sell, exchange, give away or otherwise dispose of . . .'. However, on the assumption that there is no existing discretionary power and that the British Museum Act requires amending, a bill has already been sub-mitted once for that purpose and was defeated on its second reading in the House of Lords in October 1983. The debate on that bill clearly reflected the divide of opinion on the general issue of returning cultural property, and revealed the entrenched position of existing Trustees against return. It also indicated the predominantly negative British response towards any notion of 'international obligation' regarding this matter. A large number of the Lords who took a strong line on this matter were themselves either Trustees or former Trustees of the British Museum.

In moving the second reading of the Act, Lord Jenkins of Putney (Labour: former Minister for the Arts) argued as follows:

> This Bill seeks to amend the British Museum Act 1963 to extend the powers of the Trustees of the British Museum so that international resol-utions and obligations may be complied with. In pursuance of that ob-ject it amends Section 5 of the Act . . . to extend the powers of the Trus-tees in this fashion. It adds an additional power to dispose of an object; that is to say, let it go from the collection, if . . . 'in the opinion of the Trustees it is desirable that, in fulfilment of international obligations, an object shall be returned to its country of origin'.

Section 5 of the Act lays down the existing powers of the Trustees in relation to disposal of objects. They may dispose of a duplicate. Now with modern methods of reproduction an object can be produced which only an expert can distinguish from the original. Therefore, one might say that they could reproduce the Elgin Marbles, and then send either the original or the reproduction to Greece, or perhaps some of each and no one would know – but I would wager that there would be an unholy row, so that is really no solution.

It works, however, in the case of the famous head of Queen Nefertiti, which is exchanged regularly between Berlin and Cairo,[7] and substituted when absent by a reproduction. Even to carry out such an exchange convincingly the Trustees would need to have the power to do it, whether or not they exercised it. Whether they exercised it fully, partially, or not at all they would need to have that power, and it is precisely that power which at the moment they do not possess. This bill is intended to give them that power.

At present the Trustees can only dispose of old printed matter of which they hold a copy. They also dispose of coins, although there may be some slight doubt as to whether they are in breach of the law in doing so. But they may dispose of nothing else other than objects unfit to be retained in their collection. They are hardly Trustees at all in this respect, but mere appointees of the Government. This bill frees the Trustees . . .

It is more important to emphasize that we are not here concerned with things which have been stolen, although we are able to say that we alone of all countries have never plundered another country in the course of our history. In the natural course of events of course we have, but many of the objects we now possess have been legitimately acquired. Sometimes they have been partly legitimately acquired. Therefore, we are not concerned only with plunder, and certainly we are not concerned with plunder if we are thinking at the moment of the Elgin Marbles. But Britain, not having been conquered and occupied since 1066, has never been the subject of compulsory restitution. Therefore, we probably have more objects from other parts of the world than any other country.

Recent developments include, as I have said, an agreement for the celebrated masterpiece, the head of Queen Nefertiti, to be shown in turn in Berlin and Cairo, and for reproductions to replace it while it is away.[8] The efforts of Nigeria to secure the return of the famous Benin works from Britain and elsewhere have been less successful. Similarly, while some important pieces have been returned to Sri Lanka, much of the cultural heritage of that country remains in London and in other Western capitals. Australia, on the other hand, has returned many works to Papua New Guinea and other Pacific islands; Belgium has concluded a restitution agreement with Zaire, which includes generous aid; Holland has made similar arrangements with Indonesia, and France with India and Thailand. In the United States individual agreements have been made by United States museums with Latin American countries for the restitution and exchange of objects.

In all this Britain has given the impression of dragging her feet, to say the least, and the Greek Government's request for the return of the Elgin Marbles should be seen against this background. One of our problems is that the fact that the British Museum can return nothing has set the general pattern for us. Other museums, which are not under a similar prohibition, are disposed to take their pattern and their behaviour in this matter from our premier museum – I hardly dare call it that, but I will risk it.

On 2 August this year *The Times* reported:
'The International Council of Museums yesterday passed a resolution supporting the claim by the Greek Government for the return of the Elgin Marbles, which are in the British Museum.

'At its conference at the Barbican Centre in London, the council called for the return of cultural property to its countries of origin.

'Although no specific names or examples were mentioned in the general resolution, Dr Yannis Tzedakis, director of the Department of Antiquities at the Ministry of Culture in Athens, described the decision as a "moral victory for us".'

The resolution was one of the few that were put to the conference, which was attended by nearly 1,000 museum representatives from all over the world. It was the only one that generated any considerable discussion. When the vote was taken it was carried *nemine contradicente*, but the British representatives are among a handful who abstained. There were no votes against. In spite of that this is not a bill to return the Elgin Marbles to Greece. It is, perhaps, an enabling bill. The standing of the Anglo-Saxon countries is not as high as it might be in the rest of the world. Here is an opportunity for us to abandon the role of international Scrooge.

Lord Nugent of Guildford opposed the motion that the bill be now read a second time.

He said:

The bill is of such simplicity. It is a bill simply to give power to the British Museum Trustees to return such objects as they think desirable to the countries of origin. It might be convenient to your Lordships if we were to deal with the main issue today.

One looks at a measure such as this to see just what it would mean and whether it would be possible to do what the noble Lord's bill asks for, to enable the Elgin Marbles, particularly, to be returned ...

First I should like to deal with the legal ownership. The noble Lord wisely did not touch on that, but for the interest of the general public it should be set squarely on the record that Lord Elgin acquired the Marbles in the first place entirely legally. At that time, the Greek nation was part of the Ottoman Empire. Therefore, the Greeks were under the rule of the Turkish government and the Turkish authorities ruled everything in Athens. It was from them that Lord Elgin obtained the necessary licence to acquire the marbles. Lord Elgin shipped them to England. He sold them to the British government, who gave them to the British Museum and, as a matter of historical interest, the House of Commons set up a Select Committee in 1816 to investigate the acquisition of the marbles and found that they had indeed been legitimately acquired.

The first point that must be made is that Lord Elgin's motive was, without any doubt, the preservation of the Elgin Marbles. In 1800, the Parthenon was a ruin. It had been mainly wrecked in the engagement by the Venetian navy against the Ottoman Empire in 1678, when a shell hit the Parthenon, which was being used as a gunpowder magazine, and the whole thing was blown up. Nothing had been done to it since.

There are two further points that I should make. The British Museum's conservation laboratory is foremost in the world in its techniques of protecting these ancient treasures against adverse environments and has played a major part in conserving the condition of the Elgin Marbles so significantly better than the marbles which remain on the Acropolis. The second point that I must make ... is the case for the existence of the great international museums. There are very few such museums and galleries, as I say, and they perform a service to mankind of enlightenment and enjoyment of inestimable value. In this context the British Museum is outstanding. Its exhibits are superbly shown, the Elgin Marbles in particular in the Duveen Gallery. They can be seen freely throughout the year and they are available at all times. It is a fact that the British Museum's collection spans not only the geography of the world but literally the millennia of human civilisation, so that the scope for research work on art and matters of learning and for education ... is of unique value.

All this would be set at risk if the British Museum were given the power to dispose of its major treasures like the Elgin Marbles ... If they had such a power, if the Elgin Marbles went back to Athens, that would be a precedent. Who would follow? ... Their long record of custody and conservation since the beginning of the century has provided education and enjoyment to millions of people of all nationalities. This must weigh heavily in the balance in favour of their continuing trusteeship. I would say that the balance of the moral argument is against disposal and therefore I invite noble Lords to support my amendment and reject the bill.

Lord Trend, chairman of the Trustees of the British Museum, spoke as follows:

[The Trustees] of course oppose [the bill] and they oppose it because they regard it as potentially damaging, perhaps irreparably damaging, to their main function of maintaining and enhancing a great universal museum ... It aims to present an integrated picture of the stages in the development of various civilisations of the world and their indebtedness one to another, and it has the kind of physical integrity which comes from that kind of concept of human history.

The Trustees, too, have their integrity – an integrity of purpose which is in a sense the obverse of the physical integrity of the museum. They are two sides of the one coin. But of course the integrity of purpose of the Trustees is dependent, and critically dependent, on the legal provision prohibiting permanent disposal of objects which for more than two centuries has preserved them from the random caprice of aesthetic taste of fashion, moralistic judgments and – even more important – the fluctuations of political pressure, unpredictable, random and varying from day to day. Without that protection the Trustees could not maintain the integrity of the museum; and if the integrity of the British Museum goes what will happen to other great collections in this country?

Are we really to put all those treasures at risk? If so, why? The bill, I see, speaks of 'international obligations'. It is not for me to comment on that point but I would only say that I am not conscious of any obligation accepted by Her Majesty's Government which would be binding on the Trustees in this sense. On the contrary, so far as I know, the government have always said that it is the maintenance of the great international collections of the world which does most to promote cultural understanding, and I hope they will continue to say so.

No, my Lords, I think it is something rather different which under-lies this bill. I think it is a feeling – not easy to define but one which we all recognise – that in some mysterious way the great cultural objects of the world belong, necessarily and properly, where they began. I think that the imagination – at least my imagination – boggles if I contem-plate the probable practical results if that kind of historicism were press-ed to its logical conclusion.

But the argument seems to me to ignore something else even more fundamental. It ignores the whole ethos of the British Museum and the spirit in which its Trustees administer it. There is a sense in which the British Museum is a microcosm of the whole world, and its great collec-tions certainly recognise no arbitrary boundaries of time and space in their homage to the great achievements of the human spirit. It is for that reason that the Trustees would regard it as nothing less than a betrayal of their trust to create a precedent for the piecemeal dismemberment of their collection, and it is for that reason that I must hope very much that your Lordships will reject the bill.

Viscount Eccles said:

As a former chairman of the Trustees of the British Museum ... I had some part in Section 5 of the 1963 Act, and the restrictions on the dis-posal of the objects were very strictly drawn under the leadership of the late Lord Crawford and Balcarres. I think it is true to say that at that time and ever since the Trustees have accepted those restrictions as some-thing which, as the noble Lord, Lord Trend, himself said, define the character of their trust.

Should claims for the return of objects of art put forward by an in-ternational body, or for that matter by anybody else, be encouraged? Should there be some rule or convention which might lead to the suc-cess of such claims? No one would make such claims for music or litera-ture. Mozart or Homer can be printed, translated and performed every-where and anywhere ... but it is said that the visual arts are different because they are physical objects. They can be in only one place at one time ... It is very easy to forget that the place where a great work of art is kept is less important than its careful preservation, its accessibility to a wide public and its immortal power to elevate the human spirit.

The popular campaigns which lie behind the bill now before us are quite new. In classical times, it was taken for granted that the great works of Greece should be exported to Rome and the rest of the empire. In the Middle Ages, bishops and princes vied with each other to secure the best works of art from all Europe. The Church at that time recog- nised art as the most powerful communicator of her message, and art was also seen, and it still is, to be an unrivalled source of prestige. The power to communicate and to glorify accounts for the continuing uni- versal appeal of great works of art.

No doubt from time to time we can do a little to alter for the better the course of human affairs; but neither priests nor princes nor parlia- ments can ever diminish the universal appeal of art. Like others, I salute the ancient Greeks for their wonderful history, but the Greeks of the twentieth century should know that we, too, have a history. Part of our history is expressed in our admiration for their art. We should not open the door to political campaigns for the return of works fairly acquired and now splendidly cared for. I hope your Lordships will support the amendment . . .

Lord Adrian, also opposing the bill, said:

I have to declare at the outset that I am a Trustee of the British Museum. At this stage I merely wish to put on record my surprise that so very major a change in the nation's policy towards the great treasures of which it finds itself guardian should have been put in train with appar- ently so little consultation . . . from being charged with the care of the nation's treasures we are being asked to become brokers in the interna- tional goodwill trade.

Whether we like it or not, if such is the nation's decision we shall, of course, have to implement it, but it seems to me that the Trustees should be given more guidance as to how they should carry out this task of sending back so many of the finest things in the museum. Are we, for instance, to be encouraged to give away an object which came to the museum as a specific bequest from a generous benefactor? Are we to give away an object which has been allotted to the museum in lieu of capital taxes? May we give away, if we think fit, an object whose pur- chase has been greatly assisted by the National Heritage Fund? Has the Treasury anything to say about the proposal to give away objects pur- chased with taxpayers' money, let alone with a special parliamentary grant? What shall we do if two nations claim the same object? One might, for instance, suggest sculpture imported from Italy but made in a Greek colony there. Are Hellenistic sculptures from Asia Minor to go to Greece or to Turkey?

Lord Donaldson of Kingsbridge said:

My own view is that there must be in time certain occasions when the
nation – not the museum – will say, 'This demand from someone
whose possession we have had for a long time is something we could
reasonably meet.' But I would wish for there to be national legislation
on each occasion ... My view is that the law should remain as it is and
that, if the nation ever decides that restitution of this kind should be
made, such restitution should be the result of special legislation.

The Minister of State, Privy Council Office, and Minister for the Arts (the
Earl of Gowrie) also opposed the amendment to the Act. He said:

The government are aware of no general wish to change these existing
powers and they do not propose to seek authority from Parliament to do
so. Moreover, in the government's view, the Trustees already have international obligations which they have fulfilled since the British Museum's inception as one of the world's great museums and these international obligations do reside in their existing powers. These are the true
and real responsibilities of the museum to make its outstanding collection, one of the very greatest in the world, freely available for public
viewing, research and scholarship. I could not countenance a new
obligation which would potentially and substantially diminish that collection and thus the museum's ability to fulfil these same responsibilities.

Lord Jenkins of Putney further replied:

My Lords, the distinction of the speakers in this debate has only been
exceeded by their unanimity. However, it is to be reflected that unanimity is not the same thing as rectitude ... The integrity of the museum
is important and I can understand that to him it is absolutely paramount. But the integrity of this country in the world is more important
and it is that integrity which is in charge of your Lordships and it is that
integrity which is being challenged in the world today ... This is simply a bill which enables the trustees to do what they want to do. But the
Trustees say, 'No, we want the law of the land to prevent us from doing
what most trustees in any other part of the world are entirely free to do.'

Lord Nugent of Guildford further stated:

When the noble Lord [Jenkins] says that the Trustees ought to have
this additional power so that they could use their judgment over what

they would part with and what they would keep, he, as an expert politician, knows as well as I do myself that these decisions really are political … On the *tapis* now is a formal request from the Greek Government. So what can the Trustees do except take a decision, if they have to, in a political context? It is surely wiser, in the interests of the British Museum, with its great responsibility, not just to us in this country, but with its worldwide responsibility to humanity, to defend it against pressures that really would become irresistible at times.

The vote was taken. Their Lordships divided: Contents, 49; Not-Contents, 11. The further amendment to the amending bill was resolved in the affirmative. But it was effectively defeated, by the device of postponement of the second reading. The opportunity for dealing with this problem in a general way by merely extending the powers of the Trustees of the British Museum (without imposing any obligations to exercise those powers) was lost. The question of the specific 1816 Act of Parliament vesting the Elgin Marbles in the Trustees was not raised. The arguments for special arrangements, such as exchange and the use of reproductions, as well as the arguments for outright return based on ICOM recommendations, were refuted by the majority of the Lords, who stressed the conservatory function of the British Museum and its international status. The greatest underlying fear was that the return of the Elgin Marbles would create an unacceptable precedent. Without the British Museum Act as a buffer to protect the Trustees from having to make any such decision, the very integrity of the British Museum might be threatened.

Academic opinion has also divided.[9] Sir David Wilson, as director of the British Museum, has expressed his views on the return of objects as follows:

- Legally, the museum is not allowed to alienate objects by Act of Parliament;
- the British Museum is an important part of the cultural heritage of the whole world; as it has existed for 225 years it has become a universal museum and has safeguarded material which would otherwise have been destroyed or dispersed;
- the Museum does not collect illegally exported material – and the Museum has always collected within the law;
- the Museum will continue collecting since a non-collecting museum is a dead one, although the illegal traffic in antiquities is to be deplored;
- the Museum would lend material subject to its being fit to travel, but would never give away to other countries material from its collections.
- [In particular] The marbles should not go back. If one destroyed the

British Museum then one would be destroying a centre of world culture. There would be a flood of requests for returns and then there would be no such universal institution in the world.[10]

The late Professor Glyn Daniel, Emeritus Disney Professor of Archaeology at Cambridge and editor of the review of archaeology *Antiquity*, has said:

- Dr Wilson's statement about the collecting activities of the British Museum is something of a whitewash in the light of its early nineteenth-century activities. In particular the looting by Belzoni and Rassam of Egypt and Mesopotamia enriched the British Museum's collections;
- the focus of archaeology is already shifting to the Third World, and new national museums will be developed throughout the Third World;
- there is no good reason why *some* of the objects in Western national museums should not be returned to their place of origin, such as the Benin bronzes to Africa, or the Rosetta Stone to Cairo.

(*Antiquity*, LVI, p. 4)

Professor Thurstan Shaw, Emeritus Professor of Archaeology, University of Ibadan, Nigeria, has extensive knowledge of matters that relate to West Africa and has stated that five points ought to be taken into account:

- Each case has to be considered on its merits, especially the circumstances of removal from its country of origin;
- cultural material should not be removed from good security to bad;
- cultural material should be freely available for study by international scholars. That means accessibility to all bona fide scholars, but that does not necessarily mean location in major Western capitals;
- despite these earlier considerations, in many cases it would be morally right for the holding country to return cultural material to the country of origin. Where objects were obtained by right of conquest at a time when the country of origin was weak (e.g. Benin bronzes, Ashanti gold, Burmese treasure, much from India in the Army Museum), the ex-imperial country in retaining these items is denying part of the independence 'granted' to such countries; and this is a neo-colonialist policy;
- the issue of the deprivation of rightful heritage and national pride is not one that can be excluded from this matter.

(*Antiquity*, LVI, pp. 3–4)

The director of the City Museums of Bristol, Nicholas Thomas, has said:

- It would be disastrous at the present time if the West were to consider returning such material on mainly political grounds;
- without the guarantee of stability, such return of objects could very likely result in their destruction or use for political purposes;
- the principal task of a museum is to protect and preserve its collections and at present museum professionals cannot feel assurance in their heart that by returning objects to Third World countries they are doing the best thing for the object.

(*Antiquity*, LVI, p. 3)

The director of the Science Museum, Dr Neil Cossons has said:

> If the question of restitution becomes a political one then the particular issue of the Sri Lankan treasures was a dangerous one, since it represented the tip of an iceberg.[11]

The divide of opinion appears to be that academics favour return whereas museum people generally do not. Other scholars have voiced their opinion on this matter particularly in the case of the Elgin Marbles. Peter Levi, Professor of Poetry at Oxford, has spoken in favour of the restoration of the Parthenon not only for Greece but for the international community, because with pieces scattered in far-flung locations, the rhythm and unity of one of the noblest works of art had been destroyed. This view has been supported by Professor George Forrest, Professor of Ancient History at Oxford, who has emphasized that on this basis the Elgin Marbles are now due to be returned to Greece. Other scholars such as John Gould, Professor of Greek at Bristol, have questioned the moral aspect of retaining such treasures as the marbles, and have challenged the argument of internationalism as a proper basis for withholding them, by stressing the inherent dangers of a nationally founded body claiming to be international.

Political opinion in the United Kingdom, as the Elgin Marbles debate shows, is such that the Labour and the Social Democratic parties would be more inclined to participate in some form of return of cultural property. Most editorial opinion, however, has taken a very conservative approach to this matter.

The case of the New Zealand Taranaki panels,[12] which went to the House of Lords in 1983, has shown that an English court is unlikely ever to enforce a foreign state's protective legislation providing for forfeiture in the event of the illicit export of its art treasures, since such law would be a public law and amounts to an extraterritorial exercise of the foreign state's authority. This in effect means that a foreign state enacting such protective laws will lose its treasures in such a case, unless it actually intercepts them, since it cannot expect to have them returned by an English court.

From an international point of view Britain alone amongst the major hold-ing nations remained a non-party to any major international convention dealing with the protection or return of cultural property for many years, except for the European Convention on the Protection of Archaeological Heritage (1969),[13] which came into force for the United Kingdom after March 1973. Its aim is to protect archaeological excavations, and it has no retrospective effect. Other major art-holding states with major museums, such as France and Germany, have also become parties to this convention, the former in 1972 and the latter in 1975. The UNESCO Convention concerning the Protection of the World Cultural and National Heritage was ratified by the United Kingdom in 1984 and acceded to by France in 1975.

The principal convention dealing with the return of cultural property is the 1970 UNESCO Convention on the Means of Prohibiting and Preventing the Illicit Import, Export and Transfer of Ownership of Cultural Property.[14] Bri-tain and France have failed to ratify this convention to date, and this has sometimes been attributed to the fact that the convention is unworkable, and does not provide an adequate definition of 'work of art'. The convention entered into force in respect of the United States of America in December 1983,[15] and in respect of West Germany in April 1974. As at August 1987, sixty states had become party to the convention, which aims to prevent the illicit transfer of cultural property, and to facilitate the recovery and return of such cultural property. By remaining non-parties, the United Kingdom and France abstain from any international commitment in this area. The United Kingdom Mu-seums Association supports the UNESCO Convention in principle and its policy is to press the government to ratify it.[16]

The French museum position is similar to that of the United Kingdom in its general opposition to cultural return. The Greek Minister of Culture was reported to have made an informal request for the return of the Vénus de Milo from her French counterpart, the then Minister of Culture, Jack Lang. The head of the Department of Greek Antiquities responded by saying that such a hypothesis had never even been envisaged. It was stressed that the statue was legally bought by the French ambassador in Constantinople in 1821. Accord-ing to current French law nothing could be returned even if there was a wish to do so; these treasures belonged to the French nation. Another British Museum view which is echoed by the French has been that of the past preservation of these antiquities by the holding museums. M. Amiat, the Director of Oriental Anti-quities in the Louvre, asked, for instance, 'How would the Hammurabi code have been decoded, and how many other masterpieces would have disappeared if they had not been taken away and kept in better conditions?'[17]

The royal castle of the Louvre was founded by King Philippe Auguste at the end of the thirteenth century. It was the residence of the kings of France, and the seat of the Academies until the Revolution. In 1793, the Louvre was opened to the French public. After the invasion of Belgium in 1794, Napoleon began stocking the Louvre with the artistic spoils of the countries overrun by his armies. The climax came in 1798 with the arrival in Paris of treasures taken from Italy, including the Apollo Belvedere, the Dying Gladiator, the Laocoon, the Medici Venus, nine paintings by Raphael and two famous Correggios. Later from Venice came the winged lion and the bronze horses of San Marco, and paintings by Titian and Tintoretto. The French artists of the day celebrated the occasion by putting their names to a petition in 1796 to the Directoire: 'The French Republic by its strength and superiority of its enlightenment and its artists is the only country in the world that can give a safe home to these master-pieces. All other nations must come and borrow our art . . .'

Europe got its first taste, too, of Egyptian archaeology through the activities of Napoleon. He ensured that his expeditions were accompanied by draftsmen and scientists to investigate Egyptian geography and antiquities. When he was forced to evacuate Egypt in 1801, the French collection of Egyptian antiquities fell into English hands and went to the British Museum instead of the Louvre. The museum therefore started with only a small number of mainly Roman objects. After the Congress of Vienna in 1815, foreign commissioners arrived in Paris to reclaim art works from the Louvre, and story has it that Denon, the director-general, physically resisted their removal, crying in the end 'Let them take them! But they lack the eyes to see, and France will always show her superiority in the arts, for her masterpieces were always better than those of others!'[18]

Succeeding French archaeological expeditions replenished the Louvre, giving it formidable Egyptian and Assyrian collections in particular. In 1821 the Vicomte de Marcellus, secretary to the French diplomatic mission in Athens, acting on the instructions of his superior the Marquis de Rivière, who was ambassador at Constantinople, bought the famous Vénus de Milo. It was dug up on Melos but the circumstances of its actual discovery are poorly docu-mented. There is some discrepancy between the descriptions of the state of the statue when it was found. For instance it has been said that the Louvre also received fragments of a right and left arm and a left hand holding an apple, three Hermes figures and a pedestal with a Greek inscription, all of which disap-peared and which could not be found. Therefore it was suggested that 'the worst mutilation of the Vénus actually took place within the walls of this sanctuary of the arts!'[19]

By 1848 the Louvre had been declared to be national property. It is the 1913 law of December 31 on historic monuments[20] which generally governs the disposal of art treasures by defining 'protected property', and setting out the 'rights and obligations of the owner, of the person in possession or control and of the competent authorities'.

Thus under Article 14:

> Any object whether movable or attached to immovable property the preservation of which is of national historic, artistic, scientific or technical interest may be scheduled by ministerial order.

and under Article 15:

> Movables shall be scheduled by order of the minister responsible for cultural affairs when the object belongs to the state, a department, a commune or a public institution. The scheduling order shall be notified to the persons concerned.

It is further provided under Article 18:

> Scheduled movable objects shall not be subject to acquisition by prescription.
>
> Scheduled objects belonging to the state shall not be subject to transfer of ownership.
>
> Scheduled objects belonging to a department, a commune, a public institution or public utility service may only be disposed of with the authorization of the Minister responsible for Cultural Affairs, as laid down in the laws and regulations. Ownership thereof may only be transferred to the state, a public body or a public utility service.

and under Article 19:

> The effects of scheduling shall continue in force irrespective of the person in possession or control of the object.
>
> Any private person who disposes of a scheduled object shall notify the purchaser that the object in question is scheduled.
>
> Every such transfer shall be notified to the Minister of Cultural Affairs by the transferor within fifteen days of the date of the completion thereof.

Article 20 states:

> Any acquisition effected in contravention of Article 18 (2 and 3) shall
> be null and void. Annulling actions or actions for recovery may be
> brought at any time either by the Minister of Cultural Affairs or by the
> original owner. They shall be brought without prejudice to any claims
> for damages which may be made either against the contracting parties
> that are severally liable or against the public officer responsible for the
> transfer.
>
> When the illicit transfer of ownership has been effected by a public
> body or a public utility service, this action for damages shall be brought
> by the Minister of Cultural Affairs in the name of and on behalf of the
> State. Any bona fide purchaser or subsequent purchaser, from whom
> the object is recovered, shall be entitled to the refund of his purchase
> money; if the recovery is brought by the Minister of Cultural Affairs the
> latter shall have a remedy against the original vendor in respect of the
> full amount of the compensation which he shall have been required to
> pay to the purchaser or subsequent purchaser.

The provisions of this article apply also to lost or stolen objects. Thus the
Louvre like its British counterpart is not free to dispose of its treasures, and is
therefore not free to make cultural returns. Moreover, the French like the British
have legislated to control the export of national treasures, which are not confined
to French art.

Cultural properties in France enjoy legal protection beyond the scope of the
provisions protecting historical monuments and movable works of art. This is
known as 'la protection domaniale' and applies only to public cultural property
which is inalienable.

The law of 31 December 1913 provided:

> ARTICLE 21. It shall be unlawful to export scheduled objects from
> France.

and the export law of 23 June 1941 provided:

> ARTICLE 1. Objects of national importance for historical or artistic rea-
> sons may not be exported without the authorization of the Secretary of
> State for Education and Youth who shall give his ruling within one
> month of the date of the declaration made to the Customs Authorities
> by the exporter.
>
> These provisions shall apply to items of furniture made before 1830,

and to works of painters, engravers, draughtsmen, sculptors and decorators made before 1900 and to objects resulting from excavations carried
out in France or Algeria.

ARTICLE 2. The State shall have the right to retain either on its own
behalf or on behalf of a department, commune or public institution, at a
price determined by the exporter, any objects which it is proposed to export. This right may be exercised for a period of six months.

Other European nations have taken similar steps to safeguard their heritage.
For instance the German Democratic Republic provided, by a Decree of 2
April 1953 on the protection of the German heritage of works of art, scientific
documents and materials, that:

ARTICLE 4. 1. Where the exportation of works of art, scientific documents and materials or objects of exceptional historical value involves
the disposal of such objects, the German Democratic Republic shall
have a right of preemption, which must be exercised within three
months after the receipt of the application for an export licence by the
Ministry.
2. The decision relating to the exercise of the right of preemption
shall be made, in the cases referred to in Article 2, paragraphs 1 and 3
by the Ministry of Culture and, in the cases referred to in Article 2,
paragraph 2 by the ministry responsible for universities and institutions
of higher education.

In respect of its own art and antique collections, the United Kingdom also
clearly recognizes the significance of cultural heritage.[21] Steps have been taken to
prevent the unlawful export of treasures which are more than fifty years old.[22]
(The age of objects is generally an important criterion in all countries.) So far as
works of art are concerned, the law of England rests on a statute passed on the
outbreak of the Second World War. It is the Import, Export and Customs
Powers (Defence) Act 1939. It gave the Board of Trade power by order to
prohibit the import or export of goods of any specified description. The present
order in force is the Customs and Excise Export of Goods (Control) Order, SI
1987 No. 2070. It prohibits the export (unless permitted by licence) of (among
other things) 'Any goods manufactured or produced more than fifty years before
the date of exportation', except personal property, letters, and so forth.

If works of art more than fifty years old are exported from England without
permission they are not automatically forfeited. They are only 'liable to be forfeited', and the title does not pass to the Crown until they are seized. Works

which have been imported into the United Kingdom for more than fifty years are also subject to the licensing requirements for export.

An independent six-man Reviewing Committee on the Export of Works of Art, appointed by the Arts Minister, vets export licence applications. An expert adviser applies one of three criteria on deciding whether a treasure goes before the Committee:

- Is the object so closely connected with our history and national life that its departure would be a misfortune?
- Is it of outstanding aesthetic importance?
- Is it of outstanding significance for the study of some particular branch of art, learning or history?

It can advise the Arts Minister to withhold an export licence for a fixed period, usually three months, to allow a British institution to raise funds to match the price. If this transpires, no export licence is granted. An export licence can thus be refused, and has been on a number of occasions. In practice, though, the protection of cultural heritage by an export licensing system is deficient. The attempt in 1986 to prevent the export of the 3,000-item George Brown collection of South Pacific art at Newcastle University, valued at £600,000, failed. It was sold through Sotheby's to the National Museum of Ethnography in Osaka, Japan. The export controls were evaded because on Sotheby's advice the £16,000 minimum limit on value could be overcome by exporting each piece separately. However, in July 1986, it was reported that Mr Richard Luce, the Arts Minister, had successfully embargoed nineteen of the most valuable pieces in the collection. Although these pieces were saved from export the collection was broken up (contrary to the former wishes of George Brown). They were purchased by several institutions including the British Museum, which pur-chased four items – a mask from Tolai of East New Britain and three Malangan carvings from New Ireland, both islands being part of Papua New Guinea.

British concern has been greatest over the purchasing power of foreign museums, like the Getty Museum in California, and the loss to overseas buyers of such paintings as Lord Clark's Turner seascape. However, all art treasures within the United Kingdom from whatever source are clearly included under the umbrella of 'English cultural heritage'. Interestingly, the treasures covered by British legislation[23] are not limited to English art. Cultural heritage in this context has a wider application to a legacy of world art.

The sale in 1986 at Christie's (London) of the Italian Vincenzo Foggini's sculptures brought the cry 'Save our sculpture'.[24] This view of world art and archaeology as being a part of British cultural patrimony has reinforced the steadfast resistance to the concept of cultural return of historic materials as well as to contemporary foreign purchase.

Whilst European states have taken individual measures to protect their own cultural heritage, the collective European position can be seen to run counter to the idea of national cultural protection, and to positively impede the concept of cultural return within Europe. In 1983 the Council of Europe passed a resolution (see Chapter 2, pp. 79–81) stressing the unity of European cultural heritage and the notion of Europe as a regional cultural entity.

In the past the effect of the EEC has been to prevent countries especially rich in art treasures, such as Italy, from effectively controlling the export of their cultural property. This is because the Treaty of Rome (1957) setting up the EEC provided that member states would abolish customs duties on exports between each other (Article 16). For example, in 1962, when this provision came into effect, the EEC Commission submitted a dispute with Italy to the Court of Justice of the European Economic Community.[25] This concerned the Italian law of 1939 (June 1), which had sought to protect objects of historic and artistic value by imposing an export tax of between 8 and 30 per cent of the value. Italy sought to argue that this was a case which came under Article 36 of the Rome Treaty, which said that Articles 30 to 34 (dealing with the elimination of quotas between member states) 'shall not be an obstacle to prohibitions or restrictions in respect of importation or exportation or transit which are justified on grounds of . . . the protection of national treasures of artistic, historical or archaeological value . . .' The court, however, held that the Italian law was one of a fiscal nature and did not come under the terms of Article 36, which relates only to import, export or transit.

Indeed, there is evidence that with the development of the EEC, which has meant the relaxation of tariff barriers and hence the desire to simplify or abolish customs procedures along frontiers, the possibility of controlling the illicit movement of cultural property has been reduced. The Netherlands, for instance, explains its reluctance to become a party to the 1970 UNESCO Convention by the impracticality of the kind of customs controls which would be required.[26]

Therefore legislation within Europe to restrain, reduce or control the movement of art treasures could not be achieved in this way. However, even the Council of Europe in 1983 was prepared to make a special distinction over the issue of cultural return *vis-à-vis* the Third World. There are great museums in Europe with sizeable archaeological and colonial collections, such as those in Germany and the Netherlands (the latter of which has made returns). However, certain objects within British museums have gained the greatest notoriety because of Britain's primacy as an exploring, collecting and colonial power and attention has increased as certain states have called for their return.

CHAPTER FOUR

SOME BRITISH CASES

Egypt: The Sphinx's beard

Early in 1982 the British Foreign Office refused a formal request by the Egyptian government for the return to Cairo from the British Museum of part of the beard of the 4,000-year-old Sphinx. Carved in 2600 BC, the Sphinx stands as a guardian to the pyramids of Gizeh, and is being eroded by wind and sand. The purpose of the request was the restoration of the whole monument, since for thousands of years the beard acted as a functional buttress for the head of the statue (which weighs nine hundred tons). The date of the plaited beard is uncertain. It is believed that the beard was probably added during the reign of the pharaoh Tuthmosis IV.

The Sphinx remains an enigmatic structure to this day:

> South of the Great Pyramid complex and near the Valley Building of the Second Pyramid lies the Giant Sphinx. A knoll of rock, which had been left by the builders of the Great Pyramid when quarrying stone for its inner core, was fashioned in the time of Chephren into a huge recumbent lion with a human head. It was probably overlaid with a coating of plaster and painted. The length of this colossus is about 240 feet, its height 66 feet and the maximum width of the face 13 feet 8 inches. On the head is the royal head-dress; other emblems of royalty are the cobra on the forehead, and the beard, now largely missing, on the chin. Although the face has been severely mutilated, it still gives the impression of being a portrait of King Chephren and not merely a formalized representation. A figure, possibly of the king, was carved in front of the chest, but scarcely any trace of it now remains. Between the outstretched paws stands a large slab of red granite bearing an inscription which purports to record a dream of Thutmosis IV of the XVIIIth Dynasty before he ascended the throne. According to this inscription the prince, when hunting, decided to rest at midday in the shadow of the Sphinx. During his sleep the Sphinx, which was regarded at that time as an embodiment of the Sun-god Harmachis, promised him the Double Crown of Egypt if he would clear away the sand which had nearly engulfed its body. Unfortunately, the latter part of the inscription is too badly weathered to be legible, but it may be surmised that it re-

lated how the god's wish was fulfilled and how the prince was finally rewarded with the Crown of the Two Lands. In addition to clearing away the sand, Thutmosis IV may have repaired damaged portions of the body by the insertion of small blocks of limestone – an operation which was repeated in Ptolemaic or Roman times, when the sand was once more removed and an altar was erected in front of the figure. The first excavation of the Sphinx in modern times was conducted by Captain Caviglia in 1818 at a cost of £450. Sixty-eight years later it was again freed of sand by Gaston Maspero and lastly, in 1925, the *Service des Antiquités* undertook once more its clearance and restoration.[1]

The Egyptian Ministry of Culture was not exactly clear when or how the two- to three-foot-high fragment of the beard of the Sphinx had been moved to Britain. According to a Ministry research document fragments of the beard were first discovered between the giant paws of the sixty-five-foot-high statue in the early nineteenth century, and rediscovered more than a hundred years later. It may have been given to the British Museum around 1818.

The British government made it clear in the House of Commons that such a request would be turned down, on the grounds that by law the British Museum can dispose of objects only in specific instances, including where they were clearly pilfered or stolen, and it was denied that this could be applied to the beard of the Sphinx.

The Egyptian Minister of Culture, Mr Abdul Hamid Radwan, in lieu of pressing for the return of the beard, accepted the guarantee of future assistance from Egyptologists from the British Museum in protecting the Sphinx from further deterioration. It was suggested that the Minister had not actually made a formal application for the return of the beard but had held talks with the museum officials about its possible eventual restoration to Egypt, perhaps 'on permanent loan'. It was also suggested that the object in question was actually devoid of any aesthetic interest and had been kept out of the way in a storeroom of the British Museum for many years. It constituted only a very small percentage of the total beard.

Finally, in November 1983, Egypt succeeded in securing an agreement for the return of the beard from the British Museum, apparently using control of British archaeological missions in Egypt as a persuasive lever.

A small fragment of the beard of the Great Sphinx of Gizeh was to be lent to the museum to form part of the restoration of the beard to the Sphinx's chin. In exchange, Egypt offered part of a statue of the jackal-headed god, Anubis, from Thebes, of which the British Museum already has the head.

As negotiations about the beard were prolonged for over eighteen months, it was rumoured among foreign Egyptologists in Cairo that British archaeological missions to Egypt, the most important of which are at Memphis, Saqqara and Tell el-Amarna, might not be welcome to stay if the British Museum remained unyielding.

Reports from London that the fragment would stay in the Cairo Museum, which houses the country's pharaonic collection, were dismissed by the Cairo Museum director, who said that the piece would be sent straight to Gizeh for restoration. There was no other reason to press for its return, he said, since it was otherwise undistinguished.

The piece, less than a yard high, forms part of a plan devised by a Cairo professor to re-attach the beard to the Sphinx, in the hope of helping to stop the disintegration of its limestone head.

American archaeologists working on the Sphinx were said to be sceptical about the plan and the reasons for it. The plaited beard, in their view, did not form part of the original, 4,000-year-old statue, but was attached 1,300 years later as part of a New Kingdom restoration. The fragments in London and Cairo make up less than 50 per cent. The rest, they said, would have to be constructed from concrete and plaster – and the structural support would be negligible.

Nevertheless, the seemingly successful recovery of the fragment was described as a political triumph for Egypt's Minister of Culture. But there followed much discussion about sidestepping the 1963 British Museum legislation. The British Museum, obviously fearing just such an interpretation by other claimant states, insisted that the beard was being given to Egypt as part of a loan and exchange agreement. To circumvent any wider claims by other states, an actual period of a ten-year loan was mentioned, but Egyptian sources insisted that the loan was permanent.

On the other hand Mr T.G.H. James, keeper of the Department of Egyptian Antiquities of the British Museum, was reported as explaining that 'Even if the British Museum wanted to give the fragment back – which would be the most practical solution – it could not legally do so. Instead we hope to negotiate a renewable loan. This way the British Museum will retain legal ownership of the fragment even if it is replaced in the Sphinx's beard . . . Our dealings with the Egyptians have always been extremely friendly. They have never suggested that we stole the fragment, or that we are in any sense illegally in possession of it. The piece was acquired by the British Museum by perfectly legitimate means.'[2]

By the middle of 1984, the beard had not yet actually been returned, but at the end of November 1984, a return was announced in the press, together with the uraeus or diadem from the Sphinx's brow. The draft agreement which was to be sent to Cairo for signature was said to embody the principle that the fragment of the beard was to be restored with other fragments of the beard now in the Cairo Museum in such a way that it could theoretically be returned. This was obviously done to cover the principle of 'loan', which the British Museum had maintained throughout the negotiations. Yet, in 1985, in a somewhat surprising twist to this story, Sir David Wilson, the director of the British Museum, finally indicated that the beard of the Sphinx had not in fact been returned and was no longer required.[3] The Egyptians have held a replica for some time.

Considering the vast quantities of material which found their way from Egypt to the museums of the world, particularly in Europe and North America, the Egyptian request for a fragment of the Sphinx appears to have been a singularly modest one. Many thousands of objects were removed from Egypt over a 2,000-year period, including mummies, frescoes, figurines, tools and papyri. Three of the more commonly known objects were the two-hundred-ton obelisks, one of which now stands in Central Park, New York, one in the Place de la Concorde in Paris, and the other, known as Cleopatra's Needle, on the Victoria Embankment, London. The last originally adorned the approach to the Temple of the Sun at On, and in the reign of Augustus, in 23 BC, it was moved to Alexandria. It was obtained as a gift to King George IV from the Turkish Viceroy Mehemet Ali in 1821 but did not actually arrive in London until 1878 after an epic sea voyage. This was described in *The Times*, on 8 October 1878, as 'the weather worn monument of the greatest of the Pharaohs, which two or three private citizens have saved for us from being broken up to metal the Alexandrian highways . . . .'.

During the Napoleonic occupation in 1799, an unknown French soldier uncovered a large black basalt stone with inscriptions among the ruins of Fort St Julian near the Rosetta mouth of the Nile; it is interesting to see how this came into British hands.

The Rosetta Stone (as it came to be called) is a substantial monument, measuring 114 cm in height, 72 cm in width and 28 cm in thickness, its weight being calculated as just under 762 kg. The inscriptions on the Rosetta Stone are written in two languages, Egyptian and Greek, but in three scripts. The first of the Egyptian texts is written in hieroglyphs, and the second in demotic script; the Greek inscription is written in Greek capitals.

After the operations of Sir Ralph Abercromby, in the spring of 1801, threatened Cairo, the scholars of the French expedition decided to leave the capital for the safety of Alexandria, taking with them their notes, specimens and collected antiquities, among them the Rosetta Stone. If they had remained in the capital they would have benefited from the terms of its capitulation and would have been allowed to return to France with all the objects in their possession. But under Article XVI of the Capitulation of Alexandria they were compelled to surrender the Rosetta Stone and several other large and important Egyptian antiquities to General Hutchinson at the end of August 1801.

In Alexandria the stone had been transferred to a warehouse. In September 1801, when Colonel (later Major-General) Turner claimed it under the terms of the treaty of capitulation, the French General Menou refused to give it up, affirming that it was his private property. It was surrendered with difficulty. An eyewitness account by Professor Edward Clarke of Cambridge, an English traveller and antiquary, records that the stone was handed over to him 'in the streets of Alexandria' by a French officer in the presence of Sir William Hamilton (a fellow English traveller and antiquary) and a Mr Cripps.[4] Thus the Rosetta Stone was acquired by the British as the result of war.

Colonel Turner embarked with the stone on HMS *L'Egyptienne* and arrived in Portsmouth in February 1802. On 11 March the stone was deposited at the headquarters of the Society of Antiquaries in London, where it remained for a few months while the inscriptions on it were submitted to a very careful examination by a number of Oriental and Greek scholars. In July the president of the Society had four plaster casts made for the universities of Oxford, Cambridge, and Edinburgh, and Trinity College, Dublin, and had good copies of the Greek text engraved and sent to all the great universities, libraries, academies and societies of Europe. Towards the end of 1802 the stone was removed from the Society of Antiquaries to the British Museum, where it was mounted and immediately exhibited to the general public. It has remained on exhibition there ever since.

Although the stone is often cited as a good example of an object which could be restored, since it has long been deciphered, there has been no formal, governmental claim for it.

Ghana: Ashanti gold

In the early sixteenth century, Europeans began to establish bases on the coast of West Africa, which because of gold and slaves came to be called the 'Gold Coast'.

The kingdom of Ashanti was a complex society centred around the divine king (Asantehenes), whose power was said to be vested in a golden stool which according to legend had descended from heaven with the first Asantehenes. In the late nineteenth century the British demanded the golden stool from the Ashanti nation on several occasions. Because the stool was not a symbol of political sovereignty but rather the shrine of the 'sensum' of their soul, the Ashanti refused to comply and buried the stool (Fig. 25).

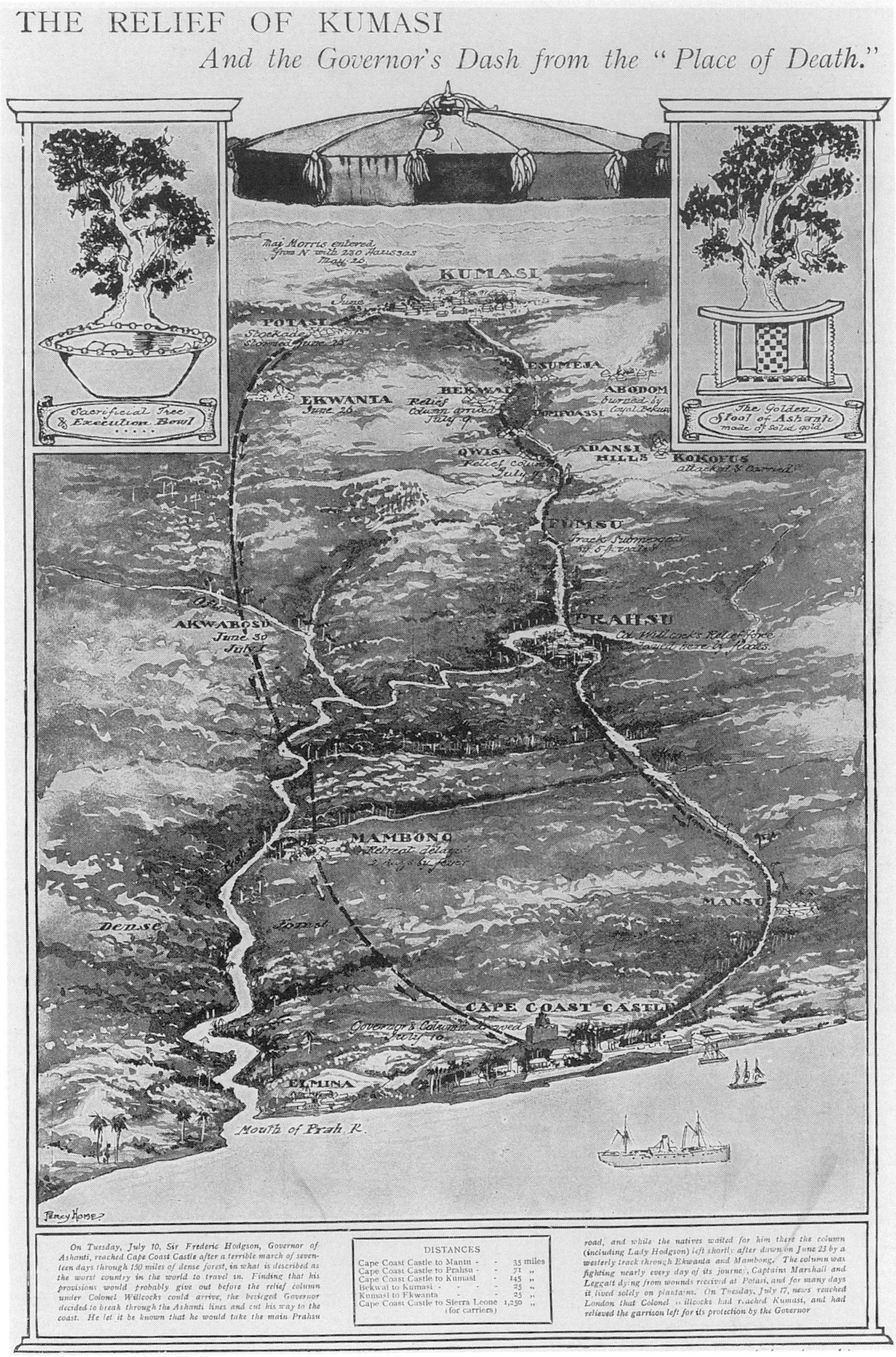

Fig. 25. Illustration from the *Sphere* magazine 1900 recording the relief of Kumasi, emphasizing the desire of the British to remove the royal regalia from the Ashanti, and in particular the golden stool.

In 1867 the British came into conflict, over a coastal fort, with a new Ashanti ruler, King Kofi Karikari. The Ashanti wars, known as the Sargrenti
War, followed. In 1874 a punitive expedition led by Sir Garnet Wolseley
entered the city of Kumasi, the tribal capital of the Ashanti kingdom. The city
had been reported to have seemingly unlimited amounts of gold, which were
used to adorn the lavish trappings of royalty. The entire society was founded on
gold, the nature and function of which had mystical associations. The metal was
extracted from mines worked by slaves, or through lakes. Gold dust was the
established currency. All nuggets were to be surrendered to the Asantehenes, in
return for part payment in gold dust. There was an estimated reserve equivalent
to about one and a half million pounds of gold dust.

The king escaped from Kumasi, but the capital and his palace were taken
by Wolseley and ransacked of every valuable object: the king's sword, pure
hammered gold masks in the shape of a ram's head or that of a man, massive
breastplates, coral ornaments, silver plate, swords, ammunition belts, caps
mounted in solid gold, knives set in gold and silver, bags of gold dust and
nuggets, carved stools mounted in silver, calabashes worked in silver and gold,
embroidered and woven silks, and numerous other treasures, including in particular a $7\frac{3}{4}$-inch-high golden head, the largest known gold work from anywhere
in Africa, outside Egypt (now in the Wallace Collection in London) (Fig. 26).
The town of Kumasi and the palace were then destroyed by fire. Many of the
ornaments of the royal regalia found their way to the Museum of Mankind,
where they still remain; it has been suggested that many of these items came as
gifts or by purchase.

In 1971 Lord Montagu of Beaulieu raised the question in the House of
Lords about the possible return of the Ashanti regalia, which he said had been
removed as 'war booty'. The Under-Secretary of State for Foreign Affairs said
that that was not an appropriate term in this case, since the regalia had been 'part
of an indemnity which [had been demanded and] was agreed by the former
King of Ashanti'. This issue of 'indemnity' has not been challenged. It has also
been suggested by some that tribal differences within Ghana would now make
return complicated.

And what of the famed golden stool? Its whereabouts eluded the British for
years, and at times the Ghanaians as well, it seems. In 1921 it was unearthed and
gradually stripped of its sacred gold accoutrements by Ashanti robbers. Although partly destroyed it actually remained with the Ashanti and was subsequently placed in a royal mausoleum. A replica of the *Sikadwa*, as it is called, is
in the Museum of the National Culture Centre, Kumasi.[5] The regalia of the
monarchy has not been the subject of any formal, governmental claim, but King
Opoka Wace II has requested the return of gold regalia and other Ashanti

objects taken from his kingdom. Following negotiations between Ghana and Britain in 1985 an Ashanti stool was returned by the family of a Captain Jackson, who had received it in 1874.

Fig. 26. From Ghana. This is the largest known gold work from anywhere in Africa and measures 20 cm in height. In 1874 Sir Garnet Wolseley led a punitive expedition to Kumasi, the capital of the Ashanti kingdom. This gold mask and much of the royal regalia were removed to Britain and it is now in the Wallace Collection, London.

Nigeria: The Benin bronzes

Until 1960 Nigeria was ruled by Great Britain. After the Republic of Nigeria came into being in 1963, it led the African campaign for the return of treasures.

In 1977 Nigeria requested the loan of a fifteenth-century Benin ivory mask for a pan-African cultural exhibition centred in Lagos. The mask had also reportedly been sought in 1974 and 1976. This was but one item of many which Nigeria had lost to the West. The British Museum first requested an insurance bond of £2 million for the mask, but then argued that the mask was too delicate to be moved out of its carefully controlled environment. The Museum of Mankind presently houses the mask at special temperature and humidity. In the event the mask was not lent. As a measure of Nigerian desperation over the issue of return, a James Bond-type film called *The Mask* was made in 1980 which indicated that the only way of achieving its return was theft from the British Museum. Ivory was the second most important material in Benin art after bronze.

Over two thousand bronzes, taken in a British naval expedition as a punitive action against the king of Benin, the Oba, came to London in 1897. The Oba received tribute from the people of Benin, known as the Bini, who had supported a trading link with the Portuguese from 1485. The Oba, who was rich and powerful, maintained a specialist guild of bronze casters to make the bronzes, which were owned exclusively by the king himself and stored in his palace. Although made solely for him, they could be given as a special honour if he chose. The art of Benin, therefore, was entirely a royal art.

The Benin empire produced brass castings and ivory carvings for several centuries. There appear to have been two particularly important periods: first in the reign of Esigie (*c.* 1550), when brass supplied by the European traders became plentiful and new forms such as 'Queen Mother' heads were introduced; and second, in the reign of Eresonye (*c.* 1735–50), when brass became even more plentiful and new forms again appeared. Benin art thus continued its evolution up until the 1897 episode.

The vice-consul of the British Trading Post, G.R. Philips, pressed a visit on the Oba with the purpose of reprimanding him for failure to keep a trading agreement. He sent his message at a time when the Oba was enacting the year's most important ceremony, the Igue – a time when the king's body is sacred and he becomes a divine person. It was a ceremony performed to ensure the continuity of the dynasty and the welfare of the entire empire.

Ignoring the Oba's reply, that he should refrain from coming at that moment, Philips pressed on with his mission. Two of the king's chiefs arranged an ambush, reportedly without his knowledge, and most of Philips' expedition, including porters, were killed. Only two Europeans escaped, and after they raised the alarm a naval expedition was mounted. One thousand five hundred men led by Admiral Rawson marched on Benin in a punitive raid, and took Benin City (Figs. 27 and 28). They found an abandoned city with objects from shrines, human sacrifices, and especially bronzes in astonishing quantity. There were embossed figures on plaques, large metal heads, carved tusks, portrait heads, statues, and carved ivory figures of animals. The large number of human sacrifices is now explained as a sacrificial step taken by the Oba to stave off the coming disaster at the hands of the white men. On the other side European commentators have said that the raid was aimed at putting an end to the human sacrifice rituals. An eyewitness to the taking of Benin City, Commander R.H. Bacon, used the phrase 'city of blood' to describe the sight that met them, and there is little doubt from viewing archive pictures of the time that Benin society was a gruesome one.

Fig. 27. In 1897 a punitive expedition was mounted against Benin led by Admiral Rawson. Members of the expedition photographed with some of the bronze plaques which were removed to the UK. Described in an *Illustrated London News* account of that year as being 'grotesque', these bronzes were later hailed as great works of art.

Fig. 28. The members of the 1897 punitive expedition against Benin with a collection of ivories and bronzes. Contemporary photograph by Rear Admiral H.S. Mearsham.

The bronzes thus obtained were dispersed among museums all over the world. It has been said that the British government was not concerned with scholarship, and the sale of the bronzes was to defray the costs of the expedition. The king was deposed and exiled, and hundreds of years of traditional Benin art came to an end. It was not until 1913 that the Oba was reinstated. The old palace has been restored, and Benin is now a major city of Nigeria.

The 160 brass heads taken away by the expedition are the Benin equivalent to chronological records. Since each head represented an Oba, this recorded a dynasty back to the twelfth century. When an Oba died, a formal head was cast in bronze as a furnishing for an altar erected to his memory. The Benin bronzes were and are so important in the artistic cultural heritage of Nigeria because they presented a record of important events. The royal palace in Benin, which covered about half of Benin City, had wooden columns supporting the roof. About a thousand rectangular bronze plaques gave a detailed picture of the Benin court at the height of its glory and power. These were fixed to the pillars of the court, and are a particularly captivating art form.

These plaques are provisionally dated from early in the sixteenth through the seventeenth century. Many show European traders in the costume of that period. According to a Benin tradition, after a group of Portuguese had assisted the people of Benin on an expedition against an enemy early in the sixteenth century, it was suggested that their success should be commemorated in the same way that Europeans commemorated such events. It is said that the rectangular form may be based on the shapes of pages in illustrated books, for this shape is not usually found in traditional African sculpture. The plaques show an evolution in style from low to high relief as, for example, in those representing more than one man. One or two plaques seem to make an attempt at Western perspective, presumably copying illustrations in the books which gave rise to the new shape. Many of the plaques represent animals including crocodiles, fish, leopards, and snakes, and a whole host of motifs from ceremonial swords to crescent moons. The roof of the palace had a huge bronze bird and python, and the entrance was guarded permanently by figures. The bronzes of this period were thin and fine and represented a high water mark of sculptural inspiration in the whole of Africa. The Benin bronzes thus represented a unique and large collection from one of the great medieval empires of Africa reflecting the concept of 'divine kingship'.

In 1938, eighteen fine bronze heads were discovered near the palace of the king, with regalia linking them with the Portuguese centuries earlier. All these pieces are in Africa. But the great bulk of Benin art is scattered throughout museums and private collections all over the world. A number of plaques were presented to the British Museum and more were purchased at the sales. One bronze figure has fetched as much as £185,000. In 1986 it was reported that four Benin carvings, two ivory and two bronze, including a very rare one of a figure blowing a horn (one of only four in existence) had been sold to the Royal Museums of Scotland for £300,000. They had been given to the McLean Museum in Greenock in 1925.[6]

In October 1897 the principal librarian reported to the Committee of the British Museum that a collection of castings in bronze from Benin City, which had been offered by the Crown Agents of the Colonies on behalf of the Foreign Office for temporary exhibition in the museum, had been put on display in the Assyrian Saloon.[7] This was the avenue by which the British Museum came to hold its most extensive collection of plaques (Fig. 29). The Trustees approved and directed that their thanks be expressed to the Secretary of State for Foreign Affairs.

Since that time the British Museum has repeatedly based the legality of its possession on the legitimate authority of the British at that time. On the other hand it has been pointed out that the Benin chiefs signed a treaty in 1894 under the threat of war.[8] Nigerian displeasure at the lack of response to requests for the

CURIOS FROM BENIN.

The city of Benin has proved a mine of ethnographical treasure, quite eclipsing in this respect the more familiar capital of Ashanti. The number and excellence of the carved ivory tusks and castings in bronze or brass which have already reached this country have taken experts completely by surprise. The accompanying Illustrations represent a few specimens belonging to the latter category.

1. EUROPEAN WITH MATCHLOCK.

They are bronze or brass plaques with figures in relief, selected from a collection of about three hundred now exhibited by the courtesy of the Secretary of State for Foreign Affairs in the British Museum, whence it is hoped that the greater part will never be removed. For what purpose these plaques were used we have at present no accurate information, but the holes at the corners suggest that they were nailed against the walls of a house or temple. They nearly all show signs of having been buried in the earth; and it seems that they were not, like the ivory tusks, actually seen placed in the positions for which they were designed. The high relief and extreme elaboration of the figures make it clear that the process adopted in their manufacture can only have been that known as the cire perdue, a process generally necessitating the destruction of the mould after use upon a single occasion. The briefest of summaries of this method may not here be out of place. A model is first

and a tree, which appears to be the Palmyra palm, with its fruit depending from it. The first and largest of these classes is the most interesting from almost every point of view, but more especially because the artists have not entirely confined themselves to the representation of their own countrymen. A glance at Nos. 1, 3, and 5 will at once suggest the non-African origin of their subjects. The figure in No. 1 has a matchlock in his hand, and appears to be wearing a kind of ruff. It seems incontestable that he is a European of the sixteenth century. Nos. 3 and 5 present us with a variant on this type. The full-bearded faces are certainly not those of negroes, while the noses are of the pronounced aquiline contour usually associated with the Semitic race. It is not necessary, however, to seek their prototypes in Asia; for even if Semites had a monopoly of

3. HEADS OF EUROPEAN TYPE.

the hooked nose, the fact that the features of No. 1 are modelled in a very similar way should make us cautious in emitting any theory of an Asiatic origin. Opinions on a subject requiring so much further elucidation are naturally subject to revision; but there seems nothing inherently improbable in the guess that Nos. 3 and 5 represent Europeans of rather earlier date than No. 1. Antonio Galvano tells us that the kingdom of Benin was discovered by one Sequeira about 1472; and that about 1485 "one John Alonso d'Aveiro came from the kingdom of Benin, and brought home pepper with a taile: which was the first of that kinde seene in Portugall."

In the long period of commerce and adventure which ensued, European fashions changed more than once. In this connection it is interesting to remark that another plaque in the collection wears a kind of hood with a Vandyked edge, which, as Mr. C. H. Read has pointed

for a ruff. This kind of theme has several parallels. In No. 2 we see two native executioners, each bearing the axe of their office, and wearing on their breasts the bell which announced the doom of their victims. In the Ethnographical Gallery at the British Museum may be seen a dress laced with red cloth and fringed with long pendants, terminating in little bells, which may well be the kind of garment from which those worn by these cast figures were modelled. In the same place may be seen the originals of the bell which is

5. FIGURE OF A EUROPEAN.

so constantly seen worn round the neck, and of the curious horned box which is constantly held in the hands. The three persons in No. 4 are more remarkable. The two lateral figures may be attendants, supporting the arms of a central princely or divine personage. There are other analogous groups in the series, in which the lateral figures are kneeling, while the central figure is seated on a stool. In other casts, again, the arms of a central figure are similarly supported, while he holds in his hands knives or other objects not easy to determine, for in most cases they have, unfortunately, been broken off.

Much might be written about these interesting objects. They abound in illustration of native costumes, weapons, musical instruments, and, in a less degree, of African fauna and flora. And yet they only represent one style of the castings which have reached us from Benin, for the more life-like figures in the round are not represented among them. The portraits of Europeans give us some idea

2. NATIVE EXECUTIONERS.

made in wax. This is then covered with a coating of finely levigated clay. A hole is now made in the clay, and heat is applied in order that the wax may run out. Into the clay mould thus formed the molten metal is poured. From such facts alone some idea may be formed of the artistic and mechanical skill possessed by the unknown artificers to whom these remarkable casts are due.

The subjects represented may be roughly divided into three classes. The first consists of human figures and principally those of native chiefs, warriors, or musicians, either singly or in groups. The second draws its inspiration from the animal world, leopards, crocodiles, serpents, and fish being especially conspicuous. The third embraces such inanimate objects as amulets, knives, a leopard's skin,

4. FIGURES SUPPOSED TO REPRESENT A NATIVE CHIEF AND HIS ATTENDANTS.

out, had almost, if not quite, gone out of fashion in the sixteenth century.

The remaining Illustrations have not quite the same high interest for us as those already mentioned. No. 6 represents leopards tearing the body of what may be meant

6. LEOPARDS DEVOURING A SLAIN ANIMAL.

as to date; possibly a chemical analysis of the material out of which they are cast might furnish us with further evidence. For if they are brass, a knowledge of the date when brass was first exported to West Africa might have an important bearing on the question. Whatever may be the origin of some of their peculiarities of style or ornament—and these are both curious and remarkable—it seems unlikely that a very antiquity can be ascribed to the bronzes themselves. But whether they are the work of negroes or of some wandering tribe of alien craftsmen, with whom casting was a hereditary occupation, they are certainly the most interesting works of art which have ever left the western shores of the Dark Continent.

Fig. 29. The October 1897 edition of *The Illustrated London News*, the year of the punitive expedition. The exquisite Benin bronzes were described as an ethnological treasure, and the hope was expressed that, having been deposited courtesy of the Secretary of State for Foreign Affairs with the British Museum, they would remain there permanently.

145

return or loan of objects has been expressed on occasion with threats of political repercussions, but there has been no formal, governmental request for the return of some or all of the bronzes.

Some plaques have been sold to the National Museum in Lagos (Figs. 30, 31). However, the Nigerians hold only the third largest collection in the world *after* Berlin and the British Museum. That is to say it has only a *minority* holding

Fig. 30. Benin plaque depicting tattooed boys with necklaces. One of several Benin bronzes bought back by Nigeria.

146

Fig. 31. Two Benin plaques showing a crocodile catching a fish, and a warrior bearing a sword.
Both bronzes were bought back by Nigeria in 1951.

147

of its own art. When the National Museum in Benin was opened in the late 1970s, an appeal was made through the International Council of Museums to give long-term loans, or to return one or two pieces to Benin City so that its ancestral art could be exhibited in this museum. The resolution was adopted and the appeal made without any response. The museum was therefore left to display lesser objects and mere casts and photographs of the pieces that once belonged to Benin.[9]

Pakistan/India: The Koh-i-noor diamond

The Koh-i-noor, which according to one version means 'Mountain of light', weighs more than 109 carats, although before it was cut to its present shape and brilliance in London in 1852, when it was valued at $700,000, it weighed about 191 carats. It would by now have at least doubled in value.

This is an object where the difficulty of the issue of 'return' is amply illustrated. Although it is formally claimed by Pakistan, the means by which this diamond finally came to rest as part of the Crown Jewels in the Tower of London today has been the subject of much anecdotal interest. If one were to combine various press accounts, they would tell the following story:

> It is probably the stone mentioned in the *Baburnama*[10] as having been originally acquired by Aluddin Khalji (emperor in Delhi, 1296–1316), which came into the hands of the Hindu ruler of Gwalior, and was presented to Babur's son, Humayun, by the family of Raja Bikramajit (killed at Panipat in 1526) as a token of gratitude for protection. Humayun in his turn presented it to his father, Babur, who returned it to his son with his blessing. Thereafter for over two centuries it formed part of the Mughal treasure. Nadir Shah, the Turkmen (Shah of Persia), seized it when he captured Delhi in 1739. When Nadir was murdered in his tent by Turkmen in 1747, Ahmed Khan (later Ahmad Shah Saddozai), the captain of his Afghan bodyguard, got possession of it along with other items of Nadir's treasure, and with its aid was able to found the kingdom of Afghanistan. Ahmad's family, the Saddozai dynasty, held it until 1800, when his grandson, the fugitive Shah Zaman, secreted it in the wall of Mulla Ashiq's fort in Shinwari country (Afghanistan). From there it was retrieved by his brother, Shah Shuja, who held it until 1813, when on the break-up of Saddozai dynasty Shah Shuja took refuge with Ranjit Singh, the Sikh ruler of the Punjab. Ranjit Singh extorted it from Shah Shuja as the price of sanctuary. When after the two Sikh wars the British annexed the Punjab, it

came, in 1849, into the hands of the East India Company, who presented it to Queen Victoria. It was seen by Mountstuart Elphinstone set in
a bracelet which Shah Shuja was wearing when receiving the envoy in
the Fort at Peshawar in 1809.

The jewel was thus in Mughal possession in Delhi for 213 years, in Afghan
possession in Kandahar and Kabul for 66 years, in Sikh possession in Lahore
for 36 years, and in British possession for 127 years. It is true that, when acquired
by the British, it was at Lahore, now in Pakistan, but it is clear that there are
other prior claimants in the field. The Mughals in Delhi were of Turkish origin,
and the rulers in Lahore, when the stone came into British hands, were Sikhs,
in which case it has been stated the word 'return' to India would hardly be
applicable.[11]

However, the vital facts that the diamond is definitely of Indian origin and
initially belonged to various rulers within the Indian territory have been used to
support India's claim. On this account it is said that India would be the legitimate claimant. It has been stated that the mere fact of the diamond being acquired by the British from the Lahore treasury of the descendants of Ranjit Singh
of Punjab in 1849 does not make it the property of Pakistan. That the British
took possession of the diamond at Lahore, which was then the capital of undivided Punjab and the Sikh kingdom but now happens to be in Pakistan, has
been said to offer absolutely no justification for Pakistan's request for its return to
that country.[12]

By way of variation another account went as follows:

> As a matter of fact the Koh-i-noor diamond did not stay with the
> Mughals for two centuries after the battle of Panipat. Humayun kept it
> until 1544 when he gave it to Shah Tahmasp of Tabriz as payment for
> the year he and his household spent in exile at the Safavid court. Shah
> Tahmasp then sent it with an ambassador named Mahtar Jamal to Bur-
> han Nizam, Shah of Ahmednagar, in the Deccan in 1547. The dia-
> mond was returned to the north in 1656 when a Persian diamond
> merchant known as Mir Jamla, who had become one of Aurangzeb's
> generals and served in the Deccan, came to the Mughal court with the
> Koh-i-noor, which he presented to the Shah Jahan, and the Darya-i-
> noor, which he gave to Aurangzeb. The two diamonds then went west
> with Nadir Shah in 1739.[13]

The complexity of these tales seems a little unreal; they are hard to follow and
are certainly no longer (if they ever were) clearly verifiable. It is a classic case
where the passage of an object is obscure and is open to much debate and
storytelling.

There even appears to be some disagreement about the final steps by which it reached Queen Victoria. A descendant of Lord Dalhousie, the then governor-general of India, has written that it would be a mistake to think that the diamond reached Queen Victoria through the East India Company. On 30 May 1849, Dalhousie wrote from Ferozepore: 'Yesterday the Council of the Regency and the Maharajah . . . surrendered the Koh-i-noor to the Queen of England';[14] and in later letters he records the anger of the company at his having sent it direct to the Queen rather than through the company. It is said that his correspondence indicates that he personally took charge of the diamond.

On 16 May 1850, he wrote:

> The Koh-i-noor sailed from Bombay in HMS Medea on April 6. I could not tell you at the time, for strict secrecy was observed, but I brought it from Lahore myself. I undertook the charge of it and never was so happy in all my life as when I got it into the Treasury at Bombay. It was sewn and double sewn into a belt secured round my waist, one end fastened to a chain round my neck. It was detained at Bombay for two months for want of the ship, and I hope, please God, will now arrive in July.

In 1976 Pakistan asked Britain for the return of the Koh-i-noor diamond, which is one of the most famous gems in the world, its history stretching back over seven hundred years. Mr Bhutto, the then Prime Minister, made the request to Mr Callaghan, Prime Minister of the UK. It was not known what constitutional processes would have to be gone into if Britain had decided to accede to the request. Subsequent to the claim from Pakistan, the Indian news agency, Samachar, said that the Koh-i-noor diamond was 'completely of Indian origin'[15] and only India would be its legitimate claimant. The diamond was unearthed from a mine in southern India and was owned successively by several Indian rulers. The last Indian owner was Prince Dalip Singh, a descendant of Ranjit Singh, who was forced to surrender the diamond when Punjab was annexed by the East India Company.

In particular, there has been a specific claim on behalf of the Sikh community:

> If Koh-i-noor is to be returned to its last owner, then fairly and squarely the only legitimate claimant is the Sikh community from whose ruler, Maharaja Dalip Singh, it was forcibly taken by the East India Company when the British annexed Punjab in the year 1849. In particular it belongs to that part of divided Punjab which can safely be considered as 'homeland' of the Sikhs in India. In all fairness to the Sikhs, Koh-i-

noor should, therefore, be returned to the Government of India to be restored somewhere in Punjab as part of Sikh heritage. Undoubtedly, the Sikh claim is based on moral and historical grounds.[16]

In addition to this claim, the *Kaghan* newspaper in Iran also claimed that the diamond belonged to Iran: the name of the diamond was Persian for 'mountain of light'. Ingeniously this was countered by the argument that the word is in fact Urdu which is a form of Hindu which uses many words of Arabic and Persian origin.

In the event Pakistan's claim was rejected. Mr Callaghan's reply was delivered in Islamabad by the British ambassador, Mr John Bushell. Although the Pakistan Prime Minister expressed disappointment over this decision, it was not apparently further pursued. The British government decided to take a firm line for fear of an increase in claims from other foreign governments for 'national treasures' presently kept in British collections.

The British government's view was that the history of the diamond was confused and that Britain had a clear title, because the diamond was not seized but was formally presented. Mr Callaghan was reported to have consulted the Queen's advisers before making his decision. An assurance was given that the Koh-i-noor diamond would not be handed over to any other country either.

In 1983 the matter was revived by India. A formal list of Indian antiques and works of art in Britain was drawn up by the Indian High Commission in London, including the Koh-i-noor diamond. The list was to be used to bring pressure on Britain to return them to India.

The disclosure that the High Commission had been requested to draw up such an inventory, under guidelines given to them for the purpose, emerged during a debate in the Indian parliament over the return of the Koh-i-noor diamond. The Deputy Minister of Education, Mr P.K. Thungon, came under particularly strong pressure over the Koh-i-noor. Mr Subramaniam Swamy, a prominent member of the Janata Party, declared that it was the demand of the entire country that the Koh-i-noor should be returned. He was vociferously supported by other opposition members. Mr Thungon said that the question of a return did not arise in this instance since the Koh-i-noor was given as a gift, by the Maharajah of Lahore, Dalip Singh. This was furiously opposed. The Speaker of the Lower House, Mr Balram Jakhar, suggested to the minister that the question to be answered was whether the Maharajah was the proper authority to make such a gift. The question should be whether he 'was independent to do so'. Mr Thungon told members of the Lower House that there was no inventory of Indian antiques in Britain, and furthermore Britain did not accept the principle that cultural property which had been acquired freely and legitimately over the years should be returned to other countries. But he added that India would continue to pursue the matter through international forums.

It had been suggested that in 1977, the Royal Jubilee year, it would have been appropriate for Britain to make the return of the Koh-i-noor – thirty years after India and Pakistan won independence. On the other hand it was argued that any grand gesture of restoration was bound to misfire. The final result was no return.

India: Ranjit Singh's throne

Linked to the loss of the Koh-i-noor diamond was the loss of Maharajah Ranjit Singh's throne (Fig. 32). It was lost through conquest when his kingdom was annexed by Lord Dalhousie in 1849. In July 1983 Sikh politicians, reportedly anxious to increase their popular support, began demanding the return of the nineteenth-century throne held in London's Victoria and Albert Museum.

The throne, once sheathed in gold, was built for the diminutive Maharajah Ranjit Singh, who ruled over an independent Punjab state for forty years.

The return of Ranjit Singh's throne is the latest demand in a programme of action drawn up in recent years by the Sikh political party, the Akali Dal. The Akalis have the enthusiastic support of Sikh landowners in the Punjab, the richest province in the Indian union. They backed a series of protest marches, starting in August 1982, aimed at gaining a large measure of home rule for their province. Harchand Singh Longowal, the moderate president of the Akali Dal, lent his support to the campaign for bringing back Ranjit Singh's throne. His office is in the precincts of the Golden Temple in Amritsar, the Sikh's most sacred shrine. He has been reported as saying: 'Many things were taken in the Sikh wars – some as booty, but this throne was taken by deception. It was the personal property of the royal family.'[17]

Sporadic attempts to borrow Sikh antiquities for exhibition in India have been only partly successful. Jagtar Singh Garehwal, vice-chancellor of Guru Nanak Dev University, headed a delegation that visited Britain in the late 1970s and requested that Ranjit Singh's throne be lent to India. His request was rejected by the Victoria and Albert Museum. The response of the museum authorities was reported to have been that the throne was 'too fragile' to be moved.[18]

The Sikhs have retained some prize antiquities. The Sikh museum, in the tower overlooking the sacred lake at the Golden Temple, is open to visitors five times a year. One of its most treasured valuables is a solid gold canopy meant to hang over the Maharajah's throne. A peacock, shaped from a single piece of

Fig. 32. The Sikh throne of Amritsar in the Victoria and Albert Museum, London. The Maharajah Ranjit Singh's throne was lost through conquest when his kingdom was annexed by Lord Dalhousie in 1849. Sikh politicians began demanding its return in the 1980s.

sapphire, stands at the apex and the main body of the canopy is encrusted with 3,600 diamonds. The canopy was taken into safe-keeping soon after annexation of the Punjab. According to legend the Maharajah's youngest son, Dalip Singh, later a favourite of Queen Victoria, had it smuggled out of the royal palace at Lahore. It stands still, bereft of the throne it was meant to cover.

Sri Lanka: Bronze statues, ivories and manuscripts

Sri Lanka has been a sovereign state from about the fourth century BC. However, between 1505 and 1815 the maritime provinces of the island were under foreign occupation, and from 1815 to 1948 this extended to the whole of the island. During this entire period of foreign occupation from 1505 to 1948 a large number of Sri Lanka's antiquities, palm-leaf manuscripts and historical records were removed from the island.

The Sri Lankan government has been the first to make an official bilateral approach to the British government, as opposed to informal lobbying, for the return of specific objects. Sri Lanka has been intent on rebuilding its own collection of ethnic art lost to colonial powers in the nineteenth century.

Sri Lanka compiled a list to be delivered to six other Western countries besides Britain.[19] These were France, Holland, Austria, Belgium, West Germany and the United States. The director of Sri Lanka's National Museums, Dr P. de Silva, has stated that the list related to especially significant items that expressed to the world and to Sri Lankans the country's unique cultural heritage.

The full list of thirty-five items requested from Britain is as follows:

From the British Library: the Hugh Neville Collection of palm-leaf and other manuscripts; and two letters from King Raja Simha II to the Dutch.

From the British Museum: a bronze double-figure of Padmapani and his consort, and ten other bronze statues; an ivory casket; a silver ladle with an elaborately carved handle; and one Sinhala sword of the sixteenth/seventeenth century.

From the Victoria and Albert Museum: a cabinet of carved ivory with silver mounts, *c.* 1700; an ivory casket with dancers, musicians and lions; brass dishes chased with leaf scrolls; masks and heads with elephants and representations of the monkey god; a silver waist chain said to have belonged to the last King of Kandy, early nineteenth century; a hanging bronze lamp in the shape of an elephant; and seven other items.

From the Royal Scottish Museum, Edinburgh: a bronze figure of a seated Buddha found in 1826, near the king's palace at Kandy; and a bronze Buddha seated on a coiled cobra.

From the Tower of London: an elephant goad of exquisite workmanship with wooden handle, turned and lacquered.

From the Ashmolean Museum, Oxford: one carved ivory comb.

From the Pitt-Rivers Museum, Oxford: a carved ivory double-headed comb.

From the Royal Collection, Windsor Castle: a Sinhalese flintlock gun of 1740.

A full description of these objects was given in the statement that Sri Lanka submitted to UNESCO in 1980.[20] In particular the manuscript items were more fully described as follows:

> *Hugh Neville Collection of palm-leaf and other manuscripts* (in the British Museum Library): Hugh Neville served in Sri Lanka, from 1 September 1869 to 14 October 1889, in various capacities under the British government. During this period of service in Sri Lanka he amassed a collection of Palm Leaf manuscripts from various Buddhist temples etc. which he took to Britain for publication and which have been subsequently acquired by the British Museum.
>
> Also: two letters from *King Raja Simha II* to the Dutch gifted by Sir Alexander Johnston in 1833 to the British Museum. King Raja Simha II was king of Sri Lanka from 1635 to 1697 (British Library Registration no: 9380). Sir Alexander Johnston was an official of the British government under Sir Thomas Maitland (1805–12) serving as Advocate General and Chief Justice. These two letters have been acquired by him in his capacity as a British official and removed from Sri Lanka during the British occupation of the island. They are more particularly a letter from King Simha II from Badulla to the Dutch Governor Jacob van Kittensteyn dated 5 September 1652 on a sheet of thick paper 38″ × 15″ and written on both sides. It is folded twice. And a letter from *King Raja Simha II* to 'The Admiral-General of the Naval Fleet, Captain-General of the Sea and Land and Superintendent of the Dutch Nations', written from Kandy on 20 December 1658, on a sheet of paper with writing on the first two pages, the other two ornamental borders in red and at the head and tail of the letter are crowned figures in the attitude of supplication and other ornaments.

Negotiations were commenced with Whitehall in June 1980, but the British government refused the Sri Lankan request in September 1981 after notification by the Foreign Office and with the support of the heads of leading British museums. Sri Lanka has indicated that it will persist in its claims to the objects that 'rightfully belonged' in Sri Lanka.[21]

Sri Lanka has actively expressed an interest in the subject of the return of cultural objects for a number of years, and in 1976 at a summit of non-aligned countries in Colombo, it successfully sponsored a resolution calling for the return of treasures to former colonies.

In February 1980, Sri Lanka lodged with UNESCO in Paris a list of about one hundred items of cultural value removed by the Portuguese between 1505 and 1656, the Dutch between 1656 and 1796, and the British after 1796.

The decision of the British government to refuse the Sri Lankan request has been based on political and legal grounds. The government could not support such a request since it would represent a precedent, and it has been decided after investigation that the objects referred to were all legally acquired by the institutions holding them. It was stated by the Foreign Office that the general policy was to return treasures only when they had not been 'obtained legally'.[22]

In this context the British Museum has maintained that all the objects it holds were legally given or purchased. It has said that it always operates within the *laws appertaining at the time*; that, administered as it was by Britain in the nineteenth century, Sri Lanka had a set of laws different from those brought into being since independence; and that the precedent of returning an object would result in the museum holding a collection purely native to Britain, and that was not the premise on which the British Museum was built.

Despite these views, however, there are doubts about several objects. Whilst the monkey god figure in the Sri Lankan list at the Victoria and Albert Museum was a gift from a civil servant returning in 1869, the mode of its acquisition is unknown. Another object, the statue of the goddess Tārā, which has been in the British Museum for over 150 years, was taken by Sir Robert Brownrigg from the king of Kandy, when the kingdom was annexed in the early part of the nineteenth century, but is described in the Museum catalogue as 'found near Trincomalee'. In any event the Sri Lankan Ministry of Culture has rejected the argument claiming 'legality of acquisition', on the grounds that those acquiring had no title.

Australia: Aboriginal skulls

The arguments for the return of 'cultural objects' are by no means limited to man-made treasures and can be extended to other items of ethnic and palaeontological significance.

The Tasmanian aboriginal centre in Hobart, at the end of 1982, made a written request to the university of Edinburgh for the return of the skull of a Tasmanian aboriginal chief, King Billy, together with ten other Tasmanian aboriginal skulls.[23] The skull was part of a collection made up by Sir William Turner, Professor of Anatomy at Edinburgh from 1867 to 1903. The contemporary Professor of Anatomy, George Romanes, responded by emphasizing the value of keeping the large Edinburgh University collection of skulls from different racial groups together.

In the year following the negative British response, the Australian aboriginals began national claims within Australia itself for their relics as their religious property. These had been stored in universities and museums around the country. In Victoria, the state government agreed to place aboriginal remains under special controls, among them the Murray Brown collection, including skeletons more than 10,000 years old which were removed from Melbourne University to be kept in special care.

In 1985 there was a ceremony to cremate Tasmanian aboriginal remains at Oyster Cove. This revived aboriginal community concern at the worldwide dispersal of their tribal remains. In that year Michael Mansell, solicitor of the Tasmanian Aboriginal Legal Service, went on a fact-finding mission to European institutions to seek a response to the aboriginal request for the return of their remains.

The Tasmanian Aboriginal Centre in Hobart traced aboriginal remains to the following centres in Britain (in addition to Edinburgh University): the Royal College of Surgeons of England, the Royal Army Medical College, the British Museum (Natural History), King's College, London, the Middlesex Hospital and the Royal Scottish Museum. In the rest of Europe the centres were the Musée de l'Homme (Paris), Institut Royal des Sciences Naturelles de Belgique (Brussels), Etnografiska Museet (Stockholm), the university of Vienna, the Natural History Museum (Vienna), the Anthropological Museum of the university of Wrocław, and the Museum of Natural History (Chicago).

The response of English institutions was legalistic, and that of Scottish ones scientific, both in opposition to the concept of return. In the United States the response was more favourable on condition that the possibility of a special keeping place for such remains be considered and accommodation be made on preservation and scientific access. In Sweden, and to a lesser extent in France and Ireland, this view was reiterated. In Belgium and Austria there was opposition to any return, the reported view of Dr Oliver Paget, the Director of the Natural History Museum of Vienna, being that it was a 'fact' that the Tasmanian aborigines were extinct (Fig. 33).[24]

Because of the apparent destruction of the Tasmanian aboriginal population over a hundred years ago, a myth has prevailed that these people were finally extinguished with the death in 1876 of Truganini, who was the daughter of Mangerner, a chief of the Recherche Bay people, and was considered to be the last full-blood aboriginal woman. However, there are several thousand surviving descendants in Tasmania, and their claim is an ancient and universal one for the disposal of ancestral remains. Yet aboriginal claims have also met with the suggestion that they would have no right to bones over 10,000 years old because aboriginal culture was at that time not developed!

THE WORLD OF SCIENCE.

THE NOW EXTINCT TASMANIANS.

By W. P. Pycraft, F.Z.S., Author of "The Infancy of Animals," "The Courtship of Animals," etc., etc.

THE discussions on the relations between Religion and Science which took place during the recent conference at Oxford mark an important change in the attitude of theologians and men of science towards one another. Nothing but good can come of it. We shall make still further progress if we can persuade the politicians to join hands with us. It is not suggested that Politics and Science have anything in common, but that the politician, to whatever school he may belong, cannot afford to ignore the facts which the man of science has gathered in regard to the history of the evolution of the human race. These would afford him an insight into the "warp and woof" of the human mind, and its potentialities for good and evil. They would furnish an insight into human mentality and passions, which would afford ballast of a very practical kind in regard to schemes for the betterment of society at large. To the lack of appreciation of this aspect of human affairs on the part of our legislators and colonists, we owe the shameful extermination of a primitive race of men from whom, to-day, we could have learned much in regard to matters which must now remain in dispute.

I allude to the Tasmanians. Until the middle of the nineteenth century they stood a race apart from the rest of mankind, dating back thousands of years to the Old Stone Age. They were a people of medium height, almost black in colour, and having black woolly hair, which grew in ringlets. Though well-built, their features were the reverse of beautiful, the nose being extremely wide, and without a "bridge," the eyes deep-set, and the mouth large (Fig. 1). Save during the winter months, they habitually went about absolutely naked. But as a protection from the cold they used the skins of kangaroos. Even then, however, the use of skins was by no means general. To protect their bodies from the rain, they smeared themselves with a mixture of grease and ochre. Yet, as Professor Sollas remarks, they were not without their refinements. The women adorned themselves with chaplets of flowers, or bright berries, and with fillets of wallaby or kangaroo skins, worn sometimes under the knee, sometimes around the wrist or ankle, as the fashion of the moment dictated. The men, especially when young, were also careful of their personal appearance: a fully-dressed beau wore a necklace of spiral shells, and a number of kangaroo teeth fastened in his hair.

They paid great attention to their hair. It was cut, a lock at a time, with the aid of two stones, one placed underneath as a chopping block, the other used as a chopper. A sort of pomatum made of fat and ochre was used as a dressing. Tattooing was not practised, but a more barbarous kind of decoration, produced by gashing the arm so as to give rise to cicatrices, was not uncommon.

While they would seem sometimes to have made use of caves as shelters, they had, as a rule, no home, nor any fixed abode, but wandered about from place to place in search of food. Their only protection from wind and weather, in a climate sometimes bitterly cold, was furnished by a rude screen (Fig. 4) made of strips of bark fixed to wooden stakes. A fire, whenever this could be lighted and kept burning, was placed in front of such screens, but they could have derived but little warmth therefrom.

The record of their implements and weapons is of special importance to us. The former were of wood or stone, but their weapons, whether for the chase or war, were of wood. The spear was the most important. It was fashioned out of the shoots of the [...] tree, on account of their natural

straightness. Nevertheless, the fashioning of a spear was a matter calling for no little skill. The selected stick was first warmed over a fire to render it pliable, and, if it were not quite straight, it was made so by

FIG. 1.—OF AN EXTERMINATED RACE FROM WHOM MUCH MIGHT HAVE BEEN LEARNED ABOUT THE OLD STONE AGE: ONE OF THE NOW EXTINCT TASMANIANS.
The photograph shows the great breadth of the nose, the absence of a bridge, the large mouth, and woolly hair.

holding it between the teeth and bending it with both hands. The end was hardened by charring in the fire, and sharpened by means of a notched flake

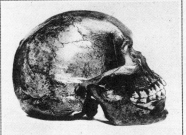

FIG. 2.—SHOWING THE "PROGNATHISM" (PROTRUSION) OF THE JAWS, A COMMON FEATURE OF PRIMITIVE RACES: A SIDE VIEW OF THE TASMANIAN SKULL.
The suture down the forehead, shown in the adjoining photograph (Fig. 3) occurs more frequently among primitive peoples than civilised.—[Photograph by E. J. Manly.]

FIG. 3.—SHOWING THE GREAT SIZE OF THE JAWS AND TEETH, AND A SUTURE DOWN THE FOREHEAD: THE SKULL OF A NATIVE TASMANIAN—FRONT VIEW.

of stone, after the fashion of the old Neander man. When finished, it was a formidable weapon, since it could be hurled for a distance of sixty yards with sufficient force to pass through the body of a man.

FIG. 4.—THE NATIVE TASMANIAN'S ONLY PROTECTION FROM WIND AND WEATHER: ROUGH WIND-SCREENS, WITH FIRES BURNING BEFORE THEM.
Such wind-screens were set up by the Tasmanian natives when camping out in exposed places during stormy weather. [Photograph by E. J. Manly.]

Up to forty yards, one of these spears could be thrown with unerring aim.

The only other weapon known to have been used was a club of about two feet long, notched or roughened at one end to afford a grip, and knobbed at the other. This also could be hurled with precision up to a distance of forty yards, but whether it was also used as a club is generally used does not seem to be certainly known. As with the spear, the stem was smoothed by means of a notched flake of stone, such as was also used by the men of the Old Stone Age.

Their stone implements, used for a variety of purposes, were made of a fine-grained sandstone, flint being unknown in the island. They were made by striking off chips from one flake of stone with another. But, perhaps owing to the intractability of the material, they do not show the finish of flint implements. Besides the notched "spokeshaves" used for polishing spear and club-shafts, there were disc-shaped weapons with a cutting edge, and smaller flakes with finely serrated edges. One of the commonest tools was the scraper. This was a stone flake of about two inches in diameter, dressed by chipping one edge only of the flake, and requiring great skill in the making. It was used for flaying purposes.

Kangaroos, opossums, bandicoots, and the kangaroo-rat provided them with ample food. The animals were roasted whole in the skin, and cut up with stone knives. Emus, black swans, mutton-birds, and penguins were also largely eaten, as also were various kinds of shell-fish whose shells to this day form huge mounds, or "kitchen-middens," in no way differing from the "middens" of the Stone Age man of Europe. Fire they made by rubbing the pointed end of a stick vigorously backwards and forwards in a groove cut in another piece of wood, or by rotating one piece of wood in a hole sunk in another.

One secret they carried with them to the grave. This concerns their use of stones, flat, oval, about two inches wide, and marked with black and red lines. A woman was one day seen arranging a number of such stones, apparently to represent absent friends, but with what motive could not be ascertained. The chief point, however, about this observation is the fact that precisely similar painted stones have been found in the cave of Mas d'Azil, Ariège, which marks the conclusion of the Palæolithic Age. These stones have always puzzled ethnologists, and, had but a remnant of these people been saved for us, we might have solved the riddle.

The early settlers in Tasmania seem to have treated these aboriginals with shocking brutality, which naturally provoked reprisals. At last the remainder were rounded up, made prisoners, and deported to an island in Bass's Straits. This was in 1835. Seven years later there were only fifty-seven survivors, and these gradually died out before their habits, customs, and beliefs could be properly studied by trained observers.

Whence came the Tasmanians we do not definitely know. But some years ago I was able to show that they passed through New Guinea, and crossed Australia on their way to their final home in Tasmania. This evidence was furnished by the skull, which presents features found in no other human skulls. The curious shape of the root of the skull, the frontal region, and the huge jaws and teeth, are the most noticeable of these features, and they are well shown in the accompanying photographs (Figs. 2 and 3).

Fig. 33. *The Illustrated London News*, September 1924, carried an article entitled 'The now extinct Tasmanians', from whom it was stated we could have gained insights into human mentality and passions. The aboriginal skulls are used to illustrate the distinction between the primitive peoples and the civilized.

158

Zambia and Kenya: Fossil remains of early humankind

In 1981 Zambia sought help from UNESCO in its efforts to recover the skull of Broken Hill Man (Fig. 34). The skull, which was a Middle Stone Age contemporary of European Neanderthal Man, was sent to the Natural History Museum in London after being found by miners in 1921 in Broken Hill, which is now the central Zambian town of Kabwe.

Mr A. Mofya, the director of Zambia's National Political Museum, stated that the skull was a unique historical treasure. He intended to apply through the special UNESCO form so that the United Nations agency could act on Zambia's behalf in negotiations with the National History Museum. To date the Natural History Museum has refused the return of the skull, although it has provided Zambia with a replica.

This is to be contrasted with the return after many years of the fossil remains of *Proconsul africanus* to Kenya, which took place in 1982 (see pp. 270–2). Presumably Egyptian mummies could also come under the head of palaeontological claims, but to date the Egyptians have shown no interest in making any such claims.

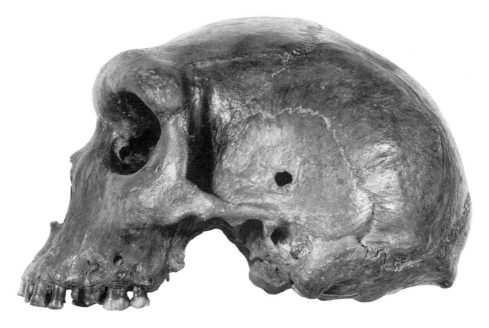

Fig. 34. Found in 1921, the skull of 'Broken Hill Man' from Zambia is kept in the Natural History Museum, London. A 1981 request for its return was refused but a replica has been provided.

Scotland: The Stone of Scone

This stone is also known as the Coronation Stone or the Stone of Destiny. It is described as a roughly rectangular block of coarse-grained reddish sandstone, similar to rocks found in Perthshire in Scotland. It weighs about 450 lb, with iron rings at each end for carrying. King Edward I, the 'Hammer of the Scots', had the stone brought to Westminster Abbey in 1297. The stone was inscribed:

> Ni fallat fatum, Scoti hunc quocunque locatum
> Invenient lapidem regnare tenentur ibidem
> (If Fates go right, wher'er this stone is found
> The Scots shall monarchs of that realm be crowned)

According to James Fergusson, keeper of the Records of Scotland: 'The Stone has a documented history of nearly nine hundred years: a presumed history of a further two hundred: a conjectural but still probable history of a century or two more; and who knows what possible antiquity even beyond that.'[25] Legend identifies the stone with the pillow of Jacob at Bethel, the stone upon which the biblical patriarch Jacob laid his head when he had his dream about the ladder stretching to heaven. The stone was taken to Egypt by a Greek, who married the pharaoh's daughter Scota (from whom the name of Scotland was derived), then to Spain and Ireland and finally to Scotland, which it was supposed to have reached about 330 BC. It was then taken in AD 846 by Kenneth II to Scone where it was later used in the coronation of all Scots kings.

The first known documented use of the stone for a coronation was that of Lulach the Simple, the half-witted stepson of Macbeth, who reigned for only seven months in 1057. However, James Fergusson has said: 'There is no reason to doubt that it had been observed at the inauguration of all Scottish Kings back to Kenneth MacAlpin, who conquered the Picts and assimilated their kingdom with his own in the middle of the ninth century.' Almost certainly the Picts themselves had used the stone for the same purpose in their capital of Scone, from which the stone took its name. In 1296, when Edward I deposed King John Balliol and overran the country as far as Elgin, the Stone of Scone, which he removed, had a powerful aura as the 'oldest native royal relic' of Scotland. The victory of Robert the Bruce over Edward II at Bannockburn, in 1314, secured the independence of Scotland, and this was fully and formally acknowledged by Edward III by the Treaty of Northampton on 4 May 1328.[26]

The Lanercost Chronicle records, in 1328, that:

> The King of England acting on the pestilent advice of his mother

[Isabella] and Sir Roger Mortimer (they being the chief controllers of the king, who was barely fifteen years of age) . . . was forced to release the Scots by his public deed from all exaction, right, claim or demand of the overlordship of the kingdom of Scotland on his part, or that of his heirs and successors in perpetuity, and from any homage to be done to the Kings of England. He restored to them also that piece of the Cross of Christ which the Scots call the Black Rood, and also a certain instrument or deed of subjection and homage to be done to the Kings of England, to which were appended the seals of all the chief men of Scotland, which they delivered, as related above, to the king's grandsire, and which, owing to the multitude of seals hanging to it, is called 'Ragman' by the Scots. But the people of London would in no wise allow to be taken away from them the Stone of Scone, whereon the Kings of Scotland used to be set at their coronation at Scone. All these objects the illustrious King Edward, son of Henry, had caused to be brought away from Scotland when he reduced the Scots to his rule.[27]

After the stone came south to Westminster Abbey, a special chair was constructed for it which was originally used by the priest conducting the coronation ceremony and by the early 1400s became the throne in which the monarch sat at the actual moment of consecration. The chair has only left the Abbey twice: once, with the stone, when it was taken across the road to Westminster Hall to be used for the installation of Cromwell as Lord Protector, and the second time, during the Second World War, without the stone, when it was taken for safekeeping to Gloucester Cathedral. The stone itself was secretly buried in the Islip Chapel and a chart showing its exact location was sent to Canada.

On Christmas Day 1950 – 665 years after it had first been brought south – the stone was removed from the coronation throne. The English press called it 'theft' while the *Glasgow Bulletin* and Scots Nationalists referred to the act as 'restoration'. It turned out that the stone had been removed by four young Scots, and it was not finally recovered until April 1951. Throughout that time there was a great argument about the stone between politicians, press and the public – sometimes humorous, sometimes serious – while the police and the Special Branch engaged in a hideandseek wild goose chase across the English and Scottish countryside.

In April 1951, the stone was found draped in a saltire in front of the altar of the ruined Arbroath Abbey, where the Declaration of Arbroath, proclaiming Scottish independence, had been signed in 1320. It was brought back to Westminster in a subdued lowprofile operation, and no prosecutions followed this event. Scotsmen apparently were not aroused in sufficiently great numbers to prevent the stone's return. But, ever since, rumours have continued that only a copy was returned and that the real stone remains hidden. At least two copies were made by Glasgow sculptor Robert Gray.

That was not the end of the matter. In August 1984, it was reported that a Scottish body, known as the Scotland–UN Group, composed mainly of Nationalists, had appealed to the UNESCO Intergovernmental Committee for Promoting the Return of Cultural Property to its Country of Origin, for the return of the stone. Mr John McGill, secretary of this group, justified their move on the grounds that the Stone 'is, after all, the sole, single surviving cultural object that is sacred to our nation, and we felt that it would be better in Edinburgh Castle along with the Scottish Crown Jewels than languishing in London any longer'.[28] It should go back to London only for future coronations. Their purpose was to lay down a marker for further claims. They had sought to establish that Scotland had a legitimate claim to the stone, as it was symbolic of the nationhood of Scotland. The group alleged that it had been agreed thirty years previously, after it was taken from Westminster, that the then government would discuss its possible return within a year, but the promise had not been honoured. The response of the United Nations Cultural Committee was to rule that it could not intervene over the question of ownership. It was a problem which existed within a national entity and was therefore an internal matter between the Scots and the English.

China: The Aurel Stein Collection from Tunhuang

Although periodically China has protested against the removal of her treasures, the Chinese government has not made any formal claim to specific items. The vast and prolific Chinese civilization created hundreds of thousands of artifacts, many of which grace the museums of the world. It remains the site of extraordinary and perennial archaeological interest. Today it is the Administration Bureau of Cultural Relics under the Ministry of Culture which is responsible for the protection and management of China's cultural heritage. It was less than a hundred years ago, at the turn of the century, that the route of the Silk Road in Central Asia attracted a number of expeditions which led in particular to the creation of a vast collection, at present in the British Museum, known as the Aurel Stein Collection. Stein was an Orientalist, originally from Hungary, who began his Central Asian travels as a British civil servant in India. He was rewarded for his exploration and collecting efforts with a knighthood.

In 1907 Sir Aurel Stein made what was regarded as one of the most wonderful discoveries of this century: a walled-up rock chapel and its priceless treasures in one of the 'Caves of the Thousand Buddhas' at Tunhuang in Gansu Province, China. Tunhuang was an oasis on the Silk Road in the Gobi Desert, and over a thousand temples, said to date from AD 366, were carved out of the cliff face. It was a centre of the Buddhist world for hundreds of years, and 469 grottoes remain today. Stein's description may be quoted:

> Farther up there were to be seen hundreds of grottoes, large and small, honeycombing in irregular tiers the sombre rock faces, from the foot of the cliff to the top of the precipice, and extending in close array for over half a mile. This bewildering multitude of grottoes all showed paintings on their walls or on as much as was visible of them from outside. Among them two shrines containing colossal Buddha statues could at once be recognized; for in order to secure adequate space for the giant stucco images of the Buddhas, close on ninety feet high, a number of halls had been excavated one above the other, each providing light and access for a portion of the colossus (Fig. 35A)

Aurel Stein eventually persuaded a Taoist priest named Wang Yuanzhuan to reveal a cache of manuscripts and pictures that had been uncovered in a concealed shrine (Figs. 35B, 35C). It is thought that this 'library' was sealed about AD 1000. As the door was opened, Aurel Stein described the scene:[29]

> The sight disclosed in the dim light of the priest's little oil lamp made my eyes open wide. Heaped up in layers, but without any order, there appeared a solid mass of manuscript bundles rising to ten feet from the floor and filling, as subsequent measurement showed, close on five hundred cubic feet. Within the small room measuring about nine feet square there was left barely space for two people to stand on.
> . . . Even before detailed examination of colophons had shown exact dates, reaching back in some cases to the beginning of the fifth century AD, there were to be noted unmistakable signs of great age in the writing, paper, arrangement, etc. An extensive text in Indian Brahmi characters written on the reverse of a Chinese roll left no doubt about the bulk of the manuscripts dating from a period when Indian writing and a knowledge of Sanskrit still prevailed in Central-Asian Buddhism. I could not feel surprise at such relics of ancient cult and learning having escaped all effects of time while walled up in a rock-cut chamber in these terribly barren hills. They were hermetically shut off from what moisture, if any, the atmosphere of this desert valley ever contained.
> Already the search of those first hours carried on in a state of joyful

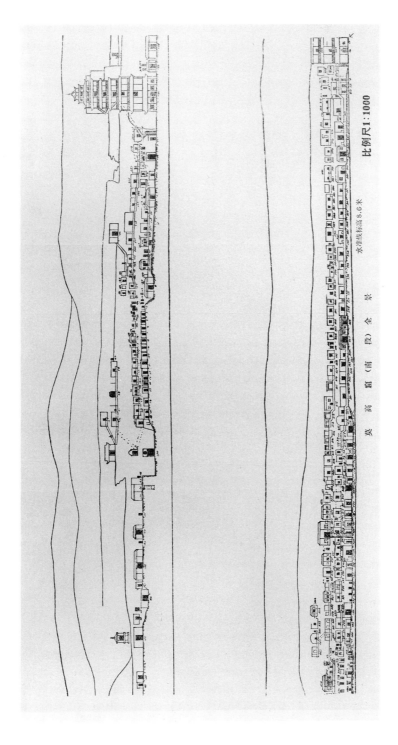

比例尺1:1000

水准线标高8.6米

莫高窟（前段）全景

Fig. 35. A: The Mogao grottoes of Tunhuang visited by Aurel Stein in 1907 are one of the wonders of the Buddhist world. According to legend they were founded in the fourth century by the Buddhist monk Lezun. Today there are five hundred caves containing about two and a half thousand statues and 45,000 square metres of murals. Among these is the formerly hidden grotto 17 (bottom right), where Stein made his momentous find.

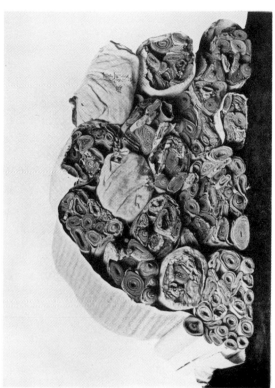

B: Bundles of manuscripts from the secret grotto at Tunhuang photographed by Aurel Stein. The ancient Buddhist scrolls were first uncovered in 1900 by the monk Wang Yuanzhuan, together with piles of scriptures, embroidered pictures and musical instruments used in Buddhist ceremonies.

C: Old Chinese manuscripts and block prints from the walled-up Temple Library of 'Thousand Buddhas' site.

excitement showed how varied were the remains awaiting here excavation of a novel kind. As bundle after bundle was brought out by the
priest to be opened by us with an eagerness which it was hard to disguise, there emerged also in plenty Tibetan manuscripts, long rolls as
well as whole packages of leaves, both belonging to the huge Buddhist
canon of Tibet. These obviously dated from the period of Tibetan domination which we know in this frontier region of China to have extended from the middle of the eighth to the middle of the ninth century.
That the closing up of the chapel had taken place some time after this
period was clear from a fine Chinese inscription on stone dated AD 851
which the priest had first come upon within the recess and subsequently
set up outside.

Mixed up with the Chinese and Tibetan texts and in utter confusion there were plenty of oblong paper leaves with Indian script belonging to different manuscripts, some in Sanskrit, some in one or
another of the indigenous languages which the Buddhists of Turkistan
had used for their translations of the sacred texts. None of my previous
finds of such manuscripts equalled these in extent or in excellence of
preservation.

But even more grateful I felt for the protection afforded by this
strange place of deposit when, on opening a large package, carelessly
wrapped in a discoloured sheet of stout canvas, I found in it paintings
mostly on fine gauze-like silk or else on linen. They were mixed up with
miscellaneous papers as well as a mass of small pieces from fine figured
and printed silk textiles suggesting ex-votos. Most of the paintings first
found were narrow pictures from two to three feet in length. By their
triangular tops and floating streamers they could at once be recognized
as having been intended for temple banners. When unfurled, these silk
banners showed beautifully painted figures of Buddhist divinities, retaining their harmonious colours in perfect freshness.

The silk used for these banners was invariably a transparent gauze
of remarkable fineness. The risks attending the use of such a delicate fabric were demonstrated only too clearly when subsequently I came upon
convolutes containing silk paintings much larger in size. Though
provided originally with borders of stronger material, these large silk
hangings had often suffered a good deal, obviously in the course of long
use while displayed on the temple walls. They must have been closely
and carelessly folded up at the time of their deposition, and were much
creased and crumpled in consequence.

After centuries of compression, I could not have attempted to open
them out completely at the time of discovery without obvious risks of

further damage. But by lifting a fold here and there it was possible to see that the scenes represented were often elaborate and crowded with fig‑ures. . . . My main care was how many of them I might be able to res‑cue from their dismal imprisonment and from the risks of their present guardian's careless handling. To my surprise and relief, [the Taoist priest] attached little value to these fine art relics of T'ang times.

In this way the British Museum acquired 260 paintings and prints dating from the seventh or eighth centuries to the tenth century and more than eight thousand manuscripts dating from the fifth to the eleventh century. The delicate and difficult process of unfolding and cleaning all the paintings occupied expert hands at the British Museum for some seven years. The manuscripts are now kept in the British Library. Stein himself did not read Chinese, and it took half a century to catalogue all the material collected.

China has never made a formal, governmental claim to these treasures carried away from Tunhuang, but informal expressions of bitterness at the mode of their removal have been attributed to the Chinese by a number of writers.[30] In early 1986 a Reuters report from China stated that Mr Duan Wenjie, the Direc‑tor of the Tunhuang Research Academy and curator at the caves of Tunhuang, had expressed a plea for the return of the forty thousand precious scrolls of manuscripts which had been removed in the early twentieth century to the museums of Western Europe. He expressed the hope that Tunhuang could be reconstituted as a single unit. The scrolls came to be distributed primarily in the British Museum (about 10,000 items), with about 8,000 in French museums, while the remainder, estimated to be around 20,000 items, were divided among fourteen other countries. As the result of such wholesale removal it has been alleged that China has been left with only about a sixth of its cultural relics.

One single item in particular emerges from the Stein collection. The most famous manuscript taken from the chamber, which some contemporary Chi‑nese writers refer to as 'stolen', was the Diamond Sutra. It was not famous for its text since there were innumerable copies of it including more than four hundred complete or incomplete versions in Aurel Stein's collection alone. The work is described in *Encyclopaedia Sinica*[31] as follows:

The 'Chin kang ching' called in the original Sanskrit 'Prajna‑Paramita' is one of the most metaphysical of the works ascribed to GAUTAMA, esteemed in China above almost any other Sutra. It is known in Tibetan, Mongol and Manchu translations. The first Chinese translation was made by KUMARAJIVA (384–417), and another is as‑cribed to HSÜAN TSANG.

The great intrinsic value of the copy at present in the British Museum is that it is apparently the earliest known printed book, produced well over a thousand years ago from blocks. According to the British Museum, however, it is not the earliest example of blockprinting, but the earliest which bears an actual date. In a 1961 publication on the history of printing the National Library of Peking described the Sutra as 'printed in the year 868 . . . the world's earliest printed book, made of seven strips of paper joined together with an illustration on the first sheet, showing the Buddha preaching to his aged disciple Sidhati'. This scroll measures sixteen feet in length and bears an exact date, 11 May 868, and includes the name of the man who commissioned and distributed the Diamond Sutra: 'made for universal free distribution by Wang Si, on behalf of his two parents on the 15th of the 4th moon of the 9th year of Xiantong'.[32]

The Diamond Sutra still remains on display in the King's Library in the British Museum with the most famous book in the West, the Gutenberg Bible. The cultural significance of this manuscript for the Chinese, comparable to that of *Codex Regius* for the Icelanders, makes it the one most likely to attract the attention of China in the future.

New Zealand: The Taranaki panels and the Ortiz case

These five wooden panels probably formed the end wall of a Maori *pataka* (raised storehouse), and were carved before 1820 by the Atiawa tribe of the Maori people, the pre-European inhabitants of New Zealand (Fig. 36). During the 1820s, the Atiawa tribe, living in the area around the present town of Waitara in northern Taranaki, was attacked by the Waikato tribes from the north. To protect the treasures of the tribe and their *mana*, the local people hid them in nearby swamps, intending to recover them when the fighting ended. However, the tribe was defeated and dispersed; their carvings were abandoned and the hiding-places forgotten. From time to time since then, individual Atiawa carvings have been adventitiously recovered, usually when swamps in the Waitara area were drained for development into pastoral land. This particular set of panels was dug up in 1972, and found its way to London via New York and Switzerland in 1978.

The carved wall represents the single most exciting unit of the now-extinct Taranaki style. It was carved with stone tools, or possibly soft metal, in a local style which was one of the most interesting and distinctive of the dozen or so different classic regional Maori styles. This is characterized by the sinuous and ridged bodies of the main figures, and peaked triangular heads. There are usually

Fig. 36. The Taranaki panels, originating before 1820, are a series of five Maori carved totaro wood panels forming the front to a food store known as a *pataka*. New Zealand unsuccessfully sought their return in the English courts between 1978 and 1983. Although illicitly removed from New Zealand, the panels were placed on auction in London by Mr G. Ortiz and appeared in a Sotheby's auction catalogue in 1978 under a false provenance which read: 'Formerly the property of Mr Robert Riggs, Philadelphia, who parted with them in 1966. He had originally purchased them in an antique shop in New-London, Conn., around 1935' (*Sotheby's Catalogue*, 29 June 1978, p.123).

two to six short curved wedge-like ridges, called *pu wereure*, 'the flowers in the maiden's hair', interrupting the flow of the long curved eyebrow or mouth ridges on the faces. Taranaki carving has been extinct since the early nineteenth century.

The five associated Taranaki panels are all different in detail; four of them are of essentially similar composition with two interwoven sinuous figures, although one has a single sinuous figure. It has been suggested that the panels may be a composite group from different sources, but this does not necessarily mean that they were not part of one building in their last functional configuration.

The precise symbolism of these panels is unclear but it is thought that they may be ancestor sculptures, with the interwoven bodies expressing ideas of fertility and abundance, appropriate to a storehouse.

The panels are of major significance for New Zealand's cultural heritage. Sotheby's catalogue of 1978 described them as 'the most important sculpture of their kind outside New Zealand and of the highest importance'. A survey in the early 1980s by David Simmons of the Auckland Museum showed that there are more Maori artifacts in collections outside New Zealand than inside. Many pieces from the whole range of regional styles left the country during the nineteenth century in the hands of explorers, traders, collectors, dealers, and private individuals. The need has been expressed to keep as much traditional woodcarving as possible in New Zealand to inspire modern carvers to work in their own tribal tradition, and to provide a cultural background for all New Zealanders, Maori and Pakeha (New Zealanders of European descent) alike.

As early as 1908, New Zealand had imposed legislative controls over the export of Maori antiquities through a succession of Acts of Parliament. The 1975 Antiquities Act vests the ownership of Maori artifacts found in New Zealand, in circumstances where their Maori ownership is not clear, in the Crown. The export of early Maori artifacts or any significant antiquities is forbidden without a permit from the Department of Internal Affairs. This law replaced an earlier Historic Articles Act 1962, and introduced a new concept in that the Crown automatically assumes ownership, on behalf of New Zealand as a whole, of any Maori artifact whose traditional owners are unknown.

This law also gave New Zealand museums, and the National Museum in particular, a great deal of responsibility. Museums act as registration centres for newly found objects, report on the cultural and historical significance of finds or objects intended for export, provide advice to those administering the Act, and in many cases hold and display important pieces acquired by the Crown under the Act. The National Museum of New Zealand also takes the initiative in repatriating significant cultural items that become available overseas. Large, or especially valuable, items are often handled directly by the cultural section of the Department of Internal Affairs. All cultural items so repatriated with public money become part of the 'national collections' and are registered in the National Museum, National Art Gallery, National Library, or National Archives. It was hoped that the Taranaki panels which were put up for sale in London would one day be returned for display.

In May 1978, the New Zealand government accidentally became aware of an impending auction on 29 June of items from the George Ortiz collection at Sotheby's in London. New Zealand museum authorities were particularly interested in lot No. 150 which consisted of the five carved *pataka* panels, and lot No. 141, a carved *pare* (lintel for a meeting-house doorway) from the eastern Bay of Plenty near Te Kaha, in the Whakatohea tribal area. Pre-sale estimates indicated that New Zealand museums lacked the financial resources to bid for the *pataka* panels. However, with assistance from the New Zealand Lottery Board and strong support from the tribe concerned, the Whakatohea, the director of the Canterbury Museum, Dr Roger S. Duff, bid for the *pare*. It was purchased for £40,000 and repatriated to New Zealand, where it is displayed in the Canterbury Museum.

It was only by chance that the New Zealand government came to pursue the return of the *pataka* panels. In June 1978, a television broadcast featured some of the items from the forthcoming London auction, including the panels of lot 150, and these were recognized by a Mr Meads of Inglewood in Taranaki, who recalled that the panels were identical to some he had seen about six years earlier at the home of a nearby resident. He mentioned this to Ronald Lambert, the director of the Taranaki Museum in New Plymouth, who contacted Dr John C. Yaldwyn, chairman of the New Zealand National Committee for ICOM and president of the Art Galleries and Museums Associations of New Zealand. He in turn contacted the Department of Internal Affairs, which administered legislation designed to protect the country's cultural heritage.

Arrangements were made for a copy of the auction catalogue to be sent quickly to New Plymouth. From the illustration in the catalogue, Mr Lambert concluded that the lot 150 panels were those which had been in Taranaki in about 1972, and the Department of Internal Affairs confirmed that no export permit had been granted.

The department requested the police to interview the person who had been in possession of the panels seen by Mr Meads. He admitted he had dug up the panels in about 1972 and had originally intended to give them to the Taranaki Museum. However, he had been approached early in 1973 by a dealer in ethnic art, Mr Lance Entwhistle, who had offered him an unexpectedly high price. He had agreed to sell, and he confirmed that the five panels in the auction catalogue were the ones he had sold.

This information totally contradicted the details of the provenance cited in Sotheby's catalogue, and convinced the New Zealand officials that a *prima facie* case could exist to claim that the panels were forfeit to the Crown because they had been unlawfully exported.

On 23 June 1978, the Department obtained the approval of its Minister, the Honourable D.D. Highet, 'to instruct Crown Counsel to brief Counsel in London to seek an interim injunction'. Subsequently the solicitors for Ortiz and Sotheby's made an extended undertaking to withhold the panels from auction pending the court hearing. At that time the possibility was raised that New Zealand might negotiate with the vendor, George Ortiz, to buy the panels.

171

(Interestingly, it emerged from the facts of the case that it had been the kidnap of the daughter of Mr Ortiz in 1977 that had caused him to put the panels up for sale to obtain funds for a ransom.)

At the beginning of December 1978, the vendor, a Swiss citizen, served two affidavits on the New Zealand government. One contained a Swiss legal principle that a person who had, in good faith purchased something and retained peaceful (i.e. unchallenged) and uninterrupted possession of it for five years 'became the owner thereof by prescription'. The second dealt with how Mr Ortiz had bought the panels in New York around 23 April 1973 from Mr Entwhistle after the latter's purchase of them from New Zealand in early March. The sale was on condition that Mr Ortiz was 'not to show the carvings or a photograph of them to any New Zealand scholar or any scholar of New Zealand extraction for a period of two years nor to entrust a photograph of them to any third party'. There was also an invoice of a purported earlier sale which was annotated with the subsequently discredited provenance published in the auction catalogue.

The statement of claim was served in February 1979 after it had been decided to join Mr Entwhistle as third defendant in the case. The statement of defence of the first defendant, Mr Ortiz, was received in early April. In it, Mr Ortiz admitted most of the known facts and made it clear that he intended to defend the case on legal grounds. His argument was that the vesting of the panels in the Crown (the Queen of the United Kingdom is also Queen of New Zealand) would have required seizure to have taken place in New Zealand; that Mr Entwhistle had good title when he sold the panels in New York; and that by the law of the State of New York, as the proper law at the sale, the present holder, Mr Ortiz, gained good title.

Alternative contentions were: (a) under Swiss law uninterrupted possession for five years gave good title, and (b) even if the Crown, in respect of New Zealand, was held to retain valid title, that title would be unenforceable in the United Kingdom, either because it would be based on a foreign public law, or on grounds of public policy. Although Sotheby's had been joined in the action as second defendant, the firm had agreed to take no part in the action and simply to abide by the outcome. The statement of defence of the third defendant, Mr Entwhistle, was received on 26 July, and it followed closely that of Mr Ortiz.

The Department of Internal Affairs sought evidence to show that 'the law of New Zealand, which seeks to protect its articles of historic importance, is very usual'. Dr Lyndall V. Prott and P.J. O'Keefe of the university of Sydney, Australia, specialists on laws relating to the protection of cultural property, stated that New Zealand's law fell within a group of over seventy-one jurisdictions which had some provision for forfeiture or confiscation of cultural heritage items which were being illegally exported.

In July 1981 the case went before the Queen's Bench Division of the High Court and the plaintiffs were successful in applying the 1962 Historic Articles Act. However the case was subsequently taken to the Court of Appeal by the first and third defendants. The case in summary went as follows:[33]

In 1973 the third defendant, an art dealer, had purchased a valuable Maori carving in New Zealand, which was a historic article within the meaning of the New Zealand Historic Articles Act 1962. By s. 5(1) of that Act, it was unlawful to remove such an article from New Zealand without a certificate of permission from the Minister of Internal Affairs. Section 12(2) of the Act further provided that 'an historic article knowingly exported . . . shall be forfeited to Her Majesty' and that the provisions of the New Zealand Customs Act 1913 relating to forfeited goods were to apply 'subject to the provisions' of the Historic Articles Act 1962. The third defendant exported the carving to New York without obtaining a certificate of permission and sold it to the first defendant, a collector of Polynesian art. In 1978 the first defendant placed the carving for sale by auction in London with the second defendant. The plaintiff contended that the words 'shall be forfeited' in s. 12(2) of the 1962 Act meant that forfeiture occurred automatically when the forfeiting act or event took place (i.e. the export of the article without a certificate), and that title to an article so forfeited passed to Her Majesty at the same time, and therefore the Crown was not seeking to enforce foreign penal or public laws but was merely claiming possession of an article to which it had title. The plaintiff also contended that since the overall purpose of the 1962 Act was to preserve articles relating to the heritage of New Zealand in New Zealand, the forfeiture provisions were incidental to that main purpose and did not bring the Act within the category of foreign penal or public law. The Queen's Bench accepted the plaintiff's contentions and held that Her Majesty had become the owner of the carving and was entitled to possession of it, and that while there was no specific category of public law of foreign states which could not be enforced in England, s. 12(2) of the 1962 Act was neither revenue nor penal in character and consequently was enforceable in England. In his judgement Mr Justice Staughton stated: 'Comity required that we should respect the national heritage of other countries by according both recognition and enforcement to their laws which affected the title to property remaining in their territory.'

Section 12 of the 1962 Act in full, provided:

(1) Subject to the provisions of this Act, the provisions of the Customs Act 1913 shall apply to any historic article the removal from New Zealand of which is prohibited by this Act in all respects as if the article were an article the export of which had been prohibited pursuant to an Order in Council under section 47 of the Customs Act 1913.

(2) An historic article knowingly exported or attempted to be exported in breach of this Act shall be forfeited to Her Majesty and subject to the provisions of this Act; the provisions of the Customs Act 1913 relating to forfeited goods shall apply to any such article in the same manner as they apply to goods forfeited under the Customs Act 1913.

(3) Where any historic article is forfeited to Her Majesty pursuant to this section, it shall be delivered to the Minister and retained in safe custody in accordance with his direction:

Provided that the Minister may, in his discretion, direct that the article be returned to the person who was the owner thereof immediately before forfeiture subject to such conditions (if any) as the Minister may think fit to impose.

In the event, however, these provisions were ineffectual in retrieving the objects for the New Zealand government through the English courts. The Court of Appeal held that: firstly, on the true construction of Section 12(2) of the 1962 Act, the words 'shall be forfeited' did not mean that there was automatic forfeiture but that forfeiture took place only when the goods had been seized, whereupon title related back to the time when the cause of forfeiture arose. It followed that since there had been no seizure of the carving, there had been no forfeiture and accordingly title had not passed to Her Majesty.

Secondly, even if Section 12(2) of the 1962 Act did provide for automatic forfeiture it infringed the principle that English courts would not enforce a foreign law which was penal or public in character because, as Lord Denning said, English courts would not enforce any public law of a foreign sovereign state by which that state purported to exercise sovereignty beyond the limits of its authority, and that included legislation prohibiting the export of works of art and providing for their automatic forfeiture if they were exported.[34]

Lord Justices Ackner and O'Connor also said that although the general purpose of the 1962 Act was to preserve in New Zealand its historic articles, the substance of the right which the plaintiff sought to be enforced was a public right which a foreign state sought to be vindicated by confiscation. It therefore amounted to a penal measure by a foreign state.[35]

In his conclusion Lord Denning said:

I am of opinion that if any country should have legislation prohibiting the export of works of art and providing for the automatic forfeiture of them to the state should they be exported, then that falls into the category of 'public laws' which will not be enforced by the courts of the country to which it is exported or any other country: because it is an act done in the exercise of sovereign authority which will not be enforced *outside* its own territory.

On this point, therefore, I differ from the judge in the Commercial Court, but I would express my gratitude to him for his most valuable contribution to this important topic. He held that our courts should en-force the foreign laws about works of art by ordering them to be de-livered up to the foreign government. He hoped that if we did this the courts of other countries would reciprocate and enforce our laws which prohibit the export of works of art. I regard this as too sanguine. If our works of art are sold to a dealer and exported to the United States with-out permission, as many have been, I doubt very much whether the courts of the United States would order them to be returned to England at the suit of our government, on the ground of forfeiture.

The retrieval of such works of art, must be achieved by diplomatic means. Best of all, there should be an international convention on the matter where individual countries can agree and pass the necessary legislation. It is a matter of such importance that I hope steps can be taken to this end.

From Lord Denning's judgement it may be concluded that without such enabling legislation to effect return no similar action could succeed in an English court, irrespective of the protective legislation regarding export or removal by the state from which treasures are removed. Earlier cases have resulted in an injunc-tion to prevent the disposal of state-owned property illegally removed,[36] but English courts have refused to enforce a foreign state's sovereign authority *outside* its territory. The penalty attaching to a prohibition of export is such an exercise of sovereign authority and therefore unenforceable. To date there has been no enabling legislation in the United Kingdom to effect returns of cultural objects nor any bilateral agreements with other countries.

The Attorney-General of New Zealand appealed to the House of Lords. The court, consisting of Lord Fraser, Lord Scarman, Lord Roskill, Lord Brandon and Lord Brightman, gave its judgement on 21 April 1983.[37] All agreed to dismiss the appeal on the grounds set out in the judgement of Lord Brightman.

He said that it was not in dispute that the carving was exported in breach of the 1962 Act. The resolution of the first issue, whether the Queen had become the owner, depended on whether, on the true construction of Section 12 of the 1962 Act, incorporating certain provisions of the Customs Act, the carving was forfeited immediately it was unlawfully exported, so that it thereupon became vested in the Crown, or whether the unlawful export of the carving merely rendered it liable to forfeiture in the future, the forfeiture taking effect only on the seizure by the New Zealand customs or police, which had not taken place. There is an express provision in the Customs Act 1913, and it is a necessary implication from a provision in the Customs Act 1966, that forfeiture under those Acts is not complete until seizure.

> In reserved judgements the Court of Appeal had unanimously decided that there was no ambiguity in s. 12(2) of the 1962 Act, that forfeiture under that section took effect only on seizure, and that, since the carving had not been forfeited, the Crown was neither the owner nor entitled to possession of the carving.
> That decision was sufficient to dispose of the first issue. If the first issue were decided against the New Zealand government, there was no need to discuss and decide the second issue, as O'Connor pointed out. The court did, however, deal with the second issue, and expressed opinions thereon. [However] My Lords, I take the view that the opinions expressed by the Lords Justices on the second issue were, in truth, *obiter*.

The effect of these statements was to confine the judgement of the House of Lords to the question of statutory interpretation. Lord Denning's judgement on the enforceability of the New Zealand Act as a foreign public law was relegated to the status of *obiter dictum* (meaning only an observation on a legal question raised in such a way as to not require a decision), and therefore could not be regarded as binding or as a precedent.

Lord Brightman continued:

> There is no offence committed under the 1962 Act by the export of a historic article unless it is done 'knowingly'. No cause of forfeiture is capable of arising by reason of an 'unknowing' export of a historic article, apart from a forfeiture for an offence under the Customs Act which has nothing to do with the fact that the subject matter of the export is a historic article. It is only to s. 12(2) of the 1962 Act that one can look in order to find a cause of forfeiture of a historic article as such. Then, to ascertain the process of forfeiture, one turns to the 1966 Act. There one finds that s. 274 requires seizure as a preliminary to forfeiture. . . . It is not in my opinion possible to reach any conclusion save that (a) the penalty of forfeiture of a historic article as such is imposed only for an

offence under s. 5(1) of the 1962 Act and (b) such forfeiture is not complete until seizure.

Lord Brightman said he had every sympathy with the New Zealand government's claim; New Zealand had been deprived of an article of value to its artistic heritage through an unlawful act committed by the second respondent. However, he did not see any way in which, on a proper construction of the 1962 Act, the Crown was able to claim ownership thereof. Thus, the appeal of the Attorney-General for New Zealand was dismissed.

The result of the judgement was that what had been described as New Zealand's 'most valuable indigenous antique' was *not* forfeited to the New Zealand government. Mr Ortiz retained possession even though the panels had clearly been exported in breach of the 1962 Historic Articles Act.

Sotheby's was reported to have been embarrassed by the whole affair. The carvings originally cost Ortiz £30,000 and it was estimated that they would fetch around £500,000 at auction. During the case Sotheby's then faced the prospect of being asked to sell a knowingly smuggled work of art – and decided to await the outcome of the case before deciding whether or not to handle it. The item never reappeared in its catalogues.

The outcome of this type of illegal export case in the English courts is to be contrasted with the situation in the United States and Canada, which has developed as a result of their national legislation, their customs policies, and their being party to the 1970 UNESCO Convention on Illicit Traffic.

However, there follows another English case where restitution has been successfully effected through the establishment of superior title based on a foreign state's cultural patrimony laws and where the non-signatory status of the UK to the 1970 UNESCO Convention on Illicit Traffic made no difference to the outcome.

India: The London (Pathur) Śivapuram Natarāja case

This Śivapuram Natarāja statue (Fig. 37) was at the centre of a High Court dispute over title to it in London between 1984 and 1988. It was alleged to be the same one which was unearthed in about September 1976 in the grounds of the ruined Śiva temple, Arul Thiru Viswanatha Swamy, in the village of Pathur. This is situated in the Nannilam Taluk of Thanjavur East District in the state of Tamil Nadu. The Tamil country extends from Madras in the north to the southern tip of the subcontinent.

The bronze is a twelfth-century statue of the Hindu god Śiva from the

Fig. 37. The London (Pathur) Śivapuram Natarāja was illicitly removed from India in 1976 and purchased for Mr Robert Borden, chairman of the Canadian Bumper Oil Co. Although the statue was purchased in good faith in 1982 it was bought under a false provenance. The Natarāja itself was named as a party in the ensuing action for its recovery in the London High Court. In 1988 the court held that the temple Arul Thiru Viswanatha Swamy in the state of Tamil Nadu, whence it came, had superior title.

Chola period. He is depicted in the famous dancing posture, surrounded by a circle of flames. This representation of Śiva is peculiar to the Tamil people of south India, and is called Natarāja. When consecrated such Natarājas are themselves deities and are worshipped. But they are also highly valued as works of art and antiquity in the world market. This particular case presented an opportunity for an English court to examine in some detail the religious significance of these much coveted statues.[38]

The transcript of the High Court judgement put the Natarāja in its historical and artistic context.

178

The Tamil country and its people have since the earliest times had a separate identity, civilization and culture. Different dynasties dominated the area at different times. The Cholas, with whose period this case is concerned, first reached prominence in the middle of the ninth century AD, and their empire continued until about 1300. It reached its zenith during the eleventh century, at which time the Chola emperors ruled over the whole of modern Tamil Nadu as well as over parts of Andhra Pradesh, Karnatik and Kerala and, across the sea, over Sri Lanka. Their period of great economic prosperity was reflected in the number and grandeur of their temples, and in the magnificence of the religious bronzes associated with their worship.

The purpose of the dedication of a temple is to 'localise' Śiva in that particular place. The focus of the worship in a temple is upon the Śiva Lingam, a phallus-shaped piece of stone. The religion involves the worship of other idols in addition to the Lingam; these idols may be made of bronze, stone or other material. The idols within any temple may be very numerous: there are some twenty-five different representations of Śiva, all of them in human form (save that the majority have four arms), and each showing some different aspect of his being. It is thus possible for there to be something in the order of a hundred idols without duplication. But there may be duplications; and there can be as many examples of a particular idol as donors can offer and temple authorities accept.

When a new temple is founded, and a new Śiva Lingam is established and consecrated, a suite of idols will be made for that temple, and in the Tamil country each such suite will include a Naṭarāja. The texts prescribe exactly where, when and how these statues shall be made, and their making will be part of the whole process of establishing and consecrating the new temple. Every idol is peculiar to its own Śiva Lingam, and each will have its appointed place within the building. Each will be consecrated and each is a deity. While in its appointed place any idol's divinity is secondary to that of the Śiva Lingam, but when it is carried in procession it assumes the full sanctity and power of the main deity. The principle is that once a deity is created it is a deity for all time, and therefore there can be no question of any idol becoming surplus or being discarded. Subject to going out in procession, each idol will remain within its own temple and in dependence upon its own Śiva Lingam.

Each suite of idols would have a Somaskanda which represents the Shivan holy family. In the Pathur example only Śiva remains but originally he would have been accompanied by his consort Parvati, in this manifestation usually known as Uma, and Skanda, their son. A Naṭarāja and a Somaskanda would each have been accompanied by its own and separate example of the goddess Parvati. Thus in the case of the Somaskanda group, Parvati would be represented twice: once as the seated figure of Uma, and once in a separate statue as Tani

Amman. The Parvati which accompanies a Nataraja is called Śiva Kami, which means the lover of Śiva.

The other idols include Chandikeswara, the gate-keeper of a Śiva temple, and a trio of saints known as the Teveram trio, St Appar and St Jnanasamban-dar and Sundarar. St Appar is always represented as an old man because he travelled about the country offering praise to Śiva until his death at the age of eighty. St Jnanasambandar is represented as a happy, dancing youth because he was occupied in singing praise to Śiva until his death at the age of sixteen. There would also be Ganesh, the elephant-headed god, a son of Śiva, seen as the god of common people, and Subramania, another of the sons of Śiva. Another manifestation of Śiva in a terrifying form is Bhairava.

The temple at Pathur is attributed to the second half of the twelfth century through its architectural style. It was established that the temple was in being in June 1346 as a recorded dispute with another temple was inscribed on stones in each of them. When it fell into ruin was unclear. By the fourteenth century Mohammedan invaders had established themselves in north India in the area around Delhi, and Hindu temples were desecrated and destroyed. There is much evidence that to avoid seizure idols were buried in the ground and down wells, and evidence suggested that this particular statue had lain buried for centuries in the Cauvery Delta, a vast area which encompasses Pathur and many other villages.

In 1976 a landless labourer named S. Ramamoorthi, digging the soil, found this Śiva and eight other idols lying face downwards, together with 'poojah' articles – ritual objects such as incense burners – food vessels and pieces of toranas (the hoops which encircle an idol). The statue passed through a chain of buyers: Meival, acting for another – Chandran – Maglal Hussain and Balraj Nadar. Evidence showed it had not left India before November 1976. The other eight idols which had been found with the Pathur Nataraja were seized by the Indian police before they could be disposed of.

The Bumper Development Oil Company of Canada, represented by a Mr Michael Dolland, bought the Nataraja together with three other objects from a Mr Julian Sherrier on 10 June 1977 for around a quarter of a million pounds. The company is incorporated in Alberta, Canada, and the objects were bought for its chairman, Mr Robert Borden, a philanthropic collector of art and antiqui-ties. The statue went in turn to a Miss Enderley, an expert conservator at the British Museum, who was acting in a private capacity. She was to do the necessary conservation work on it to enable the safe transportation to Canada. In August 1982 the police took custody of the statue, although there was no indica-tion of at whose instance this was done. The oil company took an action against the police to recover the statue. The police interpleaded between them and the state of Tamil Nadu, who claimed title to the bronze.

The case came before the High Court in 1984 before Mr Justice Ian Kennedy. The central question of fact was whether the London Natarāja and the Pathur Natarāja were one and the same. If so, questions of Indian and English law arose, also giving rise to further questions of fact. The case was of great interest in its detailed examination of the means of identification of a cultural antique and in its determination of title.

The plaintiffs sought to prove that the identity of the seized Natarāja was that of the Pathur Natarāja mainly by bringing witnesses who handled it in India in 1976 and on the stylistic similarity between it and the other idols found with it. Evidence was also introduced as to the similarities in metallurgical composition, termite runs, and adherent soils from the site of the find.

Evidence showed that the provenance upon which Bumper bought the Natarāja was completely fictitious. However, evidence regarding the coincidence of the date between the London and Pathur Natarājas was insufficient. By the end of the twelfth century there would have been thousands of temples in the Tamil country, and hundreds of ancient Sivaite temples in the Thanjavur district alone.

The theft of idols is a serious problem in Tamil Nadu. There was evidence of up to a thousand thefts in ten years, about twenty to twenty-five of which involved Natarājas. These were a matter of public and governmental concern for religious and temporal reasons.

The London Natarāja is identifiable by, amongst other things, distinctive damage to its features. The top flame in the torana is broken and the snake on the front proper right hand of the statue is broken away, leaving merely the impression of a bracelet; the flame in the front proper left hand is broken; there is some damage to the free end of the scarf and some damage within the jetta, particularly the missing river god; something is broken in the hand of the dwarf lying under the statue's feet; and there is minor damage to the proper left front corner of the top of the peedam or plinth.

In late 1982 when photographs of the London Natarāja were taken to Tamil Nadu each of the four in the Indian chain of buyers and sellers – Ramamoorthi, Meival, Hussain and Balraj Nadar – claimed to recognize the Pathur Natarāja. Chandran and the police were not called by the plaintiffs. Neither Nadar's nor Hussain's evidence was considered reliable. There was, however, no evidence of orchestration of the witnesses, and greater credence was given to Meival and Ramamoorthi. There were discrepancies and inconsistencies. There was some suggestion that, since the Natarāja had been distinctively damaged, the witnesses may have been coached in describing its features for identification. But evidence showed that this was unlikely. The defendant's witness Dr Alain Presencer failed to establish that he saw the Natarāja in London in May 1976. If he had succeeded in doing so this would have meant that the London and Pathur Natarājas were two different figures. There was evidence that the Pathur Natarāja did not leave India until November 1976. Moreover, the London statue had not been sent to Oxford University much before July 1977, which further suggested that this was indeed the Pathur Natarāja. There was also no evidence of when the London Natarāja had come into the UK.

The plaintiff's case on style was that the Pathur bronzes are a coeval suite compatible with each other in style, and that the London Natarāja is identical in style and can be paired with one of the Pathur bronzes, which is its consort. Their expert witness was Dr Nagaswamy. The defendant contended that the Pathur bronzes are not such a suite, but extend in date from the first half of the eleventh century to the first half of the thirteenth century and are dissimilar in style, and that the 'pairing' is wrong. Their expert witness was Dr Schwindler. There is no dispute as to the fact that the Pathur bronzes were found in the pit at Pathur, and it follows that if they belong to that temple they cannot antedate its foundation, although they could be later in time, either because they are replacements for an earlier idol or because they are second and later examples of the god they represent.

As to style, ordinarily one studio would make all the idols that would be required for a particular temple at its inception. If one studio was at work one would expect to find a constant 'signature' or common style within the particular group or suite of idols. Dr Nagaswamy believed that idols would be dated by comparison with one which was inscribed or where there is a control, which, though not inscribed, is so closely associated with a dated temple that scholars are agreed that the control idol is contemporaneous with the temple. Finally comparison would be made between the style of a stone statue in the fabric of a dated temple with the idol in question. This triple approach was favoured by the court.

There were the usual dissimilarities between the Pathur idols – in the ciras chakra (the halolike object at the back of an idol's head) and the peedams (the base). However, Mr Justice Kennedy pointed out that it was tempting but erroneous to conceive of the idols as a set of chessmen. The suite was not intended to be seen as one group. There was no material to suggest that one should apply Western notions of symmetry and unity to a group of idols created in Tamil Nadu in the twelfth century. No importance could be attached to the difference in findings of the idol to the frame or the torana to the idol. At the root of the dispute was the question of date – whether the individual idols dated from various dates between 1000 and 1250, as Dr Schwindler contended, or whether, as Dr Nagaswamy believed, they were all of the same period. Despite further points made as to the comparative size of the idols, and expression, the judge inclined to the view that the Pathur idols were indeed a group, coeval in date and the product of the same family or studio of workmen.

To determine its association with the Pathur group the London Nataraja was also compared with both Parvati to see if either could be shown to be its consort Siva Kami. It was observed that two pieces could be made in sympathy with one another and yet have different facial features. It was impossible to say that there were any points of style so distinct as to show that the two pieces were not a pair.

As to the metallurgical evidence the alloy from which the Chola bronzes were formed was called panchaloga, meaning the five metals of copper, lead, gold, silver and bronze. There was an attempt to see if there was a consistency between the trace elements of Pathur bronzes, which would tend to support the conclusion that something other than chance had brought them together, and more importantly to see whether the trace elements in the London Nataraja tended to associate it with the Pathur bronzes. It was found that there were not sufficient samples to demonstrate possible differences between twelfth-, four-teenth- or sixteenth-century copper by reference to which a particular piece could be dated. Also the Nataraja and Parvati would not necessarily have been made from the same batch of copper. The metallurgical evidence was therefore inconclusive regarding the decision of the case. Evidence relating to termite runs and soil particles strengthened the connection between the London Nataraja and Pathur. In conclusion the judge was entirely persuaded that the London Nataraja was the Pathur Nataraja. The Nataraja had been proved to be that found and sold by Ramamoorthi in about September 1976, and so proven to a high degree of probability. It was found that there was no evidence that could attach the Pathur find to the Pathur temple. However, the fact that they are nearly a complete set in twelfth-century terms and that there are no obvious duplications, and that the trident and poojah articles are present, suggest a probability that they are from one temple and are not a random collection. The probability must be that these idols belonged to the Pathur temple.

The court then turned to the questions of law and as to which was the correct and appropriate plaintiff of the five. The court held that the wording of the issue directed to be tried recognizes the proposition that the defendant, by its agent Miss Enderley, had possession of the Nataraja at the British Museum at the time of its seizure by the police, and that therefore one or other of the plaintiffs must show a title superior to that of the defendant if its possessory title is to be dis-placed. The position of the first plaintiff, the Union of India, may quickly be disposed of in that it has no claim to the Nataraja. Although there is Union legislation protecting the nation's artistic and cultural heritage there is no provision which would enable the Union to assert any title to any particular work of art or antiquity. Any 'government' right can only rest in the second plaintiff, the state of Tamil Nadu. The state of Tamil Nadu is one of the states which make up the Union of India. Each state has its own legislature, its own system of law and its own High Court. The seat of government and the place of sitting of the High Court in Tamil Nadu is Madras. The state bases its claim to the Nataraja upon its own legislation: (i) under the Tamil Nadu Hindu Religious and Charitable Endowments Act 1859, Tamil Nadu Act No. 22 of 1959, as amended by the Tamil Nadu Hindu Religious and Charitable Endowments (Amendment and Special Provisions) Act 1976 (President's Act 24 of 1976), and (ii) under the Indian Treasure-Trove Act 1878 (Act 6 of 1878). There is a long history of detailed enactments in each of these fields, and they originate from legislation for the Madras presidency of the East India Company in the early nineteenth century. Throughout the case the 1959 Act, as amended, was referred to as 'the HR and CE Act', and the 1878 Act, as amended, was referred to as 'the Treasure-Trove Act'.

Many, if not all, of the states of India have enactments corresponding to the HR and CE Act. A Hindu temple is autonomous: there is no religious hierarchy. With any charitable endowment anywhere there is a potential for abuse, a potential which will be enhanced by the absence of any hierarchy to control abuses. The secular power has intervened to limit the opportunity for such abuse. The HR and CE Act provides for the superintendence of the property or religious institutions and for the identification, preservation and application of the funds and property of those that are defunct. The state of Tamil Nadu asserts that either it, or the commissioners appointed under and for the purposes of the HR and CE Act, can make a claim to the Nataraja.

The third plaintiff was Thiru (Mr) R. Sadogopan, a public official appointed to control the affairs of the Pathur temple under the HR and CE Act. The fourth plaintiff was the temple itself. The fifth plaintiff was the Śiva Lingam of the temple, which was added to the proceedings to meet a point taken by the defendant that a temple is not a juristic person in Indian law. The claims of the third, fourth and fifth plaintiffs were similar to this extent – that they represented claims by the 'institution' founded in Pathur in about 1175 as a public temple for the Hindu population of the area. Effectively these three plaintiffs claimed in the alternative.

As to the plaintiffs' rights to sue, it was found that the commissioner could not claim as trustee under the HR and CE Act and therefore that the second plaintiff, the state of Tamil Nadu, had no claim through any supposed right of the commissioner. Also the appointment as trustee of R. Sadogopan, a public official, to control the affairs of the Pathur temple under the HR and CE Act had not been validly made but was saved by the statute from being overthrown. He would, however, have been a competent *de facto* trustee plaintiff. In any event the law of England admits a foreign corporation to sue. The temple (or the Śiva Lingam) is a foreign corporation. In India the appropriate plaintiff was the trustee, and in England the appropriate plaintiff was the temple.

The plaintiffs contended that in Tamil Nadu a temple is a juristic person, and that the fourth plaintiff is the party that is entitled to claim the Naṭarāja. The defendant replied that this is not so: it is the idol which is the juristic entity, and that is so throughout India. The importance of this point is that the defendant went on to argue that the fifth plaintiff (the idol) cannot sue in England as a matter of English law and public policy because it is, at best, Almighty God or, at worst, a piece of stone. Whether the plaintiffs or the defendant is right, an action, if brought in India, would have to be brought by the trustee of the juristic person. Two questions arise: is the defendant right when it claims that the third plaintiff was not validly appointed, and is therefore no trustee; and, secondly, if the defendant is right, does that invalidity disentitle the fourth or fifth plaintiffs from asserting a claim in the court?

The next major question is whether a consecrated idol, here the Naṭarāja, is 'property' in Indian law. The plaintiffs claimed that it is; the defendant that it is not. There is no question but that in Indian law the trustee of an idol has a right to have it in his custody, a right that will be enforced by the courts of India. That right of custody has not been examined in detail, but it is inferred that it arises out of the relationship between the idol and its trustee and does not essentially depend upon rights of property in the everyday sense. Mr Justice Kennedy had to decide whether in fact there is such a right of property by Indian law which would entitle the 'owner' to enforce that right outside the jurisdiction of the courts of India, and thus assert a title which is superior to the possessory title of the defendant.

It is a classical statement of Hindu law that a consecrated idol is a juristic person, capable of holding property, of suing and being sued. It does so through its human ministrant, who is frequently referred to as the trustee or manager of the idol. The term trustee is acceptable if it is not equated to that of the trustee under English law.

The juristic personality was but one fact of the idol's character. The Śiva Lingam would, as the central deity of the temple, be the juristic person, not the Naṭarāja. In Indian law idols could be subject to theft and were also treasure trove, and were therefore property. The institution has a right to possession of the idol apart from such rights of custodianship as may attach to the trustee. Evi-

dence established that the courts of Tamil Nadu would accept a suit in the name
and on behalf of a temple. The fact that personality here was focused by Indian
law into a piece of stone was immaterial.

A further objection was that the courts of England and Wales would not
recognize a god as having standing to sue. Indian law also recognized that
neither a god nor any other supernatural being would be within its purview. It
could not, however, be said that there would be no property in something stolen
because it was the symbol of a god or because by legal fiction it belonged to the
god.

In determining who was entitled to the statue the question also had to be
considered whether Ramamoorthi acquired a title to the Naṭarāja by taking it
into his possession by a lawful act. By the law of Tamil Nadu, where an article
is hidden in land, that is evidence that the owner does not intend to abandon it.
The place where it was found was part of the consecrated grounds of the temple
and remained the property of the foundation. Under the Tamil Land Encroachment Act 1905 private encroachments upon government land are regulated.
The evidence showed Ramamoorthi was not lawfully in possession of the area
where the idols were found. Without the right of occupancy he could not be said
to have that possession of the land which entitles to possession to all that lies
within it. The temple is the owner of the Naṭarāja and has superior title to the
defendant.

The evidence showed Ramamoorthi was behaving dishonestly when he
took and kept the idols, and that he knew they were not his to take, even though
he may have believed that it would be difficult to decide to whom they then
belonged. He was guilty of criminal misappropriation under Indian law, and
his acquisition of the Naṭarāja was unlawful, although not necessarily theft. The
evidence showed that the defendant, through Mr Dolland, bought the Naṭarāja
in good faith in June 1982.

Under the Indian Treasure Trove Act, if Ramamoorthi had given notice
of his find then the treasure would have been divisible between him and the
temple. The Act has two effects in this case: (i) the principles of *Attorney-General
of New Zealand* v. *Ortiz* have no application, because the forfeiture or vesting
took place within the jurisdiction of Tamil Nadu; and (ii) the government of
Tamil Nadu by virtue of the vesting has a better title than the defendant whose
possession was bare of any lawful origin. The defendant had made a plea under
the Limitation Act 1980. However, Ramamoorthi had stolen the statue and the
court applications were made at a time when six years had not elapsed since the
defendant's purchase in good faith. Mr Justice Kennedy therefore held that the
pious intention of the twelfth-century noble who gave the land and built the
Pathur temple remains in being and is personified by the temple itself, a juristic
entity which has title to the Naṭarāja superior to that of the defendant.

CHAPTER FIVE

AMERICAN AND CANADIAN APPROACHES

Museums are unevenly distributed between prosperous and poorer countries. The United States alone has about a quarter of all the museums in the world. In 1965 the American Association of Museums revealed that between 1960 and 1963 a new museum was set up every three to four days. In the 1980s there were more than twenty-one museums for every million of the population (estimated at 194 million for the USA and Canada).[1] Nearly all of these are private institutions, and in the USA, of the major institutions, only the Library of Congress and the National Archives are under federal control. Attendances at American museums and art galleries even exceeded those at popular sporting events. Museum development in Canada has also been vigorous, with much attention being given to its own rich indigenous ethnographic collections of Eskimo and Indian art. For many years the United States adopted a *laissez-faire* policy over the import and export of cultural treasures, and was reputed to be the largest buyers' market[2] in the world for stolen or illegally exported cultural property, much of it coming from South America, and often ending up in respectable museums. Cultural objects could leave and enter without restriction and were free of duty. From 1971 onwards, however, this policy began to change. Of art importing nations the United States and Canada are now among the most responsive to the issue of the origin of cultural property.

In the 1970s art museums and museum organizations[3] adopted resolutions of self-restraint in their collection policies. For instance the museum of the University of Pennsylvania decided that they would not purchase art objects without information about prior owners, place of origin, legality of export and any other relevant details. Harvard University also applied a system whereby the museum director was responsible for ensuring that the university acquired legal title to objects legally exported from the country of origin. Individual and institutional members of the American Association of Museums were urged to abstain from purchasing or accepting donations of antiquities exported from their country of origin contrary to the UNESCO Convention. Individual museums voluntarily returned illegally exported and stolen works[4] to their countries of origin. Sometimes museums were obliged to surrender imported works. In 1969 a Raphael painting was imported into the United States without declaration by the Boston Museum of Fine Arts. The unknown Raphael portrait, believed to be of a daughter of the Duke of Mantua, was supposed to form part of the museum's centenary celebration exhibition. The museum stated that the portrait was purchased from a private European collection in Switzerland. However, the Italian authorities exposed the fact that the museum had apparently purchased the portrait in Genoa, Italy, and not in Switzerland, and that it had been removed from Italy in secret. The seller was identified as an art dealer with several criminal convictions for smuggling antiques who was barred under Italian law from dealing in art. Since the painting had been brought into the United States without being declared, the US customs seized it and returned it to Italy. It was later discovered to be a fake.[5]

In the 1970s the UNESCO draft Convention on Cultural Property (see Chapter 6) was being discussed by politicians and museum officials. At its general meeting in 1970 the Council of the Archaeological Institute of America endorsed the steps to prevent illicit trafficking contained in the then proposed UNESCO draft Convention. It adopted the following resolution:

> The AIA condemns the destruction of the material and historical records of the past by the plundering of archaeological sites both in the United States and abroad and by the illicit export and import of antiquities.
>
> The AIA supports wholeheartedly the UNESCO Draft Convention on the Means of Prohibiting and Preventing the Illicit Import, Export and Transfer of Ownership of Cultural Property, and urges ratification of the Draft Convention by the United States Government at the earliest practicable moment. It further urges its members, individually and through the local societies of the Institute, to make their support of the Draft Convention felt by communications to the appropriate Governmental authorities.
>
> The AIA calls upon its members, as well as educational institutions (universities and museums) in the United States and Canada, to refrain from purchasing and accepting donations of antiquities exported from their countries of origin in contravention to the terms of the UNESCO Draft Convention.
>
> The AIA urges that, in accordance with the provisions of the UNESCO Draft Convention, concerned countries take practical steps to facilitate the legitimate export, import and exchange of archaeological materials and antiquities. The Archaeological Institute of America applauds the efforts of local authorities, both in the United States and abroad, to prevent the despoliation of archaeological sites and the illicit

export and import of antiquities and archaeological materials, and pledges its support in such efforts.[6]

In June 1971, the Council of the American Association of Museums adopted a very different resolution. This recommended:

> We urge individual and institutional members of the AAM to abstain from purchasing and accepting donations of antiquities exported from their countries of origins in contravention to the terms of the UNESCO Draft Convention. This abstention is to apply only to antiquities from a country which has adopted the farsighted policy of making duplicate material available through legal channels, or has installed a procedure for granting export licenses to material which has been approved by a board of review. We feel that this policy of combining both the abstention of questionable acquisitions, and the requirement of the foreign government to make available duplicate material is the most effective method of achieving the objective of safeguarding archaeological sites and preserving national art treasures.[7]

This clearly reflected the difference of interests which would reappear in the following years over the issue of cultural pillage. The Museums Association wanted to ensure the continued legal flow of antiquities. It therefore gave only qualified support to the UNESCO Convention, dependent upon the somewhat curious condition that there should be a supply of duplicate material.

The market for Mexican objects, in particular, has flourished in the United States. As the home of several great pre-Columbian civilizations, especially the Mayan and Aztec, Mexico is a rich source of antiquities. Looters rob its many archaeological sites, and Mayan stelae in particular have been much sought after. Carved with historical, religious and astronomical inscriptions, they are sawn into pieces to facilitate transportation and sale. There has often been looting of known monuments from known sites, and important records of the Mayan civilization have been destroyed (Fig. 38). The United States therefore entered into bilateral agreements with its neighbours.

The (1970) US–Mexico Treaty providing for the Recovery and Return of Stolen Archaeological Historical and Cultural Properties (see Appendix IV) was the first bilateral agreement entered into by the United States which provided for the *return* of stolen artifacts. The treaty was reciprocally modelled on an earlier Convention of 1936 for the Recovery of Stolen Motor Vehicles (under which the United States had mainly benefited). The purpose of the treaty was to deal effectively with the problem of the illicit international traffic in stolen arch-

Fig. 38. The Mayan Jimbal Stela 1, discovered by Gil Martinez and photographed by Christopher Jones in 1965 during the course of the University of Pennsylvania Tikal project in Guatemala. Subsequent examination after 1967 revealed extensive damage by looters who, having failed to saw off the sculptured front surface, had to destroy the upper part.

aeological, historical and cultural properties between Mexico and the United States, and was ratified by both countries in 1971.

The treaty tries to balance three major competing interests: the preservation of cultural heritage; the needs of art importers; and the preservation of artistic and archaeological values. The needs of Mexico are met by the provisions for the recovery and return of stolen Mexican cultural objects and the needs of the United States are fulfilled by the promotion of cultural exchange, and the opportunities for United States fieldwork in Mexico. Thus, the treaty encourages mutual co-operation and protects cultural property as well as effectively implementing its return.

Article I defines the items which are recoverable under the provisions of the treaty. They are art objects and artifacts of the pre-Columbian cultures of the United States of America and the United Mexican States, including stelae and architectural features such as relief and wall art, art objects and religious artifacts of the colonial periods of both countries, and documents from official archives for the period up to 1920, all of which are the property of federal, state, or municipal governments or their instrumentalities. The treaty does not cover property which is in private ownership. If the two governments are not able to agree on the application of the provisions of the treaty to a specific item, provision is made for the opinion of a panel of qualified experts. The whole treaty is subject to the limitation that the works sought will be 'of outstanding importance to the national patrimony'. This suggests that only items which have been specifically designated as such will be covered.

Under Article II each party to the treaty agrees, firstly, to encourage the discovery, preservation, excavation and study of archaeological sites and materials by qualified scholars and scientists of both countries. Secondly, the parties intend to deter illicit excavations of archaeological sites and the theft of archaeological, historical or cultural properties. Thirdly, they agree to facilitate the circulation and exhibition of archaeological, historical and cultural properties of both nations. This provision envisages that the illicit market for antiquities can be curtailed by short- and long-term exchanges between museums. One such agreement for long-term loans has taken place between the Metropolitan Museum of Art in New York City and the National Museum of Anthropology in Mexico City. This arrangement concerns exchanges of Mexican pre-Columbian artifacts from the Mexican Museum in return for Egyptian and Cypriot materials from the Metropolitan Museum in New York. Lastly, both states agree to permit the legitimate international commerce in art objects, consistent with the laws on conservation of national archaeological, historical and cultural properties.

This agreement must operate within the ambit of the Mexican regulations on cultural property. All cultural property consisting of immovable archaeological monuments and artifacts found therein belongs to the state for the purposes of conservation and exploitation. Such property is vested in the Mexican nation and is registered in an official inventory.

A criticism of this treaty has been that internal legislation enacted after ratification could alter the type and number of objects protected by the treaty. Under the treaty between the United States and Mexico, the only items covered were those owned by a federal, state or municipal government. However, in 1972, Mexico enacted a statute for the protection of archaeological sites and the stringent control of art exports, and placed even those Mexican antiquities in private ownership under state control, forbidding their exportation. This expanded the scope of the treaty's coverage. The state also maintains the right of expropriation of all cultural property and the right of reproduction. The exportation of archaeological artifacts of preColumbian origin is prohibited absolutely, except for temporary exchange purposes. It is only in the area of postColumbian historical or cultural monuments that export is now possible.

The principal means of enforcement are contained in Article III, which makes illicit the import, export or transfer of ownership of cultural property contrary to the treaty. Each party agrees to employ the legal means at its disposal to recover and return from its territory stolen archaeological, historical and cultural properties that are removed from the territory of the requesting state, if that state furnishes, with its request, documentation and other evidence necessary to establish its claim. If the requested state is unable to effect the recovery or return of a stolen archaeological, historical or cultural object located in its territory, the AttorneyGeneral of that state is authorized to institute a civil action in the appropriate federal district court. As far as the United States is concerned this provision is selfexecuting and needs no implementing legislation. Nothing in the treaty alters the domestic law of the parties otherwise applicable to such proceedings.

Article IV provides that the property be returned as promptly as possible, when the requested party has obtained all the necessary legal authorizations. All expenses incidental to the return of the property shall be borne by the requesting party. No claims for damages or loss may be brought against the returning party, in connection with its performance of obligations under the treaty.

Article V exempts the archaeological, historical and cultural property covered by the treaty from other laws dealing with the disposition of merchandise seized for having been illegally imported. Thus, no penalties or charges arising under ordinary circumstances for infringement of import laws will be imposed. This provision is also selfexecuting. The treaty shall remain in force for two years after ratification and thereafter is terminable on thirty days' written notice by either party.

This treaty of co-operation between the United States and Mexico helped to focus the attention of the Senate on the matter of stolen cultural property and illegal importation into the United States. The federal Statute[8] relating to Importation of Pre-Columbian Art (passed by Congress in 1972) is the only United States legislation which provides for the return of stolen cultural properties and the punishment of those involved in the theft.

The most important aspect of this legislation is that it represents a commitment on the part of the United States to stop an unregulated flow of articles into its territory, which have been exported in violation of a foreign country's laws. It also suggests that, in undertaking this responsibility, the United States recognizes that export controls alone are of no avail. It is necessary that importing nations make adequate provisions to ensure protection against illegal traffic.

The statute prohibits the importation into the United States of pre-Columbian monumental or architectural sculpture and murals which have been exported in violation of the export laws of the country of origin. Any object which is sought to be imported must be accompanied by a certificate which states that the exportation is legal.[9] Under the statute, the determination of what objects fall within its scope is left to the United States government. Section 205(3), however, provides that the term 'pre-Columbian monumental or architectural sculpture or mural' means any stone carving or wall art which was the product of a pre-Columbian Indian culture of Mexico, Central America, or the Caribbean Islands; was an immobile monument or architectural structure or was a part of, or affixed to, any such monument or structure and is subject to export control by the country of origin; or any fragment or part of any stone carving or wall as described.

The working of the legislation is dependent upon voluntary disclosure by the traveller or consignee at the point of entry. Any illegally imported items are to be seized and forfeited under the customs laws. Any pre-Columbian monumental or architectural sculpture or mural which is thus forfeited 'shall be first offered for return to the country of origin and shall be returned if that country bears all expenses which are incident to such return and complies with other requirements relating to the return such as the Secretary shall prescribe, or if not returned to that country shall be disposed of in accordance with customs laws regarding forfeiture'.

Import is allowed only if the importer can produce a certificate from the country of origin, in a form which is acceptable to the Secretary of the Treasury, issued by the government of the country of origin, which states that the exportation was not in violation of the laws of that country. If the consignee is unable to present the required certificate to the customs officer at the point of entry, he may still secure a legal importation by producing satisfactory evidence that such a sculpture or mural was exported from the country of origin on or before the effective date of the regulation listing such a sculpture or mural, or that the object is not covered by the list which describes the items that are regulated. After the seizure of the object, which is kept in customs custody, the consignee is given a period of ninety days in which to produce a certificate or evidence of the inapplicability of the regulations to the particular item imported.

In furtherance of United States policy on import control an amendment was made to part 12 of the US Customs Regulations to implement Title II of Public Law 92–587. This authorizes the Secretary of the Treasury to regulate the importation into the United States of pre-Columbian monumental and architectural sculptures or murals exported contrary to the laws of the country of origin. The amendment lists the types of articles to be regulated; the countries which control the exportation of such items; the documents which are required for importing the items into the United States; and the time period in which these documents must be submitted if they are not available at the time of entry. It also provides for the disposition of articles seized for failure to comply with such requirements. This amendment became effective on 1 June 1973.

There have been two landmark cases which have centred on illicit trafficking of pre-Columbian artifacts. The first of these was *United States* v. *Hollinshead* in 1974. Looters removed the rare Mayan stela known as Machaquila No. 2 (Fig. 39) from its site in Guatemala by cutting it into several pieces. It later entered the United States and was transported to California by a circuitous route. The piece was known because in 1961, when archaeologist Ian Graham discovered a magnificent collection of Maya ruins, including seventeen stelae, in a Guatemalan site, he named it 'Machaquila'. He returned in 1962 to photograph, draw and make models of various monuments. Among the stelae he recorded was Stela No. 2, a seven-foot monument intricately carved with reliefs and hieroglyphs. When he returned again to the site in 1968 he saw Stela No. 2 still intact, as it had been in 1962.

In 1971, Graham received a letter from a curator at the Brooklyn Museum, seeking his opinion about a pre-Columbian stela offered for sale by Clive Hollinshead, a Californian art dealer. Graham recognized Machaquila Stela No. 2, and notified the authorities, whose investigation uncovered an elaborate smuggling network. The stela had been cut into pieces and taken from Guatemala to British Honduras, then by air to Miami, and from Miami by road for showing to dealers and collectors in Georgia, New York and Wisconsin. Hollinshead then transported the stela to California, where he made further efforts to sell it for

Fig. 39. The Mayan Machaquila Stela 2 was at the centre of the famous 1974 Hollinshead case after it had been cut into squares and illegally exported to the United States. Ian Graham earlier identified and photographed this stela in 1962 at the ruins of Machaquila, Department de Peten, Guatemala.

around $300,000, until the offer to the Brooklyn Museum led to discovery and his arrest.

The federal grand jury indicted the dealer Hollinshead in a United States District Court for conspiracy to transport stolen goods to the value of $5,000 or more. Guatemala also filed a complaint for recovery of personal property and damages in a state court of California. The usual problem in such cases is the identification of the property, since many sites have not been excavated and the finds are not numbered or recorded. It was fortuitous that in this instance the stela had been documented. The theft was not committed in the United States, but in Guatemala and was thus a crime only under Guatemalan law. However, the transportation of the stolen property in the United States was a federal crime. There was also a suggestion that some diplomatic pressure was put on the United States. The case also raised the issue of the conflict of laws according to which one state will generally not enforce the penal laws of another state.

The Hollinshead[10] case was unusual, as it involved an archaeological item that had been well recorded, and registered as a Guatemalan national monu⁄

ment. Guatemala's ownership of the stela was uncontested. The court received expert testimony on the law of Guatemala regarding artifacts such as Macha-quila Stela 2. Under that law, all such artifacts are the property of the republic, and may not be removed without permission of the government. The court found overwhelming evidence that the defendants knew that it was contrary to Guatemalan law to remove the stela, and that the stela was stolen. However it was not even necessary for the government to prove that the appellants knew the law of the place of theft. The appellants' knowledge of Guatemalan law was relevant only in its bearing upon the issue of their knowledge, beyond a reason-able doubt, that the stela was stolen. The case served as a precedent for the McClain case, which took this principle even further.

In the McClain case[11] in 1977, the defendants were indicted before the United States District Court for the Western District of Texas for conspiracy to violate, and for violation of the National Stolen Property Act.[12] The Court of Appeals Circuit Judge Wisdom held that the Act could properly apply to illegal exportation of artifacts declared by Mexican law to be the property of the nation. The defendants were convicted of conspiring to transport and of receiv-ing through interstate commerce certain pre-Columbian artifacts (terracotta figures and pottery, beads, and a few stucco pieces) with the knowledge that these artifacts were stolen. The articles had not been registered with the Public Register of Archaeological and Historical Zones and Monuments of the Re-public of Mexico, or with any government register, and were exported without a licence or a permit from Mexico into the United States. In fact a government expert testified that some of the items in question were from Guatemala, Hon-duras, Panama, and Costa Rica, and that some were fakes.

The National Stolen Property Act (NSPA) prohibits the transportation 'in interstate or foreign commerce [of] any goods . . . of the value of $5,000 or more', with knowledge that such goods were 'stolen, converted or taken by fraud'. The Act also subjects to criminal liability 'whoever receives, conceals, stores, barters, sells, or disposes of any goods . . . of the value of $5,000 or more . . . moving as, or which are part of, or which constitute interstate or foreign commerce, knowing the same to have been stolen, unlawfully converted, or taken . . .'. The case turned on whether the pre-Columbian antiquities in question, exported from Mexico in contravention of that country's law, were knowingly 'stolen' within the meaning of the National Stolen Property Act.

The government presented no evidence as to how and when the artifacts were acquired in Mexico, nor as to when the pieces were exported. However the defendants did not dispute that the artifacts were illegally exported from Mexico. The government contended that the pre-Columbian artifacts were stolen from the Republic of Mexico; and that Mexico owned these objects despite the probability or possibility that the defendants, or their vendors, acquired them from private individuals or 'found' them – for example, by accident in overturning the soil or digging at archaeological sites on private property in Mexico.

One of the appellants' contentions was that the application of the National Stolen Property Act to cases of mere illegal exportation constituted unwarranted federal enforcement of foreign law. They argued that the word 'stolen' could not include the pre-Columbian artifacts seized in this case, for there was no evidence showing that the artifacts had been taken without consent from private individuals or that the artifacts had been in the possession of the Republic of Mexico. Mexican legislative declarations of 'ownership' of pre-Columbian artifacts were, the appellants said, not enough to bring the objects within the protection of the NSPA. The appellants argued that this United States statute employed the term 'stolen' to cover only acts which resulted in the wrongful deprivation of rights of 'ownership', as that term is understood at common law. The court however held that the question posed was not whether the federal government would enforce a foreign nation's export law, or whether property brought into this country in violation of another country's exportation law is stolen property. The question was whether America's own statute, the NSPA, covered property which was purportedly government-owned, yet potentially capable of being privately possessed when acquired by purchase or discovery. The court examined Mexican law and rejected the appellants' arguments, in line with the 1972 declaration by the Mexican government that *all* pre-Columbian artifacts were owned by the republic.

The court held that a declaration of national ownership was necessary before illegal exportation of an article could be considered theft, and the exported article considered 'stolen', within the meaning of the National Stolen Property Act. Such a declaration combined with a restriction on exportation without consent of the owner, in this case Mexico, was sufficient to bring the NSPA into play.

On a further appeal in 1979 the court upheld the conviction for conspiracy to receive, conceal and/or sell stolen goods contrary to the NSPA. The 1972 Mexican Act was clear and unequivocal in claiming ownership of all artifacts, and the NSPA applied to encroachments upon legitimate Mexican ownership, even though the goods may never have been physically possessed by Mexican agents.

The implication for the return of cultural property was considerable because criminal law was being brought to bear on illicit export of foreign cultural property.

This did not go down well with the museum establishment, nor with the many lawyers and academics who have not ceased to criticize it. The ripples it has caused have extended even beyond the particular circumstances of that one case. It is now unnecessary to prove the particular provenance of specific imported objects; or to show that they were stolen from a particular museum or archaeological site.

The strength of feeling against the case was perhaps best reflected in the *amicus curiae* brief which was submitted in the course of the appeal case by the American Association of Dealers in Ancient, Oriental and Primitive Art. It stated:

> In essence, the decision [of this case] has the extraordinary effect of converting the importation into the United States of art works exported without authorization from another country – an act never before regarded as culpable under the law of the United States – into a criminal violation of a federal statute. . . . The livelihood of the members of the association will be drastically affected if the convictions are upheld. Merely by dealing in art works that have originated – albeit many years earlier – in countries whose laws include broad declarations of national ownership in art, they will be open to charges of receiving and transporting stolen property in violation of federal criminal law.
>
> The case also has broad significance for the public at large. The art institutions of the United States have been able to assemble and exhibit ancient, oriental and primitive art only because it has been entirely lawful under United States law to collect such material, whether or not it was exported from another country in compliance with that country's export restrictions. Indeed, almost all nations which are the source of such art have traditionally attempted to curb the outflow of art by rigid export restrictions, coupled in many cases with broad claims of dominion or ownership of all such art within their territories. Thus far, the United States has refused to accede to the pressure from these art-exporting nations to make it illegal to bring into the United States all art objects exported in violation of their laws. While the United States has been willing to take steps through treaty and statute to discourage the importation of ancient art in select crisis situations, it has not been willing to deprive its museum-going public of the enjoyment of a wide range of ancient, oriental and primitive art on the basis of the policies of other governments.
>
> This long-standing policy of the United States would be reversed by a decision upholding the convictions below. The importation of ancient, oriental and primitive art into the United States would be halted and the flow of such art deflected to other art-importing nations such as West Germany, Switzerland, France and Japan. Even worse, insofar as the decision purports to give effect to Mexican law since 1897, objects of

art would now be treated as 'stolen' notwithstanding the fact that such a
novel interpretation did not obtain when they were originally introduced
into the United States. Thus, the lower court's decision would under-
mine a consistent and long-standing policy of the United States not only
for the future, but also retroactively. Museums which have painstakingly
assembled extensive collections of ancient, oriental and primitive art for
the benefit of the public of the United States would now stand branded
as receivers of stolen property. The great concern of the museum community over the implications of the decision below is illustrated by a
Statement of Concern unanimously adopted on January 6, 1976, by the
Council of the American Association of Museums, an organization representing 1,248 individual institutions. The statement concludes that
aside from its deleterious effect upon the functioning and staffing of museums, the interpretation of the National Stolen Property Act adopted
by the lower court will, if upheld, actually discourage the growing
cooperative efforts in international circles to find ways of regulating illegal traffic in cultural property.

These views were rejected by the court and, despite the dismay of the art world,
the McClain case greatly affects the illicit export of cultural treasures to the
United States. The effect of the case has been that the many countries who could
adopt sweeping 'ownership' statutes would have redress against all those who
illegally export cultural property from their territory to the United States. Moreover, it may refer retrospectively to objects unearthed long ago, since the critical
date will be that of export.

American criminal law can be used to enforce foreign export legislation,
but this is mitigated by the fact that some proof of knowledge of the foreign
legislation declaring ownership of cultural property is required.

Even before the first Court of Appeals decision in the McClain case the
Council of the American Association of Museums, an organization then representing 1,248 institutions, issued the following statement:

> The radical and novel interpretation of a domestic criminal statute,
> originally intended to deal with the problems of an altogether different
> nature . . . poses particular dangers both to American museums and to
> ongoing efforts at international cooperation. Such an interpretation may
> not only serve to brand as criminal those past actions that American
> museums have taken in good faith over the past three-quarters of a cen-
> tury but also calls into question the future ability of such museums to
> use large portions of their collections, painstakingly acquired over so

many years, for the educational and research purposes that constitute the very reasons for their being.[13]

The Court of Appeals recognized the potential impact of the case and opened its opinion in McClain I with the observation that: 'Museum directors, art dealers and innumerable private collectors throughout this country must have been in a state of shock when they read the news . . . of the conviction of the five defendants in this case.'[14] The McClain case is said to have put museum directors and curators as well as dealers and collectors in a quandary as to the inquiry they should make when offered antiquities from Mexico, or even from other countries. There was uncertainty as to whether the National Stolen Property Act would be applied against a museum director or dealer or collector who purchased an object subsequent to the McClain case.

In 1981 some significant recoveries were made of Peruvian objects which highlighted the need for a better framework for such cases in the future. At that time, although the UNESCO Convention relating to the return of cultural property had been ratified in 1972 by the US Senate, the implementing legislation to put the convention into effect had not yet been enacted. In particular there were a number of successful restitutions of Peruvian cultural property intended to go back to a new National Museum of Archaeology and Anthropology in Lima. For instance, in January 1981, US customs officials at Dulles Airport seized 154 pre-Columbian objects with a value of $288,000 from David Bernstein, who imported these as an American tourist from Peru. The basis for the seizure was a substantial under-declaration by Bernstein of the number and value of the collection of Incan gold and ceramics (dating from 900 BC to the sixteenth century). Further investigation by US customs led to the seizure of an additional 586 pieces from him in New York. The defendant was a dealer in pre-Columbian antiquities who had regularly travelled to Peru to obtain such pieces and bring them to the United States for sale. The Peruvian government, when contacted, requested the return of the objects. After extended negotiations an agreement was reached in early 1982 under which the defendant made a plea of guilty to a misdemeanour and almost all the seized pieces were handed over by the United States to Peru.[15] The sentence was a $1,000 fine, one year in prison (suspended) and one year of probation, and 200 hours of community service. The case was a routine one for making false statements to US customs officers and therefore resulted in a prosecution for fraud. The size of the recovery, totalling over $1,500,000, together with the public attention which is attracted, highlighted the problems of Peru in the loss of its cultural heritage.

Under the Peruvian law, in effect since 1929,[16] all pre-Columbian artifacts and monuments are declared to be the property of the nation of Peru, except those items in private collections at the time the law was enacted which were registered with the Peruvian government within a one-year period following the opening of the register. The law also prohibits the removal of any such objects from Peru without government permission. Although the law permits these objects to be used by private individuals within the country and such user rights can be sold and purchased, sales to non-residents of Peru are prohibited. A system for national inventory and registration of all such objects has been established. Similar legislation was enacted to cover artistic and historical objects from the colonial and republican periods of Peru's history, although such objects are not the property of the Peruvian state unless classified as monuments by official certification of the National Institute of Culture of Peru, or, in the case of structures, by the Minister of Education.

These laws represent a subject of major public interest in Peru, where cases of attempted smuggling of cultural objects, damage to and desecration of archaeological sites and recovery of stolen patrimony are frequently reported. The wealth of Peru's archaeological and cultural resources has become a matter of national pride. The recovery of a large number of high quality pre-Columbian objects in the Bernstein case was marked by a reception at the Peruvian Embassy in Washington which included a formal transfer of the objects by US officials and a display of some of the recovered objects.

Another significant recovery occurred in May 1981, when Sotheby Parke Bernet held its twice-yearly auction principally featuring religious paintings from South America. The bulk of these paintings originated in Peru, where the ancient Inca capital of Cuzco had been a centre of religious artistic workshops during the Spanish colonial period. It has been estimated that during the three hundred years of Spanish domination, over one million paintings were produced in the workshops of Cuzco for churches and private homes throughout the Spanish colonies of South America. A great part of this national heritage can still be found in Lima and in the churches, museums and convents of the Peruvian mountains. These paintings and related sculpture and furniture have become popular as objects of art commerce only in recent years. As prices have risen, so has the number of thefts from churches and museums in the Peruvian mountains.

When the Sotheby auction was announced, seven of the paintings to be offered were identified as stolen from museums in Cuzco and Arequipa. When Peru advised that the pieces were stolen, Sotheby's withheld them from the auction and notified the consignors of Peru's claim. A Sotheby's spokesman indicated that this accorded with its normal practice to respect the claim of a third party asserting ownership and to hold the disputed pieces until the parties can resolve their disagreement. Sotheby's also indicated that, if a dispute could not be resolved, it would refer the matter to the New York courts in an inter-pleader action for resolution.[17] In each of the cases raised by Peru, however, it was possible to determine the ownership of the piece without further legal action, and six paintings were ultimately returned to Peru.

In 1981 the United States also agreed to consider the execution of an agree-ment with Peru covering many of the same points as the Mexican treaty. The Agreement Respecting the Recovery and Return of Stolen Archaeological, Historical and Cultural Properties was signed in Lima on 15 September 1981 (see Appendix VI).[18]

As it was an executive agreement and not a treaty, the accord between the United States and Peru could not change existing provisions of either United States or Peruvian law. Therefore the agreement, unlike the Mexican treaty, did not include provisions authorizing the United States to bring legal actions on behalf of Peru. Nevertheless, the agreement did commit each country to 'employ the legal means at its disposal to recover and return from its territory stolen archaeological, historical and cultural properties that have been removed from the territory of the [other country]'. The agreement defined 'archaeological, historical and cultural properties' to include pre-Columbian and colonial art objects and artifacts 'that are, pursuant to the laws of the respective Parties, the property of federal, state or municipal governments . . . or of religious or-ganizations [for whom the governments act]'. Each party agreed to inform the other of cultural property stolen from it, and if so informed, to 'take such actions as may be lawful and practicable to detect the entry of such objects into its territory and to locate such objects within its territory'. If such objects were located, the party locating them would return the same if it 'obtains the necessary legal authorization', and otherwise 'shall do everything possible to protect the legal rights of the requesting Party and facilitate its bringing a private action for return of the property'. All expenses incident to the return of such property would be borne by the requesting party.

With respect to its international commitments, in 1972 the United States Senate ratified the 1970 UNESCO Convention on Cultural Property. It in-cluded one reservation and six understandings, one of which stated that the United States reserved the right to determine whether to impose export controls along with a stipulation that the Convention was neither self-executing nor retroactive. It was only after considerable political debate, lasting ten years, that the Convention on Cultural Property Implementation Act[19] (Cultural Property Law) was passed in 1982 (see Appendix VIII) to implement action as embodied in the 1970 Convention. In particular, Article 9 of the UNESCO Convention provided that a state 'whose cultural patrimony is in jeopardy from pillage of archaeological or ethnographical materials may call upon [other par-

ties to the Convention] to participate in a concerted international effort to determine and to carry out the necessary concrete measures, including the control of
exports and imports and international commerce in the specific materials concerned'. It had been the long bitter debate about how the United States should
implement Article 9 (which provided for the adoption of import controls) that
had stalled the enactment of the relevant bills until 1982.

Some extraneous pressures were applied to the United States. Peru and
Turkey refused archaeological permits to US expeditions in retaliation for the
depletion of national treasures by US buyers, and other South American states
also threatened to forbid US archaeological expeditions unless affirmative action
was taken against the illicit market in Incan and Mayan treasures.

The US State Department's position was that while the United States
'would not agree to a comprehensive system of import controls applicable to all
cultural property', it recognized that 'it is in the national interest of the United
States to help preserve the record of past civilizations. The US art market is a
major consumer of pillaged treasures. To the extent it provides an incentive for
clandestine excavations and despoliation we have a responsibility to act.' This
position was supported by art historians and archaeologists.

The central provision of the Cultural Property Law[20] is Section 303. It
provides that the US President may respond to the request of a 'state party' (any
nation which has ratified, accepted or acceded to the UNESCO Convention)
by entering into agreements to impose import restrictions on specified archaeological or ethnological material. As a prerequisite to such an agreement, however, Section 303(a) provides that the executive must first determine: (1) that the
cultural patrimony of the state party is in jeopardy from the pillage of the material
in question; (2) that the state party has taken measures consistent with the
UNESCO Convention to protect its cultural patrimony; (3) that the imposition of the import restrictions 'if applied in concert with similar restrictions
implemented, or to be implemented, within a reasonable period of time by those
nations individually having a significant import trade in such materials, would
be of substantial benefit in deterring a serious situation of pillage'; (4) that
remedies less drastic than the application of the restrictions are not available; and
(5) that the application of the restrictions is 'consistent with the general interest
of the international community in the interchange of cultural property among
nations for scientific, cultural, and educational purposes'.

The requirement of concerted international effort is then repeated in Section
303(c), which specifically denies the President the authority to enter into an
agreement to impose import restrictions under Section 303 unless the condition
of concerted action is satisfied. Finally, Section 303(d) provides for suspension
of any agreement if the President determines that a number of the parties with

significant import trade in the relevant material have not within a reasonable time implemented import restrictions similar to those imposed by the United States or are not 'implementing such restrictions satisfactorily, with the result that no substantial benefit in deterring a serious situation in the state party concerned is being obtained'.

However, the safeguards provided by Section 303, concerning concerted international effort, are partly qualified by Section 304, which provides that, in an 'emergency condition', the President may impose import restrictions on archaeological or ethnological material without the requirement of a concerted international effort. As defined by the Act, archaeological or ethnological material which entails an 'emergency condition' is:

(1) a newly discovered type of material which is of importance for the understanding of the history of mankind and is in jeopardy from pillage, dismantling, dispersal, or fragmentation;

(2) identifiable as coming from any site recognized to be of high cultural significance if such site is in jeopardy from pillage, dismantling, dispersal or fragmentation which is, or threatens to be, of crisis proportions; or

(3) a part of the remains of a particular culture or civilization, the record of which is in jeopardy from pillage, dismantling, dispersal or fragmentation, which is, or threatens to be, of crisis proportions.

The Cultural Property Law, as the comprehensive statement of US policy on the importation of cultural properties, reflected the long effort of Congress to balance the sharply differing views of archaeologists and anthropologists, art dealers and collectors, museum directors, the academic community, and the bureaucrats from the State and Justice Departments, the United States Information Agency and the Customs Service. It had therefore sought to limit to the most exceptional circumstances the powers of the US government in unilaterally barring the import of cultural property. It had been argued that otherwise an import embargo by the United States alone would simply have deflected archaeological and ethnological art to alternative foreign markets, and would have been futile in preserving art elsewhere, but would penalize American museums. The legislation had its critics for its failure to satisfy fully the original desire for compromise. This was because on the one hand the requisite of concerted international action (in Section 303) in order to bar importation could be excessively stringent; on the other hand this was offset by the provision (in Section 304) which permitted an emergency implementation of import restrictions without a concerted international effort.

Under the Cultural Property Law, however, there is a provision under which a foreign state party may be precluded from asserting a claim. The law does not apply if articles have been in the United States for a minimum of ten consecutive years and if they were on public display for at least five of those years, or if notice of their location has been received or should have been received by the foreign nation during that time (in Section 312(C)). Moreover, the 1970 UNESCO Convention has been interpreted by the 1982 Act in such a way that recovery and return of cultural property illegally exported will take effect only when the items have been specifically documented and identified.

In the face of misgivings about the Cultural Property Law, there has been one further development in the United States which has been criticized by lawyers as taking the restriction of importation of cultural property too far, and far beyond what was envisaged by the Cultural Property Law.

On 5 October 1982 a customs directive on the Seizure and Detention of Pre-Columbian Artifacts was made.[21] It is primarily intended to discourage and deter the importation of pre-Columbian artifacts from Peru and Mexico because those countries have enacted laws vesting ownership of such items in their governments and because the United States has entered into agreements with those countries to assist in recovering such items. The directive also inhibits the importation of pre-Columbian artifacts from every other Latin American country that has enacted similar legislation vesting ownership of pre-Columbian artifacts in its government. The customs service describes the background to its actions in the following way:

> In order to protect their national heritage from being plundered by treasure hunters and unscrupulous dealers and collectors, several South and Central American countries have passed laws which give title to the government to all pre-Columbian art which was unexcavated before a certain date. The unauthorized excavation and exportation of these items are illegal in these countries and, because of the claim of ownership, constitute theft.[22]

Thus the importation of pre-Columbian artifacts to the United States has been tightened up so as to make the issue of return less likely in the future. In effect the United States customs has created an embargo on ancient art coming into the United States from countries asserting legislative ownership of such art.

The customs service has justified this policy as a bureaucratic implementation of the McClain case. In practice the application of the customs policy has gone even further than the McClain case, with proof of knowledge (*scienter*) of the existence of a foreign ownership law accepted at a lower level. Nor are there time limitations in the application of the customs policy. It has been challenged as even going beyond the UNESCO Convention and the intentions of Congress in passing the Cultural Property Law, which included the replacement of the National Stolen Property Act in implementing United States policy in this area.

It is alleged that the customs service has exceeded its statutory authority. Without a federal law to prohibit imports, there should be no right to deny entry even in the event of illegal export. It is said that the customs policy goes beyond the earlier 1972 statute concerning illegally exported pre-Columbian sculpture, which covers only monumental or architectural sculpture or murals. The customs policy is being applied to all pre-Columbian art, and it has even been suggested (Fitzpatrick, pp. 813, 864–5) that the customs service might go beyond South and Central American countries in enforcing foreign ownership laws, although there is no practical evidence of this as yet.

Under the policy established by Congress in the Cultural Property Law, the executive must carefully investigate the facts and determine among other things whether import restrictions on ancient or ethnological art, if applied in concert with similar restrictions implemented by other major art-importing nations, would be of substantial benefit in deterring a serious case of pillage. Under Congressional policy, it is only on this basis that the importation of ancient or ethnographic art will be restricted. Under customs policy, on the other hand, the importation of ancient art will be restricted simply on the basis that it is pre-Columbian and that the nation of origin asserts a legislative claim of ownership. According to a customs service advisory memorandum (in 1977)[23] a number of Central and South American countries, including Costa Rica, Panama, Mexico, British Honduras and Peru, directly vest ownership of antiquities in the government; in the case of Columbia, El Salvador and Honduras, illegally exported antiquities become the property of the nation.

The 1982 customs directive states that pre-Columbian items which are improperly declared or undervalued should be seized and the Office of Investigations immediately notified. The Office of Investigations should determine the country of origin and, if the items are of Peruvian or Mexican origin, notify the cultural attaché of the appropriate embassy. If the embassy requests the return of the object, the request should be treated as a petition for relief by an interested innocent party having ownership of the goods, and as a general rule will be granted. However, return of any of the items must await criminal proceedings or forfeiture if challenges are made by the importer as to ownership.

The directive also provides that if the importer acknowledges that he is aware of 'the foreign law' or there is other evidence of such knowledge 'consideration should be given to criminal prosecution pursuant to 18 USC 2314 in accordance with *US* v. *McClain* . . .'. Further, 'the articles may be seized as evidence of a crime'.

If it is determined that the items are *not* of Peruvian or Mexican origin but are from another South or Central American country claiming ownership, the foreign country's cultural attaché should be advised of the importation. In such situations, 'if the foreign country wishes to assert a claim to the article, inter-pleader should be considered unless a National Stolen Property Act or customs violation was involved . . .'. In the latter case, the articles should be seized pending criminal proceedings.

The practical results of the development of a customs policy have been felt in effecting the return of cultural property. For instance, in 1978 an indictment was filed[24] against Daniel Weiner in the Eastern District of California, charging violations of both the National Stolen Property Act and Section 545, and seeking forfeiture of pre-Columbian art valued in excess of $100,000, which was alleged to have been brought illegally into the United States from Panama, Peru, Costa Rica and Mexico. The Weiner case was settled with a guilty plea and the return of the objects in question to their putative countries of origin.

Early in 1981, Miami customs detained Peruvian antiquities which David Goldfarb sought to import into the United States. He was apparently handling the antiquities in good faith and made full disclosure to customs. Customs was apparently satisfied that he had no knowledge of any Peruvian laws claiming ownership of pre-Columbian antiquities. Nevertheless, customs continued to detain the antiquities for several months and then filed an interpleader action in the federal court[25] in which it joined Peru and the importer as defendants and, in effect, asked the court to determine who was entitled to the antiquities. Faced with the prospect of long and costly litigation, the defendant settled the case by returning the antiquities to Peru.

There have been calls by academics and lawyers to reverse the effects of the McClain case by statute and for the customs policy to be applied in a restrained fashion consistent with the intentions of Congress as evidenced in the Cultural Property Law. However, it could be said that the US customs policy is being applied in the true spirit of the UNESCO Convention, and that in practical terms it represents simply the most effective method of returning illicitly, and contemporarily, removed cultural property to its place of origin. As such it is the correct model for regional and international co-operation. The pre-emptive conduct of US customs men ensures the least impediment to the return of cultural treasures. To date this has been confined to pre-Columbian objects from Central and South America.

As far as its own 'cultural patrimony' is concerned, the United States has in contrast with the United Kingdom concentrated its legislation on indigenous art. Congress has passed laws to preserve, restore and maintain the 'historic and cultural environment of the nation'.[26] However, this is confined to historically, architecturally or archaeologically significant objects on lands owned or controlled or acquired by the government. It does not cover all works of cultural interest to the United States, and is limited to works of art either created by American artists or concerning American topics – so that, for instance, the Statue of Liberty would be included. There is provision for an inventory system to catalogue protected cultural objects and prohibit the transfer, sale or alteration of property without the consent of the Advisory Council on Historic Preservation.[27]

In Canada in the past the loss of its heritage to foreign buyers was thwarted by the *ad hoc* purchase of items by the government when Canadian museums lacked the resources to keep collections together. In 1922 a national museum policy with the provision for an emergency purchasing fund was implemented. Among other things this fund retrieved the private Speyer collection of Canadian Indian artifacts from West Germany (Figs. 40–5) between 1973 and 1974. However, these were only interim measures, and legislation on export control was necessary.

The 1975 Cultural Property Export and Import Act of Canada, which implements the 1970 UNESCO Convention on Cultural Property, came into force on 6 September 1977. The Act governs the export of cultural property from Canada and the import into Canada of cultural property illegally exported from foreign states. This federal legislation seeks to ensure that the best examples of the nation's cultural, historic and scientific heritage are preserved in Canada. Specific protection is given to objects worth more than Can. $500 which are made by or relate to the aboriginal peoples of Canada. The Act also aims to protect the legitimate interests of foreign states concerned with the preservation of their own heritage in movable cultural property, where 'foreign cultural property' means any object specifically designated by that country as being of archaeological, prehistorical, artistic, literary or scientific importance.

The instrument used to establish these provisions is the Canadian Cultural Property Export Control List. Items falling within the Control List are subject to control under the Act. The export of an object falling within the Control List can be postponed if a person denied an export permit appeals against the decision and the Canadian Cultural Property Export Review Board decides that a reasonable delay period should be created. The Review Board is equally representative of Canadian custodial bodies, art dealers and collectors. This delay period enables interested public authorities and custodial institutions in Canada to purchase the object at a fair market price as determined by the Review Board.[28]

Figs. 40–45. In 1922 an emergency purchasing fund was implemented in Canada which enabled the repatriation of Canadian cultural treasures including the private Speyer collection of Canadian Indian Ethnography from West Germany. It is now kept in the Canadian Museum of Civilization in Ottawa. This collection consisted of hundreds of objects of great diversity, including the following items: (40) pipe bowl; (41) mittens; (42) moccasins; (43) saddle; (44) container; (45) pouch.

If the object is not purchased within the delay period, an export permit must be issued.

The Act followed the precedent of other countries, such as France and the UK, which have adopted similar legislation by defining objects which form part of the protected cultural heritage in such a way as to include not only indigenous objects but objects of foreign provenance.

The Control List thus covers items of cultural property situated in Canada without regard to their place of origin or the nationality of their creator, but which are none the less regarded as important to the cultural heritage of Canada. The major criticism was that as the Control List included works of foreign origin this would inhibit trading on the international market.

The Act was designed to ensure the co-operation of collectors and dealers in Canada. Experience in other countries has indicated that without their co-operation no system of export control will work smoothly, efficiently and fairly. Prior to its consideration by parliament, representatives of the various interested groups, such as the custodial institutions, collectors and the trade, were consul-ted about the proposed control system. There was general agreement that the legislation was fair and designed to protect the legitimate interests of all.

In the debate on the second reading of the bill the Secretary of State said:

> The movement of cultural property from one country to another can no longer be a casual and informal matter. Just as I believe that the Cana-dian government has a responsibility to act as a guardian of the heritage of Canadians, I also believe that this responsibility extends to the cul-tural heritage of mankind. During the negotiations to repatriate the Speyer collection of Canadian Indian ethnography from West Ger-many, to which I referred earlier, it was axiomatic that the West Ger-man authorities should be kept informed of our intentions. In fact, they facilitated our obtaining this important collection for Canada. I think hon. members would agree that we should not become a point of entry for illicit traffic in cultural goods.[29]

In recognition of world concern about illicit traffic in cultural property, the Act prohibits the import into Canada of any cultural property illegally exported from a country which is a party with Canada to an international agreement preventing such traffic (Section 31(2)). At the request of the reciprocating state, the Attorney-General of Canada can institute an action in the Canadian courts to recover the property.

Canada's application of the UNESCO Convention through its enabling legislation is far more liberal in its approach than that of the United States. A simple request from the country of origin is sufficient to bring the Convention into operation. However, the claiming country must compensate innocent purchasers or holders of such property before the property is confiscated and returned.

In March 1981, the first request was received from a foreign government for the return of cultural property which had been illegally exported. The Mexican government requested the return of two pre-Columbian statuettes which had been illegally exported from Mexico and which were subsequently forfeited under the Customs Act because they had been falsely described. In keeping with the Cultural Property Export and Import Act, the statuettes were delivered to the Mexican embassy in Ottawa.

Despite the progress that has been made in the North American context and while the American penal law has been applied through the National Stolen Property Act to deter illicit trafficking, such cases do not necessarily result directly in restitution of the property in question. In the case of *United States* v. *Hollinshead*, while the United States government obtained a criminal conviction and fine of $5,000 the Guatemalan government pursued and settled a civil action taking five years to obtain the return of the Mayan stela, said to be worth at least $200,000. The McClain case, although it resulted in a criminal conviction, involved many small and not specifically described archaeological objects, and no civil action was brought actually to recover these items.

In the United States, then, cultural returns have been effected by civil actions, bilateral agreements and inter-museum arrangements. Civil actions, although lengthy and expensive, have the advantage that the claim need only prove ownership, without the proof of knowledge that the property is stolen, as required under the criminal law. Criminal prosecutions have acted as a deterrent in illicit trafficking, but were not directly responsible for achieving returns.

Even where laws exist restricting the entry of illegally exported material and both states are parties to the 1970 UNESCO Convention, recovery may not always be possible. In 1983 a legal case was commenced by the Canadian government in the Provincial Court[30] of Calgary over a Nigerian Nok terracotta human figure. Nok culture flourished in Nigeria between 900 BC and AD 200, and tests had shown the figure to be between 1,800 and 2,900 years old. The figure first appeared in the art world at an auction in Paris held in the summer of 1977. It formed part of a large collection of African antiques owned by Alfred Muller, a collector, and was priced at 25,000 francs – about £2,100. The figure had been imported into Canada in 1981 by Isaaka Zango, the defendant, who reported to customs officials to have it authenticated. He declared it to be worth £390,000. After endeavouring to take it to the Glenbour Museum of Calgary, Zango and Heller, both American citizens, and Kassam, a Canadian, were charged with having unlawfully imported cultural property into Canada, contrary to the Cultural Property Export and Import Act (1974–75–76) in contravention of Section 37 of the Act, and thereby committing an offence against Section 39(1)b of the Act.[31]

It is assumed that such sculptures were of some religious or political significance to members of the Nok culture. Dr Eyo, an internationally recognized authority on ancient Africa, testified that there were only four other such sculptures known to exist, all smaller in size. He further testified that the sculpture was a Nigerian antiquity, within the meaning of current Nigerian legislation.

To succeed on their motion for committal, the Crown had to adduce evidence on the following matters:

(a) That the object was 'foreign cultural property'.
(b) That there existed between Canada and Nigeria on 1 December 1981 a 'cultural property agreement', within the meaning of the Canadian legislation. 'Cultural property agreement' is defined thus in Section 31(1): 'cultural property agreement', in relation to a foreign State, means an agreement between Canada and the foreign State or an international agreement to which Canada and the foreign State are both parties, relating to the prevention of illicit international traffic in cultural property;
(c) That Nigeria, on 1 December 1981, was a 'reciprocating state', within the meaning of the Canadian legislation. 'Reciprocating state' is defined as follows in Section 31(1): 'reciprocating state' means a foreign state that is a party to a cultural property agreement.
(d) That the foreign cultural property was imported into Canada after the coming into force of the cultural property agreement between Canada and Nigeria.
(e) That the Nok sculpture was illegally exported from Nigeria.

The court was satisfied, on the evidence of Dr Eyo and Miss Eroku (a Nigerian government lawyer), that the Nok figure was 'foreign cultural property' within the meaning of Section 31(1) of the Cultural Property Export and Import Act. The definition contained in the Canadian legislation is as follows:

> 'foreign cultural property', in relation to a reciprocating State, means any object that is specifically designated by that State as being of importance for archaeology, prehistory, history, literature, art or science.

The court was also satisfied that there was evidence to support claims (b),

(c) and (d). As to illegal export there was considerable discussion and debate in the submissions of counsel on the constituent elements of the offence. The Crown argued, on the basis of Nigerian law, that it is now, and always was, an illegal act to export such artifacts from Nigeria.

Counsel for Heller argued that the illegal exportation must be shown to have occurred 'from and after the coming into force of the cultural property agreement' between Canada and Nigeria, namely 28 June 1978. Counsel for Zango advanced a similar proposition, and argued further that there must be some evidence that the antiquity was exported illegally from Nigeria at some time prior to 1 December 1981. He also argued that there was no evidence whatsoever as to when the exportation of the object from Nigeria took place. There was some evidence that the artifact was removed from Nigeria prior to 1977, as it was tested for authenticity in Paris that year.

The Canadian legislation brought into force the substance of the UNESCO Convention, dealing with the prevention of illicit traffic in cultural property (see Appendix XVII). Article 7(a) of the international convention to which Canada and Nigeria are parties specifically states that the convention only applies to cultural property 'which has been illegally exported after entry into force of this convention in the states concerned', and further, '(which has been) illegally removed from the state after the entry into force of this convention in both states'. Similar words are found in Section 7(b). The court therefore concluded that the meaning to be attached to the words 'illegally exported' must be restricted to that time following Canada's entry as a party to the international convention. Because of the lack of evidence on a constituent element of the offence charged, all three of the defendants were discharged.

The case went on appeal to the Queen's Bench,[32] which upheld the decision of the lower court in its findings that there was insufficient evidence regarding the expropriation of the sculpture from Nigeria. In this case, therefore, although Canada was a party to the 1970 UNESCO Convention and had imposed import regulations, the case for restitution was defeated because it could not be shown that illicit export had occurred after Canadian law came into effect. It highlighted the limitations of the 1970 UNESCO Convention in this respect, and brought into relief the difficulties in achieving cultural returns which exist on an international level.

CHAPTER SIX

INTERNATIONAL AND REGIONAL REGULATION

The second half of the nineteenth century saw the birth of archaeology from antiquarianism, history and geology, and the discovery of the ancient civilizations of Egypt, Assyria and Sumeria. Systematic archaeological techniques were introduced for excavation, field survey and conservation. More slowly there was what Seton Lloyd, formerly Professor of Archaeology at the University of London, called 'the birth of a conscience' regarding the expropriation of antiquities from other countries.

In the twentieth century the idea has emerged that cultural property is a matter of international concern, and is part of the 'heritage of mankind'.[1] Concern has centred around looting from and destruction of archaeological sites, the illicit traffic of art in the international market, and the return of cultural property. Controls have been sought to establish the protection of cultural property in time of war as well as peace.

Under the auspices of the United Nations agency, UNESCO, in the early 1970s the concept of the restitution of cultural property began to crystallize around two basic issues: the removal of such property as the result of the previous colonization of newly independent states, and the issue of the continued illicit worldwide traffic in art treasures. Because of the main direction in which such objects flowed this has inevitably became primarily an issue for Third World countries, in opposition to the more developed countries, and in particular for former colonial nations. This last aspect has continued to colour the approach to the return of cultural property. Although illicit trafficking in art treasures might be seen as a quite distinct matter, it is often dealt with alongside the issue of cultural return.[2] It could be strongly suggested that although these two matters may sometimes be linked, the resulting overlap in dealing with the problem of returning specific treasures is not necessarily helpful.

UNESCO's primary activities in this area are the making of recommendations, the passing of resolutions, and the drawing up of multilateral conventions.

Recommendations are adopted by the General Conference of UNESCO by a majority of member states, but serve only to indicate a preferred course of conduct without imposing any legal obligations. All member states are required to submit the recommendations to their own competent national authorities, and within a year to submit a report on actions taken on the basis of such recommendations.

In the sphere of the return of cultural property, or closely related matters, major recommendations have included:

The Recommendation on International Principles Applicable to Archaeological Excavations (New Delhi) 1956 (see Appendix XI). It particularly sought to restrict the trade in antiquities and the illicit export of archaeological finds, and to facilitate the recovery of objects from clandestine excavations or theft. It encouraged international co-operation through, amongst other things, the responsible and licit acquisition by museums, and also by bilateral agreements between member states.

The Recommendation Concerning the Protection at National Level of the Cultural and Natural Heritage (Paris) 1972. This is embodied in the Convention of the same name. Under cultural property is included monuments, groups of buildings and various sites. Works of cultural heritage are to be considered in their entirety as a homogeneous whole, and generally none of them should be dissociated from its environment.

The Recommendation Concerning the International Exchange of Cultural Property (Nairobi) 1976 (see Appendix XIII). Under cultural property here was included a far wider range of items: zoological, botanical and geological specimens, archaeological objects, objects and documentation of ethnological interest, works of fine art and the applied arts, literary, musical, photographic and cinematographic works, archives and documents. This recommendation sought to facilitate international co-operation in the circulation of cultural property between institutions. The development of exchanges was to accompany the extension of action against every possible form of illicit trading in cultural property.

The Recommendation for the Protection of Moveable Property (Paris) 1978 (see Appendix XIV). Moveable cultural property here was defined as all moveable objects which are the expression and testimony of human creation or of the evolution of nature and which are of archaeological, historical, artistic, scientific or technical value or interest; long categories are more specifically listed. It includes property belonging to the state or public bodies or to private bodies or individuals. Amongst other things steps should be taken to facilitate international exchanges, and international co-operation on the circulation of information about illicit trading in cultural property.

The Recommendation of the World Conference on Cultural Policies (Mexico) 1982 (see Appendix XV). After the Conference, attended by states' Ministers of Culture, the final report contained a number of general recommendations. Amongst others there was one to member states to initiate bilateral negotiations between the holding authorities and countries of origin with a view to returning cultural property (Recommendation No. 53). There was also a recommendation that UNESCO support world efforts for the recovery of national monuments and cultural property illicitly transferred to other countries; and promote its programmes for training and exchange of information on preservation of historical cities, and inform world public opinion on these matters (Recommendation No. 54). Only one specific recommendation was made in respect of a specific item of cultural property, and that recommended return of the Elgin marbles (Recommendation No. 55).

UNESCO resolutions are passed by the General Conference for the future implementation of international regulations, and have in the past concerned the preservation of cultural heritage. Under these resolutions the Director General is authorized to act on the organization's behalf and reports annually. For example, in 1976 one study concerned the legal questions involved in making international agreements for the exchange of original objects.

There have been several important international Conventions, including the Convention on the Protection of Cultural Property in the Event of Armed Conflict (Hague) 1954 (see Appendix XVI).

This convention was the first comprehensive international agreement for the protection of cultural property. It came into force in 1956 after the minimum necessary number of five states had ratified it. As at June 1987 seventy-five states had become a party to it. It is basically concerned with the protection of the respect for cultural property in time of war or armed conflict. In this convention cultural property was defined as: (a) moveable or immovable property of great importance to the cultural heritage of every people, such as monuments of architecture, art or history, whether religious or secular; archaeological sites; groups of buildings which, as a whole, are of historical or artistic interest; works of art; manuscripts, books and other objects of artistic, historical or archaeological interest; as well as scientific collections and important collections of books or archives or of reproductions of the property defined above; (b) buildings such as museums, large libraries and depositories of archives, and refuges intended to shelter, in the event of armed conflict, the moveable cultural property; (c) centres containing a large amount of cultural property to be known as 'centres containing monuments'.

The Convention provides, in general, for protection against theft, pillage or misappropriation of cultural property, and reprisal against or requisitioning of movable cultural property. In the Protocol to the Convention (see Appendix XVI), the parties undertake to prevent the exportation of cultural property from an occupied territory in time of war. If such property is however exported to a party state's territory from any occupied territory, directly or indirectly, it is to be taken into custody and returned after the war to the previously occupied territory. As at June 1987, only sixty-three states had become a party to the Protocol. The United Kingdom and the United States are non-parties to both Convention and Protocol.

The Convention on the Means of Prohibiting and Preventing the Illicit Import, Export and Transfer of Ownership of Cultural Property (Paris) 1970 (see Appendix XVII) was the culmination of attempts over many years to achieve international agreement on cultural protection and return. In 1933 a draft Convention on the Repatriation of Objects of Artistic, Historical or Scientific Interest which have been Lost, Stolen or Unlawfully Alienated or Exported was submitted to member states of the League of Nations but was not adopted. A draft Convention for the Protection of National Historic or Artistic Treasures was submitted to member states of the League of Nations in 1936, but was referred back for further study. A draft Convention for the Protection of National Collections of Art and History was drawn up in 1939 which would have applied only to objects individually catalogued as belonging to a state but which were stolen and unlawfully expatriated. This was never adopted because of the outbreak of war.

The 1970 Convention is the one which deals most directly with the return of cultural property, its concern being with illicit traffic. 'Cultural property' was given a very wide meaning, including property which on religious or secular grounds is specifically designated by each state as being of importance for archaeology, prehistory, history, literature, art or science. Article 1 provides that the categories shall include:

(a) rare collections and specimens of fauna, flora, minerals and anatomy, and objects of palaeontological interest;
(b) property relating to history, including the history of science and technology and military and social history, to the life of national leaders, thinkers, scientists and artists and to events of national importance;
(c) products of archaeological excavations (including regular and clandestine) or of archaeological discoveries;
(d) elements of artistic or historical monuments or archaeological sites which have been dismembered;
(e) antiquities more than one hundred years old, such as inscriptions, coins and engraved seals;
(f) objects of ethnological interest;
(g) property of artistic interest, such as:
   (i) pictures, paintings and drawings produced entirely by hand on any support and in any material (excluding industrial designs

and manufactured articles decorated by hand);

   (ii) original works of statuary art and sculpture in any material;

   (iii) original engravings, prints and lithographs;

   (iv) original artistic assemblages and montages in any material;

(h) rare manuscripts and incunabula, old books, documents and pub‑ lications of special interest (historical, artistic, scientific, literary, etc.) singly or in collections;

(i) postage, revenue and similar stamps, singly or in collections;

(j) archives, including sound, photographic and cinematographic archives;

(k) articles of furniture more than one hundred years old and old musical instruments.

This is a far longer list than that adopted in earlier UNESCO Conventions and Recommendations. In addition to being designated as cultural property and falling into a relevant category, the object must also have a sufficient connection to the state which is claiming interest in it, and must form part of its cultural heritage.

There is no apparent distinction between publicly or privately owned cul‑ tural property. The Convention seeks to protect the property at its source by preventing export, and by preventing import into other states. A system of export certificates is envisaged which would specify that the export of a cultural object is authorized. This part of the Convention deals with a state's own national obligations to safeguard its own cultural treasure (see Appendix XVII, Article 6). As to the state parties' international obligations (Appendix XVII, Article 7), each state undertakes to implement measures consistent with national legislation to prevent its museums and similar institutions from acquiring illegally exported cultural property. There is to be a total prohibition on the importation of an object stolen from a museum or from a religious or secular public monument or similar institution, provided that the object was documented on an inventory of that institution. States whose cultural patrimony is in jeopardy from the pillage of archaeological or ethnological materials may call on the other state parties to participate in a concerted international effort to carry out concrete measures including controls on exports and imports and trade of the objects in question (Appendix XVII, Article 9). When the state party which is the country of origin of the object requests the recovery and return of such stolen cultural property, the importing state is to take appropriate steps to recover and return it. State parties are also to facilitate the earliest possible restitution of illicitly exported cultural property, and to admit action for the recovery of lost or stolen items of cultural property brought by the rightful owners (Appendix XVII, Article 13).

The Convention came into force in April 1972. By late 1987 sixty states had become parties to it, including the United States, but the United Kingdom remains a non-party. It is non-retroactive in effect and state legislation is necessary to implement it. It therefore does not cover any acquisitions of important cultural property which have taken place before the Convention enters into force. It enters into force in respect of state parties three months after the deposit of its instrument of ratification, acceptance or accession (Appendix XVII, Article 21).

The Convention has come in for criticism. The United Kingdom has argued that its greatest defect is that it is not confined to items of greatest importance. There is no age limit on many of the items to be protected, and it has been argued that expressions such as 'rare collections and specimens of fauna, flora and objects of palaeontological interest' are not sufficiently precise. The United Kingdom was also not satisfied with the test that the Convention applies to establish sufficient connection between object and claimant state. There is no time limit for an object to have remained in a territory before a state may legitimately claim it for the national heritage. What is required is that the work be found in, created in, or have legitimately entered the state. In practical terms the Convention has encountered difficulties in operation because of the logistical difficulties of establishing the national inventories it calls for, and in reconciling national regulations with the obligations it embodies.[3]

The Convention Concerning the Protection of the World Cultural and Natural Heritage (Paris) 1972 (see Appendix XVIII) deals only with immovable cultural property, and for its purpose cultural heritage includes monuments, groups of buildings, and special sites of archaeological interest. Its aim is to establish international co-operation in conservation, and to that end stresses the status of cultural, and natural, property as a 'world heritage'.

In 1974 UNESCO required member states to submit special reports on the steps taken pursuant to its Recommendation and Convention Concerning the Protection at National Level of the Cultural and Natural Heritage (1972). As at October 1974, only twenty-two had been submitted on the Recommendation and twenty-three on the Convention. At the 1974 UNESCO General Conference in Paris the Legal Committee expressed its concern that too many member states had not submitted initial special reports (as required by the Constitution and Rules of Procedure concerning Recommendations and Conventions) on a number of instruments, including this Convention which dealt with a matter of considerable interest and importance to the organization. The United Kingdom[4] was one of the states which responded with a limited report on both Recommendation and Convention, although it is, in fact, a non-party to it.

In 1977 the World Heritage Committee considered the issues involved in implementing the World Heritage Act. A World Heritage List of properties forming a part of cultural and natural heritage was to be drawn up. Inclusion of cultural property was to be justified on the basis of unique artistic achievement; oustanding importance in terms of influence on subsequent developments; significance as an example of a type of structure; rarity; and historic significance. In detail these criteria, one or more of which should be satisfied, were listed as follows:

(i) the property should represent *unique artistic* achievements, *masterpieces* of the human creative spirit; for example, a monument such as Borobudur, a group of buildings such as Angkor Wat, or a site such as the Valley of the Kings;

(ii) the property should be of outstanding importance owing to its *influence,* over a span of time or within a cultural area of the world, *on subsequent developments* in architecture, monumental sculpture, gardens and landscape design, related arts, or human settlements; for example, the Pantheon in Rome, a group such as the Plaza of Puebla in Mexico, or a site such as the château and gardens at Vaux-le-Vicomte;

(iii) the property should be the most characteristic or the most significant example of a type of structure, the type representing an important cultural, intellectual, social, artistic, technological or industrial development: for example, a monument such as a Mayan pyramid, a group such as the central city of Leningrad or a site such as the walled city of Avila;

(iv) the property should be *unique, or extremely rare or of great antiquity* including *characteristic examples* of traditional styles of architecture, methods of construction, or human settlements, particularly when they are by nature fragile and likely to disappear as a result of irreversible socio-cultural or economic change: for example, an Indonesian long-house, the Dogon villages in Mali, or a site such as Machu Picchu;

(v) the property should be most importantly *associated* with persons, events, philosophies or religions of *outstanding historical significances*; for example, monuments such as the Church of the Nativity at Bethlehem, a group of buildings such as the Holy Places of Mecca and Medina or a site such as Cape Kennedy, the launching pad for man's first voyage to the moon.

In addition, the property should meet the test of *authenticity* in design, materials, workmanship, and setting. Authenticity is not limited to considerations of original form and function, but includes all subsequent modifications and additions, over the course of time, which in themselves possess artistic or historical value. Consideration should also be given to the state of preservation, the opportunities afforded for *scientific* investigation, and the training in problems of preservation.

The properties included under these criteria[5] are as disparate as one could imagine. Apart from its declaratory effect, it is difficult to evaluate the practical effect of such a Convention. The question of the movement of cultural property is not raised directly, since the convention deals only with what is classed as immovable property – although it does stipulate that parties are not to damage any cultural heritage on another state's territory. As at October 1987 sixty states had become parties to the Convention.

With a more direct bearing on the return of cultural property, it was proposed in 1978 to set up an Intergovernmental Committee with the task of 'seeking ways and means of facilitating bilateral negotiations for the restitution or return of cultural property to the countries having lost such property as a result of colonial or foreign occupation'. This was eventually to be called the Intergovernmental Committee for Promoting the Return of Cultural Property to its Countries of Origin or its Restitution in Case of Illicit Appropriation.[6] It was to consist of twenty member states of UNESCO elected by the General Conference at its ordinary sessions, having regard to geographical distribution, the representative character of states in relation to the contribution they could make to the matter, and effective rotation of membership. The Committee was to be a good offices and/or arbitration committee and was to promote co-operation and negotiations, especially of a professional nature, at bilateral, multilateral and regional levels.[7]

The Intergovernmental Committee on Return of Cultural Property has had three main sessions: the first between 1979 and 1980, the second between 1981 and 1982, and the third in 1983.

It has emerged that the issue of return of cultural property is not one on which many countries speak with one voice. For example, in 1979 the Committee considered a proposal submitted by Peru[8] and a number of Central and South American and Caribbean states. This was a study on the possibilities of providing compensation in the form of cultural property of a different origin and of corresponding value, in cases where the restitution of the cultural objects claimed is impossible or not in accordance with the wishes of the requesting country.

The UNESCO Committee concluded that there were inherent dangers in such an idea, and that the emphasis should remain on bilateral arrangements.

That the alternative of compensation was ever even mooted is remarkable as it appears to contradict the basic principles which underlie the recovery of cultural property.

Another step taken by the Intergovernmental Committee has been the setting up of projects to conduct cultural inventories. An example is the Experimental Project for the Inventory of Cultural Property in a region of Mali,[9] Bangladesh, and Western Samoa, carried out by ICOM, and reported in 1981. Other inventories have included African objects outside Africa published by ICOM, a Pacific islands inventory co-ordinated by ICOM, and Oceanic objects in Australian museums drawn up by the Australian National Commission for UNESCO, the first phase of which was published in 1980. A study has also been made of Oceanic cultural objects in American museums. There have been a number of published inventories regarding Oceanic material held in museums around the world: *Survey of Oceanian Collections in Museums in the United Kingdom and the Irish Republic* (1979), *Oceanic Cultural Property in Australia* (1980) and *Pacific Cultural Material in New Zealand Museums* (1982). Other ethnographic inventories have been prepared in Switzerland (1980), in Sweden, and in France, by the Musée de l'Homme. These inventories appear to have been useful in examining the respective museum structures in countries that have sought the return of objects, and in ascertaining the extent of exported cultural materials, through the compilation of local and foreign inventories.

Whether such very detailed inventories really can serve any great purpose in actually securing the return of cultural property is not clear, but such lists help to pinpoint the existence and location of major objects. They facilitate research, and may also help as a control in the illicit movement of objects. In effect an enormous 'cultural census' is being suggested by such inventory projects. They are regarded as tools of scientific research, which are useful for cultural analysis. It has even been pointed out that their elaboration is not necessarily linked to requests for the return of cultural property. One must consider whether it would not be more satisfactory initially to record major cultural objects under a very limited number of headings, since the national inventories of major holding nations such as France are expected to take decades to complete.

There have been other case studies of Ghana and Panama,[10] which set out all their major museums, and the nature of their collections and it is to be hoped that these studies will further the cause of attracting the attention of politicians and the community, and enlisting their support in seeking the return of the more important collections.

The second session of the Intergovernmental Committee on Return of Cultural Property took place in September 1981. In addition to the member states another thirty-eight attended as observers, and observers from five international governmental organizations, including Interpol, and seven international non-governmental organizations participated in the work of the Committee.[11]

In the course of this session, the representative of Ecuador reported on the case of 12,000 pre-Columbian objects illicitly exported to Italy which was then before the Italian courts and which had been brought to the attention of the Committee at its first session. While he expressed his appreciation for the collaboration received from the Italian government in this matter since the first session of the Committee, he also pointed out the extremely slow pace of the judicial process. A hearing had taken place at Turin in May 1981 and since the final hearing was foreseen for December 1981 he requested that the Chairman express the Committee's support of Ecuador's claim to the Italian Minister of Justice. He recalled that both Ecuador and Italy had ratified the 1970 Convention on cultural property.[12]

The ambassador and permanent delegate of Italy in turn made his declaration to the Committee:[13]

> The archaeological objects in question, illegally exported from Ecuador in 1974, arrived in Italy the following year and were sequestered by the public prosecutor in Genoa, who placed them under the legal custody of the Federico Lunardi Museum. These objects are still being held by that museum, in compliance with the wishes of the Ecuadorian authorities... pending the conclusion of the civil proceedings instituted in Genoa by the Ecuadorian authorities in order to establish their legal ownership.
>
> H.E. the Ambassador of the Republic of Ecuador in Italy and, subsequently, the Minister of Foreign Affairs of Ecuador, H.E. Mr Alfonso Herrera Valverde, the latter in a communication dated 13 May last (probably following the deliberations of the First New World Conference on Rescue Archaeology, referred to in [a] letter from Ambassador Abad Grijalva), in fact drew the attention of H.E. Mr Emilio Colombo, Minister of Foreign Affairs, to the problem. Mr Colombo replied to Mr Herrera Valverde on 6 June, assuring him that he had stressed the importance of a prompt and satisfactory solution to the matter with his colleague the Minister of Justice, as desired by the New World Conference. At the same time, however, he [the Italian Minister of Foreign Affairs] pointed out to Mr Herrera Valverde that as the civil action instituted by the Ecuadorian authorities was pending, the executive could not exercise pressure upon the judiciary. On the other hand, it was incumbent upon counsel for the Ecuadorian authorities to make every effort to ensure that the case be settled with the utmost despatch.

The Italian Government, for its part, feels that it has fully discharged its responsibilities.

Satisfaction has already been obtained in one important respect. The objects have been entrusted to the care of the Ecuadorian Consul in Genoa, who has been given leave to deposit them in a place of his choice. Since no action has so far been taken in this connection, it may reasonably be assumed that their deposit with the Federico Lunardi Museum in Genoa meets the concerns and satisfies the wishes of the Ecuadorian authorities at the present time, pending the conclusion of the legal proceedings taking place.

In 1983 the Turin court declared the objects to be the full and exclusive property of the Republic of Ecuador. It ordered that restitution should be made to Ecuador, and so this case, which was initially brought to the attention of UNESCO, was successfully resolved.

Also at this second session of the Intergovernmental Committee, a case of successful cultural return was reported. The representative of Yemen, in his statement concerning measures to promote bilateral co-operation, informed the Committee of the return to the National Museum at Sana'a by the Wellcome Institute of the United Kingdom of a collection of Himyarite antiquities; and he expressed his government's appreciation of this gesture on the part of the Institute and of the assistance offered by the United Kingdom National Commission for UNESCO.

It was also recorded that in July 1981 the Secretary-General of the Ethiopian National Agency for UNESCO forwarded to the Director-General a 'Note on Ethiopian Cultural Objects Abroad' prepared by the Ministry of Culture and Sports. This document concerns several types of objects which have left the country, some of them as long as four hundred years ago: coins, paintings, crosses, inscriptions, parchment rolls and above all manuscripts. A preliminary inventory of the location of these objects in various museums and private collections of Europe, North America and the Middle East was also provided. In addition, the matter of a standard form to be drawn up for requests for the return of, or restitution of, cultural property was considered.

The draft form was originally prepared by the UNESCO Secretariat and the International Council of Museums to implement a recommendation of the Intergovernmental Committee's first session (5-9 May 1980). The draft was then submitted to the International Committee at the second session (14-18 September 1981). The final version now in use was approved by the chairman together with the Committee's Final Report.

Its intended purpose is to facilitate bilateral negotiations. It is to provide a means of recording information relating to objects whose return may be requested, and is designed therefore to contain data and observations supplied by the competent authorities in both the requesting country and the country in which they are now held. It is to be used only in cases where bilateral negotiations already initiated have made unsatisfactory progress.

The form is divided into five main sections:

(a) background data on the object (i.e. type of objects, materials, etc.);
(b) references of legislation and regulation to prevent illicit traffic in cultural property;
(c) present status of the object (i.e. public or private etc.);
(d) suggested action (negotiations, proposals etc.);
(e) other observations.

The form, completed in triplicate, is to be sent to the Secretariat, Intergovernmental Committee for Promoting the Return of Cultural Property to its Countries of Origin or its Restitution in case of Illicit Appropriation, Division of Cultural Heritage.

To assist the relevant authorities and professional institutions of member states in the use of the standard form, a draft handbook providing guidelines for its use was later drawn up in 1983. There appears to have been some difficulty over the two key concepts of 'return' and 'restitution', especially in relation to transfers of ownership during the colonial period.

However, as at January 1984, only one standard form had been officially registered by the Intergovernmental Committee. It concerned a request from Jordan for the return of the sandstone panel of Tyche with the zodiac, now in the Cincinnati Art Museum. Sri Lanka had unsuccessfully attempted to submit a number of standard forms, but without indicating whether bilateral negotiations had taken place with the holding countries and whether these had proved to be unsuccessful. In September 1984, Greece adopted the use of the new UNESCO procedure in further pursuing its claim for the Elgin Marbles from Britain.

The procedure defined by the Committee was applicable as an essentially diplomatic process; it offered a recourse to the Committee's moral support (regarded as significant in the Turin–Ecuador case). If the holding country did not respond within a year, then it has been suggested that the Committee could extend its good offices to mediation or arbitration. This is where the inherent weakness lies, for there appears to have been no agreement as to the Committee's effective role. In practical terms, it has no coercive authority or persuasive weight. Some of the Committee members themselves have stated that it would not be possible to accept 'arbitration' by the Committee, for its role is only one of mediation and moral pressure.

At the third session of the Intergovernmental Committee in 1983, the importance of bilateral negotiations was stressed by a number of members including the United Kingdom observer.[14] He made a statement in which he pointed out that his country was a pluralistic society, with a great deal of institutional independence where powers of government were strictly limited. In formulating policy, two possibly conflicting considerations had to be taken into account: the aspiration of developing countries to obtain irreplaceable objects relating to their cultural heritage and the need for great, universal museums, created over a long span of years, to be maintained for the international community as a whole. The way to resolve this potential conflict lay in international and particularly bilateral cultural co-operation. He continued: 'the fact that the United Kingdom does not accept the principle of the return of cultural property except in cases of illegal acquisition does not mean that we are opposed in principle to the return of objects. Each institution is free to act as it wished within the confines of its statutes.' The return of objects was only one of a possible range of options which could be explored bilaterally. He ended by referring to the possibility of using bilateral aid programmes to provide technical co-operation in museum management and the corresponding techniques of conservation.[15]

This meeting closed on an optimistic note regarding the possibilities of bilateral negotiations (such as had successfully occurred between Iraq and the USA, between the Netherlands and Indonesia, Belgium and Zaire, and France and certain African countries), and its fourth venue was Delphi in Greece in the spring of 1985.

Another principal body which has dealt with the issue of the return of cultural property has been the General Assembly of the United Nations. The Assembly has no general legislative power, except on a very limited number of matters (which do not include cultural property); its resolutions are only recommendations to members. A number of its resolutions on this matter have been in the context of the colonial legacy.[16]

On 11 November 1977 the General Assembly adopted a resolution[17] which:

> 1. [Invited] all Member States to sign and ratify the Convention on the Means of Prohibiting and Preventing the Illicit Import, Export and Transfer of Ownership of Cultural Property, adopted by the General Conference of the United Nations Educational, Scientific and Cultural Organization on 14 November 1970;
>
> 2. [Called upon] all Member States to take all necessary steps to

prevent, on their territories, any illicit traffic in works of art coming from any other country, especially from territories which were or are under colonial or foreign domination and occupation;

3. [Affirmed] that the restitution to a country of its *objets d'art,* monuments, museum pieces, manuscripts, documents and any other cultural or artistic treasures constitutes a step forward towards the strengthening of international co-operation and the preservation and future development of cultural values.

More particularly, on 11 December 1980 the General Assembly[18] adopted two resolutions on the preservation and further development of cultural values. Both were recommended by the Third Committee (Social, Humanitarian and Cultural). Under resolution 35/128 on restitution and return of cultural and artistic property to its countries of origin, adopted without a vote, the Assembly commended UNESCO for the work it had done in this area, and requested it to intensify its efforts to help countries find suitable solutions to these problems.

The Assembly invited member states, in co-operation with UNESCO, to draw up systematic inventories of cultural property in their territories and abroad, and appealed to all states to take adequate measures to prohibit and prevent the illicit import, export, and transfer of ownership of such property. The Assembly requested the Secretary-General, in further co-operation with UNESCO, to take the necessary measures to alert and mobilize international public opinion, in particular through the United Nations information media.

It expressed the hope that the second World Conference on Cultural Policies, to be held in 1982, would devote considerable attention to the return and restitution of cultural property with a view to improving cultural co-operation. The draft resolution, sponsored by forty-six nations, was approved in the Third Committee without a vote.

On 27 November 1981, by a recorded vote of 109 votes in favour and none against, with thirteen abstentions, the General Assembly invited member states to take adequate measures to prohibit and prevent the illicit import, export and transfer of ownership of cultural property, and to put an end to the illicit trafficking of priceless *objets d'art* and museum pieces by all necessary measures within each country's jurisdiction with the full co-operation of courts and customs authorities.

It also appealed to member states to co-operate closely with the Intergovernmental Committee in concluding bilateral agreements, and renewed its invitation to member states to sign and ratify the 1970 Convention on Cultural Property.[19]

Following a vote that was taken on the resolution, the United States indicated that it opposed any wording that far exceeded the provisions of the 1970 UNESCO Convention, saying that its abstention on the resolution as a whole in no way affected United States support for the principles of restitution, but that it was opposed to any governmental obligation for restitution that went beyond the UNESCO Convention. On behalf of the member states of the European Economic Community, the United Kingdom said that they considered that UNESCO should be the place for discussion of the problem and that they fully supported the work of the Intergovernmental Committee.

On 25 November 1983, the General Assembly[20] called for increased efforts to achieve the return or restitution of cultural property to the countries of origin. The vote on resolution 38/34 was 123 in favour to none against, with thirteen abstentions (Austria, Belgium, Denmark, France, Federal Republic of Germany, Ireland, Israel, Italy, Luxembourg, Netherlands, Sweden, United Kingdom, United States). Under the resolution, the Assembly once more called on member states to draw up, in co-operation with UNESCO, inventories of cultural property in their territory and their cultural property abroad; appealed for the conclusion of bilateral agreements for the return of such property; endorsed the view that the return of such property should be accompanied by the training of key personnel and the providing of facilities for conservation and presentation; and invited all states to ratify the 1970 Convention.

It reaffirmed that restitution of such *objets d'art* contributed to the strengthening of international co-operation and the preservation of universal cultural values. The Assembly also appealed to member states to encourage the mass information media and educational and cultural institutions to work for greater and more general conscientiousness in this matter.

UNESCO and the Intergovernmental Committee were commended for their work in various areas including the development of infrastructures for the protection of movable cultural property and reduction of illicit traffic in cultural property.

The United Kingdom said it could not accept the principle that cultural property which, over the years, had been acquired freely and legitimately should be returned to other countries. It believed that the great international collections of works of art constituted a unique international resource for the benefit both of the public and of scholars. Nevertheless, the United Kingdom remained sympathetic to the wishes of countries who wanted to develop and improve their collections, and museums in Britain would be happy to collaborate with those countries.

In addition to the resolutions of UNESCO and the General Assembly, there have been some regional measures concerning cultural property.

In 1969 the Council of Europe sponsored the European Convention on the

Protection of Archaeological Heritage.[21] It provides that 'all remains and objects, or other traces of human existence, which bear witness to epochs and
civilizations for which excavations or discoveries are the main source or one of
the main sources of scientific information, shall be considered as archaeological
objects' (Article 1). It seeks to establish co-operation in the protection of archaeological heritage, and in particular to ensure that the protection of cultural, and
scientific, interest in archaeological objects shall not be prejudiced by the manner
of their circulation internationally. States are to ensure that museums and other
institutions under their control avoid acquiring archaeological objects from
clandestine or unlawful excavations. They are to restrict the movement of archaeological objects so obtained (Article 6).

There is however no obligation on state parties to the Convention to legislate
on the matters contained in it. Moreover the Convention is designed only to
suppress illicit dealing in archaeological objects, and nowhere is the question of
the return of such items specifically considered.

Principal among the international non-governmental organizations concerned with cultural property is ICOM (see Chapter 7). In 1977 the International Council of Museums, responding to the efforts of UNESCO, declared
that the reassembly of dispersed heritage through restitution or return of objects
which are of major importance for the cultural identity and history of countries
having been deprived thereof was now considered to be an ethical principle. It
appealed to all its members 'to help disinherited countries to constitute representative collections of their heritage and to facilitate bilateral governmental negotiations in this field'.[22] The ICOM Assembly subsequently decided to assist in the
restitution or return to their countries of origin of the most significant objects and
instructed an *ad hoc* committee set up for the purpose to study the various technical aspects of the question and in particular to define an ethical code on the
restitution or return of such objects.

It was reported in August 1983[23] that a Draft Convention on Offences
Against Cultural Property was also under preparation by the Council of
Europe. The draft text provides for co-operation among contracting parties with
a view to the prevention of offences against cultural property (both private and
public property) and the recovery of cultural property removed as the result of
such offences. The offences in respect of which the implementation of the Convention would be of a mandatory nature are: (i) thefts of cultural property; (ii)
appropriating cultural property with violence or menace; (iii) receiving of cultural property, pursuant to one of the offences listed above. However, the scope
of application could be unilaterally extended by a contracting party to other
offences, including unlawful exportation of cultural property. The draft text lays
down procedural rules concerning the restitution of cultural property found on

the territory of a contracting party after its removal from the territory of another contracting party as a result of an offence covered by the Convention and committed in the territory of a contracting party. The draft also contains provisions concerning the enforcement of the part of a foreign judgement ordering the restitution of cultural property, and concerning the extension of criminal jurisdiction of a contracting party to include offences committed outside its territory by one of its nationals or cases where the cultural property concerned belongs to that state or to one of its nationals or was originally found within its territory. This draft is more far reaching than any other convention on the subject, as it comes to grips directly with the legal problems concerning the return of cultural property. It remains to be seen whether such a convention is accepted or widely ratified. The possible enforcement of a foreign judgement is certain to be a controversial point.

Another regional group, the Organization of American States, has drawn up a Convention on the Protection of the Archaeological and Artistic Heritage of the American Nations (1976) (known as the Convention of San Salvador; see Appendix v). There are seven Latin American[24] states parties to the Convention, whose aim is to prohibit illegal export and import of cultural property. It stipulates that the exportation and importation of cultural property shall be considered unlawful unless the exportation is authorized by the state owning it. It encourages the registration of collections and of transactions by establishments carrying out sales and purchases of cultural property, and the prohibition of imports without appropriate certificates of authorization. It more significantly sets out the procedure for the actual restitution of cultural property which has been unlawfully exported. It particularly provides that if the laws of the state petitioned require judicial action for the recovery of foreign cultural property unlawfully imported or removed, such judicial action shall be instituted in the appropriate courts by the competent authority of that state. The petitioning state also has the right to institute appropriate judicial action in the state petitioned in order to bring about recovery of the property that has been removed and application of the pertinent penalties against those responsible (Article 11).

In 1976 a study[25] was prepared at the request of the Commission of the European Communities[26] regarding the means of correlating theft and illicit traffic in art. It suggested that for protection of cultural property to be effective there must be a total abolition of protection for purchasers. That is to say there must be restitution without compensation in all cases. However there has not been any indication that the EEC has taken up any of the effective measures since recommended.

Apart from international and regional measures, there has been some precedent for bilateral agreements, on the restitution of illicitly transferred cultural property provided by the United States–Mexico Treaty 1970 (see Chapter 5).

Of all the major art-importing countries the United States has been the most active in responding to the need to establish a régime of cultural return. It has not restrained the use of its criminal law in dealing with the illicit traffic of cultural property. Internationally there are problems of establishing criminal jurisdiction in the area of offences to cultural property. One international lawyer, J.M.C. Bassiouni, has drafted an International Criminal Code which would define the theft of 'national and archaeological treasures' as an international crime.[27] However, he admitted that although existing international agreements to protect cultural property may implicitly establish a duty to punish or criminalize and, at times, a duty to co-operate in investigating, prosecuting and punishing those who commit offences against cultural property, the conventions fail to make such statements explicit. In comparing the agreements on the protection of cultural property with other international criminal law conventions, one notes the absence of more specific or wide-ranging provisions on jurisdiction, extradition and judicial assistance and co-operation in penal matters.[28] Nevertheless, the existing international legal framework has served to highlight the issue of return, restitution or forfeiture of cultural property.

CHAPTER SEVEN

ART THEFT AND THE
ART MARKET

Linked with the difficulties of the protection of cultural property, and the issue of its return, is the broader problem of art theft and the very active worldwide traffic in stolen art objects, which include great antiquities or archaeological treasures.

The earliest known regulation of cultural property dates back to 1464, when Pope Pius II prohibited the exportation of works of art from the Papal States,[1] and there were subsequent papal laws governing archaeological excavations.

Art treasures, however, have always been part of the plunder of war. The origin of plunder for the glory of one's country has been attributed to Napoleon Bonaparte in his conquest of Europe and Egypt. Formal treaties were drawn up by Napoleon. For instance, the treaties of Milan and Campo Formio in 1797 resulted in the removal from Venice of a number of significant objects, including the famous group of four bronze horses from the front of the basilica, the Horses of San Marco (Fig. 46), which were paraded through the streets of Paris. The horses had been taken from Constantinople by Venice and before that had belonged to ancient Rome or Greece, and they rivalled the winged lion as the symbol of the Venetian Republic. Napoleon amassed great quantities of objects from all over Europe, particularly from Italy and Germany. After Waterloo, the English sought restitution of all the stolen works of art. This was fiercely opposed by the French, and especially Baron Dominique Vivant Denon, director of the Louvre, an Egyptologist who had been Napoleon's adviser on his Egyptian campaigns and is accredited with shaping the Egyptian collections.

The restitution programme was considered by the French to be the culmina-tion of Anglo-French cultural rivalry. As a result of English action, many art treasures were indeed restored, including the Horses of San Marco in 1815, and the masterpiece of Hellenic sculpture, the Laocoon group taken from Rome, which was returned to the Vatican. Many treasures, however, had been dis-persed or sold and so were lost to their countries of origin. Other items were impossible to return because they had actually been incorporated into another structure, such as the marble pillars from the cathedral of Aachen which had been incorporated into the Louvre. Many treasures therefore remained scattered and were never returned.

Fig. 46. The much-travelled four bronze horses of San Marco seen here unusually at ground level in the Palazzo Ducale, Venice. Normally high above the front of the basilica, they were restored yet again after the Second World War. At one time they were taken from Venice by Napoleon and paraded through the streets of Paris; before that, they had been taken from Constantinople by Venice; and originally they had belonged to ancient Rome or Greece!

In more recent times, Hitler's army during the Second World War re-moved large quantities of art treasures for the glory of the Third Reich. Hitler also sought to do this by a treaty for confiscating and safeguarding the objects in question. He had planned a great art gallery and museum in a model city to be built in Linz, provincial capital of Upper Austria. The treasures unearthed by the Allies at the end of the war were comparable with the great collections of the major museums in the world. They consisted of many thousands of fine paint-ings including ones by Rembrandt, Tintoretto, Velasquez, Leonardo da Vinci, and Rubens, sculpture, silver, archaeological relics, antique tapestries, furniture, oriental carpets and rare books, porcelain, silver, gold and stained glass win-dows. Much of this treasure was housed in a mansion called Karinhall on an estate owned by Goering, forty-five kilometres north-east of Berlin. Another main storehouse of treasures was the Bavarian castle of Neuschwanstein, which was found to hold over 6,000 items. In a bizarre extension of this wartime storing of stolen treasures, thousands were moved to a salt mine at Alt Aussee in Upper Austria. But much of the treasure looted by the Nazis was scattered all over the world, and proved much harder to restore than Napoleon's loot had been. It would take a great deal of detective work to track it all down. The upheaval and confusion at that time also presented the opportunity for collectors to act un-scrupulously. A notorious example was that of the case which emerged concern-ing the Dutch collector Pieter Nicolaas Menten, who murdered to enhance his collections, and whose story came to light in 1976, 30 years after the war, only as the result of an article in a Dutch newspaper, *De Telegraaf*, which publicized a forthcoming sale of 425 of his valuable paintings. The Dutch Supreme Court in The Hague in 1980 upheld a gaol sentence, but also ordered 157 paintings confiscated by the Dutch government in 1976 to be returned to Menten because it could no longer be proved that these paintings were stolen from his victims. There were undoubtedly numerous other instances of private looting, and in-stances of theft which could never be redressed. However there were cases after the war where paintings seized from private collections which had even passed into the hands of bona fide purchasers were none the less returned to their owners. For instance, a New York court in 1966[2] permitted recovery of a Chagall painting which the plaintiff had left behind in his apartment in Belgium as he fled the Nazis. Restitution overrode traditional property concepts where the property was private property and there was no act of state defence available to combine with bona fide purchase.

During the war many treasures were simply destroyed such as, for instance, the twenty-eight paintings, mainly from Bezekhik in Central Asia, kept in the Berlin Museum, which were totally destroyed by the Allied bombing of that city between 1943 and 1945. Others were simply lost or could not be traced, like the

Amber Room of Tsarskoe Selo, from the Summer Palace near St Petersburg. This consisted of fifty-five square yards of carved amber panels backed with silver. It was built for King Frederick Wilhelm I of Prussia, 'the Soldier King', who presented it to Peter the Great of Russia in 1717, and in 1755 it had been reconstructed in Catherine the Great's Summer Palace. It was captured by the Germans in 1942 and it reportedly disappeared in 1944 from the old royal castle in Königsberg after Allied bombing. The Russians have tried to trace this treasure but its whereabouts are unknown to the West, although there have been allegations that the Allies spirited it away through Weimar, now in East Germany. This type of loss was worldwide, as evidenced by the disappearance in China during the Second World War of a major palaeontological find, Peking Man, whose location remains unknown to this day. Many other treasures miraculously survived the ravages of war. Thus, despite the loss, destruction and dispersal of numerous objects, many thousands of European art treasures were returned by the United States after the war from their occupied zone. This was organized through the Art Looting Investigation Unit of the US Office of Strategic Studies. In addition, British experts seconded to the Monuments, Fine Arts and Archives section of the Restitution Control Branch of the occupying forces were also active in this task of restitution. Eighteen hundred repositories in mines, castles, churches, monasteries and remote villages were discovered in the American zone. Some of the major finds made in 1945 by the US Third Army were at the Siegen copper mine in Westphalia, the Kaiserode salt mine at Merkers in Thuringia (Figs. 47, 48, 49), the salt mine at Alt Aussee near Salzburg, and the salt mine at Bernterode in the Thuringia forest. Jewish archives and treasures from the Rosenthal collection in Amsterdam and the Frankfurt Rothschild family were also uncovered in the brick kiln of the town of Hungen. By 1951 over a million art objects and four million books were recovered, identified and restored (Figs. 50 and 51).[3]

A 1984 report indicated that several thousand objects are still stored in a fourteenth-century Carthusian monastery in Mauerbach, forty-eight kilometres from Vienna. They include paintings, books, manuscripts, coins, medals and household furnishings. These were given to Austria by US military forces in 1955 under the Austrian State Treaty which charged Austria with making 'every effort to return the works to the extent they had already not done so'. The Austrian 1969 Final Settlement of Heirless Property Law required Austria to publish a list describing the property and to return items provided the claimant could prove ownership at the time Austria was under Nazi rule. As most claimants had no documentation they were required to describe the works and to provide information about the date and place of confiscation. The law also stipulated that any property not returned to claimants or that remained un-

Fig. 47. The collection of Berlin Museum paintings discovered by the 90th Division US Third Army in the salt mine at Merkers, Germany, 15 April 1945. The American Commission for the Protection and Salvage of Artistic and Historic Monuments in War Areas (The Roberts Commission) was set up to return plundered art.

claimed would belong to Austria. It appears that very few paintings were given back under this law. The restitution issue in the Austrian context has given rise to interesting cases in the past such as that of the Austrian Czernen-Morzen family claim made in 1946 and 1948 in the civil courts for the return of the Vermeer painting, *The Artist in the Studio*. It was claimed that it had been parted with under a forced sale to Hitler in 1939. The claims were defeated by a ruling to the effect that the painting belonged to Germany and that German property in Austria could be seized in accordance with Austrian post-war restitution laws which considered such property a form of reparation. The painting is thus now kept in the Kunsthistorisches Museum, Vienna.[4] In 1985 the Austrian parliament passed further legislation to enable a remaining 8,000 confiscated works of art, mainly paintings and books, to be returned to claimants who made written application to the Finance Ministry before the end of September 1986.

Since the Second World War, the international trade in illicit art objects has continued unabated on a huge scale and the United States has been credited

Fig. 48. Soldiers of the 90th Division, US Third Army, examine the famous painting *Wintergarden* by the French Impressionist Edouard Manet, in the collection of Reichsbank wealth, SS loot and paintings removed by the Nazis from Berlin to the salt mine vault at Merkers.

with being the largest single buyers' market for stolen or illegally exported cultural property, though this also travels to Germany, Switzerland, France, England and Hong Kong. The two main sources are plundered archaeological sites and art objects stolen outright from institutions or private collections.[5] Where theft is a matter of historic interest and the present ownership of an object is not disputed, displaying institutions are prepared to refer openly to the initially illicit origin of an object. For instance, the National Gallery of Scotland refers to its *El Medico* by Goya, in the full catalogue of Spanish and Italian painting, in the provenance section, as having been 'stolen from the Royal Palace in Madrid in 1869...'.

The contemporary problem of theft is global, and is escalating. What was described as the world's largest theft of art objects occurred at Mexico City's National Museum of Anthropology in December 1985. Objects stolen included relics of the Maya, Aztec, Zapotec and Mixtec cultures. In particular, the museum lost one of its greatest treasures, a burial mask from a Mayan pyramid in Palenque. The largest art theft of paintings in history occurred in Paris

Fig. 49. The vast collection of Reichsbank wealth and SS loot, including gold and paintings stored in the salt mine at Merkers.

at the Marmottan Museum in October 1985. Included in the works taken was Claude Monet's *Impression Soleil Levant*, which gave its name to the Impression- ist movement.[6] In May 1988 the largest ever art theft of paintings in the Nether- lands occurred at the Stedelijk Museum in Amsterdam. The three Impressionist pictures taken and valued at £30 million were Van Gogh's *Carnations*, Cézanne's *Bottles and Apples* and J. B. Jonkind's *The House of Maître Billaud at Nevers*. In terms of profitability, art theft is ranked second in the world to the drug trade, and it has been suggested that there are many 'schools' of art theft in operation. The motives vary from the criminal to the political, including roman- tic art 'collection', dishonest dealership, and ransom. A 1972-3 Interpol survey showed that twenty-six countries were most troubled by cultural property theft: thirteen in Europe, two in Africa, one in North America, five in South Ameri- ca and five in Asia. These are mostly public-art-owning countries, or those rich in archaeological treasures. The scale of this crime is so great in Italy that a specialist police command was set up to protect the artistic patrimony – the Commando Carabinieri Tutela Patrimino Artistico. The methods of theft and transportation are often ingenious. For instance, thieves may overpaint an origi-

Fig. 50. Florentine art treasures returned at the end of the Second World War. Six trunks with part of the half million dollars worth of art treasure which was taken to Belzano by retreating Germans arrive at the Piazzo dei Signora, Florence, 1945.

nal, or 'launder' stolen art by exporting it after theft, and reimporting it for auction, having thereby interposed a foreign law of title.[7]

There are frequent reports of theft: it is said, for instance, that in Costa Rica alone as many as 95 per cent of the known archaeological sites have been at least partially ruined by plunderers. In the 1960s Mayan art from Mexico and Guatemala was being plundered. Large intricately carved stelae were being damaged in the process and part of an important record of a historic civilization was lost. Many of these objects were subsequently traced to a number of respectable American museums.[8]

Grave-robbing is rife amongst all the archaeologically rich countries. In Italy tombs have been the constant source of Greek, Roman and Etruscan treasures finding their way into museums and the art market. This is said to be aided by the smuggling network of the Mafia. Early in 1987 grave-robbers in Peru uncovered at an ancient burial site at Huaca Rajada what is reputedly the largest cache of Moche gold objects ever found. It was dispersed before the authorities could effectively act to recover it.

In India 3,000 thefts of antiquities were reported between 1977 and 1979,

Fig. 51. The Florentine art treasures returned at the Piazzo dei Signora, Florence, are met with a fanfare and pass by a reviewing stand of American, English and Italian officials.

and only ten cases were solved. UNESCO has estimated that more than 50,000 art objects have been smuggled out of India in the last 10 years alone. In north-east Thailand, an archaeological site discovered at Ban Chiang in the mid-1960s revealed a culture that forged its own tools 4,000 years ago, but it was raided by local peasants for its pottery before archaeologists could fully explore it. These scenes have been repeated elsewhere, where local looters anticipating rich finds have descended on archaeological sites such as the royal tombs at Tillya Tepe in Afghanistan in 1979. Often archaeologists themselves are the culprits, smuggling artifacts out of the country of site. For instance, in 1982 a British archaeologist was arrested and expelled from Afghanistan for smuggling out archaeological finds.[9] Another major source is reported to be Third World museums. For instance, nine extraordinary bronze Benin figures and masks were stolen from the Nigerian National Museum in Lagos by an employee in 1981 and three turned up at the Pace Gallery in New York, which notified the Nigerian authorities. In Peru in 1981 thieves stole the country's national symbol, the Tumi, a sunny-faced figure atop a dagger, together with thirty other gold objects from the National Museum.

240

The art smugglers are said to come from all walks of life but are often journalists, art brokers and even diplomats who can take advantage of the immunity from search given to diplomatic bags. Apart from the adventure there is the lure of considerable profit. It has been reported that a Mayan head stolen from a Costa Rican temple was sold for $9,000 in Paris. In Geneva, a dealer was paid $90,000 for a sixteenth- to seventeenth-century Benin bronze plate from Nigeria. The best examples of Andean pottery have obtained prices as high as $45,000 in Tokyo.

With increased publicity concerning illicit traffic, and a change in attitude towards cultural property in the past decade, many Third World countries have passed laws that limit or ban the export of culturally significant art. The difficulties in enforcing these regulations have been considerable.

The differing national legal controls[10] on illicit traffic in cultural property pose considerable problems of their own for cohesive international regulation. An object may be illegally exported from its country of origin without actually being stolen. An object may be stolen outright from a museum or institution or private collection, or it may be taken away from an archaeological site which is either generally known or unknown. Most countries, with a few exceptions such as the United States, now impose some sort of export regulation on works of art or cultural property, but their terms vary considerably. It was reported in 1981 that there were only about six or seven countries without regulation of cultural property, or some form of export regulation. These included the USA, Denmark, Uganda, Singapore, and Togo.[11]

It was not until the mid-1980s, for instance, that Australia began to make a serious attempt to retrieve and protect its indigenous cultural heritage. The National Museum of Australia in Canberra has custody of seventeen objects deemed to be secret and sacred which were purchased by the Department of Aboriginal Affairs following their withdrawal from a Sotheby's auction in 1983. The museum agreed to catalogue the material thoroughly in order to prevent any further dealings in it and to contact communities with an interest in the material and to seek their views as to the future disposition of the material. In addition, the Australian Museum in Sydney has a collection of items withdrawn from a Sotheby's auction in 1985 after the New South Wales Aboriginal Lands Council obtained an injunction preventing its sale. A diversity of objects from the lower Murray River including early bark paintings, clubs, spears and spear throwers were subsequently purchased by the Lands Council at market price.

The changed perception of the value of aboriginal culture is reflected in a bill which was passed in 1986, The Protection of Movable Cultural Heritage Act. This was meant to replace various confusing Customs (Prohibited Exports) regulations, and the impetus for it came from the 1970 UNESCO Convention, which Australia sought to ratify only in 1986. The Act protects against the illicit export of items important to Australia's cultural heritage, including aboriginal artifacts. A permit is required to export any item on the Prohibited Export List. If an item is considered to be sufficiently important the permit can be denied by experts in aboriginal culture. There are high penalties – up to $100,000 or five years' jail – for the illegal export of the prohibited objects. The Australian government has also set up a working party comprising representatives from the Australian National Museum, the Australian Institute of Aboriginal Studies, the Department of Foreign Affairs and the Department of Aboriginal Affairs. Its brief is to evaluate the repatriation of aboriginal material and to compile a data base of such materials held abroad.

Different countries tend to deal with different kinds of object, so that some are more concerned with archaeological objects or antiquities, while others are more likely to deal with more contemporary fine art objects. Some countries, such as Turkey,[12] have total bans on the export of antiquities, whilst others, for example India[13] and Japan,[14] ban the export of certain categories of art treasure or impose a licensing scheme. The licensing system may vary in stringency: for instance, in France the state has a pre-emptive right to purchase the work of art, whereas in England and Canada a licence cannot be withheld absolutely and is subject to a bona fide domestic offer to buy at market value. Other countries declare all archaeological matter to be the property of the state, as for instance does China,[15] and some countries, such as Zaire,[16] place an embargo against the export of all cultural material. A 1983 Council of Europe Survey on Legislation concerning Archaeological Heritage indicated that there generally appear to be three types of state legislation dealing with the protection of archaeological finds, namely legislation dealing with accidental discovery, and with organized excavations, and regulations governing the ownership of objects found. Total bans seem to be singularly ineffective: for instance, thousands of items have been illicitly removed from Turkey over the last thirty years. One spectacular claim in 1970 was that the gold of Croesus, which had been smuggled out of Turkey, was being kept by the Metropolitan Museum in New York.[17] This was a collection of tomb paintings, jewellery and more than two hundred gold and silver objects which were the three-thousand-year-old finds taken from four tombs near Sardis, the former capital of King Croesus in Lydia in western Turkey. The Metropolitan Museum denied the existence of such a cohesive collection, and the case resurfaced in 1987 in the form of a legal suit by Turkey against the museum.

In addition to the problem of removal from archaeological sites, the mere fact of illegal export of cultural property, as opposed to actual theft, has generally not barred it from being legally imported into major importing countries such as England, the USA, France, Germany and Switzerland. One notable exception to this was a specific statute passed in the United States in 1972, dealing only with certain pre-Columbian art, which provided for the first offer of return to the country of origin, subject to payment of incidental expenses.

Even with the existence of such legislation, the Canadian case of the Nigerian Nok terracotta in 1983[18] has shown that restitution of illegally exported cultural property may not be possible, highlighting the limitations of the 1970 UNESCO Convention in this respect. Although Canada was a party to the Convention and had imposed import regulations, the case for restitution was defeated because it could not be shown that illicit export had occurred *after* Canadian law came into effect (see pp. 211–13).

In any event, import restrictions such as are imposed in Canada are very much the exception, despite the provisions of the 1970 UNESCO Convention[19] for the imposition of import regulations on an *ad hoc* basis. Without such widespread import controls, states which suffer loss of cultural property face many more difficulties and complications in seeking a legal recovery in the courts of the importing state. Nevertheless there has been a successful return of cultural property sought in US courts where it could be shown that the property was stolen.[20] And in another case the distinction between the penalties for importing illegally exported cultural property and importing stolen property has been made less significant – by indicating that where it has been exported in contravention of any unambiguous legislative declaration of ownership by the country from whence it is exported, it would be deemed to be stolen.[21]

Where there is no such special legislative provision even in cases where property is clearly stolen, further complications can arise when the property has been sold to a bona fide purchaser, since the rules governing title to it vary between different jurisdictions. In common law jurisdictions this is generally resolved by applying the law of the place where the object was situated at the time of the transfer.[22] In this way original owners of cultural property could lose their title if it was transferred in a manner which satisfies the law of the place where it was transferred. Only states could take action under conventional law to recover some such property, as for instance under the 1970 UNESCO Convention (see Appendix XVII, Article 7(b)(ii)), but private individuals would be confined to the use of the importing state's local laws.

To counter many of the difficulties in actually securing the restitution of cultural property, several international, nongovernmental bodies have been active in combating the effect of the illicit art trade. ICOM[23] has sought to establish a unified policy in museum practice. It has been involved for some 20 years in the struggle against illicit traffic in cultural property. Since the early 1960s, the

Council has pursued a vigorous line of action to curb the illicit export of museum objects from their countries of origin, to improve security in museums and to enforce ethical principles that should govern the behaviour of museum professionals responsible for acquisitions.

In 1971, the Council adopted a code of ethics consisting of twenty recommendations in which it called on professional staff of museums to observe the highest standards in the course of acquisition. It advocated that direct acquisitions (e.g. those obtained by scientifically conducted research missions) must be made with the agreement or the co-operation of and according to the laws of the host country, and that indirect acquisitions should always be made in observance of the laws and interests of the country from which the object is obtained or of the country of origin. The code states furthermore that 'if a museum is offered objects, the licit quality of which it has reason to doubt, it will contact the competent authorities of the country of origin in an effort to help this country safeguard its national heritage' (Recommendation 17). That this code has had an impact on the museum world is evidenced by the policy statements and regulations concerning acquisitions which have been issued by museums in Australia, Canada, Israel, New Zealand, the United Kingdom and the United States of America. For example, the policy of the Australian Museum is that it will not authenticate cultural property which does not meet its criteria for acquisition, nor will it make monetary valuations of such property. However, the code does not cover materials acquired prior to its adoption nor does it deal directly with the return of cultural property. Moreover it is not binding since it is dependent for its operation upon adoption by museum members.[24]

Another non-governmental body working closely with UNESCO is the International Organization for the Protection of Works of Art (IOPA),[25] which is especially concerned with the authentication of art objects, and registration to protect them against theft.

The organization charged with the task of actually suppressing the illicit traffic in art is the International Criminal Police Organization (Interpol).[26] Its aim is to provide the widest possible mutual assistance between all criminal police authorities within the limits of the laws existing in different countries.[27] It is therefore concerned with the co-ordination of different national police forces, and the principles upon which it is based are voluntary participation, the primacy of national legislation and intervention in the case of specifically criminal, as opposed to political or other acts. It is essentially a bureaucratic institution, monitoring international crime, and distributing information on stolen property and wanted suspects. It co-ordinates international investigations, but field investigations remain the responsibility of its member agencies, which include 135 nations. It has a unit which deals with stolen art, whose function is to send formal circulars covering major art thefts to all relevant agencies and national services such as the police and customs authorities, who in turn are expected to circulate these to museums, art dealers, auctioneers and art journals.[28]

From 1946 onwards a notice of stolen objects has been available to national authorities and international organizations such as ICOM. This includes the date and place of theft, description of the work, a photograph, and details of the authorities to alert in case of discovery or information. In recent years the number of circulars has doubled, indicating the increase in art theft, but the recovery rate has been reported as remaining steady at 12 per cent per year.[29] In particular Interpol circulates a special notice entitled 'The Twelve Most Wanted Works of Art' which is distributed internationally. The discernible trend in art theft is one of movement towards the money markets in America, Germany, France and South America.

However, art theft is not given top priority because of Interpol's other responsibilities, and computerization would involve considerable technical and financial difficulties. It is the national central bureaux that maintain records and who determine the passing on of requests and information to Interpol or who act as police departments in dealing with international cases. In the case of the theft of cultural property the general practice has been for the national central bureaux to inform the General Secretariat of Interpol only upon the conclusion of national investigations. An Interpol spokesman,[30] in explaining the functioning of the *avis de recherches internationaux,* has pointed out that the majority of requests were made by European countries, fewer than 100 requests per year being received from all the other countries combined. He expressed regret that the latter did not inform Interpol headquarters of losses of cultural property; national authorities, in co-operation with museums, ought to transmit relevant information regularly to the Secretary-General of Interpol, but in practice did not do so.

The response of the British government to the illegal international traffic of art was to call upon the art trade in 1984 to enter into a voluntary code of practice, similar to that already operated by museums and galleries, not to buy or handle works of art that have been illegally exported from their countries of origin. While the president of the British Antique Dealers' Association[31] responded favourably towards this concept, more sceptical members of the art world stressed the need for legislation to deter such illegal dealing.

There has been an occasion when an object was saved from auction by the pre-emptive demands of a government which alleged illegal export. In April 1986 a Goya masterpiece, *The Marquesa de Santa Cruz,* was handed over to the Spanish government two weeks before it was due to be auctioned at Christie's. There was evidence of either blatant forgery or some other serious irregularity regarding the export documents. The Spanish government successfully chal-

lenged these documents in the High Court[32] in March 1986, after both Christie's and Lord Wimborne, the owner, had unsuccessfully attempted to have the
case struck out as being outside the jurisdiction of the British court. Lord Wimborne therefore sent the painting back to Spain in return for a $6 million 'indem-
nity' received as a bona fide purchaser (but he is still reported to have made a
loss). The painting, which according to anecdote Franco once contemplated as
a gift to Hitler, was received back by Miguel Satrustegui, an official of the
Spanish Ministry of Culture, to be hung at the Prado Museum in Madrid.
Negotiations for the return of the painting were conducted in the framework of
the new code of practice for the control of trading in works of art agreed by the
British auctioneers' and dealers' association in 1985. But successful as it was, this
case showed nevertheless that it is not easy to implement a voluntary code.

The UNESCO Intergovernmental Committee on Return of Cultural
Property has said, amongst other things, that at the national level:

> The competent authorities in member states should study the possi-
> bility of obtaining the maintenance by art dealers of registers indicating
> where, when, how and from whom cultural property has been acquired
> and to whom it has been sold. The co-operation of the services respons-
> ible for the cultural heritage should be enlisted to assisted in the main-
> tenance of these registers.[33]

Despite these efforts to record and control the movement of art objects, many
thousands continue to leave their countries of origin illicitly each year, often
turning up in the catalogues of the great auction houses such as Sotheby's or
Christie's in London. The temptation to smuggle art cannot be suppressed,
because of the large sums of money to be made in the market. An example of this
has been the considerable number of major works of art said to have come out
of China. In 1984 a rare chime of nine archaic bronze bells and ten musical
stones dating from the Warring States period were left unsold at Sotheby's in
London at the reserve figure of £30,000.[34] There were fears of an official Chinese
objection or demand for their return. Often many such items, consisting mainly
of bronzes and pottery, and supposedly unearthed from tombs, have been sold
directly through the major auction rooms in Hong Kong. With the immense
profitability of such clandestine operations, illicit art traffic culminating in public sale will continue, until better guarantes of return of cultural property are
established through legislative measures in the state where the art is sold.

In December 1985 Sotheby's in London proceeded with a major sale of six
Greek and Roman vases from around 400 BC despite allegations of their illegal
excavation and smuggling out of Italy. Mr Brian Cook, keeper of Greek and

Roman antiquities at the British Museum, said there was reasonable cause to believe that these had come from robbed tombs. Professor Filice Lo Porto, superintendent of antiquities in the Apulian region of southern Italy and a central inspector of the department of fine arts in Rome, also said there was strong evidence that the vases had been smuggled. Sotheby's was asked to withhold the vases from the sale so that their origin could be investigated, but it proceeded with the sale since there was no evidence that they had come from an unofficial site. All the vases were sold. One, probably depicting Oedipus, was sold for £22,000, twice its estimate, to a private collector who also paid £11,000 for an amphora decorated with a young warrior. A third was sold for £9,350.

Although Sotheby's defied its critics in this auction, it agreed to change its procedures in future sales. It asked the Italian authorities to send it photographs of any items that are believed to have been removed without authority from archaeological sites, and, in turn, it would send to Italy photographs of Apulian vases consigned to it for auction. Sotheby's said that it would withdraw items from its future sales, if it received any evidence of malpractice.

The fact remains that the major art auction houses, like those situated in London, are subject to few legal controls. They need only satisfy themselves that the seller is a *prima facie* owner of the piece. There are practical difficulties in further investigating ownership, and they are not required to guarantee title or examine provenance (though they may include in the catalogue such details as are known to them), and they usually include in their conditions of sale an exclusion clause of responsibility for authenticity, authorship or provenance. As the United Kingdom has not become a party to the 1970 UNESCO Convention, there is virtually no possibility of obtaining the return of illegally exported items which appear at these auction rooms, even where the owner seeks their restitution. The same is said to apply in the smaller auction rooms of Switzerland, such as Berne and Zurich, and Liechtenstein, where legal title can be obtained to dubious works (even if stolen) provided the buyer can show they were bought in good faith at public auction. It has been conceded by the Federal Bureau of Cultural Heritage in Switzerland that Switzerland is the centre of stolen art from Italy and indeed from other foreign countries such as Greece, Turkey, Tunisia and Egypt. In Switzerland there is no restriction on the import or export of art treasures, which are often stored in bank vaults before being passed through various intermediaries on to foreign buyers, usually in the United States. This is said to represent an annual market of $2 billion. In other art sale countries, for instance France, the conditions of auction sales are, in theory at least, more stringent about guarantees of title. However, due to the more fragmented system of auction rooms in France, their catalogues are more likely to be vague, less well illustrated, distributed more locally and therefore less likely to lead to the detection of stolen art.

In the United States auction rooms and art dealers are not significantly regulated at the federal level. In New York State, a major art sale centre, the Arts and Cultural Affairs Law mainly deals with fraud, whereas the sale of illicitly exported art and artifacts is not regulated. Illicit art transactions can be more satisfactorily dealt with when the issue is one of outright defective title. For instance a case arose in 1984 involving a collection of more than fifty rare Hebrew manuscripts and books which came up for sale at Sotheby's New York,[35] and which had been transferred out of Germany during the Nazi era. They were formerly owned by the Hochschule für die Wissenschaft Judenthums in Berlin. Although the Attorney-General of New York in challenging the title of the consignor sought the return of the manuscripts to the Hochschule's successor institution or other charitable beneficiaries with a claim, an approved settlement was reached involving recall from purchasers and distribution of the most historically valuable manuscripts to certain institutions.

Doubtful objects will continue to show up in museums. The system in the United States whereby tax benefits accrue to individuals contributing art to museums has been questioned on the grounds of the dubious origins of such art and the lack of legal obligations on museums to make full disclosures on new works. For instance, more than 80 per cent of the New York Metropolitan Museum's works come to it from gifts or bequests.[36] In the UK the British Museum refuses to purchase antiquities which have no documented history. There is some indication that the role and function of museums is changing. They are seen less as storehouses of cultural heritage and preservers of past achievement and more as centres of education and communication. According to the statutes of ICOM in 1974, a museum is 'a non-profit-making, permanent institution in the service of society and of its development, and open to the public, which acquires, conserves, researches, communicates, and exhibits, for purposes of study, education and enjoyment, material evidence of man and his environment'.

Throughout history, museums of cultural property were established in different parts of the world, usually for religious or scholarly purposes. The earliest known example of the museum idea is said to have been the exhibition in the palace of Ur of the archaeological discoveries of Nabonidus, the king of Babylon, in the fifth century BC. The idea of communicating information was developed through the scholarly institutions of classical times to the religious collections of the Middle Ages. The forerunners of the public institutions we enjoy today were a product of the Renaissance, although at the time it was believed that art and scholarship belonged only to a few.

The first museums grew out of the private collections of kings, dukes, cardinals and scholars. The collection of Ulysses Aldrovandi (1527-1603) became the basis of the museum at Bologna. The collections of Thomas Howard, Earl of Arundel (1586-1646), found their way eventually into museums. John Tradescant and his son John, two of the earliest English collectors and naturalists, established the Tradescant Closet of Curiosities, a remarkable collection of 'varieties and oddities', popularly known as Tradescant's Ark, at Lambeth. The collection was acquired by Elias Ashmole in 1659 and added to his own. The whole was presented to the University of Oxford, and formed the basis of the Ashmolean Museum which was opened by James II, then Duke of York, in 1682.

A famous private collection was that of Ole Worm. On his death Worm's collection passed to the king of Denmark, Frederik III, who planned a new building opposite his castle of Christiansborg to house his collections and library. The second storey, housing the Kunstkammer Museum, had some seventy-five prehistoric exhibits by the end of the seventeenth century and was open to the public on payment of an admission charge which went to the curator.

One of the very largest private museums of the seventeenth century was that of Albert Seba (1665-1736). When Peter the Great was in Amsterdam in 1716 he bought Seba's museum and had it removed to St Petersburg; it formed the basis of the museum, opened to the public in 1719, which eventually developed into the Hermitage, which was officially founded by Catherine the Great as a court museum in 1764 and opened to the public in 1852.

Sir Hans Sloane (1660-1753), the famous English physician who was president of the College of Physicians and of the Royal Society, was one of the great collectors. His library and collections, valued at £80,000 when he died, was bequeathed to the nation. In 1753 an Act was passed for the purchase of the Sloane library and museum, and of the Harley manuscripts, to unite them with the Cotton library and provide one 'general repository' for these and later additions. This repository, opened to the public in January 1759, became the British Museum in Montagu House, Bloomsbury, London.

There were also two remarkable French collections: the first that of N. Fabri de Peiresc (1580-1637) of Aix, often described as the founder of the study of antiquity in France. The second was by M. le Comte de Caylus, the eighteenth-century scholar and traveller, who collected many specimens of classical archaeology during excavation in Asia Minor.

In the seventeenth century only distinguished travellers and foreign scholars were, as a rule, permitted to see the collections which belonged to the European princes. After 1700 the general public was admitted to the Imperial Gallery in

Vienna on payment of a fee, and there were similar opportunities for public viewing in Rome, at the Quirinal Palace, and in Madrid, at the Escorial. However, the collection of paintings which belonged to the French monarchy remained inaccessible to the public until half-way through the eighteenth century when about a hundred paintings were hung in the Luxembourg Palace, where the public could see them on two days a week.

There was no access to the collections of the wealthy English, who bought widely in Italy and other continental countries throughout the seventeenth and eighteenth centuries. Some of the German courts took a more liberal view, and the gallery at Dresden, for example, could be viewed without difficulty from 1746 onwards. When public museums, such as the British Museum, were established in Europe at the end of the century, they carried on the traditions of the private collections and there was still the element of exclusivity. However, the opening of the Ashmolean Museum at Oxford in 1682 and the British Museum in 1759 represent the beginning of the movement towards public museums which gained impetus in the nineteenth century.

At this time too, museums were being created in the New World. The first museum began in Charleston, South Carolina, when the city library society set up an exhibition and collections based on South Carolina natural history, in 1773. Shortly after, Charles Willson Peale, the Philadelphia portrait painter began an exhibition of his own mammoth bones, and his collections were eventually incorporated into the scientific research collections of the Philadelphia Academy of Natural Sciences. One of his sons, Rembrandt Peale, built the first American museum in Baltimore, in 1813. The great museums in America and Canada came to be developed over about a hundred years primarily on the basis of private benefaction and philanthropy, the theme being the enlightenment of all citizens. There was also an emphasis on scholarship and there followed the creation of the great college museums such as those at Harvard and Yale.

It has been suggested that for the future museums ought to be redefined[37] within the context of new technical resources and new social demands. The European development of museums has meant the removal of pictures or sculptures or other artifacts from their original environment to be viewed in isolation and abstraction. This has led to the suspicion therefore that the majority of museum visitors may only have a superficial appreciation of exhibits.

In the past twenty-five years the museum-going public has changed and continues to change. The range of interests has widened and the nature of museum displays has changed. The Great Exhibition in London in 1851 set the scene for museums as the centre of dramatic displays and special exhibitions with a wide public appeal. This led to museum exchanges, so that the concept of a museum as a stagnant entity has been altered, and for the public has become more mobile. There now exists the possibility of making perfect and undetectable replicas, and the means of communication and record through books and film have made the permanent retention of complete museum collections less pivotal to their existence.

It has been said that the focus of attention in the development of archaeology, for instance, has shifted to the Third World and other non-European countries. Although the wisdom of encouraging a proliferation of museums there on the American pattern has been questioned,[38] there is a growing development of new national museums in the Third World. Yet two-thirds of African artifacts now in the West have been acquired since the 1960s after most African countries gained independence. The call for the return of significant objects to their national museums has begun to produce some results,[39] as, for example, in the case of Australia, New Zealand, and the Pacific and Oceanic countries. But the majority of objects remain unreturned.

CHAPTER EIGHT

THE RETURN OF
CULTURAL TREASURES:
SOME CONCLUSIONS

What is 'cultural property'?

From the many situations considered in the previous chapters, one ought to reconsider firstly the meaning of the term 'cultural property'. It has been said that Anglo-Saxon countries tend to avoid the use of the world 'culture',[1] except in its limited scientific, ethnological or artistic sense. The rest of the world uses the term more readily, much more generally and without much precision. In Third World countries, for instance, it has a more political meaning equated to anything which heightens national consciousness or identity. There are obviously no aesthetic boundaries to what constitutes 'culture', since according to the same writer 'cultural property' includes both the *Mona Lisa* and a photograph of the living room of a French steelworker.

Geoffrey Lewis, the director of Museum Studies at Leicester University, has written:

> Cultural property represents in tangible form some of the evidence of man's origins and development, his traditions, artistic and scientific achievements and generally the milieu of which he is a part. The fact that this material has the ability to communicate, either directly or by association, an aspect of reality which transcends time or space gives it special significance and is therefore something to be sought after and protected.[2]

Article 1 of the 1970 Convention dealing with the illicit transfer of cultural property provides: 'For the purposes of this Convention, the term 'cultural property' means property which, on religious or secular grounds, is specifically designated by each State as being of importance for archaeology, prehistory, history, literature, art or science' and which belongs to a number of specified categories. This test of what is 'cultural property' therefore depends on each state's designation of it under a number of broad headings. It is a subjective and individual definition in each case of what is important as cultural property.

Many states legislating to restrict the export of cultural property do so by defining 'cultural property' by one of a number of systems. These have been described mainly as (a) enumeration of a specific list of types of object, e.g. ethnographical articles; (b) categorization with a general description of type of article, e.g. movable and immovable property of national interest; or (c) a specific list of named items. Other criteria exist such as age of objects and local origin.

Japanese legislation, for instance, has been taken as a model by other South-East Asian states for the breadth of protection given to cultural property. This is divided into four categories: 'tangible cultural properties', 'intangible cultural properties', 'folk culture', and 'monuments'. Japanese law then further classifies its tangible cultural property into national treasures or important cultural property, which is then registered.[3] It is seen as concentrating on what is of outstanding value from a national point of view.

According to a paper by Mr Salah Stétié, delegate of Lebanon and chairman of the UNESCO Intergovernmental Committee for the Return of Cultural Property:

> A cultural object is not just any kind of object. In the definition given by the Intergovernmental Committee – a definition which was both restrictive yet at the same time extensive – an object likely to provoke a call for restitution is defined as that object which is highly charged with cultural (or natural) significance. It therefore follows that the removal of this object from its original cultural context irrevocably divests that culture of one of its dimensions. Through the loss of this essential link in the chain the culture is no longer able to perceive itself in the natural logic of its own evolution. In other words, what is at stake is the loss not just of a possession but of part of the very essence of that culture. For it is through this cultural object that the creative and spiritual character of a human, ethnic, racial, religious or national community is transmitted – a community for whom this object is a fundamental symbol of expression.

The language in this definition is somewhat florid. It could be said that 'highly charged with cultural significance' could cover almost everything, depending on the circumstances, and begs the issue of definition.

The Intergovernmental Committee has recognized that the definition of cultural property in its terms of reference is capable of various interpretations. It has now been decided that the term 'cultural property' refers to 'property which is particularly representative of the cultural identity of a given nation'. This leads to the question of what is 'particularly respresentative' and how the lack of such material in a country can be demonstrated. Such a definition is couched in too general terms to be of any practical use in securing the return of objects.

Allied with the idea of 'cultural property' is the idea of 'cultural heritage'.[4] This further confuses any definition, since it has been sought to extend this to mean all forms of cultural and artistic expression inherited from the near or distant past of a given country or cultural area. In terms of the cultural return issue, this is so broad as to be of little use.

It has also been recognized that there is a divergence in the emerging doctrines relating to cultural property. The 1954 Hague Convention sees cultural property as the cultural heritage of all mankind whilst the UNESCO Convention of 1970 takes the view that it is the cultural heritage of each country. In 1980 the UNESCO Intergovernmental Committee defined its objectives as: 'The return of cultural property in its true context, namely that of maintaining, reconstituting, developing and serving the cultural identity of all peoples.' That is to say there are two approaches, one internationalist, and one nationalist. In the former case cultural property is referred to as the common heritage of mankind.[5] This is misleading because cultural property cannot, being within any state's sovereignty, be regarded as *res nullius* (property belonging to no one), or *res communis* (property belonging to the whole world). It is a concept which can have little bearing on the issue of the return of cultural property, because making 'cultural property' universal contradicts the notion of 'return'.

An examination of the cases relating to cultural property dealt with in this book has clearly indicated that we are really concerned with three different issues: (1) conservation, which is an ongoing issue; (2) illicit trading, which is a contemporary issue; and (3) the physical return of cultural property which may be associated with illicit trading but is also a historic issue.

The question of returning cultural property tends to become mixed up under these three headings without any distinction being drawn. When discussing conservation the concept of a 'cultural heritage' may be relevant, whilst when considering return the concept of 'cultural property' is relevant. If we examine the many definitions of cultural property these shortcomings are obvious. They are vague and they are subjective. Whilst it may be satisfactory to define cultural property in this way within a *national* context, a fixed and objective criterion is necessary if the matter of cultural return is to be dealt with on an *international* footing, as between states.

The term 'cultural property' has come to mean all things to all men. It can mean man-made things or natural objects or many different kinds of relics, and the definition can be taken to extremes. Take, for instance, the statement in one publication that 'there is a large range of natural objects that can become important to the cultural heritage. They may be derived from man, indicating his habits at a particular period, as for example, human faeces'!⁶

The term 'cultural heritage' has in its usage become a piece of international political and bureaucratic jargon, in much the same way as 'common heritage of mankind' or 'new international economic order' and so on. Such terms are ineffectual because they are too general, and are devalued by their constant and indiscriminate use.

Historically removed objects are in a different category from contemporary cases of illicit trading which are now covered by state legislation and convention, and to deal with them on a practical footing, a careful definition of what constitutes 'cultural property' is essential. The historic cases of removal of cultural property are not catered for under existing national legislations or under any convention, which in any event would not be retrospective. The matter of return is an individual issue in each case.

'Culture' is an abstract term related to perception or vision. In tangible form it is one kind of 'property'. Implicit in this process is the original creative and aesthetic intervention of human beings. For the purposes of defining *returnable* cultural property, it could be argued that while many objects such as the Stone of Scone, or the Kohinoor diamond, may be historic objects, or property whose return may be validly sought under some other heading, they do not qualify as *cultural* property, since they are natural, as opposed to humanly wrought, objects. 'Property' is also used in a legalistic sense to denote ownership. A narrow frame of reference should determine what constitutes cultural 'treasure', for the purposes of return. This would include only exceptional or unique landmark objects. The issue of return should be determined on the basis of two main criteria: (1) the means of acquisition; and (2) the nature of the object. It ought to be possible to claim legally all materials taken by force, by unequal treaty, by theft or deceit. (Such property is often held in the public sector by states' institutions; property privately held is more difficult to trace.) The class of object in which title should not be deemed to have passed would be the historic records or manuscripts of a nation, including the narrative representation of its history in an art form which has been dismembered, and objects torn from immovable property forming part of the sovereign territory of the state whence they were taken. In addition, palaeontological materials should be included in this class as human relics (although not strictly within the proposed definition of cultural treasure). This would provide for the restoration or reinstatement of indigenous historical records and ancient monuments, where this could now be safely achieved, and would cover historically removed archaeological objects.

What is a 'country of origin'?

One must clearly understand the concept of 'country of origin' in relation to a particular item. Does this mean the country of manufacture, the nationality of the maker, the last country to hold the object before its removal or, for example in the case of an archaeological item, the site of its discovery? And in view of the changing national boundaries during the course of history, one may ask what criteria are to be used in defining 'country of origin'? The current definition used by the UNESCO Intergovernmental Committee of 'the country with the traditional culture to which the object was related' is unsatisfactory. This is not always a clearly defined question, because it is often not easy to determine the strongest historic link, and it is sometimes obvious that this definition does not correlate with the country of origin. Each case needs to be separately examined on its merit with regard to the people for whom the object was made, by whom it was made, and for what purpose and place it was made – and, if acquired, the manner of its acquisition. The strongest link would determine the most appropriate home for the treasure. In the case of immovable property the answer is straightforward. In the case of records or manuscripts, such as the Icelandic manuscripts, the analysis would be more complicated. Sometimes the very origin of an object is uncertain, like, for example, the Bayeux Tapestry.[7] Although it is agreed that it was probably made in England, it is known that it was made to the order of Bishop Odo of Bayeux and such factors would have to be taken into consideration in determining its proper location.

What is 'return' or 'restitution'?

It has been said that museum directors dislike the use of the word 'restitution', which is often used in conjunction with 'cultural property'. This is because museums cling to the idea that all objects in its possession were lawfully obtained. This is not always realistic. If one wished to avoid a purely legalistic approach, as was initially done in the Icelandic case, it could be argued that in the case of principal objects, the merits of return ought to be evaluated not only according to historic disapprobation but in accordance with the sense of cultural property 'going back' (renvoyer) usually to its homeland, for aesthetic and historic reasons. 'Return' may also refer in a wider sense to restoration, reinstatement, and even rejuvenation and reunification.

How effective are existing bodies and conventions?

The main body which has involved itself with the return of cultural property has been UNESCO. In summary, in additional to general cultural policy, UNESCO's interconnected activities have been conservation, return of cultural property, measures against illicit trafficking, drawing up of inventories, the listing of different types of cultural property, and a number of special regional studies.

It would be true to say that UNESCO has fulfilled its mission in creating fruitful dialogue. Undoubtedly new concepts have been forged, such as that of cultural identity, and a new awareness has developed among many peoples regarding the rediscovery and rescue of their cultural history. The possibilities of securing the return of cultural property have been given publicity and much of the success in establishing bilateral arrangements, between states, and institutions, resulting in the physical return of objects, can be attributed to the efforts of UNESCO in raising consciousness about the special significance of cultural property.

But over the years UNESCO resolutions, recommendations and drafted conventions appear to have been largely ineffectual. It has produced many wordy documents, often bogged down in rhetoric and with little bearing on practical realities, which few could be expected to read and no one but an optimist could expect to be acted upon. Many of the reports and statements are filled with repetitious phrases and terms which cannot be easily recalled. Titles to subject matters are inordinately long. And an obsession has manifested itself for a mass of minute, and often unrelated, detail.

A close review of the record does not always enhance UNESCO's credibility, as evidenced by the surprising proposals of actual compensation[8] for lost cultural property or even substitution of other cultural property of a different origin – both an abnegation of the concept of return. Even more astonishing facts are revealed when one surveys the record of UNESCO over the concept of 'cultural heritage'. Its sense of realism and judgement in the use of terminology must be put into great doubt by some of its past assessments. For instance, the Auschwitz Concentration Camp is included, under Poland, in the list of properties in its World Heritage List (under the 1972 UNESCO Convention for the Protection of World Cultural and Natural Heritage; see Appendix XVIII). While this may be a historic monument, one must ask whether the killing fields of Poland are a part of its or the world's *cultural* heritage?

In recent years UNESCO has itself been divided, and come under attack from its own Western member states. Reforms have been urged to return the organization to its original mandate of 1945, which was to combat illiteracy and promote international understanding through the free exchange of ideas and knowledge. Its critics have attacked the organization for allowing its activities to become too politicized, and in particular anti-Western, and major contributors to the organization's budget such as the United States and the United Kingdom have withdrawn. This is bound to weaken further the already dissipated effect of UNESCO in securing the return of cultural property.

The 1970 UNESCO Convention is the only international convention which makes any direct provision for return of certain cultural property in some circumstances. But it is a convention with many shortcomings and has come under criticism on many grounds. It is dependent upon each state's own definition of what constitutes cultural property, and upon each state taking its own legislative measures.[9] The convention covers directly only property stolen from museums, public monuments or similar institutions. The scope of protection for cultural property of importance is unclear and much of the convention uses ambiguous language. It is not retroactive, and by its terms would not cover any of the historic cases of removal of cultural property. Indeed, even with more recent cases, problems can arise, as in the Canadian case concerning the Nok treasure.[10] If it cannot be shown that a treasure has been illegally exported after the convention has formally entered into force for both the exporting and importing states, it cannot be applied. Of course both such states must always be parties to the convention. For instance, in the Maori Taranaki panels case (see Chapter 4) the convention would not have applied since neither New Zealand nor the United Kingdom is a party to it. But in any event, even if they were parties to it, it would still not have applied in effecting their return because although the panels were illegally exported, they were not stolen.[11] There has been a successful case of cultural restitution between two states parties to the 1970 Convention. This occurred in 1983 between Italy and Ecuador (pp. 223–4). However, it took nine years for the property, consisting of 12,000 pieces, to be effectively returned after a civil action by Ecuador in the Italian courts (Figs. 52 and 53).

The 1970 Convention has been criticized for its lack of any formal means of resolving disputes between the states parties to it. Disputes relating to cultural property could in theory be put to the International Court of Justice in The Hague, but there are many impediments (see p. 101), and it is extremely unlikely that the practical result of restitution would ever follow. It has also been suggested that the ideal mechanism for settling cultural disputes would be through the establishment of a special international tribunal.[12] This would in theory deal with both disputes arising under the 1970 UNESCO Convention and disputes outside it. This court would consider the country of origin, the significance of the property to the claimant country, and the manner in which the property was removed from its country of origin. There is as yet no such special

Fig. 52. An exhibition in 1983 of a vast collection of thousands of objects successfully retrieved by a legal suit from Italy by Ecuador. Held at the Museo Arquelógico y Galerías de Arte del Banco Central del Ecuador, Quito.

Fig. 53. The Turin magistrature in Italy ordered the restitution to Ecuador of this important collection of pre-Columbian ceramics illicitly exported to Italy in 1974. There were almost 12,000 items, and this was a case of successful restitution between two states both signatories to the 1970 UNESCO Convention.

international tribunal in existence. On the face of it the proposal seems simplistic and impractical because it is difficult to see how the jurisdictional pitfalls which already face the existing International Court of Justice, together with the absence of any means of enforcing its judgements, could be overcome in the case of yet another international tribunal, especially in the light of the fact that even the 1970 UNESCO Convention is still not universally ratified.[13]

Instances of return

Although it is often assumed that the return of cultural property is a hopeless cause, there are numerous cases where intergovernmental or interinstitutional negotiations and domestic legal suits have successfully effected returns, often of historically acquired property.

Some examples of objects returned are given below.

- In the early 1930s objects removed by Sir Robert Brownrigg in 1815 after the conquest of the kingdom of Kandy, including the shrine, sceptre and orb of the last king of Kandy, were returned to the Colombo Museum by the British government.
- In 1950 there was an agreement between France and Laos about the restitution of Laotian objects of art.
- In 1962 upon Uganda's independence the special objects relating to the Kabaka of Buganda were returned by the University Museum of Archaeology and Anthropology at Cambridge.
- In 1964 the Mandalay regalia were returned from the Victoria and Albert Museum to Burma.
- In 1968 an agreement between France and Algeria led to the return of some three hundred paintings which had been exhibited in the Museum of Algiers between 1930 and 1962.
- In 1970 Belgium returned at least forty objects to Zaire (these are now said, however, to have reappeared on the international commercial art market). The agreement was between the Royal Museum of Central Africa, Tervuren, Belgium, and the National Museum, Zaire.
- In 1973 the Brooklyn Museum returned a stela fragment stolen from the Piedras Negras to Guatemala. Despite the fact that the museum had legal ownership of the fragments, it entered into correspondence with the Guatemalan government to determine what should be done about the section of Stela 3 in its possession. In 1970 the museum placed the fragments at the disposal of the Instituto de Antropología e Historia de Guatemala. On 6 June 1972, when the director, Duncan F. Cameron,

turned them over to His Excellency Dr Julio Asensio-Wunderlich, Guatemalan Ambassador to the United States, he noted that they 'constitute a part of an historical document more important in the land of its origin than in this country'.[14]

- In 1973 the Syrian Department of Antiquities requested a mosaic of the fifth century AD from the ancient city of Apamea from the Newark Museum, New Jersey. It was returned in 1974.
- In 1974, the National Museum of New Zealand, Wellington, by informal arrangement returned a mask to the Papua New Guinea Museum, Port Moresby.
- In 1976 the Peabody Museum of Harvard University returned a collection of jade objects to Mexico (Fig. 54).
- In 1977 Belgium returned several thousand cultural items to Zaire; in addition, Brussels undertook to assist Kinshasa with the organization of a national museum network throughout the country.
- In 1977 arrangements were concluded between the Netherlands and Indonesia for the return of a large number of items to the latter country. These included Buddhist and Hindu statues as well as items from ancient royal collections directly connected with outstanding personalities

Fig. 54. Toltec engraved disc of jadeite in Chichen style from Cenote Chichen Itza, Yucatan, Mexico. One of a collection of objects returned by the Peabody Museum, Harvard University, to Mexico in 1976.

or with events that were fundamental to Indonesia's history. The Lombok Treasures were returned from the Rijksmuseum voor Volkenkunde in Leiden to the Pusat Museum in Jakarta, as the outcome of a cultural agreement between Indonesia and the Netherlands in 1968. A programme of joint recommendations was accepted by both governments to effect the return of cultural property and these included:

The transfer of historical and archaeological objects should be implemented by stages according to a specific programme.

The first stage of this programme should consist of the transfer of state-owned objects linked directly with persons of major historical and cultural importance, or with crucial historical events in Indonesia. The transfer should be executed as soon as possible. These objects should comprise in the first instance the Prajñāpāramitā statue from Singasari, the crown of Lombok, and such other specimens from the Lombok treasures still kept in public collections in the Netherlands as would be selected jointly by experts from both delegations.

As regards objects linked directly with persons of major historical and cultural importance or with crucial historical events in Indonesia that were not state-owned, the Netherlands government should render assistance within the limits of its competence in establishing the necessary contacts with the present owners. With regard to the objects which once belonged to Prince Dipo Negoro, and which were kept in the Bronbeek Museum at Velp, the Netherlands government should be willing to find ways of transferring them to Indonesia.

Should objects of high cultural value – such as the state insignia of Luwu – which disappeared during the war – afterwards be discovered in the Netherlands, the Netherlands government should be prepared to establish contact with their holders and to further arrangements for their return to Indonesia.

Investigation into any possibly unclear ownership of specimens of high historical and cultural value should be carried out and continued by experts from both sides.

It was also decided that the most important transfer, namely that of the famous Prajñāpāramitā statue (Fig. 55), should be made in Jakarta on the occasion of the celebration of the second centenary of the Pusat Museum (formerly the museum of the Batavian Society of Arts and Sciences) in April 1978. Before that the objects which once belonged to Prince Dipo Negoro and a painting by Radèn Saleh depicting the Prince's surrender in 1825 were han-

Fig. 55. In 1978 the Netherlands ambassador and the Indonesian Minister of Education and Culture signed a deed of transfer in the Museum
Pusat to formally hand over the East Javan statue Prajñāpāramitā from
the Rijksmuseum voor Volkenkunde in Leiden.

263

ded over. On 24 April 1978 the formal transfer of the Prajña/
pāramitā statue was made when the Netherlands ambassador and
the Minister of Education and Culture of Indonesia signed the
deed of transfer in the Pusat Museum, where a special exhibition
of all the returned objects had been arranged.

- In 1977 the Peabody Museum of Harvard University agreed to make a
long/term loan to the Museo del Hombre in Panama of items enabling
it to reconstitute a pre/Columbian tomb, and Pennsylvania University
returned to that country ceramics originating from an important archae/
ological site.

Australia has been active in returning numerous objects from its museums to
newly established regional museums. Thus:

- In June 1977 the Australian Museum Trust returned to the National
Museum and Art Gallery of Papua New Guinea 17 artifacts as a gift to
mark the opening of the new National Museum buildings at Port
Moresby. One year later, in June 1978, the trust presented to the Solo/
mon Islands Museum two canoe/prow carvings as a gift to mark the
independence of the Solomon Islands from the United Kingdom (Fig.
56). Although the timing of these returns was determined by the Aus/
tralian Museum, each was the result of five years of discussions with the
receiving institutions. (The Australian Museum has powers to dispose
of its property as it sees fit within certain guidelines, and is not hampered
by rules of inalienability.)
- In 1978 Papua New Guinea recovered, by courtesy of the museums of
Sydney (Australia) and Wellington (New Zealand), various ethno/
graphic items of great value.

There are other examples worldwide:

- In 1979 a tablet was returned to Syria by the Yale University Babylo/
nian Collection, after the direction determined that its probable origin
was the site of Ugarit.
- In 1980 France and Iraq arranged for mutual long/term loans under
which fragments of Babylonian codes, contemporaneous with the Code
of Hammurabi, which had been held in the Louvre for study, were re/
turned to the Iraq Museum in Baghdad.
- In 1981 a French court ordered the restitution to Egypt of a stolen
Amon Min statue which had been illicitly traded.
- In 1981, under the terms of an exchange agreement, carved birds from
Great Zimbabwe held in the South African Museum, Cape Town,

Fig. 56. Solomon Islands carved wood and painted canoe-prow ornament from a hunting canoe, New Georgia group. This was one of several returned to the National Museum, Solomon Islands, with the assistance of the Australian Museum, Sydney. It was presented by the Australian Museum Trust to the Solomon Islands in 1978 to mark its independence from the United Kingdom.

were returned to the government of Zimbabwe.

- In 1981 the Historic Places Trust of New Zealand returned more than a thousand cultural items to the Solomon Islands.
- In 1981 the Australian Museum Trust returned a large ceremonial slit-drum to Vanuatu (New Hebrides).
- In 1981, with UNESCO's assistance, the Wellcome Institute, London, returned a collection of Himyarite items to the Museum of San'a (Yemen).
- In 1981 Harvard's Peabody Museum officially returned a collection of Mayan jars to Honduras. These had been taken 'on loan' from Honduras in the 1950s and had been the subject of requests for return.
- In 1982 the United Kingdom returned to Kenya the two-million-year-old skull of *Proconsul africanus*, which had been on loan for over forty years.
- In 1982 negotiations between Iraq and two American museums, the Semitic Museum at Harvard University and the Oriental Institute at

Chicago, had resulted in the return of 584 cuneiform tablets to the National Museum in Baghdad. The return of 1,055 more pieces was expected.

- In 1982 Italy returned the throne of Emperor Menelek II to Ethiopia, following discussions between the Foreign Ministries of both countries.
- In January 1983 the Turin magistrature ordered the restitution to Ecuador of an important collection of pre-Columbian ceramics illicitly exported to Italy in 1974.

In the 1980s in the United States there were significant instances of returns effected by museum co-operation or bilateral agreement or litigation. In 1982 the United States Court of Appeals[15] ruled that an East German museum was the true owner of two priceless Albrecht Dürer paintings stolen in Germany soon after the Second World War. The two paintings were portraits of Hans Tucher and his wife Felicitas, painted around 1489. In 1824 they became part of the collection of the Grand Dukes of Saxe-Weimar. In 1868 they were displayed in the art museum of Weimar, the Kunstsammlungen (KZW), and to protect them during the wartime bombardment they were moved to Schloss Schwarzburg. They were stolen in 1945 and disappeared during the period of transfer of the area to Soviet forces. After the war Edward Elicofon purchased the paintings in New York for $450. When the paintings came to light the Metropolitan Museum of Art hailed them as the art discovery of the century, and they were claimed by the Grand Duchess of Weimar, the KZW (now in East Germany) and the Federal Republic of Germany. There were difficult issues involved concerning the choice of law, statute of limitations in international disputes, and state succession. The case, commenced in 1969, was not resolved until 1982, with ownership eventually granted to the East German museum. The paintings had been sold by a German civil servant stationed at the castle to an American serviceman. The judgement was that as a public servant he did not have such possession as would allow him to transfer title and also that under New York law a purchaser could not obtain good title from a thief. Thus the paintings went back to East Germany.

In 1982 Nan Kelker, curator at the San Antonio Museum of Art, rejected a smuggler's attempt to sell a colonial period Colombian monstrance valued at $3 million, and regarded by scholars as among the three most important extant art pieces from the Spanish colonial period. Historical records show that in 1737 the Convent of Santa Clara in the city of Tunja, Colombia, commissioned master goldsmith Don Nicholas de Burgos to create the monstrance. The Spanish monarchy and Tunja residents contributed 813 *castellanos* (coins) and 1,500 jewels including 831 emeralds, 582 pearls, 42 amethysts, 37 diamonds, 6 topazes and 2 rubies. The convent had sold the monstrance, a one-metre-high gold-carved, jewel-studded liturgical object used to display the host during mass, to a Colombian national. This Colombian antiques dealer then sold the piece to Edouard Uhart, an art dealer who tried to make the sale in the United States. Although these sales were legal, according to a 1953 Colombian law, cultural property can be exported only for exhibition at cultural institutions. Ms Kelker wrote to the director of the Museo del Oro in Bogotá, Luis Dequet Gomez, to ask whether documentation existed for the monstrance, and it was found that the dealer had clandestinely removed the antique from Colombia in 1981. It was later discovered that the object had been brought into the United States through New York City, where the smugglers had used false customs documents to indicate that it came from Spain. Eventually, United States customs seized the monstrance on 21 January 1983.

In May 1983 an exhibition called 'Stolen Treasures – Missing Links' went on at the National Geographic Society in Washington. It consisted of five hundred pre-Columbian pieces, all of them seized by American customs in the previous two years (Figs. 57–62). After touring eight major museums nation-wide, the art works were to be returned to Peru, which considers all pre-Colum-bian artifacts to be government property by law, as part of a bilateral agreement to send back such property recovered at US borders.

In 1986, following two and a half years of negotiations, some of America's oldest historical paintings of settlers and Indians were returned to the Palace of the Governors at the Museum of New Mexico (Fig. 63). They were coming back from Switzerland after two hundred years. Named Segesser I and Segesser II, the murals, which are said to be the largest works of their kind, are done on animal hide hanging over thirteen and seventeen feet respectively. Segesser I shows Indians on horseback equipped with Spanish weapons attacking an Apache village. The defenders are armed with bows and arrows and leather shields. Segesser II shows the ambush of an expedition of Spanish and Pueblo Indians. Research had suggested that the pictures were historically linked with the American south-west and had probably been sent by Father Phillip von Segesser von Brunegg, a Jesuit priest, from Ures in Mexico to Switzerland in 1758. The paintings were returned by Dr André von Segesser on loan for eighteen months to enable the museum that period of time to arrange for ap-praisal, conservation and exhibition to raise the $2 million being asked in return.

In early 1986 a major American art museum, the M.H. de Young Mem-orial Museum, voluntarily repatriated half of a seventy-item collection of pre-Columbian murals to Mexico (Fig. 64). They went back to the National Museum of Anthropology in Mexico City. This was the outcome of long

Figs. 57–62. In 1983 a 'Missing Links' exhibition of Peruvian pre-Columbian ceramics, gold and textiles was organized by the National Geographic Society in Washington DC. This consisted of hundreds of items to be returned to Peru from the United States, including: (57) small naturalistic copper or gold mask depicting adult head with feline headdress, Moche Vicus culture, north coast of Peru, AD 600–700; (58) stirrup vessel in form of fish boat carrying mythological being, two prisoners and a monkey, cream with dark red paint, Moche culture, AD 600–700; (59) gold masks and beaten gold ornaments and ritual objects, Moche Vicus culture, AD 1200–1400; (60) stirrup spouted frog and toad vessels fired in clay, north coast of Peru, Moche culture, AD 300–400; (61) stirrup spouted portrait clay vessels, evolved from the jar form, Moche culture, AD 300–700; (62) silver vases and necklaces of chrysolite beads, pearls, shell, gold and silver, Chimu culture, AD 1200–1400 and possibly later.

Fig. 63. Segesser II. A large mural from the New World on animal hide which was loaned from Switzerland in 1986 to the Museum of New Mexico, Palace of the Governors, in Santa Fe. One of a pair, it depicts the Indians of the Southwest and is thought to be the first historical painting done in the European tradition in North America.

negotiations between the Fine Arts Museums of San Francisco and Mexico's Instituto Nacional de Antropología e Historia.

The murals, dating from approximately AD 400–700, had been removed from the site of Teotihuacan, forty miles north-east of Mexico City. This was the principal highland city of the classic period of Mesoamerican[16] civilization dominated by the Pyramids of the Sun and the Moon. The murals varied in size from a few inches up to fourteen feet. Taken from residential and administrative buildings they depicted deities, anthropomorphic animals, flowering trees and feathered serpents, using mainly the colours of blue, gold and green on a red background.

The M.H. de Young Museum acquired the murals through a private bequest from a San Francisco architect Harold Wagner, in return for payment of estate taxes. The United States customs authorities, acting under the 1970 US–Mexico Treaty, informed the Mexican government of this bequest. An attempt to intervene in the probate proceedings by the US Attorney's Office at the behest of Mexico was unsuccessful. However, the murals, which were painted on volcanic rock, were in a poor state and required restoration. The most suitable

Fig. 64. Warrior bird. Pre-Columbian mural, dated AD 400–700, from Teotihuacan, in basic colours of blue, gold and green on red. One of over thirty pieces voluntarily returned in 1986 to Mexico's National Museum of Anthropology from the M.H. de Young Memorial Museum, San Francisco.

place was considered to be the laboratories at the Mexican Instituto Nacional de Antropología e Historia. In 1977 a co-operative programme was commenced between the two institutions. Negotiations lasted several years resulting in a bilateral agreement on custody, conservation and exhibition of the murals. The culmination of this was the return of half the murals to Mexico – as a result of which it has also been possible to discover and survey their original location, a residential compound called Techinantitla.

Such returns as have been effected have not always been the result of a spontaneous outburst of gratuitous giving by the institutions in question. There have often been protracted negotiations, not always conducted in a spirit of magnanimity. Sometimes returns have been hard fought for against an institution holding a piece which had been only temporarily deposited with it. For instance, Mary Leakey has recounted the great reluctance with which the British Museum finally parted with the *Proconsul africanus* skull, to allow its return to Kenya (Fig. 65). After she herself as its original finder had delicately transported the skull to Britain on a RAF York bomber in 1948, she recalls that

Fig. 65. Mary Leakey attending a press conference at London Airport in 1948 after she had personally transported the *Proconsul africanus* skull to London aboard an RAF bomber. It would take more than thirty years to return it to Kenya after it was deposited with the British Museum on loan.

it was decided that it should be placed on long-term loan in the British Museum of Natural History in Kensington, and a very popular exhibit it proved when it eventually went on public display there in 1949. When this loan to the British Museum was arranged, the Chief Secretary of the Kenya Government wrote to confirm it, stipulating, however, that the loan was temporary and that the skull remained the property of Kenya and could be recalled at any time in the future. There was a sequel to this. When my son Richard became Director of the National Museums of Kenya many years later, he requested the return of the skull now that the National Museum in Nairobi was properly equipped to receive it and house it safely among the many other Kenyan finds of international importance. The British Museum claimed that Proconsul had been not a loan but a gift, and they refused to return the skull, which they said they had accessioned. All Richard's vigorous efforts during the 1970s failed to achieve the skull's return. But in 1982 my own secretary, Hazel Potgieter, found in the National Archives a copy of the Chief Secretary's letter of 1948, of which the British Museum had denied all knowledge. When I was in London I had a frosty telephone conversation on the subject with the Keeper of the relevant department. Even then, Kenya had to wait several more months before a meeting of the Trustees of the British Museum took place at which the skull could be 'deaccessioned', something which the Trustees alone had power to do. One might have hoped that a special meeting could have been arranged a little more rapidly. I am delighted to say that the *Proconsul africanus* skull is now safely back in Kenya, where it quite certainly belongs.[17]

There are other anecdotal accounts such as this which recall the difficulty of recovering objects left with the British Museum. For instance, Michael Price, formerly from the Department of Antiquities in Saudi Arabia, recalls that in the 1970s he recovered a large and important head of a lion which had been found at the site of Ukhdūd near Najran in Saudi Arabia in the early 1930s, deposited with the British Minister in Jeddah, and then sent to the British Museum in 1937. The British Museum resisted return, but the ownership of the Emir Sa'ud bin Abdul Aziz (King Saud) had been recorded, and the lion went back in 1972.

In 1987 in East Germany the Voderasiatisches Museum in Berlin undertook to return more than 7,000 cuneiform tablets to Turkey which had been stored in its basements for more than seventy years. Originally taken to Germany for study and restoration at the turn of the century, the tablets are an historical record of the Hittite Empire from 1700 BC to 1200BC. Several thousand were also returned between 1924 and 1943.

There have also been numerous cases of private collectors surrendering cultural treasures. For example, in 1982 a Swiss collector returned a Hellenistic bronze jug to the Ephesus Museum when it was shown by the Turkish Directorate of Museums that the objects had been stolen from the museum. There have been instances of objects handed back to Turkey by Cleveland Museum. In addition, there have been a number of successful restitutions obtained by virtue of the bilateral agreements between Mexico and Peru, Guatemala and the United States of America[18] and between the latter and Peru.[19] A notable case of return to Mexico from the United States was that of a temple facade comparable with that of the Elgin Marbles (Fig. 66). It is now a prized exhibit in the Maya Room of Mexico's National Museum of Anthropology. This temple facade was originally shipped to New York in 1968, and was offered for sale, at around $400,000, to the Metropolitan Museum. The Metropolitan decided against the purchase, and the dealer who had organized its removal from a remote site in Campeche was persuaded to make it a gift to the Mexican Museum.

Fig. 66. Joseph V. Noble, Director Emeritus of the Museum of the City of New York, stands before the Campeche Temple facade. It was returned to the Maya Room of Mexico's National Museum of Anthropology as a result of the refusal by the Metropolitan Museum of Art to purchase it in 1968.

Sometimes cultural property is returned after requests have been made through diplomatic channels. An example of this was a formal request made by the Cameroon government for the return of the Afo-A-Kom, a wooden carving sacred to the Kom people, which had been smuggled out of the country. The Afo-A-Kom is the carved representation of a man holding a sceptre and wearing a headdress and is the symbol of the royal dynasty of the Kom, a small tribe in Cameroon. A nephew of the royal family is reported to have stolen the Afo-A-Kom from the royal compound in 1966. A US Peace Corps volunteer who worked among the Kom searched for the statue and found it in 1973 in the catalogue of an exhibition at Dartmouth College, 'The Royal Art of Cameroon'. A New York dealer in African art had loaned the statue to Dartmouth College having obtained it from a Swiss dealer, although how it had arrived in Switzerland was not revealed. Anthropologists, art historians, the media and the State Department applied pressure to the dealer to return the Afo-A-Kom, because the statue embodied 'the spiritual, political, and religious essence' of the people of Kom. Private negotiations rather than legal action were used because at the time in the United States effective legal action would have required documented evidence to show that the Afo-A-Kom had been stolen. The statue was returned to the kingdom of Kom shortly after it was discovered to be at Dartmouth. However, in 1977, it was again reported to be on the international art market![20]

On other occasions museums have been forced to forfeit and return cultural treasures which under their own state laws have been seized as an illicit import. For instance, in December 1969, the Boston Museum of Fine Arts announced the acquisition of an unknown Raphael portrait as part of the museum's centenary celebration (see Chapter 5). Removed from Italy secretly, and brought into the United States without being declared, it was seized by the US customs and returned to Italy.

Sometimes a government has claimed property not in the public domain, as in the case of the Śivapuram Naṭarāja statue (Fig. 67),[21] which had been removed from a temple in India for restoration and was subsequently held for several years by a private collector in Bombay. This was accomplished by exchanging a copy as a substitute for the original at some time between 1954 and 1955. It was sent to the United States accompanied by a false export certificate and bought by the Norton Simon Foundation from a New York dealer in 1972 for a reported price of $1 million. In spring 1973 it was announced that this idol would be exhibited at the Metropolitan Museum of Art. The publicity associated with this announcement attracted the attention of the Indian government. This resulted in the identification of Mr Simon's statue as the missing Śivapuram Naṭarāja. The government of India applied diplomatic pressure to the Metropolitan, which agreed to cancel the proposed Simon exhibition. India then filed suits to recover possession of the statue in England, where the idol had been sent for further restoration, New York where the dealer who sold the piece to Mr Simon lived, and Los Angeles, where Simon lived. The god embodied in the statue was himself named as one of the plaintiffs. The matter was not pursued to a judgement since a settlement was achieved by which the Śiva would be returned to India after a ten-year period, and it duly returned to India in April 1986.

In 1984, the Kimbell Art Museum in Fort Worth, Texas, negotiated with the Indian government to return a Śiva Naṭarāja statue which it had bought in good faith in 1979. It had been stolen from the Thiruvilakkadu temple in the Thamjavu district of Tamil Nadu.

There has also been the case of movable cultural property deposited in a foreign state being returned to the country of origin. For example, in 1940 the Canadian government permitted, as property of the Polish state, the duty free

Fig. 67. The Metropolitan Museum of Art in New York cancelled an exhibition of this statue Śivapuram Natarāja in 1973 after it emerged that it had been illegally exported from India. In accord with an agreement arrived at, the Norton Simon Museum in Pasadena returned it in 1986. The Śiva is represented in numerous manifestations including the *Natarāja* (meaning the Lord of the Dance), where he is depicted in the cosmic dance of creating and destroying the universe. Large numbers of this important Hindu icon were produced in bronze during the Chola period between the tenth and twelfth centuries.

entry into Canada of a number of cases and trunks containing Polish art treasures. These had been removed from the museum at the Wawel Royal Castle in Cracow before invading German armies could seize them.

The treasures were kept in the federal Records Storage Building at the Central Experimental Farm in Ottawa, on the understanding that Canada was to assume no responsibility for their safekeeping, and no inventory of the treasures was given to the Canadian government.

In 1945, a few months prior to the unconditional recognition of the new Polish Communist government in Warsaw by Canada, most of the treasures were removed, without the knowledge or consent of the Canadian government, by representatives of the Polish government-in-exile. The majority of them were transferred to the Provincial Museum in Quebec City by order of the Quebec government, and the premier of Quebec declared that the art treasures would be released by the government of the province only in compliance with the decision of 'a competent court'. Two trunks were also deposited in a branch of the Bank of Montreal in Ottawa by the two custodians who had brought the collection into Canada. At the time of the deposit they did not disclose to the bank the nature of their contents or whether they were acting in their official capacity or as private individuals. The few treasures that remained in the federal building in Ottawa were removed by the representatives of the new Polish government and returned to Poland in 1948.

The Canadian federal government had to face serious international and constitutional problems when the Quebec government assumed control over the remaining portion of the treasures and maintained that it did not recognize the authority of the new Polish government. Despite the long tussle, and the conflicts of law issues involved, the new Polish régime finally obtained possession of the treasures, and in 1960 they were returned.

In another case of a state seeking property, Hungary requested the return from the US of the crown, sceptre and orb of St Stephen, the first Hungarian king (the crown had been received from Pope Sylvester II in 1001). Over the centuries it had been lost and stolen several times before being stored at Fort Knox, Kentucky, after the Second World War. It was returned to Hungary by agreement with the US in 1978 and stated to be a return to 'the Hungarian people'.

Extraordinarily, cultural property has on occasion been 'restored' by theft and returned to the country of origin by an individual. Such a case occurred on 19 June 1982, when a Mexican journalist, José Luis Castaneda de Valle, removed an ancient eighteen-page Aztec codex, known as Tonalamatl Aubin (Fig. 68), from its wooden box at the Bibliothèque Nationale in Paris, and took it back to Mexico. The loss was discovered long after he had left the library and

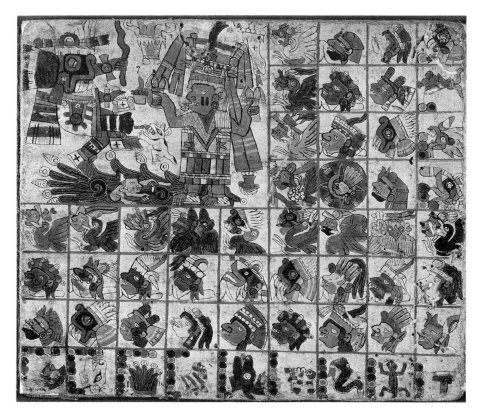

Fig. 68. The Aztec Codex (Tonalamatl Aubin) was removed from the Bibliothèque National, Paris, in 1982 by the Mexican journalist, José Luis Castaneda de Valle. Few such books, which served as genealogies and ritual calendars, survived the Spanish conquest of America because they were destroyed for their pagan images. The brightly coloured glyphs are divided by a red line horizontally and vertically and were usually read from left to right and top to bottom.

Interpol was alerted. However, the codex was handed to Mexico's Instituto Nacional de Antropología e Historia.

The French embassy requested the return of the codex but Mr Castaneda provoked a wave of nationalism by asserting that he had rescued a part of Mexico's cultural heritage that had been pilfered from the country more than a century before, following the Spanish conquest.

The codex, which originally had twenty sheets on tree bark folded like an accordion, is believed to have come from the Tlaxcala region. It consists of coloured drawings that served as a horoscope. Such codices are known as *tonala-matl*, a fusion of the Nahuatl words *tonalli* for day and *amatl* for paper.

The first known reference to the codex is in documents dating to 1740, when it was held by the Spanish viceroy. It later passed through a university library and a government office before being obtained by a Spaniard named Antonio de Leon y Gama. When he died it was sold to a German traveller, Max Waldeck, who took it to Paris in 1840 and sold it for 200 gold francs to Joseph M.A. Aubin, a French scientist, from whom it derived its name. A later owner gave it to the Bibliothèque Nationale.

Although Mexico City's Museum of Anthropology and other museums around the country preserve an impressive record of th: country's pre-Columbian heritage, many priceless items, such as the Maya Code, were destroyed by the Spanish colonizers, while others, such as the feather headdress of Montezuma, the last Aztec emperor of Mexico, were taken to Europe.

The press attaché of the French embassy in Mexico, Pierre Henri Guignard, referred to the act of returning the codex simply as robbery. Jack Lang, Minister of Culture, stressed that France could not accept robbery as a method of restitution of cultural artifacts. The type of agreement which has been drawn up between Mexico and the United States regarding return of pre-Hispanic and colonially acquired objects did not exist between Mexico and France, and France pressed for the return of the codex on a legal basis. It stated that the document truly belonged to France as it had been there since 1841, and at the Bibliothèque Nationale since 1848. It was donated by Mme Eugène Goupil, widow of the last person who had legally acquired it, and in accordance with her husband's will. There had been legal acquisition, and the codex had been kept for 140 years. However, the last record of this episode indicated that the Mexican authorities would nevertheless obstruct the return of the codex to Paris.[22]

Cultural property has also been returned by coercion after war. It is often assumed that international law in the past condoned looting, especially in time of war. However, history abounds with instances of the return of cultural treasures which a newly defeated nation had previously removed. For example, the Tyrannicides (Fig. 69), a group of figures taken away from Athens by the Persians in 480 BC, was restored to the Athenians by Alexander the Great after the defeat of the Persians in 331 BC. The armistice and peace treaty following the defeat of Napoleon (see Chapter 7) and the invasion of France did not make particular provision regarding confiscated art treasures. Yet when restitution of such property was made, no distinction was drawn between confiscated property or that taken under treaty or even property taken prior to Napoleon's activities; after the Congress of Vienna in 1815 many objects under all these headings were simply returned.

The Allies, in 1815, insisted 'on the necessity of reliving each school's work under the sky that had witnessed their birth and in the surroundings intended for them by their creators'. The rule was established that 'national heritages', by way of works of art, were not trophies of war, and if they had a home they must be

Fig. 69. The Tyrannicides, a group of figures of the Liberators of Athens, Harmodios and Aristogiton. They were taken away from Athens by the Persians in 480 BC but returned to the Athenians by Alexander the Great after the defeat of Persia in 331 BC. The original group has not survived from antiquity but is known from various copies, of which the best are these two in the Archaeological Museum of Naples.

returned to it. By the Second Peace of Paris, signed on 20 November 1815, France was obliged to restore to their owners those works of art which Napoleon had taken as the spoils of his campaign. The Prussians, without awaiting the signature of any treaty or the consent of their allies, had already packed their own works of art into wagons and sent them off to Berlin. The king of the Nether-lands recovered the Flemish masterpieces which Napoleon had housed in the Louvre. The *Venus of the Medici* went back to Florence; the horses of St Mark's were, on 30 September, taken down from the arch of the Carrousel and restored to Venice; and the Pope sent Canova on a special mission to Paris to catalogue and recover the treasures which had once been his. It was recorded that the rage of the Parisians at what they regarded as the despoiling of their capital was turned, not against those who had secured the restoration of their possessions, but against the British, who obtained nothing at all.[23]

The atmosphere prevailing in Paris at that time was recorded in the diaries of Andrew Robertson, a Scottish miniature painter:

> *September 29th*
> Still the same crowds of people looking at the horses (these are the bronze horses of St. Mark's). One or two gendarmes riding about leis-urely and whenever they saw a dozen or two people, walked through them to separate them. During the day half a dozen were so employed. The French are naturally bitter and satirical – even when they least wish it they are most so – the catalogues at the Louvre are bitter enough against themselves for as there has been no alteration they still contain their original bombast, this statue was conquered in Italy, that picture in Holland, etc. In the former catalogue they give a history of the *Venus de Medici,* her travels and the different nations which have possessed it-'but the victories of Napoleon the Great have forever fixed her destiny in France.'
>
> *October 2, 1815.*
> The public mind of Paris still continues in a state of extreme agitation; the people appear every day more and more exasperated against the all-ies. The stripping of the Louvre is the chief cause of public irritation at present; the long gallery of the museum presents the strongest possible image of desolation; here and there a few pictures giving great effect to the disfigured nakedness of the wall. I have seen several French ladies in passing along the galleries suddenly break into ecstatical fits of rage and lamentation; they gather around the *Apollo* to take their last farewell, with the most romantic enthusiasm; there is so much passion in their looks their language, and their sighs, in the presence of this monument

of human genius that a person unacquainted with their character or acc-
ustomed to study the character of the fair sex in England where feelings
is controlled by perpetual discipline would be disposed to pronounce
them literally mad – not the least of their griefs is the report that the
Apollo goes to England, the *Venus Medici* was removed yesterday.

October 4, 1815.
Groups in public places have of late increased in numbers and boldness.
The removal of the articles of art has afforded an occasion for bringing
them together and an opportunity of venting their resentment against the
allies. Upwards of 1800 pictures and other articles are said to have been
removed from the Louvre. When the *Venus* was put in the cart on
Monday, Sir T. Lawrence, Mr. Chantry and Canova burst into tears;
but a German officer who stood by kissed her and laughed at them.
When the last package was put into the cart the French mob collected
around door, hissed and goddamned the English troops who at the moment were on guard at the door just as if the pictures were going to be
sent to England. The *Venus de Medici* is said to be dispatched to
Florence.[24]

Indeed international jurists came to hold the view that cultural property was
not lawful plunder.[25] A number of codes and treaties sought to embody this
concept. Some seventeenth-century European treaties which embodied the concept of cultural return were the Treaties of Münster, 1648; Nimwegen, 1678;
Lunden, 1679; Ryswick, 1697; Utrecht, 1713; and Whitehall, 1662. The
Lieber Code of 1863 for the US army, the 1866 Treaty of Vienna and the 1907
Hague Convention contained prohibitions against seizure of historic monuments and works of art. After the First World War, the Treaty of Versailles
(1919) and Treaty of St Germain (1919) provided for the return of cultural
property. The 1921 Treaty of Riga also demanded the restitution of all cultural
property removed from Poland since 1772.

It was in the Treaties of Versailles and St Germain that the application of
a concept was for the first time fully developed. The treaties either stipulated for
the restitution of specific articles, or for authorized claims to be submitted to the
judgement of arbiters along the lines of:

(1)   special reconstitution, as reparations, of a work of art, the component
      parts of which have become separated in the course of history, even if
      such separation was the result of regular transactions;
(2)   more general, reciprocal reconstitution of the artistic and intellectual

heritage of regions dismembered through changes in territorial sovereignty;

(3) subordination of the stipulated or contemplated restitution to a respect for the unity of collections and archives and to the existence or
persistence of an historical or functional tie linking them with a given
region.

In particular, Article 247 of the Treaty of Versailles provided that, 'in order
to enable Belgium to reconstitute two great artistic works' Germany undertakes
to return to Belgium 'through the Reparation Commission, within six months
of the coming into force of the present Treaty':

(1) the wings of the triptych of the *Mystic Lamb* painted by the van Eyck
brothers, formerly of the Church of St Bavon at Ghent, now in the Berlin
Museum;

(2) the wings of the triptych of the *Last Supper,* painted by Dierick Bouts,
formerly in the Church of St Peter at Louvain, two of which are now in
the Berlin Museum and two in the Alte Pinakothek in Munich.

Restitutions also took place after the Second World War. After the war,
France, Great Britain and the United States signed the Paris Statement of Policy
with Respect to the Control of Looted Articles to Facilitate the Return of Loot.

Another area in which widespread return of cultural property has taken
place has been that of archival claims. Archives document the historical, cultural and economic development of a country and are regarded as essential to the
heritage of any national community. UNESCO and the International Council
of Archives made a special study of such claims in 1977, which indicated that
since the thirteenth century numerous treaties had governed the handing-back of
such archival material to newly independent states.[26] But its return has not
necessarily been automatic or universal. For instance, Algeria sought the return
of archival materials removed to France in 1961 for over nineteen years. However, the UNESCO study suggested that there has emerged something tantamount to an international law of archives.

There is even one precedent in modern times which has been compared
with the Elgin case, where a state has acted to pre-empt loss of a major monument. A criminal case was conducted against André Malraux, who was charged with stealing some stones and bas-reliefs from the temple of Bantea-Srei in
Cambodia while entrusted with an expedition to study the ancient monuments
of Khmer architecture (Figs. 70 and 71). Malraux later achieved fame as the
author of *La Condition humaine* and in the 1960s became the French Minister of

Fig. 70. The young André Malraux, adventurer, author and collector, later to be the French Minister of Culture, pictured with a piece of Central Asian sculpture.

Huitième année. — N° 2018   Huit pages   Le numéro : Dix cents   Huit pages   Mardi 22 Juillet 1924

L'IMPARTIAL

Organe de défense des intérêts français en Indochine

Directeur politique :
HENRY DE LACHEVROTIÈRE

Rédacteur en Chef :
GEORGES MIGNON

Téléphone : N° 289

RÉDACTION ET ADMINISTRATION :
23 à 27 Rue Catinat. — Saigon

Adresse télégr. : IMPARTIAL SAIGON

ABONNEMENTS
Indochine — Union Postale

TARIF DES ANNONCES

Agences d'informations : PRESSE ASSOCIÉE et PARIS TELEGRAMMES

Société Anonyme POINSARD & VEYRET, Agents

Concours Européen de vitesse 1921-1922
1er prix Miss Woodward
ROYAL

Le meilleur   Le plus sélect
CHAMPAGNE
KRUG & Co
REIMS
PRIVATE CUVÉE
Demi-sec   Extra-sec

Cⁱᵉ de Commerce et de Navigation
d'Extrême-Orient

Protégeons les trésors artistiques et archéologiques de l'Indochine

Angkor-Vat. — Vue générale prise du bord Ouest du bassin

Apsara volée provenant également des bas-reliefs de Banteai Srey

UN VOTE JUDICIEUX

La conférence de Londres

Divinités arrachées aux bas-reliefs du temple de Banteai Srey

BILLET PARISIEN
(D'un correspondant parisien)

JEAN BERNARD.

Dans l'Administration
Mutations

A la Philharmonique

Dans la Légion d'Honneur

COURRIER DU CAMBODGE
LE VOL DES BAS-RELIEFS D'ANGKOR
II
Malraux et Chevasson devant le tribunal correctionnel de Pnompenh

A.C.C.

Fig. 71. *L'Impartial* in Saigon, 22 July 1924, published a full account by Henry de Lachevrotière of André Malraux and Louis Chevasson's exploits in removing bas reliefs from the temple of Bantea-Srei, and illustrated this with pictures of the stones removed. The red stone chapels were built in the classical Khmer style and are dated between the tenth and fourteenth centuries. The temple consisted of shrines, libraries, courtyards and galleries and its name means 'Citadel of the Women'.

Cultural Affairs. He had quite deliberately set out to find the temple of Bantea-Srei, which he regarded as an abandoned temple in the jungle. Warned of the illegality of removing sculptures, he had in anticipation of difficulties acquired some official authorizations to cover his activities. He set out with a commission, letters of recommendation and confirmation that the authorities were to be informed of the results of their work. However, the mission, coloured by an expectation of mystery and discovery, was motivated primarily by the need of Malraux at that time to secure funds. He set out to remove stones although he knew that the official position was that they should be left *in situ*. His attitude was that the risks endured gave one the right to profit, and that the expedition was one of archaeological rescue and rediscovery, in that objects would be put into circulation which had hitherto been 'lost'. Malraux later expressed his philosophy of museums through a character (Vannec) in one of his novels, *La Voie royale*: 'Museums are places where the works of an earlier epoch which have developed into myths lie sleeping – surviving on the historical plane alone – waiting for the day when artists will wake them to an active existence....'

The Indo-China Malraux came to in 1923 consisted of four protectorates under indirect rule and one colony under direct rule, Cochin-China, whose capital was Saigon. The three Annamese Vietnamese countries of Cochin-China, Annam and Tonkin and the two Buddhist kingdoms of the west, Cambodia and Laos, came under the jurisdiction of a governor-general.

The temple he sought lay near Angkor. After trekking through the jungle for several days the group he organized came upon the temple as it had been described in art journals of the early 1900s. They chose to remove the carvings embedded in the walls, which were in better condition than those lying on the ground. It took Malraux and his companion Chevasson two days to cut away seven stones forming four great blocks decorated with very fine and well-preserved bas reliefs, which were taken away on donkey carts to be transported on the Tonle Sap river.

The group was subsequently arrested in Phnom Penh on board the boat carrying their cargo of stones. It was contended by Malraux and Chevasson that the temple was *res nullius* – abandoned property belonging to no one. However, this was not so. By virtue of a treaty concluded between France and Siam in 1907, France had acquired property rights taken by the Siamese Government in the Siam–Reap territory, which a few years later was re-attached to Cambodia under the French protectorate. Thus in 1908 the temple was classed as an historic monument and France was the owner.

During the trial, the defendants were accused of 'despoiling monuments' and of 'misappropriation of fragments of bas relief stolen from the temple of Bantea-Srei of the Angkor complex'. There were three hearings over two days.

The affair attracted public attention in France and Saigon because of its strange nature and because the principal defendant was regarded as a rather compelling personality. The original judgement was three years' imprisonment for Malraux and five years' prohibition from entering certain areas, and for Chevasson eighteen months' imprisonment. They also had to surrender the bas reliefs.

On appeal to the court in Saigon this sentence was reduced to suspended sentences of one year and eight months respectively because of the youth and character of the defendants, to which a number of famous French writers had testified. The court ordered the restoration of the bas reliefs to their original site. Malraux was so convinced as to his right to the bas reliefs that he believed that yet a further appeal to the Supreme Court of Appeal would restore them to him. In this he was completely mistaken and the bas reliefs were physically restored to the temple.

Some comparisons have been drawn between this case and the Elgin controversy: firstly, that Malraux used his official capacity under government permits to seize the materials including carvings and roof ornaments from a temple which was situated on the territory of a nation protected by France. Second, he destroyed the unity of an artistic whole – almost a ton of materials was involved. Finally, the action was sought to be legalized under the guise of an act of sale.

A principal difference between the cases is that France herself, because of treaties giving her judicial power in Indochina, applied French law through the local courts to protect the cultural patrimony of the country with whose care she herself had been charged. The statute guarded against expropriation of art treasures by France. This was not, then, a true case of return of cultural treasures but a case of a state acting to protect its 'own' cultural treasures within its jurisdiction, although the practical result was 'return' of part of a national monument to a colonial territory.

In another legal case in 1962 also involving Cambodian artifacts the International Court of Justice by a majority of seven votes to five held that cultural relics removed from the Temple of Preah Vihear by Thai authorities should be returned. The temple, which is a historic monument, was found to be situated in territory under the sovereignty of the kingdom of Cambodia. The court held that the Cambodian submission concerning restitution was implicit in and consequential on the claim of sovereignty itself. On the other hand, no concrete evidence had been placed before the court showing that specific objects of the kind mentioned (such as statues) had been removed by Thailand from the temple or temple area since its occupation in 1954. The court therefore decided that in the circumstances the question of restitution was one in which it would give a finding in principle in favour of Cambodia but without relating it to particular objects.

Sometimes other solutions to the problem of 'return' appear to have been found. For instance, it was reported in 1979 that the head of Queen Nefretiti from Egypt was to be returned from the Ägyptische Museum, West Berlin, and exhibited by turns in Berlin and Cairo. However, it has been established that no such exhibition has ever taken place, and that there has never been any formal arrangement to accomplish this. Dr Joachim S. Karig of the Ägyptische Museum has confirmed that it is not contemplated that Nefretiti would ever be exhibited elsewhere because there were conservational considerations of damage through transport or sudden climatic changes. The suggestion that Nefretiti was to be rotated had been the product of wishful thinking by a writer, Gert von Paczensky,[27] he said, and had never been discussed by the museums in question. Indeed the return of the bust has never been demanded by the Egyptian Antiquities Commission (the official body associated with ancient relics). The Nefretiti head has always been a charismatic object and it is not surprising that it had been the object of attention in the matter of cultural return, particularly in view of the circumstances of its removal by German archaeologists from Tell el-Amarna in the early 1930s. According to an anecdote from a former Egyptian attaché in the Egyptian embassy in Berlin in the 1930s, Mohammed El Kony, there was some early attempt to restore the bust to Egypt. Story has it, however, that Hitler himself upon seeing the bust determined that its obvious Aryan qualities meant that it must stay in Germany. Ironically it was amongst the finds of the Third Army at Merkers in Thuringia in April 1945. Included in the treasure trove from fifteen Berlin state museums was the polychrome head of Queen Nefretiti found in a wooden box labelled *Die bunte Königin* ('The multi-coloured queen'). And so Nefretiti has remained in Germany.

Nevertheless, there have been arrangements at the intergovernmental level for the exchange of art, such as that undertaken by the National Museum Emile Guimet in Paris with the national museums of Bangkok, Tokyo, and the Sarnath Archaeology Museum in India. The methods are by limited exchange loans, long-term loans, and indefinite exchange loans.

Sometimes a state has found the only way of effecting a return of its cultural property to be purchase back on the open market: this has been done by Nigeria, and Tahiti, through its Museum of Tahiti and the Islands. This museum has also adopted the approach of obtaining indefinite loan of objects from a number of French museums. In particular, it has purchased representative Polynesian art and ethnography, especially two parts from the Hooper Collection (Figs. 72–7) of objects from the Society Islands, probably collected by Captain Cook, from the Marquesas and Austral Islands.

Sometimes there are 'internal' conflicts within a state between the interests of its own archaeological collectors and the state itself. In Israel much controversy

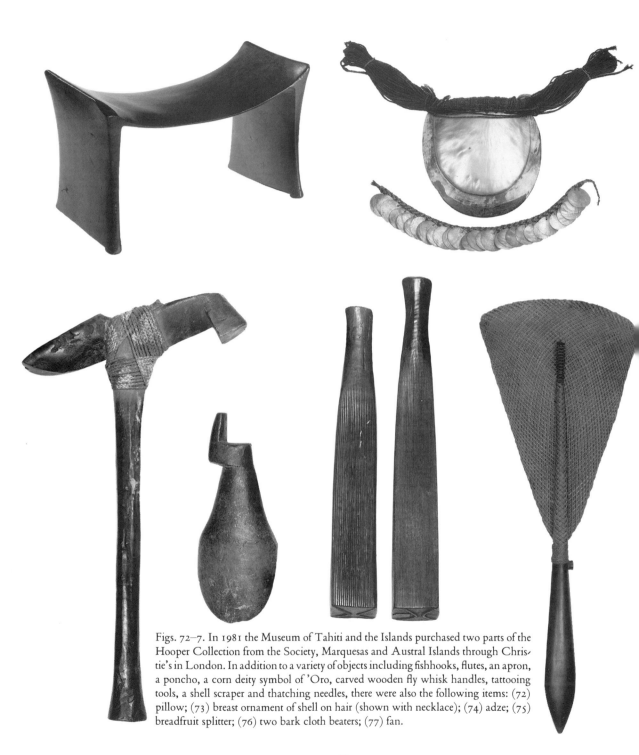

Figs. 72–7. In 1981 the Museum of Tahiti and the Islands purchased two parts of the Hooper Collection from the Society, Marquesas and Austral Islands through Christie's in London. In addition to a variety of objects including fishhooks, flutes, an apron, a poncho, a corn deity symbol of 'Oro, carved wooden fly whisk handles, tattooing tools, a shell scraper and thatching needles, there were also the following items: (72) pillow; (73) breast ornament of shell on hair (shown with necklace); (74) adze; (75) breadfruit splitter; (76) two bark cloth beaters; (77) fan.

surrounded the private collections of General Moshe Dayan, whose illegal digs turned up 10,000-year-old figurines. Ultimately his finds were purchased by a donor for the Israel Museum in Jerusalem, and put on display there in 1986. Archaeology is a particularly sensitive subject in Israel, touching upon controversial issues in law, politics, religion and culture. There have been conflicts over excavations, particularly in Jerusalem, ambiguities over property rights in buried antiques, and controversy over the trafficking of cultural objects between the territories of Israel.[28] There are internal conflicts elsewhere over the issue of the final destination of treasures on return. In Australia some aboriginal groups feel that materials should be returned to their community rather than to a national or state museum.

There have been a few instances of dismembered art works being reconstituted through museum co-operation.[29] One involved the National Gallery in Washington and the Louvre. The works concerned were two Renaissance bronzes – *Boy with a Ball*, part of the National Gallery's Kress Collection, and a figure in the Louvre identified as 'Atlas' or 'Hercules'. Louvre curator Bernard Jestaz noted the stylistic similarity between the figures while reviewing the bronzes in the National Gallery collection during a visit in 1970. Records showed that both pieces came from Gustav Dreyfus' celebrated nineteenth-century collection of Renaissance bronzes, and atomic analysis confirmed the identity of their component metals. Furthermore, when National Gallery curator Douglas Lewis brought the gallery's bronze to Paris, a projection on the boy's bottom fitted perfectly into a hole in the upraised hand of the Louvre's 'Atlas'.

Once joined, it was possible to determine the true identity of the work. The 'boy' and 'Atlas' were *St Christopher Carrying the Christ Child with the Globe of the World,* a work thought to be by Bartolomeo Bellano (1434–96), a Paduan pupil of Donatello. This discovery represents a 'significant advance for the history of art', according to National Gallery director Carter Brown. 'Every other rendition of this subject shows Christopher carrying Christ either on one shoulder or on his back. This is the only known example of the child being carried on an upraised palm' (Failing, p. 78).

Citing the unusual significance of the ensemble, National Gallery trustees authorized a permanent loan of its 'boy' to the Louvre. The Louvre, in turn, made a permanent loan to the National Gallery of a late sixteenth-century gilt bronze, *Cupid Astride a Dolphin,* also once part of the Dreyfus collection.

Another instance of reconstitution of dismembered art involved the Metropolitan Museum of Art, the largest museum in the United States. In 1974 an agreement nearly twenty years in the making joined the head of a rare Neo-Sumerian statue in the Metropolitan's collection with its body, owned by the Louvre. Ownership of the respective parts of the alabaster figure of Ur-Ningir-

Figs. 78–80. An agreement in 1974 made possible the joining-together of the head of a rare Neo-Sumerian statue, the Ur-Ningirsu, in the Metropolitan Museum of Art, New York, with its body, owned by the Louvre. Chlorite, dated 2123–2119 BC, it stands 55 cm high. Its rotation on a three-yearly basis between the Louvre and the Metropolitan is an excellent example of the co-operation of the great museums in achieving a reconstitution, mobility and display of previously dismembered works of art. (78) Joined figure; (79) head from the Metropolitan Museum of Art; (80) body from the Louvre.

su, which dates from about 2100 BC, was retained by their previous owners; the figure is shown on an alternating three-year schedule in each museum (Figs. 78–80). The Louvre and the Metropolitan also co-operate in exchanging fragments of Greek pottery and in some cases complete works have gradually been assembled. Through the conservation work and co-operation of such great museums, objects which have for one reason or another been dismembered or broken up are reunited and hence resurrected to the public gaze in their restored form.

Exhibitions can also temporarily reunite previously severed paintings, allowing the different parts to be seen together, and for the entire composition to be appreciated. For instance, the exhibition at the Dulwich Picture Gallery in England in 1986 (called 'Paintings and their Context') reunited Poussin's

Venus and Mercury, which, having been cut up into uneven parts, had been divided between Dulwich and the Louvre.

Sometimes where manuscripts are involved and physical reunification is impossible, a duplicated reconstruction through international co-operation is possible. For instance, China's largest encyclopaedia, which was commissioned by Ming dynasty emperor Yung Lo, later disappeared during the Boxer Rebellion around 1900. It had been compiled by over two thousand scholars, who laboured for more than four years to complete it. It was finished in Peking in 1407 and was an enormous work containing 22,937 volumes. The original was kept in Nanking, but two copies were made in 1567 and preserved in Peking. At the fall of the Ming dynasty the original and one copy perished. The remaining copy, which was kept at Han-Lin College (the Imperial Academy) in 1900, was presumed destroyed when the Boxers set fire to the building. However, it emerged that a number of the volumes were removed to Russia and the United Kingdom, and in the 1920s and 1930s the US Library of Congress purchased part of the collection. With the co-operation of Japan in making a microfilm of the existing different parts, China has reconstructed a set of the encyclopaedia, *Yung Lo Ta Tien,* in reprinted form.

Sometimes, happily, things which have been lost reappear,[30] and can be bought back. In April 1986 a collection of manuscripts and letters by the Norwegian composer Edvard Grieg, including his *Peer Gynt Suite*, turned up in a New York publishing house, and was sold to Norway for $615,000. The collection, taken out of Nazi Germany in the 1930s by Robert Hinrichsen, the youngest son of Grieg's publisher, includes 29 of Grieg's compositions and 371 letters by him. Lars Langslet, Norway's Minister for Cultural Affairs, said at a ceremony in New York that 'A priceless national treasure created by one of Norway's most famous sons, and thought to be lost forever, is coming home.' According to Evelyn Hinrichsen, chairman of the publishing house C.F. Peters, it is the largest collection of Grieg material in the world. The collection is to be housed in Bergen, Grieg's home city.

A case with a curious twist involving the artist's rights in the matter of cultural return occurred in 1985 when sculptor Henry Moore retrieved his *Warrior with Shield* from Florence. Photographs taken by David Finn had revealed to Moore the fact that although his work had been donated to the city preferably to be placed in the famous Saturn Terrace in the Palazzo Vecchio, the old Medici Palace, it was put into a third courtyard used as a car park. Moreover the sculpture had acquired the derisive epithet as the 'monument to the unknown (or absent) government worker'. Upon Moore's insistence the Florentine administration quietly returned the sculpture to England. Only negotiations by the Florentine mayor Massimo Boggiankino with the Henry Moore Foundation extracted the promise in 1987 that it could go back again on permanent loan subject to being put on proper display.

As a result of Australia's bicentenary in 1988, Hartog's plate, which bears the oldest piece of writing in Australian history, was returned on temporary loan for a year. It came from the Rijksmuseum in Amsterdam for display in Western Australia. Made of pewter and inscribed in Old Dutch, it had been used to mark the arrival of the Dutch navigator Dirk Hartog in 1616 on the beach south of Carnarvon in Western Australia. Over eighty years later it was taken back to Holland by another Dutch explorer, William de Vlamingh, via the Dutch East India Company in Jakarta. After the dissolution of the Company in 1795 it then went to the Royal Cabinet of Curiosities in the Hague, which was the forerunner of the Rijksmuseum. After 1964, when Australia began to seek its return, there were a series of diplomatic approaches, including appeals from succeeding prime ministers and a request to Prince Bernhard. The Dutch regarded the item as being equally significant for their own history and were concerned about the fragility of the object. However, a concession was made to allow its temporary return to Australia for the special occasion.

From the foregoing it can be seen that the concept of the return of cultural treasures is by no means novel. There are sometimes quite false reports such as that of the Nefretiti case, or that of the aboriginal artifacts kept in the National Museum of Ireland which have not been offered for return to Australia. However, returns have already been widely carried out, by coercion, by treaty, by private pressure, by diplomatic pressure, by private donations or purchase, by domestic legal actions, by gift and voluntary return, by exchanges, by indefinite loan and so on. Clearly this has not resulted in a flood of treasures going back to their source. Items have included not only major pieces, but also representative national collections of smaller objects. Often these returns have been to 'small' countries but have been of great regional significance.

The cultural property issue is often dealt with under the umbrella heading of 'protection',[31] although the issue of return is clearly separate. The main area of concern is that of objects historically removed and which are not covered adequately or retrospectively by existing international conventions or by current domestic legislation. It is these materials which ought to be designated as cultural treasures and defined as returnable under certain simple criteria.[32]

Generally, the contemporary emphasis has been on making lists[33] and preventing illicit trafficking, but what is required is strong national legislation on the actual disposal of art objects, and bilateral agreements on returning currently stolen or illicitly traded objects, and separately, historically removed materials. This requires co-operation between states. History has shown that only domestic legal action, bilateral agreements between states pursuant to formal claims, and voluntary inter-museum agreements can effect the physical return of cultural treasures. Sometimes considerable diplomatic or political intervention or participation is required.

The practice of return is becoming more widespread, and leading art-importing countries like the United States are taking a more active role. Despite the disclaimers from politicians and writers against attaching any international legal significance to the return of the Icelandic manuscripts from Denmark, since they were deemed to be a 'gift', nevertheless the international nature of the transaction and the magnitude and significance of the return make it a part of international customary practice (in which ever way this is arrived at under municipal law). However, it is arguable whether the general principle of returning cultural treasures has yet become entrenched as a *jus cogens*,[34] a peremptory norm of international law, since its terms remain to be defined.

What are the reservations against return?

Where there is no legal compunction to return cultural property, states and institutions which hold such treasures have the power to evaluate their own reservations against return. Even where the principle of return may be agreed the actual conclusion of an agreement may be a protracted affair. The Harvard University Dumbarton Oaks Museum in Washington DC and Turkey commenced negotiations in 1979 for the restoration, exhibition and eventual return of the Sion treasure, ecclesiastical Byzantine silver from the monastery of Saint Nicholas of Myra. But late into the 1980s the agreement was not yet concluded or fulfilled.

The fear that the question may become one purely of politics has been amply justified. Although the reaction of British Museum director, Sir David Wilson, to the effect that the UNESCO campaign to repatriate artistic treasures was based on Marxist–Leninist principles[35] seemed somewhat extreme, the movement for returning cultural property has sometimes become the instrument of left-wing anti-Western causes. This is arguably not the appropriate footing on which to consider such issues. However, it is equally true that the political argument cannot detract from the legal, aesthetic or historic merits of any particular return case, and that these must all be considered.

Another well-founded reservation is the potential physical danger to objects returned which may be destroyed or dispersed. There is no guaranteed place of safety anywhere in the world for any material. However, many treasures were incidentally preserved by the very fact of their original removal from countries subject to upheaval. An example of this was the terrible cultural destruction which took place in China during the Cultural Revolution in the late 1960s. Other claimant countries may still lack the resources for caring for fragile material, and arguments against the current competence of a state to receive safe custody of an object may be valid.

It is also true that the question of return can be very complicated because of the creation of new nation states (see p. 102).[36] For example, the question might arise whether Iran could validly claim Kurdish material. There are many situations in which minority, ethnic or religious groups are seeking autonomy within a state and where an object could be a focal point of this ambition, as, for instance, the Sikh throne of Amritsar.

Finally there are also the added dangers of the art market place. With continued illicit trafficking, more treasures are being lost. For instance, somewhat astonishingly it has been reported that objects returned to Zaire from Belgium have reappeared on the international market (see p. 260).

The significance of 'exchange' or 'transfer' of cultural property and its 'return'

The impact upon European art and scholarship of many of the treasures that were removed from the sites of classical antiquity, or from the numerous African sites, is not disputed. It has been said of the Benin works that their presence in Europe helped create a respect for African art, and that less than ten years later Picasso and Braque were using African art as models for their rejection of imitative in favour of conceptual art. The importance of Benin bronzes was immediately recognized by the early German Africanist Felix von Luschan. Writing in 1919, he described them in glowing terms: 'Benvenuto Cellini could not have cast them better... and nobody else either before or since Cellini. These bronzes are technically of the highest quality possible.'

Similarly, the Elgin Marbles are said to have furnished new standards of art to Western Europe and permanently modified the whole view of ancient art.

It is equally true, however, that in both these cases the works of art were lost to the descendants of the peoples who had created them, and in each case an invaluable narrative record was destroyed through dismemberment.

The importance of cultural property to the place where it is found or created can be seen, for example, by the great contemporary significance attached to archaeological finds in a land such as Israel, where archaeology, although directly involving only a small group of professionals, has been described as a national obsession. Cultural property in this context has to be understood as a significant expression of continuity with the past, a fulfilment of national legitimacy, and the reaffirmation of roots; hence the importance of such finds as the Dead Sea Scrolls.

Another situation in which cultural property may be important is where, although not created by or for the people in question, it nevertheless constitutes an important documentary record of their history. In such a situation the arguments are not really about the return of the cultural property in question but concern prior rights of acquisition. A case in point was the sale by auction at Sotheby's in 1980 of the Codrington papers, family records relating to sugar estates on the islands of Antigua and Barbuda over two hundred years. Despite arguments that they should be offered to the newly independent republic of Antigua, they were finally sold to the highest bidder, who remained anonymous. There was some doubt therefore as to their final destination.

Generally speaking it is clear that cultural property is most important to the people who created it or for whom it was created or whose particular identity and history it is bound up with. This cannot be compared with the scholastic or even inspirational influence on those who merely acquire such objects or materials. The current arguments about the retention of major objects on the grounds of scholarship are no longer tenable. In most instances the task of learning has been satisfied, as for example with the Rosetta Stone, whose hieroglyphics have already been deciphered. The Parthenon and its marbles continue their hold on the imagination but they no longer have a revelatory significance for twentieth-century Europe. The continued scholastic value of keeping the marbles in Britain is debatable and most scholars would probably welcome their return to Greece or at least not oppose it. Scholasticism can be a high-sounding motive for a selfish and unrelated purpose. Museum claims of universality are also suspect because, as Professor John Gould of Bristol University has pointed out, they cannot be invoked unilaterally but must be determined by the international community.[37] No one doubts the excellence of such institutions as the British Museum for scholarship and the maintenance and preservation of valuable treasures, but in some cases the return of treasures would be most consistent with its avowed custodial role, which could then be seen to be not purely nationalistic.

Even this argument has been inverted:

> How fortunate we are that the British Museum and the National Gallery are full of objects which are neither British nor National. It has been argued that these institutions are profoundly imperialist, and some people probably do vaguely perceive the objects they contain as trophies or tribute. On the whole, however, these institutions are far better designed than truly national collections could be to perform the vital civ-

ilizing job of reminding us of *what is not our 'heritage'*, encouraging us to love things without having to pretend that they were made for us, to take an interest in other people's ancestors, to be curious about the past be- cause our 'identity' (which generally means self-esteem) is challenged rather than reinforced by contact with it. Even if we are not clear whether or not art objects should be returned to their country of origin, we should be clear as to the purpose of museums.[38]

The retention of art treasures can be rationalized on almost any grounds, especially the sanctity of the 'collection'. However, this ignores the fact that when international collections were made, they were done so at the cost of destroying the completeness of the 'collections' of other peoples, and it chooses to ignore completely the mode by which many treasures were acquired. Account is not taken of the fact that the major Western museums are so laden with objects of every kind that there are not the facilities for them to be permanently or properly exhibited and much material is simply stored, never to be viewed by the public (Figs. 81 and 82), despite modern and innovative ideas which are emerging about museum displays.[39] Two examples of this are the ethnographic collections held by the Museum of Mankind and the Indian collections of the Victoria and Albert Museum in London, where the largest collection of Indian art treasures outside the subcontinent, consisting of 40,000 items, is mainly not shown.

The means of acquiring cultural treasures has also at times been dubiously justified. Take, for instance, the words of General H. Turner, who brought the Rosetta Stone to England:

> When the ship came round to Deptford, [the stone] was put in a boat and landed at the Custom House; and Lord Buckinghamshire, the then Secretary of State, acceded to my request, and permitted it to remain some time at the apartments of the Society of Antiquaries, previous to its deposit in the British Museum, where I trust [the Rosetta Stone] will long remain, a most valuable relic of antiquity, the feeble but only yet discovered link of the Egyptian to the known languages, a proud trophy of the arms of Britain (I could almost say *spolia opima*), *not plundered from defenceless inhabitants, but honourably acquired by the fortune of war.*[40]

In terms of the actual fate of the cultural treasure in question, the distinction between 'plunder' and 'honourable acquisition by fortune of war' seems pedan- tic.

It has been argued that, from an historic point of view, if time is not enough to confer good title then no man is secure in what he owns. History, it is said,

Fig. 81. A treasure stored: this Mexican stone is one of the items amongst the vast and intriguing British Museum collections which are not displayed. A coiled rattlesnake carved in minute detail, and remarkably realistically, and rendered accurately in the tail with the underside decorated with red spots. The snake is the most common of all the animal motifs in Aztec art, such carvings flanking the steps of the great Toltec and Aztec temple pyramids.

cannot be unravelled or turned back, and historic fact cannot be changed. 'History' is past events, but, as has been pointed out by Professor Gould, just as the 'tides of history' previously favoured the removal of many cultural treasures from their homeland, the 'tides of history' have changed and now favour return.[41] Attitudes towards the manner in which such objects were acquired have changed, together with an appreciation of their significance. And such changes in social outlook should not be dismissed purely because of inconvenience to governments or institutions.

Taken in perspective, in a world haunted by poverty, famine, war, totalitarianism, and the displacement of millions of people, the issue of returning

Fig. 82. A treasure stored: wooden figures from a spirit house in Papua, New Guinea, stored by the Ethnography Department of the British Museum but not displayed due to lack of resources.

cultural property cannot be rated very high on the list of human priorities. And this has been reflected in the conduct of states for hundreds of years, as very few governments have actually taken the formal step of seeking the restoration of major treasures. And yet the psychological and spiritual importance to all peoples of history, continuity, identity and tribal memory, as embodied in their tangible cultural treasures, cannot be ignored. Although 'cultural property' is actually created by the genius of relatively few individuals, and although 'culture', except when used by way of propaganda, is not really an active or primary interest to the majority of people anywhere, 'cultural property' still commands a collective importance through its symbolism and inspirational value.

299

There always will be an international traffic in art. The lure of treasure and the taste for 'collecting' will always prevail, whatever the psychology that lies behind it. Let us say that it is no more than the desire to possess things which are beautiful, unusual, rare and valuable. Collecting has also been said to be an essential tool of scholarship which has genuinely preserved endangered art. In any event, there will always be a difference of interests between curators, nation-alists, collectors and dealers. There is also an element of romance and piracy associated with cultural treasure. One is always intrigued by the great unsolved riddles of the missing treasures such as the 'invisible' treasure of Dorak, the lost treasure of Priam, the mysterious appearance of a fourth Mayan codex in the United States, and the disappearance of Peking Man in China. Such mysteries further complicate questions of cultural return.

For instance, the Dorak treasure (Fig. 83) has remained for over thirty years a 'phantom' treasure, known only from an uncorroborated sighting by a British archaeologist, James Mellaart, in the 1950s. Although Mellaart reported on it with detailed drawings in the *Illustrated London News* in November 1959, the treasure was never seen again.[42] It was seen in private ownership at Izmir but was attributed to the royal tombs at Dorak, and consisted of figurines, ceremonial swords, and household treasures including a carpet. The Turkish authorities gave such credence to the report as to call for the return of these objects, which they believed had been spirited away, and banned Mellaart from ever digging again in Turkey.

When Heinrich Schliemann was excavating at Hissarlik in Turkey in the late 1800s, he identified the second of seven cities on the site as Homeric Troy, the citadel of Priam, one of the mightiest kings of prehistory; and in 1873 he dis-covered a collection of magnificent gold treasures dating from the second city. Schliemann's work gave truth to Homer's poems, but his account of his find of 'King Priam's treasure' has caused controversy ever since. Its archaeological authenticity has been questioned because of his techniques and irregularities in dating and recording his finds. As a result the find has been described as a hoax. But items of jewellery and gold were undoubtedly found – diadems, brooches, chains, bracelets, plates, and buttons, golden wire and thread, which he smug-gled out of Turkey through Athens. In doing so, as the author C.W. Ceram pointed out, he was acting on a 'precedent of sorts' set by Lord Elgin seventy years earlier. The treasure was put on exhibition in Berlin, and then disappeared during the Second World War never to be seen again.

Until April 1971 it was believed that only three Mayan codices in the world had survived the Spanish Conquest of the New World. These have ended up in the libraries of Dresden, Paris and Madrid, and consist of texts and pictures on folded sheets of bark. They have been invaluable in helping scholars interpret glyphs, calendrical systems and iconography. It is speculated that possibly thousands of codices were destroyed by Spanish priests or perished in the humid forest environment. In 1971 it was announced in New York that a previously unknown fourth codex had come to light. This fourth codex was an eleven-page fragment of a calendrical book written on bark cloth and apparently dating to the late post-Classic Maya period, from about AD 900 to 1520; its contents deal with the cycles of the planet Venus. It was said to be an archaeological find of major significance made at the site of Chiapas, but it is now said to have disap-peared again, thus constituting a further loss to Maya scholars.

Equally aggravating to scholars for over fifty years has been the missing Peking Man (Figs. 84 and 85), which the Chinese would undoubtedly wish to recover. Peking Man was a skull discovered by the Chinese palaeoanthropolo-gist Pei Wenzhong on 2 December 1929, in a twelve-metre-deep cave at Zhoukoudian on Beijing's south-western outskirts. It dated hominid history back 400,000 to 500,000 years, and opened an important chapter in the study of the evolution of man. However, the war in the early 1940s caused the skull to be lost in transit to the USA, and its whereabouts are still unknown.

There are still many famous unresolved claims. The long-standing Turkish claim over the Croesus gold or Lydian treasure (Fig. 86) re-emerged in 1987 as a potential legal battle which promised to be a landmark case if taken to its conclusion. In the extent of its claims the Turkish case has been compared with those of Greece for the Elgin Marbles, although the removal was contemporary.

The story of the Croesus gold only goes back as far as the 1960s when village treasure hunters at Ikiztepe near Ushak made four illegal excavations and then smuggled about 250 gold and silver objects. These consisted of wine jugs, bowls, incense burners, often beautifully shaped and embossed with figures of men and animals. The villagers' ringleader was a man called Durmish and one of the main participants was the village blacksmith Osman. The Turks believe that the treasure was bought by an Izmir dealer named Ali Bayirlar who in turn sold it to international antiques dealer John Klejman. The Metropolitan Mu-seum of Art in New York purchased it from him through Dietrich von Both-mer, chairman of the Department of Greek and Roman Art. The museum is reputed to have paid between a half and one million pounds for the collection.

Despite exhibitions at the Metropolitan Museum in 1970 and 1975, where suspect individual objects were displayed without provenance and mixed in with objects from other sources, the Turks have never relinquished their belief in the existence of a collection. The museum continues to deny this, but when in 1984 an exhibition was held displaying a far wider range of fifty-five objects, these appeared in its summer *Bulletin* catalogued and photographed. Osman the blacksmith from Ushak was able to identify these objects. In addition the objects

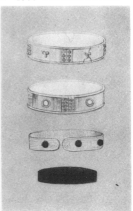

FIG. 3. THE TWO BRONZE FIGURINES: PRIEST-ESSES OR WORSHIPPERS WEARING WHAT WAS PRESUMABLY THE NORMAL DRESS OF THE YORTAN RULING CLASS (6 INS. HIGH).

FIG. 4. BACK VIEW OF FIG. 3. THE FIGURES ARE OF BRONZE WITH SILVER GARMENTS; AND HAIR, ORNAMENTS AND DECORATION IN GOLD. TWO HAIRSTYLES ARE SHOWN.

FIG. 5. ONE OF THE ATTENDANTS ON THE GODDESS. THE BODY IS ENTIRELY MADE OF SILVER, THE HAIR AND ALL THE ORNAMENTS BEING GOLD.

FIG. 6. PERSONAL JEWELLERY FROM THE QUEEN'S TOMB: GOLD AND SILVER BRACE-LETS, WHOSE PATTERN MAY ALSO BE OBSERVED ON THE FIGURINES.

FIG. 7. THE GODDESS (RIGHT) IN ELECTRUM AND HER PRINCIPAL ATTENDANT IN SILVER, ALL THE ADDITIONAL ORNAMENTS BEING IN GOLD. THE GODDESS'S GOLD BELT AND PENDANTS ARE SOLDERED ON BUT THE "GRASS SKIRT" IS ENGRAVED. LIFE SIZE.

FIG. 8. THE BACK VIEW OF THE TWO FIGURINES SHOWN IN FIG. 7. THE SILVER FIGURE, WEARING A GOLD-EDGED SILVER APRON, HOLDS A CIRCLET, WITH SEVERAL BIRDS ON IT, PERHAPS A MUSICAL INSTRUMENT OF THE SISTRUM TYPE.

It is not absolutely certain that these five amazing figurines in electrum, silver and bronze were actually found in the two tombs; and Mr. Mellaart, while convinced of their genuineness, thinks that they may be a little later. All are about 6 ins. high, cast in a two-piece mould and are naturalistic though a little flat. All the articles of dress, hair, necklaces, bracelets and anklets were made in sheet gold or wire and were added by soldering or sweating-on, or, in some cases, loosely fixed. It is noteworthy that the objects of jewellery are exactly to be paralleled among the jewellery found with the queen in the double tomb; and Fig. 6 shows a group of bracelets from that tomb — two of them were found round the queen's arms — which exactly resemble the bracelets worn by the figurines. There seems little doubt that the electrum figure represents the goddess, the two silver figures her close attendants and the bronze figures her priestesses or worshippers. The silver figurine in Fig. 8 is especially interesting. It is suggested that the rod in the left hand was used to beat the bird-studded circlet in the right hand to produce a musical note. One of the bronze figures holds a similar circlet.

Fig. 83. *The Illustrated London News*, 28 November 1959, carried an article and drawings by James Mellaart of the missing Dorak treasure. Although this was an uncorroborated find never seen again, the Turkish authorities demanded its return without success and banned Mellaart from digging in Turkey again.

THE ROYAL TREASURE OF DORAK—A FIRST AND EXCLUSIVE REPORT OF A CLANDESTINE EXCAVATION WHICH LED TO THE MOST IMPORTANT DISCOVERY SINCE THE ROYAL TOMBS OF UR.

By JAMES MELLAART, Assistant Director, The British Institute of Archæology, Ankara.

Owing to the circumstances of this discovery, no photographs whatever are yet available and all our illustrations, both black-and-white and coloured, are from meticulous scale drawings made by Mr. Mellaart and they are now published for the first time anywhere in the world. It is emphasised that the colouring is not representational, but is designed to show the materials of which this unbelievably rich treasure was made. The site of the discovery was on an estate somewhat inland from the southern shore of the Sea of Marmora, that landlocked sea which lies between the Dardanelles and the Bosphorus, between, that is, Troy and Byzantium.

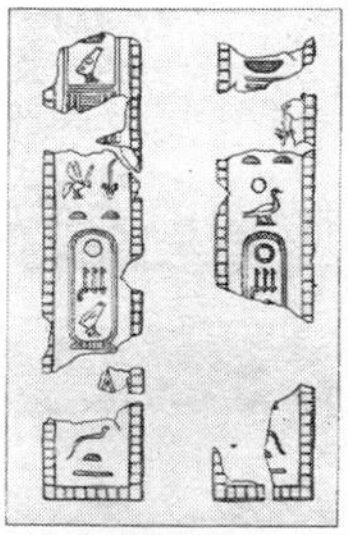

FIG. 1. EVIDENCE WHICH SECURELY DATES THE ROYAL TOMBS OF DORAK TO THE THIRD MILLENNIUM B.C.

These drawings are careful scale transcripts from fragments of gold sheet which originally adorned a wooden throne in the single tomb. They show the *cartouche* of the Pharaoh Sahure (2487-2473 B.C.) and indicate that the throne must have been a Royal gift, provide the first piece of evidence of contact between the seafaring population of North - West Anatolia and Egypt of Third Millennium and also give, as it were, a written date for the tomb.

A RICH collection of objects derived from an unpublished excavation of two Royal Tombs of the Yortan culture, undertaken at about the time of the Turco-Greek war, was rediscovered some years ago by the writer in private possession in Izmir. We are much obliged to the present owner for her permission to publish coloured reproductions of the objects and for the information from what remains of the original excavation records and from notes and old photographs, which has enabled us to reconstruct the approximate tomb lay out.

A small cemetery consisting of two Royal cist graves and two *pithos* burials of servants was found high up on a hill slope near the village of Dorak, on the southern shore of Lake Apolyont (Vilayet of Bursa) in North-West Turkey, near the Sea of Marmora. A close investigation at the time showed that no other tombs were present in the immediate neighbourhood, and it appears, then, that this site was only used for the burial of a king in Tomb I, a king and queen in Tomb II and two servants of the Royal couple. The *pithos*-graves of the commoners are similar to those found at Yortan, Babaköy and Bayindir (the best-known cemeteries of the Yortan culture), and the pottery found in the two Royal Tombs is again of Yortan type. No other Royal Tombs are known in Western Anatolia and the present find is therefore of unique importance.

FIG. 2. CERTAINLY THE EARLIEST DETAILED REPRESENTATION OF OCEAN-GOING SHIPS YET KNOWN OUTSIDE EGYPT: A CLOSE-UP OF THE ENGRAVING ON THE BLADE OF THE SILVER SWORD OF STATE FROM THE SINGLE TOMB.

The silver-bladed sword from which this detail is taken is illustrated on the third colour page and appears as Fig. 18B. Nothing like as early a picture of ships as this has ever been discovered in Asia or, in fact, anywhere else but in Egypt; and indeed it is in vessels like these that we can imagine the legendary Argonauts sailing through the Sea of Marmora, past Dorak, on their way to Colchis.

Tomb I, the smaller of the two, measured 6 ft. 1 in. (1.8 m.) x 2 ft. 8¾ ins. (0.83 m.) and contained the body of an adult male stretched out on his back with his head to the east and feet to the west. He lay on a badly preserved woollen *kilim* (or woven rug), which did not survive the opening of the tomb (Fig. 13).

Around the king's body were placed his funerary gifts: ceremonial arms, weapons, drinking vessels in precious metals, pottery and stone vessels, which may have contained food, and, most important of all, a piece of furniture, probably dismantled before being deposited in the tomb. The position of these objects, as far as still could be ascertained from the faded photographs, was reconstructed in a plan of the tomb.

On the king's right side lay a splendid sceptre with a pear-shaped fluted head of light-green stone and a diagonally fluted ivory handle with gold-capped ends, two black obsidian beakers, one smooth polished, the other vertically fluted, a vertically fluted *depas* (two-handled drinking cup) of gold (Fig. 14), and a one-handled cup with *repoussé* design.

Near his right hand lay a dagger (11¼ ins. in length) with a carnelian pommel, silver blade and hilt covered with embossed gold sheet. Between the king and the south wall of the tomb lay a group of weapons: a lance with silver head and chased midrib, the long decayed wooden shaft being encased in alternate ribbed gold and plain silver tubular pieces of casing, a bronze (or copper) battle-axe of shaft-hole type, with plain gold-encased wooden handle, a flat axe of the same material and a pile of nine swords and daggers. (*Coloured drawings of five of these splendid weapons are shown in our third colour page as Figs. 15, 18a, 18b, 20 and 21. Of the remainder the most interesting is a bronze dagger with a hilt consisting of two plaques of meerschaum, a material found only near Eskisehir, about 100 miles east of Dorak.*)

Stone bowls, cups and goblets of white marble, pink-veined white marble, or light-green stone, and black or brown burnished pottery vessels of Yortan type were placed in the four corners of the tomb. The largest pottery vessel contained the crushed remains of a silver bird-vase with a gold spout and gold ribbing, indicating the bird's plumage. The two rivets on the cut-away spout have heads of lapis lazuli set in gold granulation. Vessels of this type are extremely common in Yortan pottery, and it is now clear that their prototypes were metal vessels.

The most remarkable object, however, in the tomb was a wooden chair or throne, probably dismantled when put in the tomb and unfortunately not restorable. It was plated with thick sheet gold; one of the surviving casings of the legs shows that it had animal feet. Strips of sheet gold bear in embossed Egyptian hieroglyphs the name and titles of the second king of the Fifth Dynasty, Sahure (2487-2473 B.C.) (Fig. 1). This piece of Egyptian furniture undoubtedly represents a Royal gift, and is the first piece of evidence of contact between the seafaring population of North-West Anatolia and Egypt in the Third Millennium B.C. Even if it were an heirloom at the time when it accompanied its owner into the grave, it remains of supreme importance for dating the tomb to *c.* 2500 B.C. or a little later.

The second and larger tomb, measuring 10ft. 2 ins. x 6 ft. 6¾ ins. (3.10 x 2 m.), contained two burials: a king in the southern half of the tomb and his queen in the northern half, each accompanied by funerary gifts. Both burials were flexed, with their heads oriented towards the east. Both lay on their right side facing the lake. At the king's feet lay the skeleton of a dog, lovingly provided with its own stone bowl. Both burials lay on mats which covered the floor of the tomb, and in the case of the queen, remains of textiles were around and below the skeleton when the tomb was opened, but these have not survived.

THE KING'S GRAVE GOODS fall into the same categories as those found in the other tomb, and are on the same lavish scale, but the queen is provided with jewellery and toilet articles, objects naturally not occurring among the paraphernalia which accompanied the king's. The king was provided with a sceptre, the spherical head of which was made of pink-veined white marble. Its wooden handle was cased in gold sheet, ribbed and ornamented with gold granulation (Fig. 12). Near it in front of the king lay a drinking cup of gold with a spirally-fluted body and granulated patterns on the neck (Fig. 9). (*Under, beside and behind the king's body lay some eleven swords and daggers; and nine of these are illustrated on the third colour page as Figs. 16, 17, 18c, 18d, 18e and 19.*)

A silver lance-head, like that in Tomb I, lay along the south wall of the tomb, its shaft decorated with alternate gold and silver tubular casings. Behind the king's head there lay four ceremonial battle-axes like those found at Troy (Fig. 11). Other vessels of precious metal buried with the king included a gold jug with cut-away spout and embossed decoration (Fig. 10) and a small silver, half-corroded, two-handled *depas* (Fig. 9), with horizontal ribbing. Two silver pins with double spiral heads were found near the king's shoulder. A shallow white marble bowl and four burnished pots of Yortan type, one of them a bird vase, lay in the corners of the tomb nearest to the king.

THE QUEEN'S FUNERARY OFFERINGS: In the north-western corner, in the queen's half of the tomb, there stood two wooden tables or trays supporting several pottery vessels, one of which contained a necklace of about twenty gold beads in the form of double-spirals, such as have been found at Ur, Troy, Poliochni and Brak. Near the neck of the skeleton were found other necklaces, consisting of carnelian, rock-crystal and gold beads, or of white marble and gold, or striped onyx, or of gold-capped obsidian, and of rock-crystal beads. Below the queen's hips strips of silver and gold sheet were found, with holes along the edges for sewing on to garments, no longer preserved. Around the skull and partly slipped off, lay a badly corroded silver diadem with pendants, and behind the head were found four elaborate ear-pendants of Trojan type, made of silver. Around the wrist were found two silver bracelets (Fig. 6), one piped with gold decorated with silver, and gold double-spirals and rosettes. Near them was found a bracelet made of silver wire with electrum rosettes and a gold bracelet, made of five wire loops, the outer ones plain, the inner ones twisted. In front of the queen lay a small sceptre with a peculiar knobbed amber head and silver-cased wooden handle (Fig. 12), decorated like the king's sceptre, but in a bad state of preservation

The metal vessels and toilet articles all lay either in front of the queen against the north wall or in the north-eastern corner of the tomb. The metal vessels are all of small size, and consist of two small silver bowls, a small reddish gold cup, a small high-handled silver cup, an electrum beaker of Trojan type (Fig. 9), a silver-fluted juglet (Fig. 9), and a fluted miniature bird vase with granulation on neck and handle of characteristic Yortan type.

A set of stone vessels included a small ointment vessel of white marble, inlaid with small pieces of obsidian and lapis lazuli. It had a gold lid with a granulated handle and stood on a small pedestal made separately in pink-veined white marble. The type is familiar in Yortan pottery. The same applies to a pedestalled bowl in white marble, inlaid along the rim with black obsidian triangles. This contained a mass of silver pins of about a dozen types. A small white marble jar with lid is likewise inlaid with obsidian and lapis lazuli, and the small carinated saucer in a yellow-veined green stone has a strong Egyptian look.

A small toilet set in silver included three silver tubes with caps, decorated with ribs and hatched designs. They are said to have been found filled with a red, green and black substance, of which nothing now remains. This is reminiscent of the Ancient Egyptian use of rouge and black (kohl) and green eye-paint. With it were found a spatula, a toilet spoon and a pair of tweezers, all in silver, and fragments of a corroded silver mirror. The finest object deposited with the queen was, however, an ivory comb, worn in the hair, with a centre roundel framed by an open-work band, depicting two finely-carved wild goats or ibexes and two dolphins, the whole picked out in red and blue colour, and provided with a gold edge, carved rosettes and a carnelian rivet head surrounded by gold granulation.

With the exception of the piece of furniture from the Egyptian Old Kingdom none of the objects appear to be of foreign make, and the excellence of local craftsmen working for the ruler's court is nowhere more clearly shown than in a group of five statuettes, said to have been found in these tombs. (See colour page opposite.)

Illustrations from colour photographs of the original drawings, by courtesy of Thames and Hudson, from their forthcoming publication "Founders of Civilization."

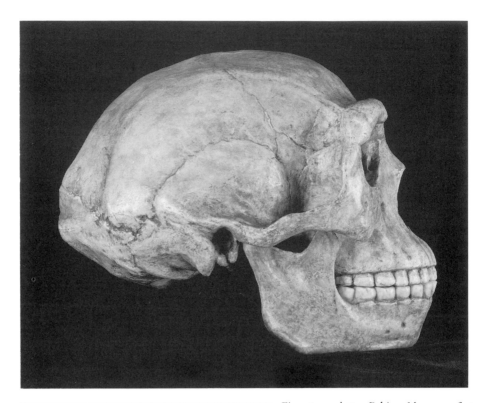

Figs. 84 and 85. Peking Man was first identified by Davidson Black, a Canadian professor of anatomy at Peking Union Medical College. In 1941 when the Japanese entered China it is thought to have been lost in a footlocker being transported by retreating US Marines. One and a half million years old, it was believed to be the link between Java Man and Neanderthal Man. (84) Reconstruction of Peking Man skull at the Museum of Natural History, New York; (85) reconstruction of the head of Peking Man, by Dr Harry Shapiro, Emeritus Curator, Department of Anthropology, American Museum of Natural History, New York.

Fig. 86. The Croesus gold or Lydian hoard from Ushak in Turkey is said to consist of individual objects which are held, and have been displayed, by the Metropolitan Museum of Art in New York. Over two hundred gold and silver embossed wine jugs, bowls and burners are claimed by Turkey to have been illegally excavated and exported in the 1960s. In a legal action commenced in 1987 in the New York District Court, Turkey claimed possession and the Metropolitan Museum maintained its denial of a cohesive and identifiable collection.

which the museum hold closely resemble other objects which were confiscated at the time of the illegal excavations and which are housed in the museums of Ankara and Ushak.

A formal demand for return was made by the Turkish ambassador in Washington in 1986, and rejected. It was therefore decided to commence legal proceedings based on Turkish ownership of the treasure under its own cultural patrimony laws. In May 1987 New York lawyers filed a complaint in the district court against the Metropolitan Museum of New York claiming that the 'plaintiff is the lawful owner and entitled to immediate possession of the Lydian Antiquities'. The museum in response indicated its intention to rely on the argument of undue delay in bringing the action, and on a Statute of Limitations. In addition it has always maintained that the Turks would have to prove the identity and provenance of each individual object and it refuses to acknowledge that there is a cohesive collection. Both parties are clearly set to go to considerable lengths to maintain their respective positions.

The history of the world is the history of an intricate web of universal plunder, of fetishism, and of the cannibalization of cultures. It would not be possible, or desirable, to have a tidy world where every artifact or relic or work of art was kept in the place of its making or the home of the maker or the person for whom it was made, or in the place where it was discovered. Cultures indeed are interrelated, but there are cases where restoration is warranted, and these are where major pieces constituting historic records have been displaced by dubious methods.

It is absurd to equate the argument that certain items of cultural property ought to be restored with the idea that every Picasso must hang in Spain, every da Vinci in Italy, and so on, or that every item from archaeological finds representing a particular epoch or civilization must be returned to its primary source. It is understood that most paintings are in any event to be dispersed and will have many owners. It is also understood that archaeological finds belong on site and to local history, so that the question of the return to source would not arise, as in the case of Roman finds in Britain. However, such arguments bear little relation to the question of an immobile monument built for the landscape, and indeed fashioned with the materials from it, such as the Parthenon, but which was destroyed. Its continued integrity must be assumed to have been desired and intended by both artist and the people for whom it was built. These marbles, known customarily by the name of the man who removed them, could equally well have been known to history as the Pheidias marbles. Professor George Forrest of Oxford University has pointed out that although the Parthenon frieze was conceived as a unity, nearly one half of it is in the British Museum, and about 176 feet in Athens, and this could be likened to a Renoir painting having been sawn in two, with one half being kept in New York and the other in Vladivostok.[43]

There is, of course, a precedent in modern times for a painting of special significance being returned to its homeland. This was Picasso's *Guernica* (Fig. 87). However, this was a special case because of the painting's particular anti-fascist symbolism, and because Picasso himself took the painting to the Museum of Modern Art in New York in 1939. After purchase by the Spanish government it was held in deposit in America on the artist's own stipulation that it should not be returned to Spain until, according to his lawyer Mr Roland Dumas, 'public liberties' had been restored there. The US Congress in any event expressed its approval for the return prior to such a declaration and the Museum of Modern Art agreed to the return of the painting, which went back to the Prado in 1982.

There is also an interesting case in the United Kingdom. In 1898 Sir Edmund Antrobus offered to sell Stonehenge to the British nation[44] for £125,000 (it was subsequently bought for £6,600 by Cecil Chubb in 1915), and there was the possibility that it could have been dismembered and actually taken abroad. This seems incredible. Yet many who would regard this as unbelievable do not regard the continued retention of major portions of foreign national monuments in distant museums as remarkable or inconsistent.

The case of the Icelandic manuscripts is the outstanding example of a major state-to-state return of cultural property. It was an unusually civilized and rational act in the face of all the common, legal, political and historic arguments against return. With time, the view that certain major treasures selected under certain fixed criteria ought to be returned may not be regarded as the pipedream of misguided liberals and scholars, nor as the abandonment of national self-interest, nor as a precipitate action which will cause the ultimate absurdity – the return of everything. For example, it was implied by a question of Baroness Trumpington[45] in the House of Lords in February 1982 that if the Elgin Marbles were returned then London Bridge (Fig. 88), which had been purchased in the 1960s, would also in turn have to be returned from Arizona in the United States where it had been taken.

The issues surrounding cultural return are complex, and the legal, political and museum arguments have not always been conducted with sang-froid. Claimants regard the removal and retention of cultural treasures as 'cultural imperialism',[46] and Sir David Wilson, director of the British Museum, has said that the return of objects, especially the Elgin Marbles, would be tantamount to the destruction of the Great Library in Alexandria. He has described this as 'cultural fascism'.[47] More diplomatic but in a similar vein is the remark attributed to the Louvre conservator Paul Vitray after a lecture by Thomas Bodkin advocat-

Fig. 87. Picasso's *Guernica* was taken by the artist himself to the Museum of Modern Art in New York in 1939. The painting was famous for its anti-Fascist symbolism, and the artist stipulated that it should not be returned to Spain until 'public liberties' were restored there. The Museum of Modern Art agreed to its return to the Prado Museum in Madrid in 1982.

Fig. 88. London Bridge being taken down for sale in 1968 before its transportation to Arizona, USA. It is cited sometimes as an example of an object which should also be returned in the event of any such precedent being set by the return of the Elgin Marbles. In 1987 the Americans were back in London trying to sell London Bridge back to the British.

ing international co-operation in reconstituting dismembered works: 'That's all very well... but remember that the Louvre never gives anything' (quoted by Patricia Failing).

Some writers and legal specialists talk about cultural property as the cultural heritage of *all* mankind.[48] According to this view the Greek desire for the return of the Elgin Marbles is 'cultural nationalism'. On the other hand the needs of 'cultural internationalism' which relate to preservation and access are not seen to support the Greek case. While cultural treasures may generate universal inspiration and appreciation they are not universally created nor can there be international possession. Is it possible that arguments about 'internationalism' may merely disguise nationalism? On the other hand, the concept of cultural property as something which should be distributed, 'allocated' and apportioned takes a commodity view of culture.

The past exercises a profound and hypnotic fascination over us and the continuing museum phenomenon and the charisma of objects are a testament to this. Cultural treasures are a part of our dreaming and memory and spiritual landscape.

But museums have been likened to churches or universities. They can become monuments to domination, privilege and wealth, and centres of ritual pilgrimage where the fame of the objects is their meaning. Despite the educative value of museums contemporary writers have described that 'tiring museum feeling' and it is sobering to remember a 1966 survey in France which showed that two-thirds of ordinary visitors to an art museum could not remember the name of a single work.[49]

Holding nations base their 'cultural patrimony' not solely on creative imagination but on possession. Authenticity, which is supposed to be the special magic of museums, is often challenged by the belated exposure of long-revered relics as excellent fakes, and sometimes master forgers have been mistakenly arrested as looters.[50] Above all it has been the evolution of Malraux's 'museums without walls'[51] – open exhibitions with the use of photography, film and art publications – which has exploded the accessibility of art and culture far beyond the artificial parameters of any museum. Art has no address.

Perhaps the notion that some of the major cultural treasures of the world should be returned to the people to whom they matter most is put into true perspective by the words of the nineteenth-century American writer Nathaniel Hawthorne. In 1856 he observed:

> [Yesterday]... I visited the British Museum; an exceedingly tiresome affair. It quite crushes a person to see so much at once; and I wandered from hall to hall, with a weary and heavy heart, wishing (Heaven forgive me!) that the Elgin marbles and the frieze of the Parthenon were all burnt into lime, and that the granitic Egyptian statues were hewn and squared into building-stones, and that the mummies had all turned to dust, two thousand years ago; and, in time, that all the material relics of so many successive ages had disappeared with the generations that produced them. The present is too much burdened with the past. We have not time, in our earthly existence, to appreciate what is warm with life, and immediately around us; yet we heap up all these old shells out of which human life has long emerged, casting them off forever. I do not see how future ages are to stagger onward under all this dead weight, with the additions that will be continually made to it.[52]

Acknowledgements

I am indebted to the late Glyn Daniel, Emeritus Disney Professor of Archaeology, University of Cambridge, who read the original draft and whose comments and observations were illuminating.

I also wish to express my indebtedness to the many individuals and institutions who directly or indirectly contributed to the content of the book, and in particular: Jónas Kristjánsson, Director of the Manuscript Institute, Reykjavík, and Magnus Magnusson, broadcaster, for assisting me with access to the Icelandic and Danish materials and for their invaluable corrections and advice concerning the account of the return of the Icelandic manuscripts; Sir David Wilson, Director of the British Museum, and Janet Wallace, archivist, British Museum, for access to, and assistance with, documents relating to the Elgin Marbles and the Benin collection; Harry Prasad, archivist, Museum of Mankind, for access to the archives; David Lance of the National Museum of Australia, and Michael Mansell of the Aboriginal Legal Service, Hobart, for furnishing significant additional information on the matter of aboriginal relics; David Collison, film producer, for access to preparation materials for the BBC *Tribal Eye* series; Susie Wong, London, for assistance on Chinese and other Asian source materials; Peter Thompson, Press Office, Greek Embassy, London, for providing detailed information about the Parthenon and the Greek case; Geraldine Norman, *The Times* saleroom correspondent, for permitting me to consult her in her area of expertise and in particular in relation to the art market map; Yudhisthir Raj Isar, Catherine André-Verdellon, and Christine Wilkinson, Division of Cultural Heritage, UNESCO, Paris, and Claude Chopelet, archive section, Division of Cultural Heritage, UNESCO, Paris, for assistance with obtaining all the relevant UNESCO documents and the UNESCO bibliography which appears on the fiche; Adrian Butler of the Council of Europe, Strasbourg, Press and Information Services, for assistance with obtaining Council of Europe documents; Ron Swerczek, Washington Archives, for assistance in obtaining photographic copies of US documents; Mr Ashok Mehta, First Secretary for Trade, High Commission for India, London, for permitting me to have the transcript of the 1988 London Nataraja High Court case; David Finn, New York, Joseph Noble, New York, Christopher Jones, University of Pennsylvania, and Ian Graham, Harvard University, for generously contributing their photographs to the book; Luis Ponce, Alfonso

Espinosa and Rosa Maria Wallach, Cultural Department of the Peruvian Embassy, Washington, Elizabeth Simpson of the Metropolitan Museum of Art, New York, Rosangela Adoum, Jefe de la Unidad Fondo Arquelogico, Ecuador, Sara Campbell and Cheryl Barton of the Norton Simon Museum, Pasadena, Dave Phillips, Palace of the Governors, Museum of New Mexico, and Charlene Androes of Stanford University Press for assistance in securing photographs contributed to the book; Professor Robert J. Sharer, University of Pennsylvania; Barbara Isaac, Peabody Museum, Harvard University; Chris Kirby, National Museums of Canada, Ottawa, for assistance in locating specific photographic material; Marie Claire Quiquemelle, Paris, for assistance in researching the André Malraux pictures; Hermione Waterfield, director, Tribal Art Department, Christie's, London, for her expertise in locating the relevant photographs from the Hooper Collection; Neeta Mainee of Zaiwalla and Co. for providing the photograph of the London Natarāja; Elin Gerslund, Cambridge, for a detailed translation of the Danish legal cases and parliamentary debates; Inger Glahn, Danish Embassy, London, for assistance with Danish terms; Paul Kuek, Melbourne, for Figs. 8, 14 and 20 and all the map drawings; Anne Robinson, Oxford, for her expertise in typing the manuscript; Vera Madan, London, for computer-setting the index.

Abbreviations

All ER	*All England Law Reports*
Alta LR	*Alberta Law Reports*
EEC	European Economic Community
F.2d	*Federal Reporter 2d Series*
ICOM	International Council of Museums
ILR	International Law Reports
IOPA	International Organization for the Protection of Art
MR	Master of the Rolls
TLR	*Times Law Reports*
UN	United Nations
UNESCO	United Nations Educational, Scientific and Cultural Organization
UNTS	*United Nations Treaty Series*
USC	*United States Code*
ICJ	International Court of Justice
Interpol	International Criminal Police Organization

On the UNESCO documents

CLT	Culture Section Series
CONF or C	Conference
CC	Culture and Communications (Section)
COM	Communications (Section)

Terms relating to international conventions

Signature:	to sign and authenticate (prior to agreement becoming binding)
Ratification:	confirmation of previous act not formerly binding (done by state parliament or equivalent)
Accession:	absolute or conditional acceptance by one or several states of a treaty already concluded between other states

Notes

CHAPTER ONE

1. Explanatory note on translation of Danish and Icelandic materials: in the case of specific clauses in documents or legal terms a detailed translation is given, but in the case of the parliamentary and legal debates much of the material is presented in paraphrase form to describe accurately the tenor of the arguments rather than give a verbatim account.
2. 'Icelandic manuscripts', *Islandica*, vol. XIX, Cornell University Library, Ithaca, New York, 1929.
3. It should be noted, however, that in 1962 a new Manuscript Institute was established in Reykjavík specifically to receive the manuscripts from Denmark; in 1970 it moved into a specially built university building, named *Árnagardur* in memory of Árni Magnússon.
4. 'Comments on the right of ownership of foundations in connection with the discussions concerning the handing over of manuscripts to Iceland', *Weekly Law Report*, Danish Law Association, 19 May 1961.
5. Section 25 of the Danish Constitution is concerned with the Royal Prerogative to make grants, and grant exemptions from statutes, etc.
6. In *The Manuscripts Case*, Setberg: Ministry of Education, 1961.
7. In 1918, Iceland had entered into a twenty-five-year period of monarchical union with Denmark, which was due to expire in 1943, when the question of total independence would be resolved.
8. *Morgunbladid*, 24 February 1965.
9. *Heimkoma Handritanna* (The Homecoming of the Manuscripts), Reykjavík, 1981.
10. Former Lecturer, University of Copenhagen, now a manuscript specialist at the Manuscript Institute in Iceland.

CHAPTER TWO

1. These drawings are preserved in the Bibliothèque Nationale in Paris.
2. This reportedly includes one bought by Elgin after its capture from the French, and 'temporarily' deposited in the British Museum.
3. For example, see 'Document shows Elgin had permission to take Parthenon Marbles' by Christopher Warman, arts correspondent, in *The Times*, 9 June 1983.
4. *Ancient Marbles in Great Britain*, translated by C. A. M. Fennell, Cambridge 1882.
5. Only one of Lusieri's drawings has survived, the 'Monument of Philopappus', 1800.
6. See, for instance, the 1916 *Journal of Hellenic Studies*. The activities were continued by Lord Elgin's son, who ordered the destruction of the Summer Palace in Peking in 1860.

7. 'Give back the Elgin Marbles', *Nineteenth Century*, December 1890.

8. Public Records Office, London, FO 371, 1941, 29861.

9. Institute of Fine Art, London University.

10. By Miss Welsford, Courtauld Institute Librarian.

11. CLT/83/CONF.216/5, Annex II.

12. The Greek resolution supporting return of the marbles was carried 56 for, 12 against, 24 abstaining.

13. Reported in 'Backing for return of marbles', *The Times*, 3 August 1983.

14. In Appendix X. The headquarters of the Council of Europe are in Strasbourg. (It should not be confused with the EEC, which is a different entity.) The Statute was signed in London on 5 May 1949, on behalf of the governments of Belgium, Denmark, France, Ireland, Italy, Luxembourg, the Netherlands, Norway, Sweden and the United Kingdom. The nineteen member states of the Council of Europe are: Austria, Belgium, Cyprus, Denmark, France, Federal Republic of Germany, Greece, Iceland, Ireland, Italy, Luxembourg, Malta, the Netherlands, Norway, Portugal, Sweden, Switzerland, Turkey and the United Kingdom.

15. This included the Social Democratic Party leader Dr David Owen, who gave a formal favourable reply in principle.

16. Charles Moore, 'Beware of bearing gifts to Greeks' in *The Daily Telegraph*, 30 January 1984.

17. The debate is reported in full in Chapter 3, pp. 115ff.

18. Hansard, vol. 49, no. 53, 21 November 1983.

19. The effect of these Conventions is considered in Chapter 6.

20. Hansard, vol. 49, no. 53, 21 November 1983.

21. For example, J.B.S. Morritt, MP, gave evidence before the 1816 Parliamentary Committee based on a three-month stay in Athens in 1795; John Cam Hobhouse, *Travels*, 1810; Frederick S. Douglas (a member of the 1816 House of Commons Select Committee), *Essay on Certain Points of Resemblance between the Ancient and Modern Greeks*, 1813.

22. *The Guardian,* 31 October 1985.

23. 'Thinking about the Elgin marbles', *Michigan Law Review*, vol. 83, no. 8, August 1985, especially p. 1899.

24. Referred to by J. Merryman; taken from accounts in W. St Clair, *Lord Elgin and the Marbles*, especially pp. 113, 159–60.

25. B.F. Cook, *The Elgin Marbles*, British Museum Publications, 1984.

26. A.H. Smith, 'Lord Elgin and his collection', *Journal of Hellenic Studies* 1916, p. 181: an account on the centenary of the purchase of the Elgin marbles based on papers handed over by the Earl of Elgin's grandson. The papers at Broomhall included those handed over by Lusieri or Hamilton, or their representatives.

27. This translation was subsequently provided by Dr Hunt to the 1816 Parliamentary Committee. It is cited thereafter as the documentary evidence upon which the removal of the marbles was legitimated.

28. *ICJ Reports*, 1962, p. 6. Discussed in further detail in Chapter 8.

29. The definition of 'good faith' and consequences varies between states. In 1982 it was reported that UNIDROIT (International Institute for the Unification of Private

Law) was trying to assemble and unify legislation on this subject, in particular on the definition of 'good faith', with respect to the purchase of objects which have been acquired illicitly.

30. H. Wheaton, *Elements of International Law*, p. 395.
31. Professor Charles de Visscher, Professor of Law, University of Louvain, Judge of the International Court of Justice, *Essays on National Protection of Works of Art*, US Department of State Publication, 1949, pp. 828–9.
32. Ian Brownlie, *Principles of Public International Law*, Oxford, 1973, p. 415.
33. 'Thinking about the Elgin Marbles', *Michigan Law Review*, vol. 83, no. 8, 1985.
34. There is a view that rules of customary law may become an overriding principle of international law known as 'jus cogens'. For discussion, see Brownlie, *Principles of Public International Law*, pp. 499–502.
35. Amravati is the ancient Buddhist site on the Kistna river in the state of Andhra Pradesh, India. The great Buddhist monument which once stood there was completely demolished in the eighteenth century, but numerous carved marble reliefs were dispersed, especially to Madras and the British Museum.
36. *The Scotsman Magazine*, vol. 4, no. 7, October 1983, pp. 11, 14.

CHAPTER THREE

1. T.G.H. James, *The British Museum and Ancient Egypt*, 1981, p. 3.
2. Seton Lloyd, *Foundations in the Dust*, Oxford, 1947, p. 193.
3. The Vatican Collections, *The Papacy and Art*, Official Publication authorized by the Vatican Museums, Harry N. Abrams, 1982, p. 226.
4. Hugo Davenport, 'Elgin Marbles surprise', *The Observer*, 15 May 1983.
5. Section 1, British Museum Act 1963.
6. Section 1, First Schedule.
7. This statement by Lord Jenkins is incorrect: see p. 287.
8. See note 7 above.
9. *Antiquity*, editorial, vol. LVI, no. 216, March 1982, pp. 2–4.
10. 'Sir David, defender of the marble halls', *Guardian*, 14 December 1985.
11. 'UK to keep Sri Lanka treasures', *The Observer*, 24 January 1982.
12. See Chapter 4; [1983] 2 All ER 93–101.
13. Prepared by the Council of Europe, Appendix IX. The UK signed in 1969 with a territorial reservation (see Article 12). (Conventions are considered in further detail in Chapter 6.)
14. Referred to often simply as the Convention on Cultural Property, Appendix XVII.
15. Ratified 1972; see Chapter 5.
16. *Museums Yearbook*, 1986, p. 7.
17. 'Qui veut la renvoyer dans ses foyers?' *La Vie*, 16–22 September 1982.
18. Dillon Ripley, *The Sacred Grove: Essays on Museums*, New York, Simon and Schuster, 1969, p. 42.
19. Claude Tarral, 'The discovery of the Vénus de Milo', *Revue Archéologique* series IV, vol. VII, 1906, reprinted in C.W. Ceram, *The World of Archaeology*, Thames and Hudson, 1966.

20. This is periodically amended by laws and decrees. For a compendium of texts on the protection of the historic and aesthetic heritage of France, see *Journal officiel de la République française*, no. 1345.

21. The protection of cultural property in Britain began with the Ancient Monuments Protection Act 1882.

22. Originally the required export licence applied to antiques more than one hundred years old, valued at £1,000, raised to £4,000 and then to £16,000. The Reviewing Committee on the Export of Works of Art apply criteria laid down by the Waverly Report issued by a special government committee in 1952.

23. For national legislation on protection of cultural property, see the 1974 *ICOM Handbook* and 1984 *UNESCO Handbook*.

24. *The Financial Times*, 12 July 1986, Anthony Thorncroft. Also *The Daily Telegraph*, 28 September 1986, 'Americans want city's gateway knights', Stephen Castle. A tussle with an American buyer over Hereford's city gate sandstone figures resulted in them being dubbed locally as its 'Elgin Marbles'.

25. 14 *Receuil de la Jurisprudence de la Cour*, 620–1 (Cour de Justice des Communautés Européennes 1968).

26. Comments by the Netherlands government to UNESCO, quoted in L.V. Prott and P.J. O'Keefe, *National Legal Control of Illicit Trade in Cultural Property* (study commissioned by UNESCO and submitted to a consultation of experts held at UNESCO headquarters in Paris, 1–4 March 1983).

CHAPTER FOUR

1. I.E.S. Edwards, *The Pyramids of Egypt*, Penguin, 1961.

2. 'Inscrutable but not immutable', *The Times*, 16 June 1984.

3. Report in the *Guardian*, 14 December 1985.

4. Carol Andrews, *The Rosetta Stone*, British Museum Publications, 1982, p. 11.

5. For full details on Ghanaian Museum Collections, see UNESCO Doc. CC-81/CONF 203/8, July 1981.

6. *The Sunday Times*, 22 February 1986.

7. British Museum Committee papers, 9 October 1897, vol. XLVIII.

8. Treaty between Great Britain and the Chiefs of Benin River and Jekeri Country – Benin, 2 August 1894, British and Foreign State Papers, LXXXVI, 1893–4.

9. For the continuing loss of Benin bronzes, see the account of Ekpo Eyo in *A Threat to National Art Treasures*, 1986, pp. 203–12. These losses include the Jebba female figure, the Ododuwa bronze head and the Ife terracotta head.

10. *Bābur-nāmeh*, Turkish work of history on the Life of the Mughal Emperor, Babur.

11. Sir Olaf Caroe, letter to editor, *The Times*, 9 September 1976.

12. Professor Harminder Singh, *The Times*, 11 September 1976.

13. E.S. Smart, letter to editor, *The Times*, 10 September 1976. Ref. to article by H. Beveridge, *Asiatic Quarterly Review*, 1899.

14. Brigadier Lord Ballantrae, letter to editor, *The Times*, 13 September 1976.

15. *The Times*, 8 September 1976.

16. Professor Harminder Singh, letter to editor, *The Times*, 11 September 1976.

17. 'Sikhs demand their throne from Britain', The *Observer*, 24 July 1983.
18. *The Observer*, 24 July 1983.
19. Sri Lanka presented a statement to the UNESCO Intergovernmental Committee dealing with these matters, May 1980, CC⁄79/CONF206/6.
20. CC⁄79/CONF 206/Col. 10. This statement listed objects in detail, which are sought for return from Great Britain, Netherlands, France, Austria, Belgium, Germany, Switzerland and the United States.
21. 'UK to keep Sri Lanka treasures', *The Observer*, 24 January 1982.
22. *Ibid.*
23. In 1988 Maori leaders in New Zealand sought the withdrawal from auction, at Bonham's in London, of a tattooed Maori chieftain's head (*The Observer*, 8 May 1988). The High Court blocked the sale pending a plea for possession by the Maori people. In the light of this unfavourable publicity, Christie's cancelled its sale in June of human heads from the Amazon Basin, Papua New Guinea and Peru (*The Times*, 24 May 1988). The owner finally agreed to return the Maori head for burial (*The Independent*, 5 July 1988).
24. Unpublished report by Michael Mansell, Tasmanian Aboriginal Legal Service.
25. In Russell Chamberlin, *Loot: The Heritage of Plunder*, Thames and Hudson, 1983, pp. 100–3.
26. For the terms of the treaty with Scotland, see Rymer, *Foedera*, II, ii, 6 (Latin).
27. *Chronicon de Lanercost*, translated by Sir Herbert Maxwell, *Scottish Historical Review*, vol. 9, p. 168 (Latin).
28. 'UN rejects stone of destiny plea', *Glasgow Herald*, 18 August 1984.
29. *On Ancient Central Asian Tracks*, University of Chicago Press, 1964, pp. 179–81.
30. For example, Peter Hopkirk, *Foreign Devils on the Silk Road*, John Murray, 1980, pp. 2–6, 174.
31. Samuel Couling (ed.), Shanghai: Kelly and Walsh, 1917, p. 143.
32. Paraphrased by Peter Hopkirk in *Foreign Devils on the Silk Road*, p. 174.
33. *Attorney⁄General of New Zealand v. Ortiz and others* [1982] 3 All ER 432–68.
34. *Don Alonso v. Cornero* (1611) Hob 212, *King of Italy v. Marquis Cosimo de Medici Tornaquinci* (1918) 34 TLR 623, *Brokaw v. Seatrain UK Ltd* [1971] 2 All ER 98 followed; *Paley (Princess Olga) v. Weisz* [1929] All ER Rep 513 distinguished.
35. The case of *Huntington v. Attrill* [1893] AC 150 applied.
36. *King of Italy v. Marquis Cosimo de Medici Tornaquinci* (1918) 34 TLR 623.
37. [1983] 2 All ER 93–101.
38. The account which follows is mainly abridged from the transcript of the judgement of Mr Justice Ian Kennedy in the High Court in February 1988.

CHAPTER FIVE

1. Alma Stephanie Wittlin, *Museums in Search of a Usable Future*, 1970, p. 174.
2. See Chapter 7 on New York auction rooms.
3. See this development worldwide under ICOM, Chapter 6, especially p. 229.
4. This was a practice followed by European museums. For example, in 1984 the Louvre returned to Italy the stolen painting, *The Annunciation*, by Jacopo del Casentino.

5. *The Economist*, 17 October 1987.

6. *Archaeology*, vol. 24, 1971, p. 165.

7. Quoted in an article by Joseph V. Noble, *Archaeology*, vol. 25, 1972, p. 144.

8. Act of 27 October 1972, title II, 86 Stat. 1296, 1297–8 (1972) (codified at 19 USC §§2091–5 (1976)).

9. See 1092 of the US Customs Laws.

10. *United States* v. *Hollinshead*, 495 F.2d 1154 (9th Cir. 1974).

11. This case was decided on two separate appeals. For the first appeal, *see* 545 F.2d 988 (5th Cir.) (hereinafter 'McClain I'), rehearing denied, 551 F.2d 52 (5th Cir. 1977) (per curiam). After a new trial was ordered in McClain I, the case came before the Court of Appeals for the second time: *United States* v. *McClain*, 593 F.2d 658 (5th Cir.) (hereinafter 'McClain II'), cert. denied, 444 US 918 (1979). Attempts have been made to legislate a reversal of the decision in the McClain case.

12. 18 USC §§2314, 2315 (1976) Note on the stolen character of goods restated in 1988 Supplement, 18USC, note 42.

13. Council of the American Association of Museums, Statement of concern (9 January 1976), unpublished, from *Journal of International Law and Politics*, vol. 15, no. 4, New York University, Summer 1983, p. 828.

14. Circuit Judge Wisdom, 545 F.2d. 988 (1977), at 991.

15. *United States* v. *Bernstein*, No. 82-00019-A (ED Va. 5 March 1982). Excepted from the terms of the settlement were certain pieces not belonging to the dealer but held on consignment, and other pieces which proved not to be genuine pre-Columbian articles from Peru.

16. Law No. 6634 of 13 June 1929. Regulations under the law were adopted as Supreme Resolution No. 49 of 31 March 1933.

17. From Frederic J. Truslow, 'Peru's recovery of cultural patrimony', *Journal of International Law and Politics*, vol. 15, no. 4, New York University, Summer 1983, p. 844.

18. Agreement Respecting the Recovery and Return of Stolen Archaeological, Historical and Cultural Properties, 15 September 1981, United States–Peru, TIAS No. 10, 136. See Appendix VI.

19. This Act was enacted by Congress, 21 December 1982, and became law on 12 January 1983.

20. Consisting of Sections 301 to 315 of Public Law 97–446.

21. Manual Supp. No. 3280-01, US Customs Service (5 October 1982).

22. Quoted by James F. Fitzpatrick, 'A wayward course: the lawless customs policy toward cultural properties', *Journal of International Law and Politics*, vol. 15, no. 4; New York University, Summer 1983, pp. 857–94.

23. 'California pre-Columbian artifacts – violations and restrictions involving importation', Office of the Regional Counsel, US Customs Service, San Francisco (15 November 1977).

24. *United States* v. *Weiner*, No. S-77-339 (ED Cal. 1979) (denying motions to dismiss).

25. *United States* v. *Pre-Columbian Artifacts, Peru and David Goldfarb*, 81-1320-Civ-JE (SD Fla.) (filed 18 June 1981).

26. Executive Order No. 11, 593, 3 CFR 154 (1971). This furthers the policies of four statutes: National Environmental Policy Act (1969); National Historic Preservation

Act (1966); Historic Sites Act (1936); Antiquities Act (1906). US basic legislation on antiquities and trafficking of goods illegally excavated is to be found in the Arch-aeological Resources Protection Act (1979) S 6, 16 USC SS 470ee(C) (1982).

27. Executive Order No. 11, 593, Protection and Enhancement of the Cultural Environ-ment, 3 CFR 154, 155–6 (1971).

28. For an account of how the Review Board operates, see Ian C. Clark and Lewis E. Levy, *Journal of International Law and Politics*, vol. 15, no. 4, New York University, Summer 1983, pp. 771–87.

29. HC Deb. (Can.) 7 February 1975, pp. 3024–40.

30. *R. v. Heller, Zango and Kassam, Alberta Law Reports*, 27 Alta LR (2d), 346–55.

31. Section 39 was deemed by the court to be penal in character providing for fines and/or imprisonment.

32. *Alberta Law Reports*, 30 Alta LR (2d), 130–8.

CHAPTER SIX

1. See, for instance, the Convention for the Protection of the World Cultural and Nat-ural Heritage (1972), which refers to the 'world heritage of mankind', and the Euro-pean Cultural Convention (1954), which refers to the 'common cultural heritage of Europe...'.

2. See further, for instance, the combining of the two concepts in the name given to the UNESCO Intergovernmental Committee set up to deal with the problem.

3. For a Canadian legal case on this Convention, see Chapter 5.

4. 18 C/23, p. 7, 18 October 1974; 18 C/22, p. 7, 19 October 1974.

5. See Appendix XVIII: List as at December 1985. CC77/CONF 001/4 June 1977. For list of endangered sites, see K. Meyer, *The Plundered Past,* Hamish Hamilton, London, 1974, pp. 203-8.

6. Hereafter, for the purposes of this book, referred to as the UNESCO Intergovernment-al Committee on Return of Cultural Property. UNESCO has differentiated between the different usage of 'Return' and 'Restitution'. The former refers to a moral right of return whereas the latter refers to a legal right where the object was stolen or illegally exported.

7. For Resumé of History of Progress in the Matter of Return and Restitution of Cultural Property, see CLT/CH 482, 11 June 1982.

8. CC79/CONF 206/3. Annex II 20/OR 132.

9. Preliminary Study CC79/CONF 206/5, March 1980. CC81/CONF 203/6, Aug-ust 1981.

10. CC81/CONF 203/Col.6.

11. For details, see Annex III, CC81/CONF 203/10, March 1982.

12. He also referred to document CC-81/CONF 203/INF.3, which contained a resolu-tion passed by the First New World Conference on Rescue Archaeology (Quito, Ecuador, 1981). The resolution referred to the illegal export of the Ecuadorian objects through an international dealer, and supported the case for restoration of this property as part of Ecuador's 'cultural memory'.

13. CC-81/CONF 203/10.

14. Final Report of the UNESCO Intergovernmental Committee on Return, 9–12 May 1983, Clause 19, p.6 (CLT–83/CONF 216/8).

15. Ibid., p.6

16. Resolutions on the Restitution of Works of Art to Countries Victims of Expropriation: Resolution 3187 (xviii) February 1974; Resolution 3391 (xxx) November 1975.

17. 'Unofficial Reports concerning legal matters in the United Nations', United Nations Law Reports, J. Carey (ed.), Volume 12, 1 December 1977, Number 4, A/RES/32/18.

18. U.N. Monthly Chronicle, vol. xviii, no. 3, March 1981, p. 68.

19. U.N. Monthly Chronicle, vol. xix, no. 4, February 1982, pp. 49–50.

20. U.N. Chronicle, January 1984, pp. 27–8.

21. Appendix ix. As indicated in Chapter 3, the United Kingdom is a party to this Convention, as of March 1973. The Convention was drawn up by the Council for Cultural Co-operation. It also prepared a draft outline for the active protection of immovable cultural property in Europe: Council of Europe. Consult. Ass. doc. 2819, 18 September 1970.

22. Quoted and referred to in UNESCO Doc., General Conference, Twentieth Session, Paris 1978, 20C/86, p. 1.

23. 22 C/93 August 1983. For recent comments on the draft convention, see Council of Europe Report on International Legal Protection of Cultural Property, Strasbourg, 1984, pp. 21–7; Draft (PC–R–OA) 33rd Sess. CDPC (84) 3 (1984).

24. 1982 UN Report by Joint Inspection Unit on the contribution of the UN system to the conservation and management of Latin American cultural and natural heritage – and a detailed record was made of Latin American regional participation in a number of conventions including those dealing with Illicit Trade in Cultural Property 1970, and Protection of Cultural Property in the Event of Armed Conflict 1954. 116/Ex./9, March 1983. See table, Appendix vii.

25. J. Chatelain, Means of Combating the Theft of Illegal Traffic in Works of Art in Nine Countries of the EEC – a Study Prepared at the Request of the Commission of the European Communities, 1976, pp. 106–7.

26. The EEC has a Council of Ministers and Commission which can deliberate and make regulations (entirely binding on members), directives (binding as to the result but not the method of achieving it), and decisions (entirely binding on states to whom directed) – Article 189, Treaty establishing the European Economic Community (1958) 298, UNTS, 14.

27. J.M.C. Bassiouni, International Criminal Law: A Draft International Criminal Code, Sijthoff and Noordhoff, 1980, pp. 98–9.

28. J.M.C. Bassiouni, 'Reflections on Criminal Jurisdiction in International Protection of Cultural Property', Syracuse Journal of International Law and Commerce, vol. 10, 1983, p. 281.

CHAPTER SEVEN

1. F.C. de Visscher, La Protection des patrimoines artistiques et historiques nationaux: Nécessité d'une réglementation internationale 'Art et Archéologie', *Receuil de Législation Comparée et de Droit International*, 1 November 1939, p. 20.

2. *Menzel* v. *List*. 49 Misc. 2d 300, 267 NYS 2d 804 (Sup. Ct. 1966), aff'd *per curiam*, 28 AD 2d 516, 279 NYS 2d 608 (App. Div., 1967).

3. Ardelia Ripley Hall of the Art Monuments Advisory to the Department of State, Washington, *U.S. Department of State Bulletin*, vol. 25, no. 4635, 27 August 1951, pp. 337-8.

4. See A. Decker, 'A legacy of shame', *Art News*, vol. 83, no. 10, December 1984, especially pp. 63-4 and details of other claims against Austria pp. 68-76.

5. For a table of major art thefts, 1911-72, see K. Meyer, *The Plundered Past*, Hamish Hamilton, 1974, pp. 219-39.

6. In 1987 this theft was linked to Tokyo and a Japanese gang; see *The Observer*, 8 November 1987.

7. As in the case of *Winkworth* v. *Christie Manson and Woods, Ltd.* [1980] 1 Ch. 496.

8. In the 1969 *Art Journal* Dr Clemency Coggins published an article, 'Illicit Traffic in pre-Columbian Antiquities', which traced much stolen Central American art to such museums as the Brooklyn Museum, the Cleveland Museum of Fine Art, the Minneapolis Institute of Fine Art and others, and highlighted the problem (p. 94).

9. *The Times*, 16 July 1982.

10. For a detailed study, *National Legal Control of Illicit Traffic in Cultural Property*, UNESCO, 1983, *Lyndel* v. *Prott and P.J. O'Keefe*. For national legislations dealing with cultural property, illicit traffic etc. see UNESCO: The Protection of Movable Cultural Property, 1984: Compendium of Legislative Texts. ICOM: 1974, Handbook of National Legislations.

11. Paul M. Bator, *The International Trade in Art*, University of Chicago Press, 1983, p. 38.

12. Antiquities Law No. 1710 of 1973. The embargo approach prevails in the Mediterranean, Middle Eastern, and Central and South American countries.

13. Antiquities and Art Treasures Act 1972.

14. Law No. 214, for The Protection of Cultural Properties, 30 May 1950. Licences may be sought to export works not designated as highly important cultural property.

15. People's Republic of China, Provisional Regulations on the Protection and Administration of the Cultural Heritage, 1960.

16. Ordinance Law 71-160 of 15 March 1971 on The Protection of Cultural Property.

17. Peter Hopkirk, 'Turks claim Croesus gold is in U.S. museum', *The Times*, 27 August 1970.

18. *R.* v. *Heller et al., Alberta Law Reports*, 30 Alta LR (2d). Following this case it was reported that the Canadian government was considering making a further appeal.

19. Appendix XVII, especially Article 9. See Chapter 6.

20. F. 2d. 1154 (9th Cir 1974); *United States* v. *Hollinshead* 495. See Chapter 5.

21. The National Stolen Property Act would apply: 48 Stat. 794 (1934). *United States* v. *McClain*, 545 F. 2d 988 (5th Cir.) [*McClain* I], 551 F. 2d (5th Cir. 1977); *United States* v. *McClain*, 593 F. 2d 658 (5th Cir.) [*McClain* II], 444 US 918 (1979). Also

Canada: Cultural Property Export and Import Act SC 75, 1975, c. 50. Return of foreign cultural property is mandatory if illegally exported from country of origin.

22. Known as the *Lex Situs*, this is a conflict of laws issue (private international law).

23. ICOM was established in 1946; its headquarters are in Paris. Its membership consists of over 3,000 institutions in over 100 countries. It is financed by its members, grants from foundations and UNESCO. ICOM acts in consultation with UNESCO.

24. ICOM Report and Recommendations, Malacca, Malaysia, 1972. As an extension of its programme on the ethics of acquisition ICOM also issued a regional report and recommendations regarding Southeast Asia in 1972. Participants at the Malacca meeting included the Philippines, Malaysia, Thailand, Singapore, Hong Kong, Indonesia, and the Khmer Republic (Cambodia).

25. IOPA was formed in 1972, in Paris. Its membership consists of individuals, organizations of member countries of the UN, and specialized institutions of the UN. See CC 77/CONF Col. 5, June 1977, for some further details concerning its work.

26. An intergovernmental organization established by text adopted by governmental delegates, and not by international convention.

27. Article 2 of its Constitution.

28. Interpol publishes 'L'officiel international des tableaux et objets d'art voles', a list of stolen works of art which is edited in six languages. An *Annual Index of Stolen Art* is also published by the International Foundation for Art Research, New York (since 1977).

29. See *Connoisseur*, October 1984, for Paul Chutkow's report on a successful recovery of paintings taken from the Hungarian Museum of Fine Arts, Budapest, December 1983.

30. The Interpol observer at the third session of the Intergovernmental Committee for Promoting the Return of Cultural Property to its Countries of Origin or its Restitution in case of Illicit Appropriation, Paris, November 1983, CLT-83/CONF 216/8, p. 13.

31. Mr Charles Lee in *The Times*, 11 March 1983.

32. Reported in *The Times*, 11 April 1986.

33. CC.81/CONF 203/10, p. 18.

34. Geraldine Norman, *The Times*, 21 December 1984.

35. *Abrams v. Sotheby Parke-Bernet Inc.*, No. 42255-84 New York Supreme Court filed 8 August 1984.

36. K. Meyer, *The Plundered Past.*

37. K. Hudson, *Museums for the 1980s: Survey of World Trends,* Macmillan, 1977, especially pp. 1–8.

38. K. Hudson and A. Nicholls, *The Directory of Museums,* Macmillan, 1981, p. viii. The concept of 'a museum without walls' has been suggested. See A. Malraux, *The Voices of Silence,* Princeton University Press, 1978, p. 13.

39. See Chapter 8 and references to Glyn Daniel in Chapter 3.

CHAPTER EIGHT

1. K. Hudson, *Museums for the 1980s: Survey of World Trends,* Macmillan, 1977, p. 34.

2. *Journal of the Royal Society of Arts, Proceedings,* June 1981, p. 436.

3. Law No. 214 for the Protection of Cultural Properties (30 May 1950). The National Commission for Protection of Cultural Properties is responsible for classification.

4. This approach appears in the new Law of the Sea Convention (1982) (not in force). Article 149 of this treaty expressly refers to archaeological and historical objects to be preserved for the benefit of all humanity, giving preferential rights to the state of origin. This article and Article 303 lay down rules for the protection of objects found on the sea bed, firstly in an 'archaeological zone' extending to twenty-four nautical miles, and secondly in the international zone beyond the limit of states' jurisdiction. See also U. Leanza, *The Territorial Scope of the European Draft Convention on the Protection of the Underwater Cultural Heritage,* Council of Europe, International Legal Protection of Cultural Property, 1984, p. 127.

5. The concept of 'culture' as the 'common heritage of mankind' was proposed at the Dumbarton Oaks Conference 1945, by Brazil as an amendment to Chapter IX of the UN Charter which was not accepted. The 1954 European Cultural Convention refers to the 'common cultural heritage of Europe...' and reasonable access thereto. This Convention encourages a policy of common action among signatory states to safeguard and encourage the development of European culture.

6. O'Keefe, P.J. and Prott, L.V., *Law and the Cultural Heritage,* Abingdon: Professional books, 1984, vol. 1, p. 33. Also, in some cultures, what constitutes a 'national treasure' is not confined to inanimate or tangible objects: e.g., in Japan, this even includes individuals having great skills in the arts.

7. The Bayeux Tapestry depicts the Norman Conquest of England; it is 900 years old and is presently in Bayeux, France. See *The Times,* 5 July 1984.

8. Proposed by Peru. Postponed by the UNESCO Intergovernmental Committee on Return of Cultural Property, 1980, 21 C/83, p. 5.

9. For example, the Philippines and Papua New Guinea have made it an offence to import into their territory cultural objects not covered by an export certificate from the state of origin.

10. See Chapter 5. Under Articles 7 and 13 of the Convention, Canada has successfully returned two pre-Columbian statues to Mexico which were seized by Canadian customs officers and forfeited, in 1981.

11. The view of American writer, James A.R. Nafziger, is that the result would have been different. However, he refers to general, enabling provisions, which are not mandatory (Articles 6, 8, 13, 15) and therefore it is unlikely that any different result could have been produced by this convention. See his article in the *Journal of International Law and Politics,* vol. 15, no. 4, Summer 1983, pp. 795–9.

12. Ann P. Prunty, 'Toward establishing an international tribunal for the settlement of cultural property disputes: how to keep Greece from losing its marbles', *The Georgetown Law Journal,* vol. 72, 1984, p. 1155.

13. It was ratified by only sixty states as at 1987 (not including the United Kingdom).

14. *Current Anthropology,* vol. 14, 1979, p. 579.

15. *Kunstsammlungen zu Weimar* v. *Elicofon* 678 F. 2d. 1150 (2d cir. 1982).

16. Central America, 14 to 21 degrees north; Mexico, Belize and Guatemala, where the Olmec Maya, Aztec, Teotihuacan and Toltec civilizations flourished.

17. Mary Leakey, *Disclosing the Past,* Weidenfeld, 1984, pp. 100–1.

18. 1970 Return from US to Guatemala of Mayan stele of the classical period (AD 600–400) from the ancient ruins of Piedras Negras (in north-western Guatemala).

19. Agreement on the Recovery and Return of Stolen Archaeological, Historical and Cultural Properties, 15 September 1981, USA–Peru.

20. As noted by Professor Leonard D. Duboff, *Proceedings of the American Society of International Law,* 1977, p. 200, at the International Protection of Cultural Property seminar, 22 April 1977, Northwestern School of Law of Lewis and Clarke College, USA.

21. *Union of India* v. *The Norton Simon Foundation,* United States District Court, Southern District of New York, 74 Cir. 5331 (SDNY 1976); United States District Court, Central District of California, Case No. CV 74-3581-RJK (CD Cal. 1976).

22. By the end of 1987, despite attempts to resolve this issue diplomatically, the codex remained in Mexico: confirmed by Mrs F. Callu, Director of the Department of Manuscripts, Bibliothèque Nationale, Paris.

23. Barnett Hollander, *The International Law of Art,* Bowes and Bowes, 1959, pp. 24-5.

24. Reprinted in F.H. Taylor, *The Taste of Angels,* pp. 580–1, 585–6. For a table of objects officially returned to the Allies, 1816, see *The Taste of Angels,* p. 589.

25. See T.D. Woolsey, *International Law,* 5th edn, 1879, p. 230. The regional inter-American multilateral Roerich Pact (1935) was the earliest document to protect cultural property in peace (as well as war). (Full title: Treaty on the Protection of Artistic and Scientific Institutions and Historic Monuments, 1935, Stat. 3267 TS No. 899. 1678 LNTS 289.)

26. There are more than eighty-five such treaties. For a detailed table of treaties, see PG1 77/WS/1, June 1977, pp. 12–20.

27. In *Musuem,* vol. XXXI, no. 1, 1979, on p. 12 reference is made to Gert von Paczensky from *Die Zeit,* 21 April 1978. He had written about the possible return of Nefretiti, but on p. 8 this is incorrectly referred to as a fact or *fait accompli.* It never happened.

28. For detailed account on Israel, see *Case Western Reserve Journal of International Law,* vol. 19, no. 3, Summer 1987, pp. 343–60, 'Antiquities in Israel in a maze of controversy'.

29. For detailed account, see Patricia Failing, 'The case of the dismembered masterpieces', *Art News,* September 1980, p. 78.

30. In particular, old master paintings which have disappeared for hundreds of years are rediscovered. For a list of the international top ten missing masterpieces, see *The Observer,* 19 October 1986.

31. See, for example, *Proceedings of the Thirteenth Colloquy on European Law,* Delphi, September 1983 (Council of Europe) International Legal Protection of Cultural Property.

32. Author's criteria suggested, pp. 255–6. See abstract values suggested as a framework for determining bilateral agreements by James A.R. Nafziger, *Journal of International Law and Politics,* vol. 15, Summer 1983, p. 807: (i) the preservation of archaeological evidence, particularly in an on-site context; (ii) the association of art with its geographical historical milieu; (iii) the preservation of the national patrimony for reasons of

awakening the national conscience, fostering community pride, socializing youth, enhancing local scholarship, and elevating national civilization; (iv) the preservation of both individual *objets d'art* and, when significant, sets and collections of them; (v) the enhancement of an exporting or loaning state's foreign policy and the financial resour⁄ ces of its museums; (vi) the enrichment of the importing state's civilization; (vii) the promotion of international understanding through the diffusion of art; (viii) the respect for cultural diversity, the acknowledgement of a global patrimony and a shared heritage of significant art, as well as the elimination of parochialism; (ix) the widest possible visibility and accessibility of significant objects; (x) the protection of signifi⁄ cant objects, under the best possible circumstances, in both the country of origin, and the importing country; (xi) the encouragement of respect for the law and the mutual development of shared controls; (xii) the enrichment of aesthetic and intellectual in⁄ terests of individual collectors, museums and museum viewers; and (xiii) restraints on the production of forgeries.

33. For example, see *Council of Europe Report,* 1983, p. 143, which suggests a proposal for build⁄up of national registers, registration of objects of special value, lists of stolen property and computerization of public property and state⁄protected as well as private⁄ ly owned objects.

34. Defined in Vienna Convention on the Law of Treaties, Article 53, as a norm accepted and recognized by the international community of states and as a whole a norm from which no derogation is permitted. It is argued by some writers that cultural return remains the exception rather than the rule. See *Council of Europe Report,* 1984, com⁄ ments of Professor Detlev Christian Dicke, Professor of University of Freiburg, Swit⁄ zerland, p. 37: he doubts the existence of a *general* practice and *general* acceptance necessary for the formation of customary law.

35. A left⁄wing Greater London Council (abolished in 1986) declared its approval of the return of the Elgin Marbles (1985).

36. Reservations expressed by Malcolm McLeod, keeper of the Museum of Mankind, London, *History Today,* Supplement, March 1984 in conjunction with a Channel 4 television programme *Today's History,* 22 March 1984.

37. See the view of Lord Strabolgi, in the House of Lords 1982, that the British Museum is as much a part of world culture as the Parthenon; Hansard, *Parliamentary Reports,* House of Lords, vol. 427, no. 40, Monday, 15 February 1982, p. 362.

38. Nicholas B. Penny, keeper of the Department of Western Art, Ashmolean Museum, Oxford, reviewing *Loot* by Russell Chamberlin in *The Sunday Times,* 18 September 1983.

39. See, for example, M.M. Ames, *Museum,* 1985, vol. XXXVII, pp. 25–31.

40. In a letter addressed to Nicholas Carlisle, Secretary of the Society of Antiquaries.

41. See the views expressed in Chapter 3.

42. There is an unproven suggestion that there is a collection of 135 Bronze Age pieces at the Boston Museum of Fine Arts that constitutes the Dorak treasure. See *Connoisseur,* July 1987, p. 67.

43. In fact there is a precedent for the reunification of a painting in its original setting: Van Eyck's Ghent altarpiece, which was dispersed by sale in the last century to museums in Berlin, Paris and Brussels, was reassembled under Article 247 of the Treaty of

Versailles. For a more contemporary reunification, see 'New delights from the auld alliance', *The Independent*, 17 October 1986. Poussin's *Venus and Mercury* was reunited for an exhibition at the Dulwich Picture Gallery, the smaller piece coming from the Louvre.

44. Referred to in *The Illustrated London News*, 12 January 1901, p. 30. Also see James Dyer, *Southern England, An Archaeological Guide*, Faber and Faber, 1973. Stonehenge was bought for the nation in 1915 but not designated as an ancient monument until over forty years later.

45. Parliamentary Debates, House of Lords, Questions, The Elgin Marbles, vol. 427, no. 40, Monday 15 February 1982, p. 362.

46. Meredith Palmer, *Syracuse Journal of International Law and Commerce*, vol. 1, 1976, p. 53, refers to the loss of identity. UNESCO statements stress restitution to countries which have been under foreign domination.

47. Interview, *Heart of the Matter*, BBC1 15 June 1986.

48. Professor John Merryman, *Michigan Law Review*, vol. 83, no. 8, August 1985, p. 1923.

49. Referred to by Donald Horne, *The Great Museum: The Re-Presentation of History*, Pluto Press, 1984, p. 16.

50. For example, see the controversy over the statue of Kouros at the Getty Museum California and other objects elsewhere (*The Times*, 9 August 1986 and *The Observer*, 13 July 1986). See also *Connoisseur*, May 1987, p. 98 and August 1987, p. 72. Finally, see the account in June 1987, p. 98, of the Mexican forger Brigído Lara, whose pre-Columbian-style statues have ended up in some of the finest collections in the world.

51. A concept expounded by André Malraux, *Museums without Walls*, Secker and Warburg, 1967.

52. Nathaniel Hawthorne, *English Notebooks*, journal entry, Thursday, 27 March 1856, p. 294.

Bibliography

Principal legal cases

DENMARK

Transcript from the Register of Judgements of Østre Landsret (The Eastern High Court) in case no. III 219/1965.

Arne Magnussen's Foundation (The Arnamagnaean Institute) v. *Ministry of Education*, 5 May 1965.

Transcript from the Register of Judgements of the Supreme Court in case no. 107/1966 (translation in Appendix 1).

Arne Magnussen's Foundation (The Arnamagnaean Institute) v. *Ministry of Education*, Supreme Court, 17 November 1966.

Transcript from the Registrar of Judgements of the Østre Landsret (The Eastern High Court) in case no. III 57/1967 (translation in Appendix 1).

Ministry of Education v. *Arne Magnussen's Foundation (The Arnamagnaean Institute)*, Eastern High Court, 13 March 1970.

Transcript from the Register of Judgements of the Supreme Court in case no. 68/1970.

Arne Magnussen's Foundation (The Arnamagnaean Institute) v. *Ministry of Education*, 18 March 1971.

ENGLAND

Court of Appeal: *Attorney General of New Zealand* v. *Ortiz and others, All England Law Reports* [1982] 3 All ER 432–68.

House of Lords: *Attorney General of New Zealand* v. *Ortiz and others, All England Law Reports* [1983] 2 All ER 93–101.

High Court: 1988, *Union of India and Others* v. *Commissioner of Metropolitan Police, Bumper Development Oil Corporation and others.*

CANADA

Provincial Court: *R.* v. *Heller, Zango and Kassam, Alberta Law Reports* 27b Alta LR (2d) 346–55, 16 June 1983.

Queen's Bench: *R.* v. *Heller et al., Alberta Law Reports* 30 Alta LR (2d) 130–8, 21 February 1984.

UNITED STATES OF AMERICA

United States Court of Appeals: *United States* v. *Hollinshead*, 495 F.2d 1154 (9th Cir. 1974).

United States Court of Appeals: *United States* v. *McClain*, McClain I 545 F.2d 988 (5th Cir.); 551 F.2d 52 (5th Cir. 1977); McClain II 593 F.2d 658 (5th Cir.); 444 US 918 (1979).

OTHER CASES CITED

Case Concerning the Temple of Preah Vihear (*Cambodia* v. *Thailand*). *International Law Reports* 1962, p. 6.

Menzel v. *List*, 49 Misc. 2d 300, 267 NYS 2d 804 (Sup. Ct. 1966), aff'd per curiam, 28 AD 2d 516, 279 NYS 2d 608 (App. Div. 1967).

United States v. *Weiner*, No. S-77-339 (ED Cal. 1979).

Winkworth v. *Christie Manson and Woods, Ltd.* [1980] 1 Ch. 496.

United States v. *Pre-Columbian Artifacts, Peru and David Goldfarb*, 81-1320-Civ-JE (SD Fla. 1981).

United States v. *Bernstein*, No. 82-00019-A (ED Va. 5 March 1982).

Kunstsammlungen zu Weimar v. *Elicofon*, 678 F. 2d. 1150 (2d cir. 1982).

Union of India v. *The Norton Simon Foundation* (United States District Court, Southern District of New York, 74 Cir. 5331 (SDNY 1976); United States District Court, Central District of California, Case No. CV 74-3581-RJK (C.D. Cal. 1976)).

Books and articles

BY AUTHOR

Abramson, Ronald D. and Huttler, Stephen B. 'The legal response to the illicit movement of cultural property'. *Law and Policy in International Business* (Washington), vol. 5, 1973, pp. 932–70.

Adams, Patricia. 'The Melanesian mission museum, Auckland: Returns solve a space problem'. *Museum*, UNESCO Quarterly Review, vol. XXXIV, no. 4, 1982, pp. 263–4.

Adams, Robert McCormack. 'Archaeology and cultural diplomacy'. *Foreign Service Journal* (Washington), June 1968, pp. 24, 49–50.

Adams, Robert McCormack. 'Illicit international traffic in antiquities'. *American Antiquity* (Washington), January 1971, pp. ii–iii.

Altes, Alexander Korthals. 'Submarine antiquities: a legal labyrinth'. *Syracuse Journal of International Law and Commerce*, vol. 4, 1976, pp. 77–96.

Ames, Michael M. 'De-schooling the museum. A proposal to increase public access to museums and their resources'. *Museum*, UNESCO Quarterly Review, vol. XXXVII, no. 1, 1985, pp. 25–31.

Andersen, Poul. 'Comments on the right of ownership of foundations in connection with the discussions concerning the handing-over of manuscripts to Iceland'. 'Ugeskrift for Retsvæsen'. *Weekly Law Report*, vol. 19, May 1961. Danish Law Association (Danmarks Juristforbund).

Andrews, Carol. *The Rosetta Stone*. London: British Museum Publications, 1982.

Anton, Ferdinand, Dockstander, Frederick J., Trowell, Margaret and Neuermann, Hans. *Primitive Art: Pre Columbian, North American, Indian, African/Oceanic*. New York: Abrams, 1979.

Bacon, Reginald Hugh Spenser. *Benin The City of Blood*. London, New York: Edward Arnold, 1897, especially Chapter 7.

Bai Liu. *Cultural Policy in the People's Republic of China. Letting a Hundred Flowers Bloom*. Studies and documents on cultural policies. China Art Research Institute, UNESCO, 1983.

Banks, George. *Moche Pottery from Peru*. London: British Museum Publications, 1980.

Baquedana, Elizabeth. *Aztec Sculpture*. London: British Museum Publications, 1984.

Barnett, Catherine. 'A special agent speaks out; an insider's look at art crime'. *Art and Antiques*, November 1986, pp. 59–60.

Bassiouni, Cherif J.M. *International Criminal Law: A Draft International Criminal Code*. Sijthoff and Noordhoff, 1980, pp. 98–9.

Bassiouni, Cherif J.M. 'Reflections on criminal jurisdiction in international protection of cultural property'. *Syracuse Journal of International Law and Commerce*, vol. 10, 1983, pp. 281–322.

Bator, Paul M. 'The international movement of national art treasures', 10 October 1969. Unpublished paper presented to the Panel of the American Society of International Law on the International Movement of National Art Treasures.

Bator, Paul M. *The International Trade in Art*. University of Chicago Press, 1983.

Berman, Shoshana. 'Antiquities in Israel in a maze of controversy'. *Case Western Reserve Journal of International Law*, vol. 19, no. 3, Summer 1987, pp. 343–60.

Boardman, John. *Greek Sculpture, the Classical Period*. London: Thames and Hudson, 1985.

Boardman, John and Finn, David. *The Parthenon and its Sculptures*. London: Thames and Hudson, 1985.

Bolton, Lissant. 'Recording Oceanic collections in Australia: problems and questions'. *Museum*, UNESCO Quarterly Review, vol. XXXVI, no. 1, 1984, pp. 32–5.

Bostik, William A. 'The ethics of museum acquisitions'. *Museum*, UNESCO Quarterly Review, vol. XXVI, no. 1, 1974, pp. 26–33.

Bostik, William A. *The Guarding of Cultural Property*. UNESCO Technical Handbooks for Museums and Monuments, 1977.

Braun, Barbara. 'The De Young ends a Mexican stand off'. *Connoisseur*, August 1986, pp. 14, 16.

Bronson, Bennet. 'The campaign against the antiquities trade'. *Field Museum of Natural History Bulletin* (Chicago), September 1972, pp. 2–5.

Browning, Robert. 'The case for the return of the Parthenon Marbles'. *Museum*, vol. XXXVI, no. 1, 1984, pp. 38–41.

Brownlie, Ian. *Principles of Public International Law*. Oxford: Clarendon Press, 1973.

Burnham, Bonnie. *Art Theft, Its Scope, Its Impact, Its Control*. New York: International Foundation for Art Research, 1978.

Cabanne, Pierre. *The Great Collectors*. New York: Farrar, Strauss, 1963.

Cardenas, Hector. 'Paradise lost; recovering Mexico's heritage'. *Museum News* (Washington), March 1972, pp. 32–3.

Cater, R.R. 'Return and restitution of cultural property. The Taranaki panels – a case study in the recovery of cultural heritage'. *Museum*, UNESCO Quarterly Review, vol. XXXIV, no. 4, 1982, pp. 256–8.

Ceram, C.W. (ed.). *The World of Archaeology (An Anthology)*. London: Thames and Hudson, 1966.

Ceram, C.W. *Gods, Graves and Scholars: The Story of Archaeology*. Harmondsworth: Penguin, 1984.

Chamberlin, Russell. *Loot: The Heritage of Plunder*. London: Thames and Hudson, 1983.

Chavez, E. Thomas. 'History comes home'. *Art and Antiques*, November 1986, pp. 75–6, 114.

Cheng Te-K'un. 'Archaeology in Communist China'. *China Quarterly* (London), July/September 1965, p. 75.

Chia Lan-Po. *The Cave Home of Peking Man*. Peking: Foreign Languages Press, 1975.

Chutkow, Paul. 'How Interpol works'. *Connoisseur*, October 1984, p. 126.

Clainen, Michael. 'Museums and thefts of works of art'. *Museum*, UNESCO Quarterly Review, vol. XXVI, no. 1, 1974.

Clark, Ian Christie. 'The Cultural Property Export and Import Act of Canada: legislation to encourage national co-operation'. *Journal of International Law and Politics*, vol. 15, no. 4, New York University, Summer 1983, pp. 771–87.

Clark, Ian Christie and Levy, Lewis E. *National Legislation to Encourage International Co-operation: The Challenge to our Cultural Heritage*. UNESCO, 1986, pp. 213–31.

Coggins, Clemency. 'Illicit traffic of pre-Columbian antiquities'. *Art Journal* (New York), vol. 30, 1971, p. 384.

Colley, Mary. 'The effects of efforts to control illicit art traffic on legitimate international commerce in art'. *Georgia Journal of International and Comparative Law*, vol. 8, 1978, pp. 462–81.

Cook, B.F. *The Elgin Marbles*. London: British Museum Publications, 1984.

Corbett, P.E. *The Sculpture of the Parthenon*. Harmondsworth: Penguin, 1959.

Cottrell, Leonard. *Wonders of Antiquity*. London: Longmans, Green and Co., 1959.

Craven, C. Roy. *Indian Art*. London: Thames and Hudson, 1976.

Crossley, Mimi and Wagner, Logan E. 'Is it a fake?' *Connoisseur*, June 1987, pp. 98–103.

Curtin, Jennie. 'Sacred art: the Pope's dilemma'. *Good Weekend* (Melbourne), 13 June 1986, pp. 6–12.

Daifuku, Hiroshi. 'S.O.S. Angkor'. *The UNESCO Courier*, December 1971, pp. 4–5.

Daniel, Glyn. *150 Years of Archaeology*. London: Duckworth, 1978.

Daniel, Glyn. *A Short History of Archaeology*. London: Thames and Hudson, 1981.

Dark, Philip J.C. *An Introduction to Benin Art and Technology*. Oxford: Clarendon Press, 1973.

Davidson, Marshall B. (ed.). *The Horizon Book of Lost Worlds*. Compiled and designed by the editors of *Horizon* magazine. Text by Leonard Cottrell. New York: American Heritage Publishing Company, 1962.

Davis, Hester A. 'Is there a future for the past?' *Archaeology*, October 1971, pp. 300–6.

Decker, Andrew. 'A legacy of shame'. *Art News* (New York), vol. 83, no. 10, December 1984, pp. 54–82.

De Visscher, F.C. 'La protection des patrimoines artistiques et historiques nationaux:

Nécessité d'une réglementation internationale'. *Art et Archéologie*. Recueil de Législation Comparée et de Droit International, 1 November 1939.

De Visscher, F.C. *Essays on International Protection of Works of Art. US Department of State Documents and State Papers*, vol. 1, no. 15, June 1949.

Dimick, John. 'The equitable distribution of antiquities: a suggestion'. *Archaeology* (New York), vol. 25, 1972, p. 144.

Diop, Abdoulaye and Sokhna, Gueye. 'Museological activity in African countries: its role and purpose'. *Museum*, UNESCO Quarterly Review, vol. XXV, no. 4, 1972, pp. 250–6.

Dontas, Georges. 'The Parthenon in peril'. *The UNESCO Courier*, June 1968, pp. 16–19, 34.

Douglas, David C. (ed.). *English Historical Documents*, vol. IV, *1327–1485*. London: Eyre and Spottiswood.

Douglas, Frederick Silvester North. *Essay on Certain Points of Resemblance between the Ancient and Modern Greeks*. London: John Murray, 1813, especially pp. 86–9.

Duboff, Léonard D. (ed.). *Art Law: Domestic and International* (collection of papers). New Jersey: Fred B. Rothman, 1975.

Duboff, Léonard D. *The Deskbook of Art Law*. Federal Publishers, 1977, pp. 71–2.

Duboff, Léonard D. and Duboff, Mary Anne Crawford. *The Protection of Artistic National Patrimony against Pillaging and Theft in Law and the Visual Arts*. Law and the Visual Arts Conference, 1974, Portland, Oregon, sponsored by the Northwestern School of Law, Lewis and Clark College and others, 1974.

Easton, Donald. 'Schliemann's mendacity – a false trail?' *Antiquity* (Cambidge), vol. LVIII, no. 224, November 1984, pp. 197–204.

Edwards, I.E.S. *The Pyramids of Egypt*. Harmondsworth: Penguin, 1961.

Eyo, Ekpo O. *The Threat to National Art Treasures: The Illicit Traffic in Stolen Art, the Challenge to our Cultural Heritage*. UNESCO, 1986.

Fagan, Brian M. *Quest for the Past: Great Adventures in Archaeology*. Reading, London: Addison-Wesley, 1978.

Fagg, William. *Divine Kingship in Africa*. British Museum Publications, 1978.

Failing, Patricia. 'The case of the dismembered masterpieces'. *Art News* (New York), September 1980, pp. 68–78.

Faith, Nicholas. *Sold: The Revolution in the Art Market*. London: Hamish Hamilton, 1985.

Fiddick, J.M. *Research Note (on Elgin Marbles)*. House of Commons, March 1983.

Finlay, Ian. *Priceless Heritage: The Future of Museums*. London: Faber and Faber, 1977.

Fishman, James J. and Metzger, Susan. 'Protecting America's cultural and historical patrimony'. *Syracuse Journal of International Law and Commerce*, vol. 4, 1976, pp. 57–76.

Fitzpatrick, James P. 'A wayward course: the lawless Customs policy toward cultural properties'. *Journal of International Law and Politics*, vol. 15, no. 4, New York University, Summer 1983, pp. 857–94.

Flanner, Janet. 'Annals of crime, the beautiful spoils'. *The New Yorker*, 8 March 1947.

Garnett, Henry. *Treasures of Yesterday*. London: Library of Modern Knowledge, 1964.

Gathercole, Peter. 'The need for ethnographic inventories'. *Museum*, vol. XXXVI, UNESCO Quarterly Review, no. 1, 1984, p. 37.

Gimpel, Jean. *The Cult of Art*. New York: Stein and Day, 1969.

Gíslason, Gylfi P. *The Manuscripts Case (Handritamálið)*. Setberg: Ministry of Education, 1961 (in Icelandic).

Gordon, John B. 'The UNESCO Convention on the illicit movement of art'. *Harvard International Law Journal*, Fall 1971, pp. 537–56.

Gould, John. 'Whose heritage?' In supplement, *History Today* (London), March 1984, pp. 26–32.

Goy, R. 'The international protection of the cultural and natural heritage'. *Netherlands Year Book of International Law*, vol. 4, 1973, pp. 117–41.

Hainard, Jacques. 'Collections passion'. *Museum*, UNESCO Quarterly Review, vol. XV, no. 3, 1983, pp. 157–8.

Halberg, Peter. 'Do the manuscripts have to stay in Copenhagen?' *Morgunblaðið*, 24 February 1965.

Hall, Ardelia R. 'The recovery of cultural objects dispersed during World War II'. *Department of State Bulletin*, 27 August 1951, pp. 337–40, 344–5.

Hansen, Tag Høyer. 'The museum as educator'. *Museum*, UNESCO Quarterly Review, vol. XXXVI, no. 4, 1984, pp. 176–83.

Hanson, Brian. *The Acquisition of the Marbles*. London: British Committee for the Restitution of the Parthenon Marbles, 1983.

Harrison, Frederick. 'Give back the Elgin Marbles'. *Nineteenth Century*, December 1890.

Hawkes, Jacquetta. *Man on Earth*. The Cresset Press, 1954, especially Chapter 4, pp. 66–114.

Hawkes, Jacquetta (ed.). *The World of the Past*. London: Thames and Hudson, 1963.

Hawkes, Jacquetta. *Atlas of Ancient Archaeology*. London: Heinemann, 1974.

Hawthorne, Nathaniel. *English Notebooks* (1856), edited by Randall Stewart. The Modern Language Association of America, 1941, especially p. 294.

Haynes, D.E.L. (ed.). *An Historical Guide to the Sculptures of the Parthenon*. London: British Museum Publications, 1962 (reprinted).

Hermannsson, Halldór. 'Icelandic manuscripts'. *Islandica*, vol. XIX, Cornell University Library, Ithaca, New York, 1929.

Hobhouse, John Cam. *A Journey through Albania and other Provinces of Turkey in Europe and Asia to Constantinople during the Years of 1809 and 1810*. London: James Cawthorn, 1813, especially letters XXI and XXIII.

Hollander, Barnett. *The International Law of Art*. London: Bowes and Bowes, 1959, especially Chapter 1.

Home, Robert. *City of Blood Revisited: A New Look at the Benin Expedition of 1897*. London: Rex Collins, 1982.

Hopkirk, Peter. *Foreign Devils on the Silk Road*. London: John Murray, 1980.

Horne, Donald. *The Great Museum: The Re-Presentation of History*. London, Sydney: Pluto Press, 1984.

Hosack, John. *The Rise and Growth of the Law of Nations as Established by General Usage and by Treaties*. London: John Murray, 1882.

Houseman, Lee Ann. 'Comment: current practices and problems in combatting illegality in the art market'. *Seton Hall Law Review*, vol. 12, 1982, pp. 506–67.

Howe, Thomas C., Jr. *Salt Mines and Castles: The Discovery and Restitution of Looted European Art*. New York: Bobbs-Merrill, 1946.

Hudson, Kenneth. *Museums for the 1980s: Survey of World Trends.* London: Macmillan (UNESCO), 1977.

Hudson, Kenneth and Nicholls, Anne. *The Directory of Museums.* London: Macmillan, 1981.

Impey, Oliver and McGregor, Arthur. *The Origins of Museums* (Collected Papers). Oxford: Clarendon Press, 1985.

James, T.G.H. *The British Museum and Ancient Egypt.* London: British Museum Publications, 1981.

Janus, Christopher G. and Brashler, William. *The Search For Peking Man.* New York: Macmillan, 1975.

Jensen, S. Haugstraup. Review of the book by Poul Møller (Conservative MP), *De Islandske Håndskrifter i dokumentarisk belysning (The Icelandic Manuscripts seen from a Documentary Point of View). Højskola bladet,* Danish Folk High School Magazine, no. 6, 12 February 1965, pp. 91–4 (in Danish).

Jore, Karen S. 'The illicit movement of art and artifact: how long will the art market continue to benefit from the ineffectual laws governing cultural property?' *Brooklyn Journal of International Law,* vol. XIII, 1987, 55–81.

Kaylan, Melik. 'Who stole the Lydian hoard?' *Connoisseur,* July 1987, pp. 66–73.

Ketchum, Linda. 'Curator refuses treasure shipped out of Columbia'. *Museum,* UNESCO Quarterly Review, vol. XXXVI, no. 1, 1984, pp. 55–6.

Killelea, Kent L. 'Property law: international stolen art, *Kunstsammlung Weimar* v. *Elicofon,* 678. F2d 1150 (2d Cir 1982)'. *Harvard International Law Journal,* vol. 23, 1983, pp. 466–72.

Kristjánsson, Jónas. *The Homecoming of the Manuscripts (Heimkoma Handritanna).* Reykjavík, 1981 (in Icelandic).

Lacouture, Jean. *André Malraux.* London: André Deutsch, 1975, especially Chapters 3 to 5, pp. 49–81.

Langlois, G. Walter. *André Malraux, the Indo China Affair.* London: Pall Mall, 1966.

Leakey, Mary. *Disclosing the Past.* London: Weidenfeld, 1984, especially pp. 100–1.

Leonhard, Adam. *Primitive Art,* Harmondsworth: Pelican, 1949.

Lewis, Geoffrey. 'The return of cultural property'. *Journal of the Royal Society of Arts Proceedings,* June 1981, pp. 435–43.

Lloyd, Seton. *Foundations in the Dust.* Oxford University Press, 1947.

Lowenthal, David. Where does our heritage belong? Unpublished paper, University College, London.

Lowenthal, David. *The Past is a Foreign Country.* Cambridge University Press, 1985.

Lubbock, Jules. 'Antiquities: whose marbles?' *New Statesman,* 20 May 1983, p. 28.

McCalee, James R. 'The McClain case. Customs and Congress'. *Journal of International Law and Politics,* New York University, vol. 15, no. 4, Summer 1983, pp. 813–38.

McGrath, Lee Kimche. 'Stolen treasures – missing links: an exhibition of art and advocacy'. *Museum,* UNESCO Quarterly Review, vol. XXXVI, no. 1, 1984, pp. 58–60.

Maclagan, Eric. *The Bayeux Tapestry.* Harmondsworth: Penguin, 1949.

McLeod, M.D. *The Asante,* London: British Museum Publications, 1981.

Magnusson, Magnus. 'Can we have our past back?' In *Magnus on the Move,* Edinburgh: Macdonald, 1980, pp. 73–80.

Magnusson, Magnus. *Iceland Saga*, London: Bodley Head, 1987.

Makagiansar, Makaminan. 'Museums for today and tomorrow: a cultural and educational mission'. *Museum*, UNESCO Quarterly Review, vol. XXXVI, no. 1, 1984, pp. 3–7.

Malraux, André. *Museums Without Walls*. London: Secker and Warburg, 1967.

Malraux, André. *Antimemoirs*. London: Hamish Hamilton, 1968.

Malraux, André. *The Voices of Silence*. Princeton University Press, 1978.

Marcheso Ho, Alan. 'Protection of art in transnational law'. *Vanderbilt Journal of Transnational Law*, vol. 4, no. 3, Summer 1974, pp. 689–724.

Mayrand, Pierre. 'The new museology proclaimed'. *Museum*, UNESCO Quarterly Review, vol. XXXVII, no. 4, 1985, pp. 200–1.

Mellaart, James. 'The royal treasure of Dorak'. *Illustrated London News*, vol. 28, November 1959, pp. 754–60.

Merryman, John H. 'International art law: from cultural nationalism to a common cultural heritage'. *Journal of International Law and Politics*, New York University, vol. 15, no. 4, Summer 1983, pp. 757–63.

Merryman, John H. 'Thinking about the Elgin Marbles'. *Michigan Law Review*, vol. 83, no. 8, August 1985, pp. 1881–1923.

Merryman, John H. and Elsen, A. *Law, Ethics and the Visual Arts*. University of Pennsylvania Press, 1980.

Merryman, John H. and Elsen, A. 'Hot art: a re-examination of the illegal international trade in cultural objects'. *Journal of Arts Management and Law* (Washington), Fall 1982, p. 5.

Meyer, Karl E. 'Jewel case for pre-Columbian gems'. *Art News* (New York), February 1964, pp. 36–9, 57–8.

Meyer, Karl E. *The Maya Crisis: A Report on the Pillaging of Maya Sites in Mexico and Guatemala*. New York: Center for Inter-American Relations, 1972.

Meyer, Karl E. *The Plundered Past*. London: Hamish Hamilton, 1974.

Michaelis, Adolf. *Der Parthenon*. Leipzig: von Breitkopf und Härtel, 1871 (in German).

Michaelis, Adolf. *Ancient Marbles in Great Britain*, translated by C.A.M. Fennell. Cambridge University Press, 1882.

Miller, Crane H. *International Law and Marine Archaeology*. Massachusetts Academy of Applied Science, 1973.

Miller, Mary Ellen. *The Art of Mesoamerica*. London: Thames and Hudson, 1986.

Nafziger, James A.R. 'Regulation by the International Council of Museums: an example of the role of non-governmental organizations in the transnational legal process'. *Denver Journal of International Law and Policy*, Fall 1972, vol. 2, pp. 231–53.

Nafziger, James A.R. 'UNESCO – centred management of international conflict over cultural property'. *Hastings Law Journal*, vol. 27, May 1976, pp. 1051–67.

Nafziger, James A.R. 'The new international legal framework for the return, restitution or forfeiture of cultural property'. *Journal of International Law and Politics*, New York University, vol. 15, no. 4, Summer 1983, pp. 789–812.

Nafziger, James A.R. 'Comments on the relevance of law and culture to cultural property law'. *Syracuse Journal of International Law and Commerce*, vol. 10, 1983, pp. 323–32.

Nafziger, James A.R. 'International penal aspects of protecting cultural property'. *The International Lawyer*, vol. 19, no. 3, Summer 1985, pp. 835–52.

Nagin, Carl. 'The politics of plunder'. *New Art Examiner*, Chicago, vol. 14, no. 3, November 1986, pp. 22–8.

Nahlik, E. Stanislaw. 'International law and the protection of cultural property in armed conflicts'. *Hastings Law Journal*, vol. 27, May 1976, pp. 1069–87.

Niec, Halina. 'Legislative models of protection of cultural property'. *Hastings Law Journal*, vol. 27, May 1976, pp. 1089–1122.

Nielsen-Becker, Hans and Widding, Ole. *Arne Magnusson, the Great Manuscript Collector (Arne Magnusson. Den Store håndskriftsamler)*, translated by Robert W. Mattila. Odense University Press, 1972.

Noble, Joseph Veach. 'A plea for sense in regard to trade in antiquities'. *Archaeology* (New York), vol. 25, 1972, p. 144.

Noorbergen, Rene. *Treasures of Lost Races: Discovering the Riches of Ancient Civilizations.* London: W.H. Allen, 1983.

Nordal, Sigurður. 'Time and vellum'. *Annual Bulletin of the Modern Humanities Research Association*, edited by L.T. Topsfield, November 1952, no. 24.

Norman, Geraldine and Hoving, Thomas. 'The Getty Scandals'. *Connoisseur*, May 1987, pp. 98–109.

Norman, Geraldine and Hoving, Thomas. 'It was bigger than they know'. *Connoisseur*, August 1987, pp. 72–81.

Nowell, W. George. 'American tools to control the illegal movement of foreign origin archaeological materials: criminal and civil approaches'. *Syracuse Journal of International Law and Commerce*, vol. 6, 1978, pp. 77–100.

O'Keefe, P.J. and Prott, L.V. *Law and the Cultural Heritage*, vol. 1, *Discovery and Excavation.* Abingdon: Professional Books, 1984, pp. xxvii, 32–187, 434.

Palmer, Meredith A. 'Harvard attacks art looting: proposes acquisition policy'. *Harvard Crimson*, 18 November 1971.

Palmer, Meredith A. 'Symposium: legal aspects of the international traffic in stolen art'. *Syracuse Journal of International Law and Commerce*, vol. 4, 1976, pp. 51–5.

Pearson, Kenneth and Connor, Patricia. *The Dorak Affair.* New York: Atheneum, 1968.

Pegden, Norman. 'A comparison of national laws protecting cultural property'. *Museum*, UNESCO Quarterly Review, vol. XXVI, no. 1, 1974, pp. 53–60.

Prott, Lyndel V. 'International control of illicit movement of the cultural heritage: the 1970 UNESCO Convention and some possible alternatives'. *Syracuse Journal of International Law and Commerce*, vol. 10, 1983, pp. 333–51.

Prunty, Ann P. 'Toward establishing an international tribunal for the settlement of cultural property disputes: how to keep Greece from losing its marbles'. *The Georgetown Law Journal*, vol. 72, 1984, p. 1155.

Pye, Michael. 'Whose art is it anyway?' *Connoisseur*, March 1987, pp. 78–86.

Ram, Mohan. 'To catch a thief'. *Far Eastern Economic Review*, Hong Kong, 17 February 1983.

Rheims, Maurice. *The Strange Life of Objects.* New York: Atheneum, 1961.

Ripley, Dillon. *The Sacred Grove: Essays on Museums.* New York: Simon and Schuster, 1969; London: Victor Gollancz, 1970.

Roth, H. Ling. *Great Benin: Its Customs Art and Horrors.* Halifax: F. King and Sons, 1903.

Rothenberg, Jacob. *'Descensus ad Terram', The Acquisition and Reception of the Elgin Marbles*. New York and London: Garland, 1977, especially Chapters 5, 7 and 8.

Ruz, Alberto Lhuillier. *Destruction and Pillage of Mayan Archaeological Zones*, Paper at the Round Table on the Protection of the National Cultural Heritage, Mexican Academy of Culture, Guadalajara, Jalisco, Mexico, December 1968.

Ryan, Lyndall. *The Aboriginal Tasmanians*. University of Queensland Press, 1981.

Schneider, Eric C. 'Plunder or excavation? Observations and suggestions on the regulation of ownership and trade in the evidence of cultural patrimony'. *Syracuse Journal of International Law and Commerce*, vol. 9, 1982, pp. 1–19.

Shapiro, Harry Lionel. *Peking Man*. New York: Simon and Schuster, 1974.

Shaw, Thurstan. 'Losing one's marbles: two views of a controversy'. *Encounter*, March 1985, pp. 70–3.

Shelley, Henry C. *The British Museum, its History and Treasures*. Boston: L.C. Page and Company, 1911.

Silverberg, Robert. *Lost Cities and Vanished Civilizations*. Philadelphia and New York: Chilton, 1962.

Silverberg, Robert (ed.). *Great Adventures in Archaeology. An Anthology*. Harmondsworth: Penguin, 1985

Smith, A.H. 'Lord Elgin and his collection'. *Journal of Hellenic Studies*, 1916, pp. 163–370.

Smith, Joseph Lindon. *Tombs, Temples, and Ancient Art*. University of Oklahoma Press, 1956.

Smith, T.B. *The British Commonwealth: The Development of its Laws and Constitutions*, vol. 1, *UK, Scotland, Channel Islands*. London: Stevens, 1955.

Sneyers, Rene. 'Stones also die'. *The Courier*, UNESCO, January 1965, pp. 26–7, 30–2.

St Clair, William. *Lord Elgin and the Marbles*. Oxford University Press, 1967.

Stein, Aurel M. *Ruins of Desert Cathay (Personal Narrative of Explorations in Central Asia and Westernmost China)*. 2 vols. London: Macmillan, 1912, especially Chapter 66.

Stein, Aurel M. *On Ancient Central Asian Tracks*. University of Chicago Press, 1964. Introduction by Jeannette Mirsky.

Strahle, Rochelle. 'The retention and retrieval of art and antiquities through international and national means: the tug of war over cultural property.' *Brooklyn Journal of International Law*, vol. 1, 1979, pp. 103–28.

Sun, Shirley. 'The preservation of cultural properties in China'. *Art Research News*, International Foundation for Art Research, New York, vol. 2, no. 1, 1983, pp. 18–20.

Sveinsson, Einar Ól. *Handritamálið – The Manuscripts Case*. Icelandic Literary Society, Reykjavík, 1959 (monograph in Icelandic).

Sveinsson, Einar Ól. *Fakta om der Islandske Handskrifter. vdg. af 'Handskriftkomitean af 1964'. Kritiske Bemærkninger*. A Critique of the Danish Pamphlet, *Facts about the Manuscripts* (monograph in Danish).

Taylor, Francis Henry. *Babel's Tower: The Dilemma of the Modern Museum*. New York: Columbia University Press, 1945.

Taylor, Francis Henry. *The Taste of Angels: A History of Art Collecting from Rameses to Napoleon*. London: Hamish Hamilton, 1948, especially Chapter 5.

Truslow, Frederic J. 'Peru's recovery of cultural patrimony'. *Journal of International Law and Politics*, New York University, vol. 15, no. 4, Summer 1983, pp. 839–56.

Tucker, T.G. *Life in Ancient Athens*. London: Macmillan, 1912, especially Chapter 3.

Upton, Richard. 'Art theft, National Stolen Property Act applied to nationalized Mexican pre-Columbian artifacts'. *Journal of International Law and Politics*, vol. 10, 1978, pp. 569–611.

De Varine, Hugues. 'The rape and plunder of cultures: an aspect of the deterioration of the terms of cultural trade between nations'. *Museum*, UNESCO Quarterly Review, vol. XXV, no. 3, 1983, pp. 152–7.

Vrettos, Theodore. *A Shadow of Magnitude: The Acquisition of the Elgin Marbles*. New York: Putnam, 1974.

Wheaton, Henry. *Elements of International Law: With a Sketch of the History of the Science*, 2 vols. London: B. Fellowes, 1836 edition.

Whitehouse, David and Whitehouse, Ruth. *Archaeological Atlas of the World*. London: Thames and Hudson, 1975.

Willett, Frank and Eyo, Ekpo O. *Treasures of Ancient Nigeria*. Boyoi Books. Alfred A. Knopf in association with the Detroit Institute of Arts, 1980.

Williams, S. 'The protection of the Canadian cultural heritage: the Cultural Property Export and Import Act'. *Canadian Yearbook of International Law*, vol. 14, 1976, pp. 292–306.

Williams, S. 'Protection of cultural property. The Canadian approach'. *Arizona Law Review*, vol. 22, 1980, p. 737.

Wilson, Derek. *The World Atlas of Treasure*. London: William Collins, 1981.

Wiseman, James (ed.). 'Greece and the Elgin Marbles'. *Context*, Boston University, Centre for Archaeological Studies, vol. 3, no. 1–2, Summer 1983.

Wittlin, Alma Stephanie. *The Museum, its History and its Tasks in Education*. London: Routledge and Kegan Paul, 1949.

Wittlin, Alma Stephanie. *Museums in Search of a Usable Future*. Massachusetts Institute of Technology, 1970.

Xia Li, Dunhuangology. 'Studying artwork and manuscripts'. *China Reconstructs*, vol. XXXVI, no. 5, May 1987, pp. 10–13.

Zaldumbide, Rodrigo Pallares. 'Return and restitution of cultural property: cases for restitution'. *Museum*, UNESCO Quarterly Review, vol. XXXIV, no. 2, 1982, pp. 132–4.

Zelle, Ann. 'Acquisitions: saving whose heritage?' *Museum News* (Washington), April 1971, pp. 19–26.

Zelle, Ann. 'ICOM ethics of acquisitions: a report to the profession'. *Museum News* (Washington), April 1972, pp. 31–3.

BY ORGANIZATION

Stofnun Árna Magnússonar, Iceland

Handritasýning á þjóðhátíðarári, An Exhibition of Manuscripts, Reykjavík, 1974. Pamphlet.

Stofnun Árna Magnússonar, á Íslandi. Paper in German by Jón Samsonarson, 1984. With bibliography of publications on the Icelandic manuscripts, published by the Institute.

Australian Institute of Aboriginal Studies
The Preservation of Australia's Aboriginal Heritage: A Report of a National Seminar, Austl. Inst. Aboriginal Studies, vol. 54, Canberra, 1975. Prehistory and Material Culture Series no. 11, edited by Robert Edwards.

Copenhagen University, Arnamagnaean Institute and the Royal Library
Arne Magnusson, 1663–1963. Det Kongelige Bibliotek, 1963. Pamphlet in Danish for Exhibition, November–December 1963.

Danish Manuscript Committee
Fakta om Håndskrifterne, Facts about the Manuscripts. Pamphlet in Danish, 1964.

International Council of Museums (ICOM)
'Protection of cultural property in South East Asia'. Report and Recommendations, Malacca, Malaysia, 1972. International Council of Museums.

International Institute of Higher Studies in Criminal Science
   (Quaderni de scienze Criminali)
Conference, Siracuse (Sicily) 1982, Chairman, Shoshana Berman. *Penal Protection of Works of Art,* especially Part Two, 'Plunder, theft and illicit trade in art', 1983, pp. 151–242.

Interpol
A report by the Interpol General Secretariat to the Organization's forty-second General Assembly, 2–9 October 1973. In *Museum,* 1974, vol. XXVI, pp. 4–9.

UNESCO
Final Report, Brussels, 19–22 November 1973. Committee of Experts on the Risks Incurred by Works of Art and Other Cultural Property, in particular the risks of theft and other forms of illicit transfer of ownership. In *Museum,* vol. XXVI, no. 1, 1974, pp. 61–4.
An Illustrated Inventory of Famous Dismembered Works of Art: European Painting. UNESCO, 1974.
Protection of the Cultural Heritage: Protection of the Underwater Heritage. Technical Handbooks for Museums and Monuments, 4 SG70 UNE, 1981.
'Prevention urged of illicit import of cultural property'. In *U.N. Monthly Chronicle,* vol. XVIII, no. 3, March 1981, p. 68.
'States asked to prohibit illicit import and transfer of cultural property'. In *U.N. Monthly Chronicle,* vol. IX, no. 4, February 1982, pp. 49–50.
'Assembly urges increased efforts for return of cultural property'. In *U.N. Chronicle,* January 1984, pp. 27–8.

The Challenge to Our Cultural Heritage, edited by Yudhishthir Raj Isar. UNESCO, Smithsonian Institute Press, 1986.

United Nations Social Defense Research Institute
The Protection of the Artistic and Archaeological Heritage, 1976, especially pp. 164–90, 'The protection of the cultural heritage: an Italian perspective'.

Vatican museums
Papacy and Art. Official publication authorized by the Vatican museums. Harry N. Abrams, 1982.

Other publications

Proceedings of the American Society of International Law, 1977, pp. 196–207, The International Protection of Cultural Property, 22 April 1977, Seminar, Northwestern School of Law of Lewis and Clark College, USA. Moderator: Professor Leonard D. Duboff. Participants: J.H. Merryman, P. Macrory, M.B. Feldman and P.M. Bator. Seminar Reporter: Alina Gonzales Aldape.

Antiquity (Cambridge), vol. LVI, no. 216, March 1982, pp. 1–4. Editorial on *The Times* article, 'Should we give back these treasures?'

Antiquity (Cambridge), vol. LVIII, no. 234, November 1984. Editorial.

Archaeology, vol. 24, 1971, p. 165. Archaeological News: Council of the Archaeological Institute of America. Resolution on the Plundering of Sites, 1970.

British Museum Quarterly, vol. XI, 1936–7, pp. 154–6, 'Bronze lion's head from S. Arabia'.

Commonwealth Arts Association Publication. *The Lost Heritage*, 1981.

Connoisseur, vol. 192, 1976, p. 178. 'Whose heritage?'

Current Anthropology, vol. 14, 1973, p. 579. 'Brooklyn presents stela fragments to Guatemala'.

The Economist, October 1987, pp. 101–2. 'Collectors or looters?'

International Directory of Arts, vol. II, 18th edition, 1987–1988. Frankfurt/Main: Müller.

L'Hebdo, Magazine suisse d'information, 12 March 1982. 'La Filière suisse. Traffic international d'œuvres d'art'. 'The Swiss connection. International traffic in art objects'.

Museum, vol. XXXVII, no. 4, 1981, pp. 200–1. 'Declaration of Quebec, basic principles for a new museology'.

Museum, vol. XXXVI, no. 1, 1984, pp. 35–6. 'Meeting to discuss surveys of Pacific cultural property in museums around the world. Statement on the development of worldwide inventories of anthropological and archaeological collections derived from Oceania'.

Museum, vol. XXXVI, no. 1, 1984, p. 57. 'Ecuador recovers an important fragment of its cultural memory'.

Museums Yearbook, 1986. The Museums Association, London, pp. 7–8.

National Geographic Illustrated Cultural Atlas of the Ancient World, 1983. 'Peoples and places of the past'.

National Geographic, vol. 169, no. 4, April 1986: pp. 452–62, Ian Graham, 'Looters rob our past'; pp. 462–6, Gillett G. Griffin, 'In defence of collectors'.

Newsweek, 30 May 1983, pp. 60–2. Ray Wilkinson, Cathleen McCuigan, Elaine Shannon, Maggie Malone, 'Art: the booming trade in smuggled art'.

Ruins of Sacred and Historic Lands. London and Edinburgh: Thomas Nelson, 1850.

The Scotsman Magazine, vol. 4, no. 7, October 1983, Art and Argument 1; 'Elgin's Marbles, the row that won't go away'; pp. 10–17, Magnus Magnusson, 'Our richest heritage of controversy'; p. 15, Melina Mercouri, 'When you took them you took our flag'; pp. 11, 14, Lord Elgin, 'Politically they are a lovely plaything'.

Syracuse Journal of International Law and Commerce, vol. 4, 1976: pp. 51–95, Symposium: Legal aspects of the international traffic in stolen art. Papers by J. Fishman, S. Metzger and A.K. Altes; pp. 96–134, 'Proceedings of the panel on the U.S. enabling legislation of the UNESCO Convention on the Means of Prohibiting and Preventing the Illicit Import, Export and Transfer of Ownership of Cultural Property'. Participants: L. Duboff, J. Nafziger, A. Emmerich, M. Feldman, J. McAlee and P. Bator.

Syracuse Journal of International Law and Commerce, vol. 10, 1983, pp. 281–351. Symposium: Jurisdictional Issues in the International Movement of Cultural Property. American Society of International Law, 22–3 April 1983. Papers by M.C. Bassiouni and J. Nafziger.

UNESCO Conventions and Recommendations relating to cultural property

CONVENTIONS

Final act of the intergovernmental conference on the protection of cultural property in the event of armed conflict, The Hague, 1954. (See Appendix XVI.)

Convention on the means of prohibiting and preventing the illicit import, export and transfer of ownership of cultural property, Paris, 1970. (See Appendix XVII.)

Convention concerning the protection of the world cultural and natural heritage, Paris, 1972. (See Appendix XVIII.)

RECOMMENDATIONS

Recommendation on international principles applicable to archaeological excavations, New Delhi, 1956. (See Appendix XI.)

Recommendation concerning the most effective means of rendering museums accessible to everyone, Paris, 1960.

Recommendation concerning the safeguarding of the beauty and character of landscapes and sites, Paris, 1962.

Recommendation on the means of prohibiting and preventing the illicit export, import and transfer of ownership of cultural property, Paris, 1964.

Recommendation concerning the preservation of cultural property endangered by public or private works, Paris, 1968.

Recommendation concerning the protection, at national level, of the cultural and natural heritage, 1972.

Recommendation concerning the safeguarding and contemporary role of historic areas, 1976.

Recommendation concerning the international exchange of cultural property, Nairobi, 1976. (See Appendix XIII.)

Recommendation on the protection of movable cultural property, Paris 1978. (See Appendix XIV.)

Recommendation: World Conference on Cultural Policies, Mexico City, 1982. (See Appendix XV.)

GENERAL

18 C/23 – Initial special reports submitted by Member States on the action taken by them upon the recommendation concerning the protection, at national level, of the cultural and natural heritage, adopted by the General Conference during its seventeenth session. 18 October 1974.

18 C/22 – Initial special reports submitted by Member States on the action taken by them upon the Convention concerning the protection of the world cultural and natural heritage, adopted by the General Conference during its seventeenth session. 19 October 1974.

18 C/22 Add. – Initial special reports submitted by Member States on the action taken by them upon the Convention concerning the protection of the world cultural and natural heritage, adopted by the General Conference during its seventeenth session. 21 October 1974.

18 C/23 Add. – Initial special reports submitted by Member States on the action taken by them upon the recommendation concerning the protection, at national level, of the cultural and natural heritage, adopted by the General Conference during its seventeenth session. 21 October 1974.

CC – 77/CONF 001/4 – World Heritage Committee – Paris, 27 June–1 July 1977. Issues arising in connection with the implementation of the World Heritage Convention. Paris, 9 June 1977.

CC – 79/CONF 206/6 – Intergovernmental Committee for promoting the return of cultural property to its countries of origin or its restitution in case of illicit appropriation. First session, Paris, 2 April 1980.

CC – 81/CONF 203/10, 1982 – Intergovernmental Committee for promoting the return of cultural property to its countries of origin or its restitution in case of illicit appropriation. Final Report, Paris, September 1981.

CLT – 83/WS/16 – National legal control of illicit traffic in cultural property by Lyndel V. Prott, P.J. O'Keefe. UNESCO, Paris, 1983. Distribution limited.

CLT – 83/CONF 216/inf 3 – Intergovernmental Committee for promoting the return of cultural property to its countries of origin or its restitution in case of illicit appropriation. Third Session press file, September 1981–March 1983. 15 March 1983. Distribution limited.

22 C/93 – Proposals for the implementation of the Convention on the means of prohibition

and preventing the illicit import, export and transfer of ownership of cultural property. 30 August 1983.

22 C/88 – Report of the Intergovernmental Committee for promoting the return of cultural property to its countries of origin or its restitution in case of illicit appropriation. 22 September 1983.

Intergovernmental Committee for promoting the return of cultural property to its countries of origin or its restitution in case of illicit appropriation. Rules of procedure. Distribution limited.

National legislation

COLLECTIONS

Index of national legislations on the protection of the cultural heritage, UNESCO, SHC/WS/ 111, Paris, 1969.

The Protection of Cultural Property – Handbook of National Legislation, Bonnie Burnham, International Council of Museums, 1974.

Synopsis of national legislations in the field of culture, January 1976. UNESCO, Working paper DOC Code SHC 75/WS/40, Microfiche 7650409.

Protection of movable cultural property. UNESCO, vols. I and II, Compendium of Legislative Texts, 1984.

STATUTES

Australia: The Protection of Movable Cultural Heritage Act, 1986 (No. 11).

Canada: Cultural Property Export and Import Act (1974–1976) 1 Can. Stat. ch. 50.

Denmark: Danish Constitutional Act 1983 (Fact sheet/Denmark, press and cultural relations. Department of the Ministry of Foreign Affairs).

United Kingdom: British Museum Act, 1963, in Halsbury's *Statutes of England*, vol. 19, pp. 168–76; National Heritage Act, 1983, in Halsbury's *Statutes of England*, vol. 53, pp. 734–77.

United States of America: Convention on Cultural Property Implementation Act, Pub. L. No. 97–446, S 301–315 (1982) (codified at 19 USC). Laws of 97th Congress, 12 January 1982, 96 Stat 2350–63.

Other documents

BRITISH MUSEUM

Original Letters and Papers (Elgin Marbles), vol. III 1810–1816, vol. IV 1816–1821.

Communications respecting purchase: Standing Committee General Meeting [GM] vol. V, 13 December 1806–13 December 1828 (*GM 1137*).

– To be opened to the Public: Committee (*C. 2644*), vol. X, 13 July 1816–10 March 1827.

Original Letters and Papers (Benin Bronzes) – Committee, vol. XLVIII, 9 May 1896–30 April 1898, especially 9 October 1897.

EUROPE

Council of Europe
European Cultural Convention, 1954, 218 UNTS, 139.
Parliamentary assembly: report on the return of works of art, 15 September 1983, Doc. 5111, ADOC 51111.C: I Draft resolution (see Appendix x) II Explanatory memorandum.
Proceedings of the Thirteenth Colloquy on European Law, Delphi, 20–22 September 1983. International Legal Protection of Cultural Property. Strasbourg 1984.
Draft Final Report of the Select Committee of Experts on International Co-operation in the field of offences relating to works of art. (PC-R-OA), 33 Sess. CDPC (84) 3 (1984).

EEC

J. Chatelain, *Means of Combating the Theft of and Illegal Traffic in Works of Art in the Nine Countries of the EEC – a Study Prepared at the Request of the Commission of the European Communities*, 1976, pp. 106–7.

DENMARK

Folketingets Fordhandlinger. Proceedings of the Danish Parliament (in Danish), no. 3, 1964–5. Meeting days (Mødedagene den 27, 28 og (&) 29 October, cols 370–453). First Reading of the Proposed Act for Changing the Founding Document of 18 January 1760, of the Arne Magnussen Foundation.
Folketingets Fordhandlinger. Proceedings of the Danish Parliament (in Danish), no. 25, 1964–5. Meeting days (Mødedagene den 12, 13 May, cols 5047–5109). Second Reading of the 1964 Law.
Folketingets Fordhandlinger. Proceedings of the Danish Parliament (in Danish), no. 26. 1964–5. Meeting days (Mødedagene den 18, 19, 29, 21 May, cols 5303–50). Third Reading of the 1964 Law.

ICOM

Study on Ethical Rules Governing Museum Acquisitions, Paris, 1970. List of 20 Recommendations.

UNITED KINGDOM

Report from the select committee on the Earl of Elgin's collection of sculptured marbles. Ordered by the House of Commons to be printed, 25 March 1816. (See Appendix II.)
Hansard Parliamentary Reports. House of Commons, vol. 32, 15 February 1816, 578, 823–28.
Hansard Parliamentary Reports. House of Commons, vol. 34, 7 June 1816, 1027–40.
Hansard Parliamentary Reports. House of Lords, vol. 427, no. 40, Monday, 15 February 1982.

Hansard Parliamentary Reports. House of Lords, vol. 444, no. 25, Thursday, 27 October 1983.

Hansard Parliamentary Reports. House of Commons, vol. 49, no. 53, Monday, 21 November 1983.

Foreign Office Records, London, R/643/19, FO 371, 29861, 1941.

UNITED NATIONS

Official report concerning legal matters in the United Nations, vol. 12, no. 4, 1 December 1977.

Reports of the United Nations Joint Inspection Unit: 'Contribution of the UN system to the conservation and management of Latin American cultural and natural heritage' (JIV/Rep/82/5) 116/Ex 9, March 1983.

UNITED STATES OF AMERICA

Council of the Archaeological Institute of America. Resolution on the Plundering of Sites (December 1970) *Archaeology*, vol. 24, 1971, p. 165.

Senate Comm. on Foreign Relations, Convention on Ownership of Cultural Property, S. Exec. Rep. No. 29, 92d Cong., 2d Sess. (1972).

UNESCO Convention on Cultural Property: Hearings on H.R. 5643 Before the Subcomm. on Trade of the House Comm. on Ways and Means, 95th Cong., 1st Sess., 30–38 (1977) (statement of Douglas Ewing, President, American Association of Dealers in Ancient, Oriental and Primitive Art).

Convention on Cultural Property Implementation Act: Hearings on H.R. 5643 and S. 2261 Before the Subcomm. on International Trade of the Senate Comm. on Finance, 95th Cong., 2d Sess. 19 (1978) (statement of Mark Feldman, Deputy Legal Advisor, Department of State).

TABLES

Table on Major Art Thefts, 1911–72, prepared by Bonnie Burnham of ICOM, appears in K. Meyer, *The Plundered Past*, pp. 219–39.

Table on Latin American Region: Ratification of International Conventions on Conservation of Natural and Cultural Heritage, March 1981, UNESCO 116 Ex/9 March 1983. (See Appendix VII.)

Principal press references

GENERAL

UNESCO Doc. CLT 83/CONF 216/INF. 3. 15 March 1983 (Distribution limited). This contains many international press items; apart from those in English there are many items in French and Spanish. (Covers September 1981 to March 1983.)

AMERICAN

New York Times, 1 September 1981. 'U.S. seeks to limit questionable art imports'.

New York Times, 6 September 1981. 'A tougher policy on art imports?'

New York Times, 4 October 1981. 'Peru acts to stem trade in stolen artworks'.

International Herald Tribune, 31 August 1982. 'Between France and Mexico: a cultural crisis'. Alan Riding.

International Herald Tribune, 8/9 February 1986. 'Books fuel search for new sources of saleable art'. Souren Melikian.

International Herald Tribune, 5/6 April 1986. 'Artwork lost and found'.

International Herald Tribune, 16/17 August 1986. 'The art market vs artistic legacy'. Stephen Castle.

International Herald Tribune, 4 August 1987. 'Grave robbing and a golden find in Peru'. Bradley Graham.

International Herald Tribune, 9 October 1987. 'Bayeux's English heritage'.

AUSTRALIAN

The Age, 29 August 1986. 'In search of religious artefacts'. John Larkin.

The Australian, 2 January 1988. 'Plate back after 291 years'. Peter Terry.

The Age, 9 January 1988. 'On the trail of Italy's lost treasures'. Robert Suro.

The Australian, 12 January 1988. 'Classic error'. Simon Jenkins.

ENGLISH

The Times, 27 August 1970. 'Turks claim Croesus gold is in U.S. museum'. Peter Hopkirk.

The Sunday Times, 18 April 1976. 'Police snap up treasures at Christies'. Rocca and der Porthogh.

The Times, 4 September 1976. 'A Jubilee portrait to please the Queen'. George Hutchinson.

The Times, 8 September 1976. 'Indian news agency claims diamond belongs to India'.

The Times, 25 September 1976. 'British P.M. rejects Pakistan's claim'.

The Times, 6 October 1976. 'Pakistan P.M. disappointed over Britain's refusal to return Koh-i-Noor diamond'.

The Times, 18 October 1981. 'Should we give back these treasures?' Richard Dowden.

The Observer, 24 January 1982. 'U.K. to keep Sri Lanka treasures'. Peter Deeley.

The Times, 9 February 1982. 'Egypt asks for return of sphinx's beard'. Christopher Walker.

The Times, 11 February 1982. 'Putting in a good word for Elgin'.

The Times, 16 February 1982. 'The Elgin Marbles will not be returned to Greece'. Parliamentary Correspondent.

The Observer, 21 February 1982. 'Beard of sphinx will stay'. Peter Deeley.

Guardian, 30 July 1982. 'Marbles are tossed into political arena'.

The Observer, 19 December 1982. 'U.K. must keep the Elgin Marbles'. Nicola Tyrer.

Guardian, 23 December 1982. 'Athens and its lost marbles'.

The Times, 15 January 1983. 'The case for sending the marbles back home'. Melina Mercouri.

The Times, 11 March 1983. 'Minister seeks art trade code on illegal exports'. Frances Gibb.

The Sunday Times, 3 April 1983. 'Maori treasures slipping through legal loophole'.

The Times, 22 April 1983. 'Collector wins tussle over Maori carving'.

The Times, 22 April 1983. 'No forfeiture of carving (Law Report)'.

The Times, 14 May 1983. 'Greece lays formal claim to Elgin Marbles'. Mario Modiano.

The Observer, 15 May 1983. 'Elgin Marbles surprise'. Hugo Davenport.

The Times, 9 June 1983. 'Document shows Elgin had permission to take Parthenon marbles'. Christopher Warman, Arts correspondent.

Guardian, 27 June 1983. 'Why the marbles are not just a museum piece'. Peter Thompson.

The Sunday Times, 22 July 1983. 'Melina and the marbles'. Susan Crosland.

The Observer, 24 July 1983. 'Sikhs demand their throne from Britain'. Shyam Bhatia.

The Times, 3 August 1983. 'Backing for return of Elgin Marbles'.

The Times, 2 September 1983. 'Britain denies damage to Elgin Marbles'. Michael Horsnell.

The Observer, 4 September 1983. 'Elgin Marbles are tip top'. Peter Deeley.

The Sunday Times, 18 September 1983. 'Gods, cash, patriotism and pride'. Nicholas B. Penney, Keeper of the Department of Western Art, Ashmolean Museum, Oxford, reviewing *Loot* by Russell Chamberlin.

The Times, 13 October 1983. 'Official demands for marbles'. Henry Stanhope (Diplomatic correspondence).

The Daily Telegraph, 15 October 1983. '40 MPs back return of Elgin Marbles'. Keith Nurse.

The Times, 28 October 1983. 'Elgin Marbles to stay in museum'.

The Times, 9 November 1983. 'British Antique Dealers Association to take action over illegal auction rings'.

The Times, 12 November 1983. 'Sphinx beard fragment to be given back'. Richard Dowden.

Guardian, 17 November 1983. 'Sphinx's beard to return to Egypt'. Kate Finch.

The Times, 22 November 1983. 'Commons: Greeks ask for Elgin Marbles'.

The Times, 23 December 1983. 'India says "Give us back our Koh-i-Noor".' Michael Hamlyn, Delhi.

The Times, 6 January 1984. 'Mercouri wins Kinnock pledge'. Mario Modiano, Athens.

The Times, 7 January 1984. 'Editorial: The expansive Mr Kinnock'.

The Times, 7 January 1984. 'Museum upset by Kinnock'. Christopher Huhne.

The Observer, 15 January 1984. 'Row over £150,000 god seized by Yard'. Robert Low.

The Financial Times, 21 January 1984. 'The marbles — how Greek?' William St. Clair.

The Times, 24 January 1984. 'Elgin Marbles: mistake to start repatriating famous museum pieces'.

The Daily Telegraph, 30 January 1984. 'Beware of bearing gifts to Greeks'. Charles Moore.

The Times, 14 February 1984. 'The arts: reply soon to Greek request'.

Guardian, 31 March 1984. 'The day the F.O. lost its marbles'. John Torode.

The Times, 11 April 1984. 'Marbles to be kept in British Museum'.

Guardian, 11 April 1984. 'Marbles return rejected'. John Torode.

The Times, 11 April 1984. 'Britain rejects request to return Elgin Marbles'. Henry Stanhope.

The Times, 14 April 1984. 'House of Lords to debate issue of preserving heritage'.

The Times, 14 April 1984. 'Put art in new framework'. Geraldine Norman.

The Times, 16 June 1984. 'Inscrutable but not immutable'. Kate Hickman.

The Sunday Times, 15 July 1984. 'Must art treasures go to the highest bidder?' Leslie Geddes-Brown.

Glasgow Herald, 18 August 1984. 'U.N. rejects stone of destiny plea'.

The Observer, 19 August 1984. 'Nok treasures stir storm in art world'. Cameron Duodee.

The Observer, 7 October 1984. 'Greek appeal to U.N. on marbles'. Hugo Davenport.

The Times, 24 November 1984. 'Sphinx to get its beard back after 166 years'. Richard Dowden.

The Observer, 24 November 1984. 'Sphinx treasure returned'. Shyam Bhatia.

The Times, 24 December 1984. 'Spectrum: turning dishonesty into an art form'. Geraldine Norman.

The Times, 18 March 1985. 'Britain to keep marbles, questions'.

The Observer, 24 March 1985. 'Sacred skulls reburied'. Robin McKie.

The Times, 12 July 1985. 'The saga of Iceland's missing myths'. Christopher Follett.

The Sunday Times, 29 September 1985. 'Whose treasures?' Leslie Geddes Brown.

The Times, 8 October 1985. 'On this day, October 8, 1878, Cleopatra's Needle'.

The Times, 12 October 1985. 'Firm line on Elgin Marbles'. David Hewson.

The Times, 31 October 1985. 'Playing for keeps in the diplomatic marbles game'. George Hill.

Guardian, 31 October 1985. 'People at large: marbles: new evidence'.

The Times, 11 November 1985. 'Elgin Marbles dispute. The struggle goes on says Mercouri'. Mario Modiano.

The Times, 7 December 1985. 'Austrians ready to hand back Nazi's haul'. Richard Bassett.

The Observer, 8 December 1985. 'Sotheby's "blind eye" on vases'. Peter Watson.

The Financial Times, 10 December 1985. 'Suspect vases find buyers saleroom'. Antony Thorncroft.

Guardian, 14 December 1985. 'Sir David, Defender of the marble halls'.

The Sunday Times, 29 December 1985. 'Artful dodges'. Tim McGirk, Rowena Webster and Brian Whitaker.

The Observer, 5 January 1986. 'How the Greeks lost their marbles'. Neal Ascherson.

The Sunday Times, 12 January 1986. 'Museum fury as treasures go to Japan'.

The Times, 29 January 1986. 'Jigsaw operation to rebuild the decaying Parthenon'. Mario Modiano.

The Sunday Times, 9 February 1986. 'How Japan blew a South Sea Bubble'. Leslie Geddes Brown.

The Times, 25 February 1986. 'Past with a rich future'. Alan Hamilton.

Guardian, 11 March 1986. 'Greek children plead for Elgin marbles'.

The Sunday Telegraph, 16 March 1986. 'Heart of stone'.

Guardian, 26 March 1986. 'Spanish approach on Goya'.

Guardian, 9 April 1986. 'Goya painting returns to Spain after £4m compensation agreed. And so to bed for the Marquesa'. Richard Wigg and Geraldine Norman.

The Times, 28 April 1986. 'China wants its scrolls'.

The Daily Telegraph, 14 June 1986. 'My vicious game of marbles at Oxford'. Gavin Stamp.

Guardian, 21 June 1986. 'Give marbles back to Greece on Byron's birthday, says Foot'.

Guardian, 1 July 1986. 'Museum makes reluctant tribal art purchase'.

The Financial Times, 12 July 1986. 'Save our sculpture'. Antony Thorncroft.

The Observer, 13 July 1986. 'Museum treasures found to be fakes'. Peter Watson.

The Times, 9 August 1986. '$7 million masterpiece – or a fake?' Geraldine Norman.

The Times, 10 September 1986. 'Art treasures in EEC'. Letter from Norman St John-Stevas.

The Daily Telegraph, 28 September 1986. 'Americans want city's gateway knights'. Souren Melikian.

The Independent, 17 October 1986. 'New delight from the auld alliance'. David Eskerdjian.

The Observer, 19 October 1986. 'Long lost old masterpieces return to excite the experts'. Peter Watson.

The Observer, 28 October 1986. 'The Henry Moore warrior that could start a cultural war'. Peter Watson.

The Times, 21 November 1986. 'Museum planned for the Elgin marbles'.

The Times, 19 December 1986. 'Strange tales of a head'. Geraldine Norman.

The Times, 30 December 1986. 'Plundering the underworld'. Geraldine Norman.

The Observer, 15 February 1987. 'Statue of liberties'. Peter Watson.

The Times, 27 March 1987. 'Monument to a fraudster'. Geraldine Norman.

The Times, 1 May 1987. '"Egyptian" bronze probably a fake'. Charles Brenner.

The Observer, 3 May 1987. 'Trail of looted treasures leads to U.S.' Tony Catterall and Paul Lashmar.

The Times, 28 May 1987. 'Tomb robbers guide to history'. Geraldine Norman.

Guardian, 6 June 1987. 'Object lesson'. Mohini Patel.

[London] *Evening Standard*, 19 June 1987. 'Scandal of V & A's Indian art cover-up'. Steve Clarke.

The Sunday Times, 21 June 1987. 'The case of the invisible treasures'. Alison Beckett.

The Sunday Telegraph, 28 June 1987. 'Onassis move on marbles'. Stephen Castle.

The Times, 29 June 1987. 'Elgin seen as noble saviour'.

The Observer, 5 July 1987. 'Ripping off the marbles'. Christopher Hitchens.

The Observer, 12 July 1987. 'The glory that was Greece'. Christopher Hitchens.

The Observer, 8 November 1987. 'Japan gang stole French treasures'. Peter McGill and Robin Smyth.

The Times, 24 November 1987. 'Elgin marbles to stay in Britain'.

The Independent, 29 January 1988. 'Legal tussles over Croesus' smuggled treasures (Art-World)'. Geraldine Norman.

The Sunday Times, 21 February 1988. Sueing Shiva dismays art dealers'. Alison Beckett.

The Times, 6 June 1988. 'Foul deeds of desecration'. Bernard Levin.

The Independent, 14 June 1988. 'Smugglers hoard worth $10 m'. Geraldine Norman.

The Independent, 17 June 1988. 'Why grave robbing is no longer ethically acceptable'. Geraldine Norman.

The Independent, 5 July 1988. 'Maori head to return for traditional burial'. Geraldine Norman.

FRENCH

L'Express, 23 September 1982, 'La loi du retour' (The law of return).

Le Matin, 1 September 1982. 'Un codex Aztèque subtilisé à la Bibliothèque Nationale' (Aztec codex stolen from the Bibliothèque Nationale).

Le Pèlerin, 2 May 1982. 'Faudra-t-il vider nos musées?' (Will we have to empty our museums?).

La Vie, 16–22 September 1982. 'Qui veut la renvoyer dans ses foyers?' (Who wants to send her back?).

ICELANDIC

Morgunblaðið, (*The Morning Paper*) (Conservative), 28 May 1965, 'Handritin Heim', (The manuscripts are home).

Althýdublaðið, (*People's Paper*), 16 February 1965, Halldór Halldórsson, 'Annáll Handritamálsins' (Annal of the Manuscripts Case).

Appendices in microfiche

DENMARK

UNITED KINGDOM

USA AND LATIN AMERICA

EUROPE

Bibliography: Items on restitution of Cultural property available at UNESCO, archives,
Paris.

* In translation from the Danish.
(R) Ratifications, etc.

Index

For individual collectors, see under collectors; for collections of cultural treasures and individual objects, see under cultural property; for individual museums and institutions, see under museums and institutions; for individual treaties or national laws, see under treaties or statutes.